GUMSHOE AMERICA

1/30/01

NEW AMERICANISTS *A Series Edited by Donald E. Pease*

Hard-Boiled Crime Fiction and

the Rise and Fall of New Deal

Liberalism

GUMSHOE AMERICA

Sean McCann

Duke University Press   Durham & London   2000

© 2000 Duke University Press
All rights reserved
Printed in the United States of America
on acid-free paper ∞
Designed by C. H. Westmoreland
Typeset in Sabon with Frutiger display
by Keystone Typesetting, Inc.
Library of Congress Cataloging-in-
Publication Data appear on the last
printed page of this book.

CONTENTS

ACKNOWLEDGMENTS

I am grateful to many friends and colleagues for the advice and support they gave me while I worked on this project. Rachel Adams, Jesse Ashlock, Jennifer Ashton, Daniel Born, Deirdre Day-MacLeod, Dewar MacLeod, Mary Esteve, Maria Farland, Hilene Flanzbaum, Noah Isenberg, Natasha Korda, Doug Mao, Marybeth McMahon, Bob Mirandon, Ross Posnock, Joe Reed, Carlo Rotella, Peggy Samuels, Richard Slotkin, William Stowe, Michael Szalay, Betsy Traube, Michael Trask, Joe Vizcarrondo, Ingrid Walker Fields, Mark Weiner, David Weisberg, and Chris Zinn read all or portions of the manuscript and offered helpful responses and superb advice. Henry Abelove and Richard Ohmann gave me invaluable guidance. George Donahue provided vital material support at a key point in the book's progress. Morris Dickstein, William Kelly, Louis Menand, and Walter Benn Michaels gave the benefit of their wisdom and, more importantly, provided models of scholarly and intellectual excellence.

I am also indebted for their assistance to the librarians at the Harry Ransom Humanities Center of the University of Texas, the UCLA Special Collections Library, and the Fales Library at New York University. An NEH Summer Seminar Fellowship and a fellowship at the Wesleyan Center for the Humanities each gave me time for research and provided me with perceptive audiences at an early stage in the project's development. I am thankful, too, to Lesley Himes for permission to quote from Chester Himes's letters, to Sharon Thompson Reed for permission to quote from Jim Thompson's letters, and to the Literary Property Trustees Under the Will of Lillian Hellman for permission to quote from Dashiell Hammett's letters and unpublished writings.

I could not have completed this project without the support of my family. I am deeply grateful to Moira McCann, Helena Moraski, and Ray Moraski for their unflagging interest and enthusiasm, to Jay McCann for his sharp questions, and to Bryan McCann for the many generous readings he gave the manuscript and for his brilliant advice.

My deepest debt is to Minou Roufail, to whom this book is dedicated. Her intellectual excitement, her wonderful sense of humor, and, most of all, her love made it possible.

UNCIVIL SOCIETY

Hard-boiled Crime Fiction and the Idea

of a Democratic Culture

If democracy is not an institution or a set of institutions, what is it?
It is an atmosphere and an attitude; in a word — a culture.
— Jacques Barzun, *Of Human Freedom*, 1939

My argument is and always has been merely that there is no such
thing as serious literature. — Raymond Chandler[1]

James M. Cain's 1937 novel *Serenade* is that classic Depression-
era story, a tale of exaggerated good fortune and terrible bad luck.
Though it might just as easily have told the history of an engineer, an
athlete, or a gangster, Cain's particular version of the tale features an
operatic tenor named John Howard Sharp, and it relates with grim
fatality his rise and fall through the world of music. A poor boy
blessed with talent and a strong will, Sharp rises by dint of hard
work to a minor level of international recognition, but he loses his
way when he falls beneath the influence of an avant-garde impre-
sario and homosexual Svengali named Winston Hawes. Subject to
Hawes's cosmopolitan corruption, Sharp's will evaporates, his talent
disappears, and he plummets rapidly to become a penniless bum on
the streets of Mexico City. There he is saved by the love of a good
woman, a Mexican Indian prostitute named Juana, and, regaining
his talent, he claws his way back to stardom in radio and movies — a

cheap success he despises — and prepares to return triumphantly to the world of serious music to which he aspires. Just as he is about to claim the grail of a season at the Met, however, disaster strikes Sharp yet again. Winston Hawes reappears on the scene, Juana murders him to protect her man, and the lovers flee to become international fugitives. By the story's conclusion, Juana is dead and Sharp's talent has departed along with her. He ends the novel a broken and anonymous man.

Pausing midway through his narrative to consider this melodramatic course of events, John Howard Sharp ties all of his problems to a single moment of weakness. In the midst of his early success, he admits, he grew weary of his fame and dismissive of his audience. "Singing is a funny job," he explains:

> You go out there and take those calls, and it's so exciting that when you get back to your dressing room you want to sing. . . . But that excitement is all from out front, from a mob you only half see and never know, and you get so you'd give anything for somebody, for just one guy that knew what you were trying to do, that spotted your idea without your telling him, that could appreciate you with his head and not with the palms of his hands. And mind you, it couldn't be just anybody. It has to be somebody you respect, somebody that knows.[2]

That longing for the appreciation of the coterie audience was his original sin, Sharp suggests. It made him vulnerable to the predatory desires of Winston Hawes, led him ironically to embrace the mass culture that he himself despises, and ultimately drove him toward the aimless life of the wanted man. Had he been able to address an audience that was not an ignorant mob but an engaged public, Sharp might have had a happy life, Cain implies. As it is, his many disappointments can all be traced to that one mistake and to the simple but corrosive evil of artistic professionalism.

Such a premise makes for an unusual crime story, but *Serenade* is in several respects the most revealing of Cain's many novels. It is his most patently autobiographical work, the ambivalent response to the mass popularity he had attained with *The Postman Always Rings Twice* three years earlier. And it may illuminate more clearly than any other single text the constellation of problems that lay at the heart of the hard-boiled crime fiction whose recent success Cain's work exemplified. Like John Howard Sharp, James M. Cain despised both the high art of the contemporary literary elite and the cheap entertainment purveyed by the mass media, and he imagined himself like his protagonist a figure striving heroically to overcome the limits of cultural division. Like Sharp, too, though, Cain felt sure that any such effort would be bound for failure and that it would be doomed by the very features of the literary marketplace that enabled it in the first place. Just as Sharp yearns for a public that is neither the coterie nor the mob, and just as he sees that possibility constantly slipping away, Cain sought — with little hope for success — to split the difference between the "intellectual snob[bery]" of the avant-garde and the mindlessness of commercial sensation.[3] In this regard, he was typical of the whole generation of artists who reinvented the American crime novel during the middle decades of the twentieth century. The style of hard-boiled crime fiction that flourished in the United States between 1930 and 1960 tended to echo *Serenade*'s populist cynicism and its air of fatality, and the major writers who shaped the development of the genre tended to share Cain's ambivalent literary attitudes. All of them were like Cain both intensely ambitious and acutely sensitive to their own failures. Having moved in most cases from pulp anonymity to relative prestige, none was willing to think of his work as pop entertainment alone. Nor, though, could any of them imagine that he had achieved unequivocal literary success. Raymond Chandler, who claimed that he could write for "the avant-garde magazines" and in "the rough tough vernacular," also worried that no convincing way could be found to bring the two together. "You cannot have art without a public taste," Chandler claimed, "and you cannot have a public taste without a sense of style and quality throughout the social structure." But such a common culture could not compete, Chandler admitted, against the perils of aesthetic elitism and the seductions of pop entertainment. The contemporary United States simply offered "too limited a public." Dashiell Hammett echoed the sentiment, arguing that any decent writer should seek "fame, fortune and personal satisfaction," popular success and artistic legitimacy. "You're not likely to ever get all these things," he acknowledged, but "anything less is kind of piddling." Jim Thompson could have spoken for all of them when he claimed, despite the commercial success he achieved by bringing modernist techniques to the suspense novel, that he was "probably the world's most self-doubting writer."[4]

Driven by ambitions that they felt certain could not be realized, the major hard-boiled writers became, in effect, pulp avant-gardists — figures whose determination to overcome the limits of intractable cultural institutions could be measured by their willingness to embrace failure.[5] That combination of grandiose ambition and fateful resignation offered them the creative license they needed to rewrite the popular crime story, and it made their fiction both a product of, and a reflection on, their literary endeavor. Their novels became, I will argue, entries in an ongoing meditation on the difficulty of imagining a democratic culture in a literary marketplace shaped by the institutions of mass communication and professional expertise. Indeed, like *Serenade*, hard-boiled crime fiction consistently suggested a direct connection between the very form of the crime story and the latent vision of frustrated cultural reunion that inspired the genre's major writers, a connection implicit in their shared complaints against a too limited public.

Traditionally, the classic detective story celebrated the victory of public knowledge and civic solidarity over the dangers of private desire. It registered that victory formally by bringing the arcane knowledge and peculiar abilities wielded by the detective to bear on the challenge to the social order represented by the villain, suggesting thereby that there was no specialized learning that could not prove socially useful just as there was no strife or dissension that could not be absorbed by a healthy civil society. Hard-boiled crime fiction transformed that story by radicalizing its tensions. In the novels of Cain, Hammett, Chandler, and their peers, civil society can no longer contain private desire, public knowledge rarely trumps specialized expertise, and the idea of a common culture seems both profoundly appealing and ultimately unbelievable.

In this manner, hard-boiled crime fiction became, as it developed during the years between the wars, not just a style of popular entertainment, but a kind of literary critique — a metaphorical account of the possibilities for public life in a society newly acquainted with the power of the mass media and with the preeminence of a national, professional elite. By the same token, it amounted to a telling political fable for an era in the midst of profound transformation. In their renditions of a vanguardist and ultimately doomed effort to assert public values over private interests — and in their attempts to reconcile the world of literary expertise with the spirit of a pulp fiction largely associated with the urban working class — the genre's major writers echoed the rhetoric that ran through the contemporaneous development of New Deal liberalism. The various methods they chose in which to pursue or to depict that effort mirrored particular strains of New Deal thinking, and the frustrations they inevitably encountered in their pursuit of a utopian, democratic culture dramatized the conflicts and contradictions that would dog New Deal liberalism as it evolved from the 1930s through the 1950s and beyond. A pop genre, a cultural complaint, and a political myth, hard-boiled crime fiction thus became a symbolic theater where the dilemmas of New Deal liberalism could be staged.

OUR COVENANT WITH OURSELVES
The Classic Detective Story as a Parable of Classical Liberalism

Franklin Delano Roosevelt pointed to the common ground shared by New Deal politics and the hard-boiled crime novel in his second inaugural address, given in March of the same year that Cain's *Serenade* was published. The difficult effort to make a public culture out of private experience that hard-boiled crime fiction depicted lay also, as FDR explained in his speech, at the heart of the New Deal project to redefine the tenets of traditional American liberalism. This "new chapter in our book of self-government," Roosevelt announced, turned on an effort to assert "our common welfare" — "[o]ur covenant with ourselves" — over the liberties of "heedless self-interest." The challenges that faced the nation exceeded the reach of mere "individual or local solution." If the New Deal were to succeed, those outmoded methods would have to be abandoned, and "private autocratic powers" would need to be brought into "their proper subordination to the public's government." Such efforts would depend, moreover, on the ability of "popular government" to discover and represent the "common ideals" of a "single-minded" nation. Out of "the confusion of many voices," FDR asserted, presidential leadership must bring forth the "united purpose" and the "dominant public need" of "one people."[6]

At the heart of this vision of the New Deal, in sum, lay an image mirrored by the avant-gardist ideals of writers like Cain and Chandler—the invocation of a latent, collective spirit whose realization would overcome the limits of narrow institutions. The echo was not merely fortuitous. The detective story had always been a liberal genre, centrally concerned with a fundamental premise of liberal theory—the rule of law—and with the tensions fundamental to democratic societies that constantly threw that principle into doubt. Though the complex roots of the genre may lie deep in cultural history, the detective story first sprang to life in its recognizable form in Edgar Allan Poe's stories from the 1840s, when the United States under Andrew Jackson's presidency had recently experienced both the advent of populist democracy and the transformative energies of a "market revolution"—in a society, in short, that had definitively traded its republican and agrarian legacy for a liberal, capitalist order.[7] Employing Arthur Conan Doyle's innovations, the detective story leapt to mass popularity, first in England and then in the United States, near the turn of the century—at a time when the rise of organized capitalism and the evident failure of the unfettered market to deliver a just society gave rise to the first serious challenges to liberalism in both countries. Those key moments in the making of the genre came, in short, during periods when liberalism itself was in profound transition and when the social forces prodding its development threatened to tear the very idea of a liberal society to pieces.[8] The detective story both registered that threat and turned it into a manageable tale, a political myth for that "anxious man" who "emerges as the creation of liberalism."[9] It comes as no surprise, then, that detective fiction experienced its next major period of innovation in the United States during the interwar years, when a whole generation of intellectuals and politicians joined FDR in the effort to adjust liberalism to the special demands of an industrialized economy and an urbanized nation. Hard-boiled crime fiction followed a parallel track.

We can best understand the drama staged by the formal detective story created by Poe and perfected by Conan Doyle — and in turn the way in which hard-boiled crime fiction revised that story — by seeing it in light of the problem of law basic to modern, secular societies. Put simply, all classical liberal theories presume that political society is formed by the consent forged among free individuals.[10] A basic question that presupposition raises, however, concerns the binding force of such consent. If the social order is grounded by no inherited beliefs or religious truths but only by the abstract rules that people give to themselves, why should individuals submit to laws with which they may disagree or which they do not feel are their own? What can hold a society of individuals together *as* individuals and how can it overcome the competing forces that always threaten such an order — such forces, that is, as the ties of blood, family, ethnicity, community, or religion that constitute an alternate image of social responsibility; or the uncontrolled passions, unchecked desires, and unconstrained power that threaten to dissolve any stable order altogether?

For most theorists of classical liberalism, the prime answer to this question could be found in the power of rational self-interest. Heeding its call would convince individuals to live by the dictates of a civil society whose spontaneously created order was nothing more than the combined action of every rationally self-interested member of the community. Because each reasonable individual hoped to prosper in society, everyone had good reason to accept the minimal demands of sociability, responsibility, and self-control that society placed on its members. Those very demands emerged not from the transcendent source of tradition, religion, or political authority, but from the action of society itself; they were the natural creation of the many combined daily interactions of social and economic life, the self-generated rules of the game. The law itself merely formalized the most basic of these requirements and served neutrally to protect the independent workings of society; the state became, in Wilhelm von Humboldt's famous phrase, a mere night watchman. Thus, people had good reason to live by the laws and expectations of their worlds.

By doing so, they were in effect only following rules they had given to themselves, and adhering to those rules would enable them to prosper in the world they had chosen.[11]

The traditional detective story offers a similar answer. But before doing so it points to the thinness and fragility of the classical liberal vision by raising the prospect of its nightmarish inversion. In the moments before its climactic resolution, the traditional detective story depicts civil society as a regime of doubt and confusion — one where individual freedom results not in spontaneous order, but in an anarchic war of all against all, in which everyone schemes, acts duplicitously, and is motivated only by squalid purposes or irrational passions. If "the clash of unsupervised individual opinions" created by liberalism were to produce not social harmony, but "only skepticism, which destroys everything," as the great antiliberal polemicist Joseph de Maistre warned, then the classic detective story provides, until the moment of crisis, an image of the general fear and paranoia that would result from such a condition. "Everybody is suspected," Edmund Wilson states in summing up the dynamic. The "streets are full of lurking agents whose allegiances we cannot know. Nobody seems guiltless, nobody seems safe; and then, suddenly, the murderer is spotted, and — relief! — he is not, after all, a person like you or me."[12]

The classic detective story, in other words, articulates a tension basic to the classical liberal vision of society. It depicts a world in which the freedom of the individual creates an anarchic or a soulless society. It is a society where communal bonds are absent; where human relations are cold and manipulative, or violent and warlike; where the law is corrupt, abstract, or impotent, and people are driven by heedless self-interest or primal urges — only then to reverse that image by banishing a pair of scapegoats (murderer and victim) who embody the worst of those evils. This is the story that Poe created in "The Murders in the Rue Morgue." His detective genius Dupin regards ordinary social life as analogous to a game of whist — a pattern of strategy, conscious calculation, and unconscious self-revelation, where "mind struggles with mind" in the pursuit of "legitimate advantage." That game is the perfect image of civil society seen as the intersection of rationally self-interest agents, and the patterns that Dupin discovers in it enable him to recognize what exceeds them: in this case, the brutal slaughter of Madame L'Espanaye and her daughter by a Bornese "Ourang-Outang"—an animal that is crucially both nearly human and of "intractable," and hence inhuman, "ferocity." In short, only the genius whose "analytic ability" allows him to view human action sociologically or ethnographically, as a neutral game played by nameless self-interested players, can separate bestial fury from the ordinary patterns of civil society, thus reassuring us that random violence is truly idiosyncratic and that most people are tractable rather than ferocious. Once violence is shown to be "without motive" and "absolutely alien from humanity," society can return to its ordinary workings, just as in "The Purloined Letter" communication can return to its normal channels once the threat of criminal interference is removed.[13]

As Edmund Wilson, W. H. Auden, and countless later critics of the genre have noted, nearly every example of detective fiction follows that basic outline—a pervasive skepticism, or paranoia, or guilt is dispatched, and life returns to its normal channels when the detective-genius banishes a criminal scapegoat. One way to describe this scenario would be to say that the classic detective story plays on our experience with what the philosopher Ernest Gellner calls the "naïve realism" and "naïve mentalism" of ordinary life: the assumption that "things are as we think they are," reflected simply in our minds, and that "our inner habits and motivation, our susceptibilities and competences" are similarly self-evident. The truth, of course, is that, though we habitually take them for granted, both our knowledge of the world and our mental susceptibilities and competences are far from self-evident. What makes them seem so, Gellner points out, is the "system of . . . seemingly self-evident connections . . . known as a culture." And what the detective story does is to take advantage of that fact. Playing on the classical liberal assumption that modern societies are ungrounded by tradition or religion—that they are based solely on the free consent of individuals—the genre acts momentarily as if the self-evident assumptions of culture had been erased. No facts can be assumed, no behavior is predictable, no mental actions are reliable. (Hence Jim Thompson's claim that "there is only one plot — things are not as they seem," and hence also Poe's introduction of "the imp of the perverse" alongside his genius Dupin.) Then the detective steps in and, viewing the world ethnographically, shows that, though we may have doubted it, such a culture existed all along. Indeed, the seemingly anarchic terrain of civil society turns out to be not a soulless market but a reassuring culture, exacting unstated obligations, punishing outrageous actions, and rewarding reliable behavior. By the lights of detective fiction, modern societies are thus simultaneously ungrounded and basically predictable.[14]

A more robust and revealing version of the story can be seen in *A Study in Scarlet*, the novella in which Arthur Conan Doyle introduced Sherlock Holmes and began to expand on the possibilities established by Poe's model. In doing so, Doyle made the liberal presuppositions of the detective story more cogent by registering more clearly the challenges that modern societies could present to such assumptions. As Holmes himself explains, crime serves a similar purpose for Conan Doyle that whist does for Poe. Though here it operates as a contrasting negative rather than as the analogy that Poe sees in whist, the "scarlet thread of murder" is significant because it runs through "the colorless skein of life" to reveal its otherwise invisible order, thus bringing forward the tacit bonds of liberal society.[15] In a different example, Doyle makes the point still more clearly when he has Holmes imagine floating above London and removing the city's rooftops to see "the strange coincidences, the plannings, the cross-purposes, the wonderful chains of events, working through generations and leading to the most *outré* results." This vision of a neutral and omniscient viewpoint is not merely voyeuristic fantasy, as some critics have suggested, but much as in Poe, an appeal to the unplanned order that emerges from seemingly anarchic, individual acts. Vicariously granted the superior viewpoint of the detective, Doyle's readers can discover along with Holmes the elements of the structure that is always invisible amid everyday interactions — the common pattern created by the merely individual plannings and cross-purposes of the city's individual residents — and they can thus experience a central aesthetic pleasure of the mystery story:

the tension between pattern and event, structure and agency, the plotted and the outré that organizes every example of the genre.[16]

For Conan Doyle, as for Poe, the hidden structure that Sherlock Holmes discovers in the city becomes most significant when society appears, in fact, most anarchic. When *A Study in Scarlet* begins, we first meet Doctor Watson who has returned as an invalid from war in India to London, "that great cesspool into which all the loungers and idlers of the empire are irresistibly drained." With neither "kith nor kin in England," Watson stays in "a private hotel in the Strand, leading a comfortless, meaningless existence," until he is introduced by a former schoolmate to Holmes and decides to move in with him — because, as he explains, he is running through his savings and "should prefer having a partner to being alone" (2, 3). Later, when Watson and Holmes first come upon the scene of the murder at the center of the novel and find the word "rache" (German for revenge) scrawled in blood on the wall, the implicit significance of these minor features is redoubled. For, the word appears to indicate the presence of "the secret societies" of revolutionary anarchism (116), and the portrait of the city of London that results from these and other carefully assembled details is a picture of liberal society as its most vehement critics describe it. The metropolis appears cold and anonymous, riven by class tension and submerged political struggle, its solitary and weak individuals like Watson thrown back cruelly on their own pitiful resources. The criminal violence that runs through the city appears an emblem of its very political order. For, as Watson points out, the popular press attributes the crime at the heart of the story either to the absence of authority characteristic of "a Liberal administration" or to the "despotism" of "Continental governments," whose "hatred of Liberalism" spawns an international network of political resistance and violent subversion (46, 47). For Conan Doyle, at least, it seems clear that crime raises the question of the very legitimacy of a liberal society.

Of course, true to the detective story form, *A Study in Scarlet* will ultimately show that the murder at its center is not at all "a political one," but rather the fruit of a "private wrong" (121). And the novella will suggest consequently that, at least for Doyle, murder does not truly question the liberal order, but only makes its virtues clear. Those virtues are figured most tellingly in the "partner[ship]" of Watson and Holmes — an image of the free association at the core of civil society — and they are implicitly cast in relief by the history of the "private wrong" contained in the story's central murder narrative. That history is explained to us in a complex but revealing background narrative detailing the story of Jefferson Hope, an American frontiersman who comes into conflict with the Church of Mormon. As a young man, Hope had been betrothed to Lucy Ferrier, a young woman who had grown up within the church's territory in Utah and who had adhered to its rules without ever being a true believer. Learning of their engagement, however, the church fathers determine that, in order to preserve the institutions of polygamy, Lucy must marry a Mormon saint, and they exercise all the "formidable machinery" of their "terrible despotism" to compel her assent (83, 96). In the end, a lascivious pair of Mormon brothers kidnap Lucy and force her into marriage, an indignity that leads to her death. Jefferson Hope, "possessed" by "a power of sustained vindictiveness which he may have learned from the Indians among whom he had lived," swears revenge and pursues Lucy's kidnappers throughout the United States and Europe (101). He finally runs them down in London and, wreaking his vengeance, leaves the corpses and the scattered clues that establish the novella's mystery.

The most obvious significance of this melodramatic tale is to reveal Holmes's remarkable powers, for he intuits most of its features without needing to be told the details. Its more significant purpose, though, is to set up two alternative images of moral action to be contrasted to the friendship of Watson and Holmes. On the one hand, there is the despotism of a patriarchal religious society, whose surface appearance of order, harmony, and prosperity is belied by the coercion on which it rests. Although the Mormons build what seems an Edenic community in the Utah desert, that order depends on an "omniscient and omnipresent" system of enforcement that denies personal freedom and gives rise to rapacity and terror (83). (It is surely no coincidence that Doyle displaces attention to the "secret societies" of socialist and anarchist radicalism with the "secret society" of the Mormon patriarchy. While the Mormon patriarchy was reassuringly distant from late Victorian England, each promises to create a utopian community, and for Doyle, each kind of clandestine utopian society exemplifies the danger of hidden power and violent coercion.) Almost as troubling, though, is the noble spirit of vengeance represented by Jefferson Hope. We are plainly meant to feel, as Watson does, both sympathy for Hope's righteous pursuit of justice and revulsion at his all-consuming determination to exact a revenge for which he alone will be "judge, jury, and executioner" (109). Closely aligned with the Noble Savage of the Native American, he is implicitly, like the Latter-Day Saints, outside the order of liberal society — like the Mormons, Doyle's parodic image of a premodern traditional culture. Though Hope's actions are heroically individual, where theirs are cruelly authoritarian, each refuses to be bound by the rule of law or to adhere to the claims of rational self-interest built into civil society. For, though noble in one case and squalid in the other, both the Mormons and Jefferson Hope are driven by unyielding passion and uncontrolled desire, and both defer to the values of tradition and affiliation over abstract claims of individual right.

The effect of such excess is to cast the friendship of Watson and Holmes, and the social bonds they exemplify, as free and reasonable by comparison. Placed in contrast to the nightmarish world of Utah or the unbending obsession of Jefferson Hope, metropolitan London looks less like a coldly anonymous city and more like an open but coherent society, a place where personal freedom and civic tolerance flourish. As the emblem of those virtues, the fraternal partnership of Watson and Holmes is all but explicitly contrasted to the violent bonds between Hope and his victims. When Watson decides to room with Holmes, his schoolmate warns about the detective's eccentric interests, claiming that he could imagine Holmes "giving his friend a little pinch of the latest vegetable alkaloid . . . out of a spirit of inquiry" (5). Later, we learn that this is precisely the method that Jefferson Hope uses to poison his victim, and the implication — which will be made still more patent in later comparisons of Holmes to his slothful brother Mycroft and to the criminal genius Professor Moriarty — is clear. Hope is a noble figure who must die because he will not yield to the formal demands of law and because he cannot be assimilated to a liberal and democratic order. Holmes is a similarly aristocratic figure, but, like his predecessor Dupin, he is an aristocrat willing to live by the rules of liberal democracy, and he is admirable because he turns his extravagant abilities not to self-aggrandizement or pointless specialization, but to the larger benefit of society.[17]

What such a contrast should bring out is the strongly ethical component of the classic detective story — a component that, like the classical liberal vision of civil society, disguises itself beneath an impression that it records merely the amoral actions in society's elaborate game of whist. Classical liberal theory sometimes suggested, as in Bernard Mandeville, that society as a whole benefited when individuals heedlessly pursued their personal desires — that private vices combined to produce the public good. More frequently, though, liberal theory contended people were in fact at their best when they listened to the dictates of rational self-interest. They were most peaceful, tolerant, responsible, reasonable, and open-minded — though perhaps not most heroic or noble — when, in order to advance their own interests, they lived by the demands of civil society. The classic detective tale is a paean to those humble bourgeois virtues in the guise of a parable of their disappearance. In the tales of friendship, neighborliness, and openness that make up a crucial aspect of the genre's apparatus, and which are only heightened in their significance by the fiction's contrasting images of cruelty and paranoia, decent and democratic folk prosper and the arrogant and obnoxious suffer.

A similar thing is true of the work of detection itself, which as a number of critics have suggested is the heart of the fiction, and which they often read as the expression of an oppressive form of disciplinary surveillance — "the exercise of lucid power over an identified enemy of society." To see the fiction in this light, however, is to capture only half its mythic import. It is true that mystery stories often cast the detective's abilities as a kind of terrifying intellectual power capable of submitting human idiosyncrasy to order, just as they habitually suggest that society is vicious and the law absurd. In each case, though, that negative image is raised solely so that it can be banished. The point of the detective's work, from the perspective of detective fiction, is not that it submits society to a disciplinary grid, nor that it represents the "triumph of a superior mind."[18] Indeed, each of those dangers is best represented by criminal geniuses like Professor Moriarty who exist to provide inverted images of the detective hero. The significance of the detective, rather, is that he or she sees as we do ordinarily — reading the signs of clothing and manner, inventing life histories from casual remarks, reconstructing the tacit drama of society — only with more acuity. In doing so, the detective separates, with far more confidence than we ever could, the venial sins of mundane life from actions that truly threaten the fabric of society; simultaneously, the detective commits himself or herself to live within the patterns of that fabric. The detective is, in this light, not significant because he or she is "an exceptional individual" and the mystery story is not quite "a form of traditional heroic 'discourse' in modern guise."[19] The classic detective, instead, is an exceptional individual who matters because he or she finally chooses not to be exceptional and thus is a hero who surrenders, all but completely, heroic virtues for bourgeois habits. Seen this way, the ethical drama of the detective story is a drama of the commitment to civil society.

AN INDIAN HAS NEVER HEARD OF A CONTRACT
The Hard-Boiled Challenge to the Classical Story

In perfecting that drama, Conan Doyle fashioned a myth of liberal society, and he celebrated its tenets — personal freedom and the rule of law, especially — against the problems of aimlessness and amoralism internal to liberalism and against the cultural, intellectual, and political challenges to liberal theory that were already becoming prevalent by the late nineteenth century. (Holmes, who is a parody of the scientist is also famously an echo of the decadent aesthete, and he thus yokes an unlikely image of intellectual and cultural harmony at the very moment when the implausibility of that harmony was growing increasingly apparent.) In effect, the classic detective story exploits and then symbolically remedies the weakest features of the classical liberal vision of society. Most people are not guided consistently by rational self-interest, but often, like Jefferson Hope, by selfless, irrational, and destructive passions. Liberal society cannot claim, like the Mormon church or the anarchist utopia, to be built on shared faith and common purpose, but flourishes instead, as Ernest Gellner points out, "on doubt, compromise, and doublethink."[20] The rule of law is often not fair or just, but frequently rigidly bureaucratic and a weapon of the powerful. The role of the detective, however, is to take the long view enjoyed by the social scientist in order to suggest that such sources of skepticism are ultimately insignificant. Out of the combination of ordinary habits and the disparate movements of isolated individuals, civil society produces a stable order that can survive violence and abuse. Out of the darkness of hidden power, obscured crimes and abuses can be brought to public light and resolved. And the legal order, which is often impotent or an obstruction, can thereby be brought in line with the demands of justice. As Inspector Lestrade explains at the conclusion to *A Study in Scarlet*, "the forms of the law must be complied with" (118).

By the turn of the century, however, the assumptions behind this story were already coming into doubt. To many of the era's leading intellectuals, the corporate concentration of economic power, the rapid growth of the state, and the prevalence of deep social ills and political conflicts all seemed to make the classical liberal theory at the core of Doyle's stories outmoded, and the tacit moral center of his fiction — the image of a society of free and responsible individuals — looked ever more like the nostalgic myth that it would plainly be in the "golden age" mystery of the twenties.[21] By the 1930s, the poverty of liberal theory seemed apparent. To the most significant of the era's political thinkers and actors, the idea of a society of free individuals was not just a remnant of a simpler era of economic and political decentralization, but a reactionary force in and of itself — one that protected the rights of the powerful and ignored the needs of the weak. Among those who sought to defend it, the assumption was common that if liberalism were not to perish altogether, it would need to be fundamentally revised.

This was what FDR referred to when he spoke of a "new chapter in our book of self-government." The crisis of the Depression had finally made it clear, Roosevelt contended, that a complex, urban industrial society demanded a "redefinition" of the nation's traditional liberal principles. As the "intricacies of human relationships increase," he explained, "so power to govern them must also increase." And that meant that, facing the realities of a "changing and growing social order," the tenets of nineteenth-century liberalism — the primacy of personal liberty and freedom of contract especially — would have to yield. "[P]rivate economic power is, to enlarge an old phrase, a public trust as well," FDR argued, and thus in a centralized industrial economy, "property rights" and personal liberties would need to be reconceived so that they would not conflict with the larger claims of the "public welfare."[22]

Such arguments echoed throughout the political discourse of the interwar decades, expanding on a tradition of social criticism that had been developing in the United States since the Progressive Era but that came to wide academic and popular prominence only during the twenties and early thirties. Developing rapidly throughout the era, the newly formed disciplines of the social sciences established their credibility in good part by pointing like FDR to the gap between the dogma of traditional political theory and the unacknowledged facts of social reality. If the dominant political creed of the nineteenth-century United States amounted, as Louis Hartz would later argue, to a tacit "Lockean consensus" — envisioning a society joined only by the rational consent of free individuals — academic writing in the interwar era would consistently point to the unreality of those assumptions.[23] In legal scholarship and political science especially, "realist" or "naturalist" thinkers transformed their disciplines by arguing that the classical liberal vision of a decentralized society built on free consent was outmoded. In fact, if not in theory, they argued, society was held together by superstition and prejudice and was governed not by a democratic citizenry, but by potent economic and political elites. To deny that reality in order to preserve outworn ideals of individual freedom and democratic participation would be to live in a dreamworld. It would also mean surrendering the tools of "social control" necessary to govern a complex civilization while ceding political authority to the most powerful members of society. As one prominent legal realist claimed in a denunciation of the fictions of individual right and the rule of law, "men have used philosophies to maintain the *status quo*"; they might employ them, though, as "naturalistic jurisprudence should be used" — to shape "social arrangements" in "preparation for an intellectual tomorrow."[24]

Like FDR, in short, the dominant schools of social thought during the interwar era argued that if liberalism were to survive in an industrialized society, it would need to be saved from itself. Both directly and indirectly, the major hard-boiled writers echoed those "realist" critics of traditional liberal theory. James M. Cain's first book, a work of journalistic political speculation called *Our Government*, drew explicitly on "realist" arguments to assert that useful knowledge depended on abandoning the "theological perspective" of traditional political dogma in favor of "the muddy waters of experience." One should hope not to "know what government was intended to be" or "what it ought to be," but "what government actually is" — and what it usually was, he suggested, was inefficient and corrupt. Dashiell Hammett similarly mimicked contemporary "realists" by arguing that a fundamental divide fell between the empirical facts of ordinary existence and the "metaphysical" principles of moral philosophy.[25] More important, though, the hard-boiled writers' very efforts to revise the detective story form depended on a logic that mirrored the "realist" critique of traditional liberal theory. The classic mystery story had been itself a parable of liberal society. Depicting the challenge to the social order posed by some anomalous example of unconstrained passion or personal desire, the classic detective tale banished that evil to create an image of a community ruled by law and formed by the consent of free agents. At its center thus stood, as one early critic noted, "not the state . . . but instead the individual."[26] When they attacked that genre for being unrealistic — or, in Raymond Chandler's revealing terminology, "formal" — then, the hard-boiled writers implicitly cast the classic detective story in the same role that "realists" attributed to liberal theory. The traditional mystery tale was a political myth, illegitimate because it no longer corresponded to the complex realities of an urban, industrial society. In Chandler's implicit description, it was a "fiction" at odds with "the tangled woof of fact."[27] If the genre were to survive, then, it would need, like the liberalism it echoed, to be saved from its own worst tendencies — an effort that, as in contemporary political thought, would depend on displacing the centrality of the individual with an emphasis on the significance of the state and the problems of "social control" that the state exemplified.

That was the problem to which James M. Cain pointed implicitly in *Serenade* and throughout his work, where he retold the story underlying *A Study in Scarlet* and "The Murders in the Rue Morgue" in order to emphasize its untenability. For Cain, who praised Conan Doyle's "easy intimacy with the reader," the classic detective story suggested an image of public communication that echoed the genre's celebration of civil society.[28] In his own reworking of the form, though, Cain made the hard-boiled crime story a tale of the *absence* of popular voice and civic freedom, as if to make clear just how outmoded the classic detective story and its vision of society had become.

The very awkwardness of Cain's tale and his characterization drew attention to this problem. For, if the classic detective story depicted the victory of public knowledge over social fragmentation, a victory echoed by the fiction's very "intimacy" with its popular readership, *Serenade*'s unusual premise pointed to the unlikelihood of that story. In his earlier novels, *The Postman Always Rings Twice* and *Double Indemnity*, Cain had made a hero out of a figure who had obsessed him since his youth, the tough-talking common man. Cynical, appetitive, and ruthlessly self-interested, men like Frank Chambers of *Postman* or Walter Neff in *Double Indemnity* are in Cain's description, "worried souls — people who may not have education or culture," but who for that very reason, "ain't tepid." Such protagonists embodied Cain's distaste for pretense. They did nothing, however, to address the writer's other great love, the fine art of operatic music. Cain's first ambition as a young man, acquired around the same time that he became fascinated with the tough-guy vernacular of the urban working class, had been a career in opera. Professional writing, he claimed later, "was distinctly a consolation prize." And throughout his life he remained a passionate amateur singer, fiercely dedicated to protecting the divide between great music and cheap entertainment.[29] *Serenade* emerged as the product of the combination of these strangely disparate interests. Juxtaposing the untepid spirit of hard-boiled populism with the redemptive air of great music, Cain sought to meld the two by plunging them into the same cauldron of sex and fatality that had powered his previous fiction. The result was a novel whose unusual, often awkward features cut directly to the tensions at the heart of Cain's novelistic career and, more broadly, to those characteristic of the whole hard-boiled genre.

Those difficulties appear most directly in the characterization of the novel's protagonist and narrator, John Howard Sharp — a figure who resembles Frank Chambers in station and demeanor and (as his name might suggest) Cain himself in aesthetic sensibility. Like Cain, Sharp is a failed tenor. Like Frank Chambers, he is a tough guy on the bum, with an eye for the main chance and a weakness for dangerous women. When the story begins, Sharp is stranded in Mexico City. The failure of his operatic career has left him penniless and in doubt of both his abilities as a singer and, more fundamentally, of his masculinity. In the novel's first scene, however, Sharp encounters Juana, and he soon discovers that she will be the means to his salvation. When the two are stranded together in an empty church at the height of a tropical storm, Sharp forces himself upon Juana and soon recovers all his powers as a result. The rape, he assures us, was "only technical, brother, only technical," and he gains from it not just Juana's undying love and a renewed sense of his own masculine prowess, but the return of his once lost voice. "Something in me had died. And now . . . had come back, just as sudden as it went," he exults. "I was . . . like a man that had gone blind, and then woke up one morning to find out that he could see."[30]

Cain's rape scene earned his novel predictable controversy, though more for its reputed sacrilege than for its celebration of sexual violence. But, in truth, the core concerns of *Serenade* followed this moment, in the effects on Sharp's singing career that Cain traced to the rape. The most immediate of these is awesome artistic power. Sharp not only recovers his voice; it is full of new force and vitality, and returning with Juana to the United States, he calls on it, first to rocket to overnight stardom in Hollywood musicals and radio variety shows, and then to rejuvenate his operatic career, rising to assume the role of star tenor at the Met — "the best opera company in the world" (112). As in Cain's earlier fiction, though, such happiness is bound to be short-lived. Sharp's new stardom brings him to the attention of Winston Hawes, the homosexual impressario who once directed the singer's career, and when Hawes again begins to assert aesthetic and erotic control over Sharp, Juana rises to defend her man — murdering her rival in a parodic reenactment of a bullfight. The two lovers must flee, therefore, to Central America and eventually back to Mexico where they live in hiding. Sharp, who has been made internationally famous by American mass media, is forced to conceal his identity and, more important, to restrain his remarkable voice. Like the sexual potency with which it is closely linked, though, his vocal power is irrepressible. Unable to restrain his extraordinary virility, Sharp lets loose a burst of *"Canta y no llores"* in the center of Mexico City. The song immediately identifies the fugitives, and Juana is promptly shot as she flees. The novel ends with Sharp lost, broken, and doomed to the failure he had briefly escaped.

Like his previous novels, then, *Serenade* tells the story that obsessed Cain — that of the "terrifying concept" of "the wish that comes true."[31] Like Frank Chambers in *The Postman Always Rings Twice* and Walter Neff in *Double Indemnity*, John Howard Sharp gets everything he desires and is destroyed by that satisfaction. But far more explicitly than in Cain's earlier fiction, *Serenade* also makes a problem of the very fantasy of public communication that he praised in the classic detective story. Sharp is literally made and destroyed by popular voice. That is the power he longs for and that ultimately ruins him, and the novel's central problem is the fact that no ground seems to exist between Sharp's extraordinary fame and his public vulnerability — or between the primitive authenticity represented by Juana and the effete specialization embodied by Winston Hawes. Cain's point resembles Raymond Chandler's complaint against the limited public: there seems to be no institution that can shape and guard popular expression and thus no intermediate ground between Sharp's massive power as a media figure and the anonymity he rediscovers once that authority is lost.

The events of Cain's narrative give greater weight to this impression, and they lay out Cain's complaint in terms close to those relied on by Chandler. For, if Sharp was intended to combine Cain's democratic sympathies and his elite tastes, the character does far more to emphasize their antagonism and weak resolution. Sharp speaks of

Rossini, Beethoven, and the Met in the same laconically cynical voice that Cain used for the narration of Frank Chambers and Walter Neff, and the awkwardness of that combination points to a discomfort that Cain felt was central to his career. On the one hand, his political impulses and aesthetic inclinations were deeply populist in orientation. He disdained both Republican conservativism and Harvard liberalism, he claimed, and he likewise sneered at any sign of aesthetic pretense or elitism. The "conscious creation of art is a form of literary smugness," he argued in the forties, and throughout his career he denounced the "virtuously cultivated aestheticism" and the "ideation[al]" preoccupations of his most prominent contemporaries. His own mind, he bragged with reverse snobbery, was one of "appalling usualness, . . . filled with trade goods right off the national stockpile," and when he spoke about literature, he sometimes turned similarly to the market-driven methods of pulp fiction, popular theater, and the movies for an image of a "literature of the people." Yet Cain was equally inclined to see mass culture as cheap, shallow, and manipulative. Speaking of his own work in Hollywood, he claimed about screenwriting that it was "not art, but . . . money, and the older I get the more I wonder whether the two are not the same thing." The interesting, and exemplary, feature of that remark is the way in which Cain sought to align commercial craft and literary art without finally eliding the distinction between the two. As many of his hard-boiled contemporaries would do, he called on the demands of the market to rebuke aesthetic pretense and on artistic value to denounce mass-cultural shoddiness; thus, he could be finally comfortable neither thinking of himself as a literary artist nor proclaiming himself a commercial producer.[32]

The narrative voice that Cain called on for his crime-fiction protagonists was intended to address this difficulty, since it was supposed to be at once antielitist and noncommercial. Around the time he was writing *Serenade*, Cain confidently denounced both modernist literary experiment and middlebrow snobbishness by calling on the rhetoric of populist nativism. "We have striven so hard for culture," he complained, "and on the whole so unhappily, that it ought to be clear by now that there is something screwy about the whole quest; that we are not as other nations are and that our culture cannot be forced to take the form that their cultures have." Against that tendency, then, Cain would call on "the language of the western roughneck" whose value stemmed from the fact that it was neither tepid, nor hackneyed, but seemed by contrast "elemental." Thus, implicit in the creation of Frank Chambers and Walter Neff—and in their common vernacular in particular—was Cain's vision of a program of cultural nationalism, one in which the effort to refuse European sophistication would culminate in the reclamation of a primitive national authenticity. Rediscovered, "our culture"—an implicitly democratic and common inheritance—would overcome the dangers of both sterile sophistication and commercial vulgarity and would thereby reproduce the "easy intimacy with the reader" that had been lost in the pursuit of foreign learning.[33]

That vision is implicit in both *The Postman Always Rings Twice* and *Double Indemnity*, both of which, however, portray its failure. In each, the vernacular wisdom embodied by Cain's protagonists cannot contend with a bureaucratic and commercial order—represented by courts, laws, insurance companies, and roadside restaurants—indifferent to its survival. Cain returned once again to the promise of cultural nationalism in *Serenade*. But as if in response to the frustration it suffered in his previous work, that vision became here far more direct and elaborate, and ultimately far more problematic, than it had been in its initial appearance. The antagonistic and predatory relations among Sharp, Juana, and Winston Hawes lent Cain's sense of an embattled national culture a dramatic and nearly allegorical form, and if that drama were not itself clear enough, Cain paused midway through the novel to make his aesthetic theory explicit. Fleeing Mexico for the United States, Sharp falls into debate with Captain Conners, the honest old salt who pilots the tramp steamer on which Sharp and Juana are traveling. Their topic at first is classical music and the relative merits of Italian opera and German symphony. From there, though, the two quickly turn to Cain's real concern—the relation between high art and popular expression and their intimate connection in the elemental source of the national tongue. "I'm a bit of a bug on that subject of language," Sharp announces, and he goes on to explain the reasons for his obsession. Different languages bear within themselves fundamentally different artistic possibilities, and those aesthetic principles correspond with the spiritual resources of the people to whom the languages naturally belong, he argues. Language is thus less a medium of communication than the expression of a collective soul. It is "born in . . . [the] mouth" of its speakers, the vehicle of their common "being." The true artist must be a bug on the subject, therefore, because it is the language one naturally speaks that distinguishes authentic expression from both shallow entertainment and decadent aestheticism. In the common tongue, suffused with the "knowledge of what lurks below the surface," high art and popular voice come together. Without it, Cain suggests, "true beauty" drifts toward the corruption of either elite alienation or lowbrow ignorance.[34]

Given the mutually antagonistic authorial stances that Cain seemingly wanted to invoke throughout his career, it is perhaps obvious why he might be drawn to such a vision of organic culture. But if that theory was intended to address the aesthetic tensions that dogged Cain's career, *Serenade* revealed it to be less a solution than a problem in itself — both as an ethical principle informing Cain's novel and, more obviously, as a formal aspect of its narrative. Thriller novels do not usually interrupt their action to insert the kind of philosophical dialogue pursued by Sharp and Captain Conners. Something is plainly ill-fitting about the effort to graft theoretical speculation onto the narrative of the pulp thriller — a hybrid as misplaced in its way as the decision to make an opera singer the hero of a hard-boiled crime story — and the sheer awkwardness of this passage in Cain's novel emphasizes less the writer's synthetic abilities than the unlikely combination of stances he was attempting to manage. Traditionally, cultural nationalism has been the special province of marginal literary intellectuals. As critics and historians have noted frequently, the kind of romantic vision of profound national spirit on which it depends may be especially appealing to isolated artists and intellectuals because its central claim — that it is up to the solitary and gifted figure to articulate an obscure national identity — can compensate well for the actual fact of popular marginality. Nationalism thus allows such people to claim a transcendent popular authority while allowing them simultaneously to deny the authority of the pop culture market.[35] When Cain sat down to write *Serenade*, however, he was far from a marginal intellectual. Indeed, the massive success of *The Postman Always Rings Twice* placed him at the throbbing heart of the industries of American mass culture, and he exemplified the commercial and popular success that could come to the writer in that world who identified himself less as an artist than as a professional craftsman. Indeed, the cultural nationalism invoked by Sharp depends on just those "ideation[al]" literary concerns that Cain sought to disavow when he pointed to the value of commercial success. If he believed as he claimed that the only legitimate motivations for writing were "money and recognition (which leads to more money)," then he was far out of keeping with the main line of cultural nationalism, whose central claim tends always to be that there are values — national or cultural values — more fundamental than those determined by the market.[36]

In short, like nearly all his literary reflections, the philosophical dialogue at the heart of *Serenade* testified less to the coherence of Cain's aesthetic vision than to the fundamental tensions that divided it. Though he may have imagined that an "elemental" voice, emerging from the common spirit of the nation, could overcome the limitations of a fragmented literary culture, his own narrative methods pointed both to the appeal of that vision and to its impossibility. "The only way I can keep on the track at all," he acknowledged of his writing, "is to pretend to be someone else — to put it in dialect and thus get it told. If I try to do it in my own language I find I have none."[37] That is the dilemma that *Serenade* explores, the yearning to invoke a common culture and the realization that no such thing exists. For the central irony on which the novel relies is the fact that, just as Cain found he lacked a language of his own, John Howard Sharp discovers that he has no voice without the primitive authority of Juana and that, however much he may need it, he can never fully possess that authority. After a climactic moment in which he attempts to fend off his weakness before Winston Hawes by literally nursing at Juana's breast, Sharp comes to a late understanding: "I know now," he admits, that "all my life comes from there," and the exclamation illustrates Cain's point in brief (145). Sharp can sing only when he makes himself both Juana's lover and her child. But the fact that her elemental language is Spanish and his is English emphasizes just how tenuous their connection must inevitably be.

Cain raises that implication for the first time after the pivotal rape scene, when Juana renames Sharp, dubbing him "Hoaney." At first, Sharp is disappointed by this endearment. "I half wished she had picked out something different than what she called every Weehawken slob that had showed up at her crib." The name Honey, he complains, resonates with the false sentiment and empty repetition of the purely commercial relationships exemplified by prostitution. But Sharp's attitude suddenly alters when he realizes that in fact Juana is translating his name into *her* vernacular — calling him not Honey but, in effect, Juany — and he is accordingly overwhelmed by the beauty and sincerity of her expression. "[S]omething caught my throat. . . . She was calling me Johnny — her way" (70). The exchange sums up Cain's central problem. Juana can give Sharp the authenticity and power that she represents only so long as she translates him into the world of the Mexican past, a world that seems so deeply primitive that it lacks even an awareness of the fundamentals of commercial civilization. ("An Indian has never heard of a contract," Sharp points out in describing Juana. "They didn't have them under Montezuma, and never bothered with them since" [112]). When he rapes her in the heart of the Mexican jungle, then, Sharp rescues Juana from the world of contractual relations exemplified by prostitution — a world that she both lived in and could never understand — and returns with her to a more authentic form of relationship. And, although Sharp himself is slow to grasp its implications, the pathos of that story is that the beauty of the authentic past must always remain foreign to the commercial civilization represented by Weehawken. The point is thus not that Sharp possesses the language of a common people when he sings, but precisely that he does not possess it, and that the potency he gains from Juana must be impermanent. Indeed, as the novel's conclusion finally makes clear, the very effort to give it expression will ultimately kill the authentic spirit that Sharp has had the good fortune to discover.

In this respect, the irony of *Serenade*'s conclusion is a reiteration of the ironic development of John Howard Sharp's early career and indirectly of Cain's dissatisfaction with his own literary errand. He was not always an effete intellectual, Sharp takes care to intimate to his readers. He grew up an honest, working-class kid, blessed with the talent and opportunity that enabled him to rise to artistic prestige. But his career took a wrong turn, he explains, when he grew dissatisfied with the rewards of operatic success. The result of that frustration, however, is the disaster that encapsulates Cain's diagnosis of the cultural marketplace, an account that is at once an acute sociological analysis and an ugly example of homophobic moralism. The very enormity of his popular success, the singer explains, reduces his public to a faceless mob, and, casting the star into isolation, it naturally leads him toward the intimacies of professional appreciation. But, where his modernist contemporaries would tend to see that development as a story of emancipation — of the freedom to be gained by embracing the expert coterie over the mass audience — Cain makes it a tale of decadence.[38] For in his confusion Sharp turns to Winston Hawes, the avant-garde conductor and homosexual Svengali who embodies the evils of elite privilege, decadent aestheticism, and sexual corruption. The wealthy scion of a meat-packing industry dynasty, Hawes represents for Cain both modernist experiment and commercial degradation. With his "Petite Orchestra" and his commitment to artistic excellence, Hawes does "more for modern music than anyone," Sharp admits. But because that innovation is premised on Hawes's financial ability to "own a composer, . . . own an audience, . . . own the orchestra, . . . own the singer," it seems plainly "unhealthy" to Sharp. "He made a whore out of music," Sharp complains, and the ultimate extension of that attitude is that he seeks to make a gigolo of Sharp. First seducing Sharp by his appreciation of the tenor's abilities, then enticing him into his company by the promise to lead Sharp to artistic "perfection" (he "had a live stick" as a conductor, Sharp says, and "threw it on you like a hypnotist, and you began to roll it out, and yet it was all under perfect control"), Hawes finally gains complete emotional control over Sharp and attempts to convert that power to sexual possession. The result is the destruction of the hero's voice (127–30).

Were that story the only dimension of Cain's account of contemporary culture, his novel would be an inventive but familiar attack on cultural elitism. The equation of sterile aesthetic expertise with homosexual prostitution is a nastily ingenious translation of common wisdom into pulp narrative. But that association is only one aspect of *Serenade*'s critique. Like Chandler, Cain can be happy neither as elitist nor as anti-intellectual, and he balances his distaste for aesthetic professionalism with an attack on the very populism of the market he could sometimes celebrate against snobbery. When he comes back to the United States from Mexico with Juana, Sharp first returns to his singing career by working in the movies and radio. With only the slightest effort, he becomes an international star — "a household institution, name, face, voice and all, from Hudson Bay to Cape Horn and back again" — and for Sharp the ease of that success serves as a testimony to the convenient shallowness of popular entertainment. Though he sneers at the bad taste of the mass audience and at the philistinism of the merchants who pander to it, he can take pleasure in the fact that pop culture seems so easily manipulable. By contrast to the world of Winston Hawes, where Sharp fell beneath the hypnotic stick of the avant-gardist, here he seems master of every arrangement. Indeed, at one pivotal moment, while singing on a radio show broadcast throughout the Americas, Sharp pauses, despite the fact that radio "messages to private persons are strictly forbidden" by federal law, to insert a greeting to Captain Conners (138). The implicit comparison to Sharp's time in Paris with Hawes underlines the appeal of mass culture. While a prisoner of the avant-garde, Sharp discovered that the liberty of aesthetic elitism was actually a form of imprisonment. The world of pop culture may seem shallow by contrast, but it appears to allow Sharp the freedom to exert his will over bureaucratic restrictions and to nourish the sentimental brotherhood he has established with Captain Conners. Mass media seem to replace the homoerotic captivity of the cultural elite with populist, homosocial affection.

Except that this fraternity, too, quickly becomes a kind of constraint. Later in the novel, after the climactic murder scene, when he and Juana must flee the authorities, Sharp discovers the depth of his error. Because of the illegal broadcast he made to Captain Conners, the single person certain to help the fugitives will be under constant surveillance. In his arrogance, Sharp thus effectively closed off his one clear route to escape, and that mistake illuminates the problem with mass culture in general. Since it covers the entire Western hemisphere in a web of publicity and communication, Sharp and Juana can find no place to run where they will not come under suspicion. The very media that made him powerful, now make Sharp pathetically vulnerable. "Show business is all one giant hook-up," a minor character notes earlier in the novel when Sharp finds himself ensnared in a complex set of entertainment contracts (125). By the novel's conclusion, the frustration that those contracts embody has become a kind of fatality, and the network of mass-cultural affiliation has become an iron cage.

To emphasize that point, Cain makes Winston Hawes a secret partner in the contracts that imprison Sharp. The obvious reason for that detail is to stress the book's twinned nightmares — the oligarchic structure of the entertainment industries and Hawes's satanic determination to own Sharp. The more subtle implication comes, however, in Cain's suggestion that high art and mass culture are obverse faces of a single coin. Each finally makes art "something you buy, for whatever you have to pay," thereby reducing culture to terrible effeminacy (the province of "a castrated eunuch"), and each holds out a promise of freedom and community that becomes ultimately a prison (99, 62). Juxtaposed to the vision of romantic nationalism embodied by Juana, each stands as an inadequate distortion of the promise of a common culture. Between them, drawn to each and satisfied by neither, stands Cain's stranded artist, a figure who exemplifies the impoverishment of the civil society that classic detective fiction once celebrated. The freedom of association and the public intimacy that Doyle represented in the friendship of Holmes and Watson has been narrowed in Cain's work to the freedom of contract — a liberty exemplified by Juana's prostitution and Sharp's servitude to Winston Hawes — and such freedom protects only the right of the strong to exploit the weak. Likewise, the rational self-interest that the classic detective story apotheosized by dispatching its criminals becomes in Cain an all-but-universal predatory desire exemplified by the rapacious power of tycoons and the banal appetites of consumers. In both senses, the liberal vision of a society of self-governing individuals culminates in the libertarian image of a universal law of the market. For Cain, then, it is only in the traditional world explicitly rejected by classic detective fiction—the organic, patriarchal culture exemplified by the Mormon church and embodied by Juana—that freedom is not empty, and community remains meaningful. As John Howard Sharp's fate makes clear, though, that world is no longer available in the contemporary United States.

THE INDIVIDUAL, THE BODY ECONOMIC, AND THE STATE
The Varieties of New Deal Liberalism and the Styles of Hard-Boiled Crime Fiction

Like FDR and the realist critics of liberalism, then, Cain worried about the compatibility of traditional individualism—exemplified by the swaggering machismo of John Howard Sharp—and the trend toward what Roosevelt labeled "economic oligarchy," a dynamic embodied by the shadowy power of Winston Hawes. Like FDR, too, Cain appeared to suggest that the only way to resolve that conflict was by turning toward a "greater social contract," a profound sense of national identity that could constrain the powers of "a highly concentrated economic system."[39] Thus, like FDR's account of the New Deal, *Serenade* hinged on the attempt to discover a united purpose out of the confusion of many voices—a vision of national community that seemed more profound than the classical liberal vision of civil society. Each thereby depended on the intuition that Jacques Barzun later made explicit: if a democratic society could not be guaranteed by the traditional institutions of American liberalism—representative government and individual freedom—it would depend on a more potent source of equality and mutual commitment—a common culture. The difference between the two, however, came in the fact that where Roosevelt viewed that prospect with apparently boundless optimism, Cain suggested that any such effort was bound to fail. Through much of *Serenade*, John Howard Sharp believes that he can triumph over the petty interests of media barons, the narrow restrictions of law and bureaucracy, and the hidden powers of economic oligarchs—and that in doing so he can submit the "system of Government and economics," as FDR put it, to the popular spirit articulated by his voice. He resembles, in sum, a heroic embodiment of the New Deal. In the novel's conclusion, however, Sharp realizes the futility of such confidence and discovers himself to be, not the resonant popular spirit he imagined, but an impotent and isolated figure, unable to assert "the common end" of popular government over "private advantage" and private weakness.[40]

In this respect, Cain's novel and FDR's second inaugural address represent contrary ways of evaluating the fortunes of the New Deal in the later thirties and, more broadly, of the contemporary redefinition of liberalism. Speaking early in 1937, Roosevelt looked back on what seemed the success of the first New Deal and anticipated the promise of similar reforms to come, seeing in "popular government" an "instrument of unimagined power for the establishment of a morally better world." Cain's novel pointed toward a different reality, anticipating the frustrations and recession that would dog Roosevelt's second and then third terms and, in effect, dramatizing the fact that 1937 would mark, in historian Alan Brinkley's description, the end of "the active phase of the New Deal."[41] By extension, the two documents exemplify two extremes among the various ways to describe the era's reconstruction of liberalism. For FDR in early 1937, the promise of government remained what it had been since his first campaign for the presidency, a means of "enlightened administration." From this perspective—exemplified by the diverse policies of antimonopolism, centralized planning, and NRA-style corporatism—the redefinition of liberalism meant "a changed concept of the duty and responsibility of government toward economic life." Though it might call on varied and perhaps inconsistent means, the expanded power of the federal government would take an active hand in reforming the structural problems endemic to industrial capitalism.[42] Cain's novel pointed toward another conception of liberalism, one that began to emerge among policy makers during the later thirties and that would come to dominate political thought only after World War II. From this perspective, the role of the state would be not administrative, but "compensatory." Rather than restructuring economic life, the federal government would work to stimulate growth, to negotiate among the various interest groups that domi-

nated social and economic life, and to protect citizens from the unpredictable fluctuations of the market—goals exemplified by the
new prominence given to fiscal policy and social insurance during
the later thirties and the forties. Instead of the managerial collectivism that FDR's inaugural address appeared to invoke, New Deal
liberalism by the end of the war would come to stand for an American Keynesianism.[43]

As many historians have noted, the policies of the Roosevelt administration during the thirties were an evolving, confusing, often chaotic
amalgam of these attitudes. It was only in the later forties, during the
Truman administration, that a settlement would be reached defining
military-based deficit spending as the core responsibility of the federal government. In its depiction of the effort to make an inclusive
public culture out of small, private notions, hard-boiled crime fiction—as both a style of popular myth and a literary movement—
would range similarly between analogs of the era's changing ideas of
liberalism. On occasion it envisioned, like FDR, the emergence of a
redemptive popular voice, one capable of overcoming social fragmentation and bureaucratic restriction to reform the basic order of
society. Indeed, however frequently the genre's writers portrayed the
failure of that dream, it remained always the horizon against which
they cast their dissatisfactions. At the other extreme, hard-boiled
crime fiction would sometimes echo Cain's suggestion that no such
redemptive common expression could be imagined—that public life
was fated to remain an aggregate of alienated private meanings. More
frequently, hard-boiled crime fiction landed somewhere between
these poles, divided between a utopian vision of a collective, "public
taste" and a realization of the irresolvable plurality of contemporary
society.

Each of these ways of reimagining political society contained an
implicit view of the role of the state and—more significantly for
hard-boiled crime fiction—of popular citizenship. If the central
problem of the era's reconstruction of liberalism concerned the relation between activist government and the prerogatives of personal
liberty, rethinking that balance would inevitably alter assumptions
about the part to be played by individual citizens—"creating new
relationships," as James Landis, the chair of the new Securities and

Exchange Commission, explained in 1938, "between the individual, the body economic, and the state."[44] At one extreme, a managerialist strain in contemporary thought narrowed the political significance of the ordinary voter to a slim and virtually insignificant range. This view — prominent among New Dealers like Landis who staffed the era's expanding state bureaucracies and the social science academics who provided their philosophy — suggested that the ability of ordinary citizens to direct their government was as limited as their capacity to control an industrial economy. Where the tacit Lockeanism of traditional liberalism imagined a citizenry that directed its affairs by rational consent, the "realist" and "naturalist" thinkers of the New Deal era emphasized that society was held together by myth, superstition, prejudice, and popular inertia. Political change depended, therefore, on what Landis called "expertness" — the leadership of an elite capable of directing the "bold, persistent experimentation" and the "social planning" that FDR placed at the heart of the New Deal. It was up to the representatives of "intelligence," the prominent political scientist Charles Merriam explained, to "shape forms and general understandings appropriate to the emerging order of things."[45]

From this perspective, the New Deal's commitment to defending the public interest against private selfishness would depend on an administrative cadre capable of seeing beyond merely "individual or local" perspectives. Even when committed to democratic ends, progressive politics would require the sacrifice of certain democratic means. As one contemporary observer, the sociologist and documentary filmmaker John Grierson, explained, "because the citizen, under modern conditions, could not know everything about everything all the time, democratic citizenship . . . [seemed] impossible." But the reconstruction of liberalism could also point in another prominent — if somewhat vaguer — direction. The patent obsolescence of the traditional liberal theory of citizenship might suggest the need, not for state paternalism, but for a renewed and reinvigorated vision of participatory democracy. As Grierson himself explained, once "the old liberal individualist and rationalist theory" was finally dismissed, it would be possible to develop a "deeper sort of national story" — one where society would be seen not in "the aggregate" but in its "quintessence." Here "the intimate drama of . . . citizenship" would depend on "bridging the gaps between citizen and community" to create a realization of "the corporate nature" of political action. Though Grierson's vision was intentionally vague and hortatory, it corresponded with intense New Deal efforts to foster popular involvement in local political agencies and with the rhetoric of communal engagement that ran throughout the era. That commitment to what Tennessee Valley Authority (TVA) director David Lilienthal called "grassroots democracy" found its most cogent theoretical expression in the work of writers like Lewis Mumford and John Dewey who argued that political reform would be significant mainly in its ability to foster new modes of popular citizenship.[46] In Dewey's description, the "Great Society" of a complex metropolitan civilization could become a "Great Community" only through the self-expression and self-realization of popular citizenship. A "public articulated and operating through representative officers *is* the state," Dewey claimed; "there is no state without a government, but also there is none without the public."[47]

Both this vision of popular engagement and that of paternalist administration ran powerfully through the complex policies and rhetoric of the New Deal. Neither, however, would be the dominant legacy of the era's political transformation. Rather, the same settlement that in the late forties made an American Keynesianism the answer to the redefinition of the economic tenets of liberalism also made interest-group pluralism the resolution of the political reconstruction of liberal citizenship. By the terms of this postwar realignment, the state would be not the "night watchman" of classical liberalism, nor the engineer envisioned by New Deal planners, nor the self-expression of an engaged public imagined by John Dewey. The citizen likewise would be neither free agent, passive subject, nor participatory democrat. Rather, the liberalism that emerged after World War II would envision the federal government as a "Broker State" intervening among various competing and organized interest groups.[48] By the same token, it would cast citizens not as prostrate victims or public actors, but as members of various population groups whose interests were represented by a complex web of interlocking and competing national bureaucracies. To be a democratic subject in this view did not entail a direct role in self-government; nor did it make one a faceless member of a mass constituency. It meant, rather, that one belonged to one or more of the various "support group constituencies" that negotiated through the state over the direction of society.[49]

In their efforts to imagine a democratic literature and a reformed literary marketplace, the creators of hard-boiled crime fiction turned successively to analogs of each of these political visions. When he attempted to "make literature" out of the pulp detective story during the late twenties and early thirties, Dashiell Hammett implicitly cast himself in a role much like that imagined by the era's "realist" critics of classical liberalism. He attributed Landis's "expertness" to himself and described pulp fiction as a form of popular mystification that he was called upon to shape and articulate. By implication, a democratic literature in his view would be the product of a gifted intellectual's ability to discover the meaning latent in popular confusion — one where art was somehow made out of trash materials. When Raymond Chandler turned away from that vision in the mid- and late thirties because it seemed arid and sterile, he embraced against it a populist sentimentalism that echoed the appeal to national community articulated by critics like Grierson and Dewey. The aim was no longer to give shape to commonplace delusion, but instead to preserve and to communicate an evanescent popular vitality. A democratic literature would not be one in which shape had been imposed on mundane confusion, but rather, as in Dewey's vision of the democratic state, one where an inclusive public seized hold of rigid and desiccated cultural institutions in order to make them newly representative. In the last major stage of its development, however, hard-boiled crime fiction abandoned each of these ambitions. During the late 1940s and through the 1950s, suspense novelists like Jim Thompson and Charles Willeford developed the vision first articulated by James M. Cain in order to create a popular myth well-suited to the regime of postwar liberalism. In the works of these writers, neither the elite leadership imagined by Hammett nor the populist sentimentalism embraced by Chandler appeared plausible. The public seemed neither a confused body in need of direction nor a vital common spirit demanding the transformation of political and cultural institutions, but rather an abstraction represented solely by bureaucratic organizations. In the work of Thompson and Willeford, those developments signaled the death of the detective story and its vision of cultural and social mediation. For Chester Himes, who had come of age with the New Deal coalition, and who had looked to its populist rhetoric as an answer to the history of American racism, they seemed a concession to prejudice and injustice as well, and he used his crime novels as a means to define and indict the decline of the New Deal.

As the rest of this book will attempt to explain, each of these literary strategies was both an echo of contemporary political issues and a response to the structure of the literary marketplace at a particular stage in its development. It was because they approached that marketplace with unusual ambition, hoping to overcome the limits of literary institutions, that the major hard-boiled writers developed such grandiose literary visions and in turn mirrored the major political aspirations of the New Deal era. Because they knew those literary ambitions were bound to fail, though, hard-boiled crime fiction was uniquely positioned to bring out the contradictions and ironies that dogged the period's reconstruction of liberalism. Dashiell Hammett cast himself as the literary correlative to the era's democratic realists, but his fiction tended less to celebrate the victories of intelligence over myth than to portray the delusions that undermined the pretense to intellectual leadership. Raymond Chandler imagined a redemptive public taste inspired by popular vitality. But his fiction constantly depicted the exploitation and erasure of that popular spirit. More tellingly, it revealed the way that the "corporate" vision of democratic life which he shared with Grierson and Dewey might easily culminate in an invocation of an imperiled racial republic. Jim Thompson and Charles Willeford took advantage of the postwar consumer market to envision a unified literary public, but the noir paperback novel they invented depicted the dissolution of that common people and the consequent disappearance of the popular artist. Chester Himes's novels invoked a nonracial civic realm and a morally transcendent law and then portrayed the ways in which they fell before racism and greed. Each of the major styles of hard-boiled crime fiction thus portrayed the hopes and failures of its authors' cultural ambitions and, more broadly, dramatized the problems that lay at the heart of the New Deal.

1.

CONSTRUCTING RACE WILLIAMS

The Klan and the Making of Hard-Boiled Crime Fiction

In an emergency Americans will enforce their own law — not merely their statutes but also fundamental laws that they believe essential for their own or the national good — and . . . they will use lampposts if it should become necessary. — Stanley Frost, *The Challenge of the Klan*

The flash of my gun showed me nothing. It never does, though it's easy to think you've seen things. — Dashiell Hammett, *Red Harvest*[1]

From its first appearances in the pulp magazines of the 1920s, hard-boiled crime fiction emphasized its populist credentials. These were stories, the genre's writers and fans claimed, with a privileged purchase on "real life" and a fundamental antipathy to genteel fantasy. Against the "bunk" of oversophistication, they promised to deliver the stark truths of contemporary society — "ugly, vicious, sordid, and cruel." And, at their most grandiose, they linked this antiliterary sensibility to a complaint against social corruption. Revealing unpleasant reality was not just pulp sensationalism, the fiction's writers and editors implied; it was part of a moral struggle against dishonesty. The fiction thus railed against social decline — indicting "graft," denouncing "parasites," and complaining against "unjust . . . wealth" and "tainted power." As one influential editor implied when he claimed that his fiction offered a "public service" to its readers, the champions of the genre were rarely content to see it as a form of entertainment alone. Hard-boiled crime fiction, they suggested, offered a popular critique of a decadent society.[2]

In short, as many commentators have since noted, the hard-boiled detective story created a pulp version of the populist jeremiad.[3] What has been less apparent about this antielitist fiction, though, is the way it developed in close proximity to a nonfictional variety of nativist populism. During the early twenties, as the hard-boiled genre emerged in *Black Mask* magazine, the recently revived Ku Klux Klan rose to prominence in American society by championing a social fantasy that closely resembled the mythology implicit in hard-boiled crime fiction. Like the heroes of *Black Mask*'s "new type of detective story," Klan ideologues during the twenties railed against class parasites and social decadence. Like the jaundiced private detective, they, too, spotted the signs of corruption in urban vice and moral decline. And, like the hard-boiled heroes, Klansmen imagined that the only effective response to social ills was a form of vigilante justice that imposed order on the confusions of an urbanizing society. The common ground was apparent in the title of an early Dashiell Hammett story, "Women, Politics, and Murder." In both Klan ideology and hard-boiled crime fiction, the American city was riven by illicit sexuality, corruption, and crime — closely linked forms of social disarray that demanded the control of vigilant men.[4]

Such notions have, of course, a long lineage in the traditions of American populism, and their common presence in pulp fiction and the rhetoric of the Klan might seem merely coincidental were it not for a suggestive accident of publishing history.[5] During the later months of 1923, at the same time in which hard-boiled crime fiction was gaining prominence in the magazine, *Black Mask* also featured an ongoing discussion about the Ku Klux Klan and its place in the moral regeneration of American society. Indeed, the first successful hard-boiled private detective, Carroll John Daly's tellingly named Race Williams, made his debut in a special issue of *Black Mask* dedicated to a fictional debate over the Klan—a dispute that Williams entered as an enemy of the Invisible Empire. And for the next six months, as Daly's and Dashiell Hammett's stories gained popularity in the magazine, *Black Mask* continued to run a "Klan Forum" in which its readers debated the KKK and its relation to "Americanism." This unusual event created a small sensation in the magazine, and it coincided with important changes in *Black Mask*'s tone and direction. But its most important effect came in the way that it placed the magazine's "new type of detective fiction" in direct contact with Klan ideology at the moment when nativist politics were approaching their high-water mark in American history.

In the person of Race Williams, hard-boiled crime fiction began life directly opposed to the Klan's nativist populism, and, as we will see more fully, the fiction did its utmost to undermine the racial ideology and moral authoritarianism vital to Klan thinking. As the name of Daly's protagonist implies, however, the contest was a deeply ambivalent one at best. In Carroll John Daly's fiction, Race Williams and the Ku Klux Klan battled for the right to possess and define the spirit of "race," struggling over the characteristics of American inheritance and its meaning for national politics and culture. The Klan and hard-boiled crime fiction developed different answers to the questions implicit in this contest, and as the Klan's vision disappeared from both national politics and the pages of *Black Mask* during the later twenties, hard-boiled populism rose to supplant it in the magazine—so that the genre invented by Daly and Hammett gained a reputation, first as *the Black Mask* and later as the peculiarly American version of the detective story. What *Black Mask*'s Klan Forum reveals, however, is that hard-boiled fiction and nativist fantasy competed on the same ground during the twenties. Each sought to fashion a convincing populist account of contemporary life, and each supported that vision with a particular idea of race and its uses. The results of that competition would be apparent in hard-boiled crime fiction's characteristic ambiguities long after the Klan faded from view. In order to recognize those effects, though, it will be helpful to trace the thinking against which the genre contended and the context in which it first appeared.

A SIDE JOURNEY INTO THE INVISIBLE EMPIRE

Black Mask's unusual Klan debate began with few expectations apart from a desire to cash in on the recent and surprising popularity of KKK membership. During the early twenties, the Klan had risen from obscurity to become a nationally prominent mass movement of disaffected white Protestant men, and *Black Mask*'s editors sought little more than to get in on the sensation. Describing the KKK as "the most picturesque element that has appeared in American life since the war," they presented their readers with a special issue dedicated to the group in June 1923. This "side journey into the Invisible Empire" was an unexpected success, prompting strong reader reaction and a wave of enthusiastic letters. For the remainder of the year, therefore, the magazine attempted to exploit its good fortune by running a "Klan Forum" in which reader letters and occasional essays debated the KKK and its relation to American citizenship. It was, the magazine claimed, the "only open, free, absolutely unbiased discussion for and against the Invisible Empire published anywhere in America."[6]

That description was much exaggerated, but *Black Mask* did publish a series of letters from ordinary Klansmen and their opponents, and those often unlettered accounts of the appeal or repugnance of Klan politics were rare in the early twenties. The source of the magazine's surprising success with its Klan debate, moreover, seems to have been precisely its shallow pretense to neutrality. As pulp magazines were always apt to be, *Black Mask* was proudly deferential to its readers in the early twenties. But the magazine was also deeply uncertain of its market. "Enthusiastic readers bring joy to our soul. We publish this magazine entirely for them," the editors claimed in the midst of their Klan sensation, "but the trouble is that not all people are enthusiastic over the same kind of stories." To appeal to as many readers as possible, then, the magazine needed to pretend to a modicum of indecision about the Klan, and in that effort hit upon a marketing device that was well-suited to generating sensationalism. Casting their Klan number as a "literary experiment," the editors explained in their introduction to the special issue that the Klan had been drawn on not as a problem of political argument or critical investigation but as "a background for fiction stories" in which the magazine's writers expressed their personal "reactions" to the organization. These stories offered varying images of the Klan, allowing *Black Mask*'s editors to claim that the magazine offered a "neutral" field for discussion. At the same time, by emphasizing narrative and emotion over analysis and argument, and by explicitly disowning any claim to authoritative commentary, *Black Mask* appealed to Klansmen who felt that their beliefs were "shunned, . . . jeered [at], and . . . misrepresented" by the mainstream press. For a brief period, the magazine thus unwittingly came to provide a home for readers who claimed to represent the neglected spirit of true Americanism.[7]

The passion with which these Klan sympathizers and their enemies responded to the KKK in *Black Mask* mirrored the moral fervor that the organization attracted throughout much of American culture during the first half of the twenties. To many observers at the time, the Invisible Empire appeared to have sprung up from nowhere, confronting its allies and its opponents with the image of a "vigorous" popular movement of "incalculable" strength. In fact, this modern incarnation of the Klan had been in existence since 1915, when — inspired by Thomas Dixon's novels and fraternal organizations like the Masons — William Simmons took the name of the Reconstruction era vigilante force for an order of his own invention. It was only after 1919, though, that the modern Klan began to expand beyond its Georgia origins. Drawing on grassroots organizing tactics conceived by public relations executives Edward Young Clark and Elizabeth Tyler, the Klan spread rapidly throughout the South, West, and Midwest during the post-World War I economic downturn and continued to expand as the national economy began to boom. By 1924, the Klan could boast of several million members in some four thousand local "Klaverns" throughout the country, and Klansmen played prominent roles in the civic and political life of hundreds of cities and towns and several states. Perhaps more importantly, as the KKK's prominent role in the Democratic Party's national convention of 1924 and its support for the drastic immigration-restriction legislation of the same year suggested, the beliefs espoused by the Invisible Empire enjoyed wide public support at the time. During the

twenties, Klan politics combined two broad dispensations: a populist critique of social corruption; and a nativist defense of "Americanism" against various "strangers"—especially Catholics, Jews,
and immigrants. Both aspects of Klan belief were commonplaces of
the era's social discourse. In fact, to the extent that the organization
came under attack, many of the group's critics stressed the dangers
posed by a renegade vigilantist society, or they scoffed at the Klan's
moralism and its elaborate regalia. Fewer took exception to the
Klan's vision of social crisis or attempted to defend a nonracial conception of citizenship against the Klan's nativist vision of "100 percent Americanism."[8]

In and of itself, *Black Mask*'s forum added little to this national
debate over the Klan. The few dozen letters and the handful of essays
that the magazine printed through the later months of 1923 hardly
amounted to serious political discussion, and they raised few new
issues. What *Black Mask*'s Klan Forum did reveal, though, was just
how robust and ordinary Klannish views were at the time—indeed,
of the way they would be defended precisely as the ordinary beliefs
of ordinary citizens. Imperial Wizard Hiram Evans claimed that the
Klan spoke for "the plain people," and *Black Mask*'s patina of neutrality and its deference to its readers brought out this populist spirit
strongly. Perhaps for this reason, the magazine's debate over the KKK
presented a watershed for the development of hard-boiled fiction
and its institutional home, both of which, as they evolved, would
rely heavily on the notion of popular legitimacy. In any case, the Klan
Forum appears to have influenced *Black Mask* in ways that its editors did not at first anticipate. When its KKK debate began, the magazine featured unconvincing images of polite society, and its mis-
cellany of stories and columns tended to invoke the ideals of "good
taste," "education and breeding." Over the second half of 1923,
though, the magazine began to turn away from this pseudogentility
and to emphasize thriller fiction built around masculine community
and popular justice. By the following year, *Black Mask* had begun to
define the market niche—"stories of virile, realistic action"—that
would make it the most influential publication in its field.[9] During
this same period, both Daly and Hammett were just beginning to
define the basic features of their fiction, and each specifically took up

the Klan in the process. Though Daly did so with greater earnestness, both writers mocked Klan ideology and simultaneously stole KKK rhetoric in order to turn the group's fantasies about race and conspiracy to different purposes.[10] In Daly's case in particular, the basic qualities of the hard-boiled protagonist—his ability to move between law and crime, his ostensible commitment to self-interest, his fluency and wit—emerged specifically as weapons to be used against the Klan and its fantasies of moral and ethnic control. By 1924, such features would lead *Black Mask* readers to declare the two the magazine's most successful writers.

It would be a mistake, however, to overemphasize the role played by the Klan in the development of either hard-boiled crime fiction or *Black Mask* magazine. After 1924, the Klan faded quickly from political and social prominence, the victim of a series of public relations disasters. Likewise, the group (and nativist varieties of fiction that it may have helped inspire) disappeared from *Black Mask* after the mid-twenties, and neither the magazine nor hard-boiled crime fiction ever made direct reference to the Klan again. It seems unlikely, then, that the KKK provided an essential element for the success of the genre or that the fiction could not have developed as it did without the Klan. Rather, the Invisible Empire functioned for Daly, Hammett, and *Black Mask*'s editors much as it did in a broader way for the country at large. In historian Stanley Coben's phrase, the Klan served as "the most visible and powerful guardian of Victorianism during the 1920s," supplying both its adherents and its enemies with an exaggerated representation of beliefs that were prevalent throughout American culture at the time.[11] For Daly and Hammett especially, the Klan and its analogs came to represent an absurd antimodernism and served by contrast to highlight the distinctive features of their own aesthetic. The Klansmen in their stories were fantasists, dedicated to wild racial theories and outmoded dreams of social order. They defined everything that the hard-boiled protagonist would refuse to be.

In particular, the generic protagonist fashioned by Daly and Hammett defined himself in opposition to the emotional core of Klan rhetoric—the ideal of community. The heroes of the hard-boiled genre are notoriously far from communally minded, and they are rarely — to use a phrase crucial to Klan rhetoric of the twenties — good citizens. Seen in the context of *Black Mask*'s KKK debate, though, that often resentful independence can be understood, at least in part, as a tactic aimed against the affective force of nativist ideology. Klansmen *were* communally minded, intensely so, and they thought of themselves as exemplifying the traits of good citizenship. In the estimate of most recent historians of the group, moreover, those qualities reflected the central impulses of Klan politics. The KKK succeeded as a popular movement during the 1920s because it offered a cogent interpretation of the changes that were transforming twentieth-century American society and because it promised a compelling set of political responses to those changes. Vital to both features of Klan ideology was a charged image of "community." When Klansmen described the deleterious effects of modernity, for instance, they pointed to the decline of local control and intimate society. Ordinary men, they argued, exercised ever less influence over the moral qualities of their families and their worlds. More seriously, Klan leaders complained, the same difficulties dogged American society at a national level. The rise of political bureaucracy, of economic and managerial concentration, of "oligarchy" generally meant that the bonds of the republic were beginning to wither; a country built upon the fellowship of independent men was devolving toward a society of decadent elites, servile workers, and unhealthy parasites.

For the "middling men" — small farmers, small businessmen, lower-level clerical employees, and skilled workers — who made up the heart of Klan membership in the twenties (and who most likely supplied much of the era's pulp readership as well), that was a compelling diagnosis. As one Klan sympathizer who wrote to *Black Mask* worried, "greed and lust" appeared to be "undermining our country." But if those men saw "community" as a terribly vulnerable entity, prey to powerful outside interests, they also envisioned communal spirit as a latent force of nearly transcendent authority. Rescued from predation, Klansmen and their allies contended, both local societies and the community of the nation itself would be capable of subduing the disintegrative forces unleashed by industrial capitalism and mass culture. The Klan's mission, therefore, was to intensify the bonds of community and to tap into its dormant strength — forging, as one *Black Mask* essay exhorted, "sacred, solemn, binding, and patriotic obligation." Only the achievement of such an "*orderly* community," as historian Christopher Cocoltchos puts it, would be capable of rescuing a fraternal republic from an incoherent society and of thereby restoring what several *Black Mask* readers called a "wonderful nation."[12]

In short, Klan politics during the twenties amounted to an early, and especially reactionary, version of what we now call communitarianism or civic redemptionism. The champions of the Invisible Empire trumpeted the values of communal obligation and mutual feeling. They demanded that political and economic elites act as responsible members of local societies and the national community, and they sought, perhaps more strenuously, to impose a respect for common principles of good behavior on social deviants. Like today's celebrants of civil society, too, they placed great importance on the value of civic action and public association, describing their own order as the exemplary instance of a popular organization that mediated between the sanctuary of the home and a distant or arrogant state. Even the Klan's most unusual or extremist actions were defended by Klansmen as part of the group's commitment to orderly community. The organization's elaborate regalia — its "mystic words" and "exalted ritual" — for instance, came directly from fraternal orders like the Masons and worked for the KKK, as it did for other groups, to legitimate fellowship by giving it liturgical form. Endowed with titles and dignified by costumes, Klansmen could claim to act not as self-interested individuals but as a unified common body that represented a local community — and, more extensively, the larger community of the white race. Likewise, Klan leaders defended vigilantism as a means to supplement corrupt institutions with the force of popular righteousness. An essay in *Black Mask* summed up the principle: "What is right and what is wrong is governed by the community's sense of justice." From this perspective, vigilantism not only imposed order, it summoned a reformed community into existence by calling on the latent will of the people.[13]

HONORABLE CITIZENS VS. MYSTERIOUS ORGANIZATION

The Klan's vision of orderly community may have appealed to *Black Mask*'s readers, and it may have had a particularly strong impact on the magazine itself because of the way it helped to make sense of a dynamic built into the periodical's very mode of publishing. When *Black Mask* bragged that it offered the nation's only open and unbiased discussion of the Klan, and when the magazine's readers responded by complaining about the way they were jeered at elsewhere, each drew implicit attention to the marginal status that *Black Mask* enjoyed in its role as a pulp magazine. During the interwar decades, pulp magazine publishing came to define a distinct subfraction of the American periodical marketplace — one at sharp ideological, aesthetic, and economic odds with both the era's elite journals of opinion and with the much larger realm of mass-market entertainment. Over the coming decades, *Black Mask* and its imitators would give ever greater weight to that marginal status, fashioning from it a particular subcultural ethos that in turn would play a vital role in the development of hard-boiled crime fiction. With the exception of James M. Cain and Chester Himes, every major writer in the genre began his career in the pulps or in the "digest" magazines that evolved out of them in the late 1940s and the 1950s. Many began as writers for *Black Mask* itself, the most prestigious and influential magazine in the field, and each of the most innovative figures capitalized in distinct ways on their pulp experience and on the values cultivated by pulp publishing when they left the magazines for more prestigious literary venues. Ironically, though, when *Black Mask* began its Klan Forum, the pulps were still a young and poorly defined industry, and *Black Mask* was a magazine without a clearly delineated market niche. The magazine's KKK controversy in fact would play a pivotal role in sharpening its focus. It may have helped, moreover, to develop the subcultural ethos that would characterize the pulp world throughout the later 1920s and the 1930s.

At bottom, that ethos was rooted in pulp publishing's economic basis. The pulps earned their name from the particular type of paper they used — the cheapest, most disposable grade of wood-pulp paper. But that paper itself spoke to a more fundamental feature of this particular segment of the publishing market and the one that most sharply divided it from its competitors. Unlike the mass-circulation magazines (or "big slicks") that had been a constantly expanding feature of the periodical industry since the turn of the century, pulp magazines made their money not from advertising but from circulation. A host of immediate effects and many less tangible results followed from that fact. The most fundamental was that, by virtue of its very mode of profit, the pulp world tended to be cut off from the developments that were transforming both the nation's larger consumer market and its growing network of national media.

That network had sprung up rapidly since the last years of the nineteenth century. Since the 1890s, the magazine business in the United States had been booming — driven largely by the concomitant expansion of advertising, consumer capitalism, and a new, highly educated, "professional-managerial" middle class. Beginning in 1896, when Frank Munsey discovered that he could sell magazines below cost and thus expand circulation by making up income on advertising sales, periodical publishing had grown ever larger, richer, and more competitive. As consumer marketing expanded, magazine publishers drew on the heavy capitalization brought in by advertising dollars to create increasingly luxuriant and ambitious publications. In effect, the new advertising business literally underwrote the new, twentieth-century magazine, enabling publishers to invest in technological innovation; to print on high-quality laminated paper with color illustrations and photographic reproduction; to pay the high salaries and rates that brought talented writers, artists, and editors to the magazines; and to create the systems of distribution and marketing that built vast circulations. By the early 1920s, the big slick magazines constituted the most prominent face of the newly developing national mass media. The largest of them, the *Ladies' Home Journal* and the *Saturday Evening Post*, reached several million readers with every issue; the industry as a whole sold more than 200 million magazines a year and carried nearly $3 million in advertising. Alongside those crucial ads, the slicks brought their audience a vision of the bright promise of modernity — a future defined mainly by the freedom and satisfactions of "consumption mobility." Their readers, the big slicks implied, were the vanguard of a sophisticated and wealthy middle class, with a yearning to improve their lives and the disposable income to spend on the goods that made such development possible.[14]

The pulps, by contrast, took little part in these developments. Like the slick magazines, they had been around nearly since the turn of the twentieth century, and like the slicks, their market boomed during the 1910s and especially after World War I as literacy and income levels grew. By the thirties, the pulp audience would include some ten million regular purchasers and a readership of perhaps three times that number. But, unlike the slicks, the pulps had descended from the late-nineteenth-century dime novels and story papers that were targeted toward an urban, working-class audience, and like those earlier styles of sensational publishing, they remained almost completely reliant on circulation-based income throughout the life of the industry. Assuming that the pulp audience was made up of young people and working-class readers with little disposable income, mass-market advertisers never took much interest in the magazines. The pulps were thus deprived of the enormous capitalization that drove their competitors. They survived only by taking in more money from subscriptions and newsstand sales, mostly the latter, than they spent on their combined expenses. As one pulp editor put it, they lived beneath "the Damoclean sword of the budget."[15]

Nearly every aspect of pulp publishing was shaped by these minor budgets. To begin, of course, the magazines could afford only low-cost pulp paper, but everything about their appearance separated the pulps from their "smooth paper" rivals. Where periodicals like the *Ladies' Home Journal* and the *Saturday Evening Post* were massive, glossy, and packed with features and advertisements, the pulps were small and flimsy. They usually had a striking color reproduction on the cover; inside, the magazines contained page after page of double-columned type, broken by an occasional line drawing. More generally, the pulp world developed at a distance from the booming consumer culture championed by the slicks, and as the industry expanded, the magazines' publishers, editors, and writers gave increasingly positive emphasis to that fact. Though little is known definitely about the magazines' purchasers, most people inside and outside the industry assumed that the pulps spoke to "a new reading public" of high-school educated, skilled and unskilled laborers.[16]

The big slick magazines were studiedly indifferent to that audience, and pulp writers and editors eventually took advantage of that fact by playing up their populist alienation from the world of mass-market consumerism. Defending themselves from recurrent charges of cheapness and sensationalism, "pulpsters" (the term was their own) gradually defined their world as a refuge of honest, manly labor, independent of the "terribly effeminate" world of solicitation and image-mongering that they saw in the slicks. The pulps were "honest and forthright," Raymond Chandler later claimed; their slick competitors, which "cater[ed] principally to the taste of women," were "artificial, untrue, and emotionally dishonest."[17]

Perhaps the most important consequence of the pulp industry's marginal status was the editorial ethos associated with the magazines. Here, too, pulpsters defined themselves against their slick competitors. Fighting for ever larger shares of the periodical market and for more secure brand recognition, the mass-circulation magazines developed giant editorial operations. They staffed large organizations devoted to developing, planning, and packaging their magazines and often paid exorbitant rates to attract the most renowned contributors to their pages. As a consequence, the slicks not only offered a wealth of information and entertainment, they tended to speak to their audience as experts, celebrities, and prophets. In response, pulpsters celebrated the local, intimate, and antielitist tendencies built into their industry. Pulp publishing lacked capitalization compared to the slicks' massive expenditures, and, for pulpsters, name recognition carried only slight value. Because their magazines cost little to produce, publishers could erect few barriers to entry, and the most successful magazines soon attracted imitators and competitors that could offer readers nearly the same product. The typical pulp magazine could thus afford to staff only a tiny office of two or three people, and it usually paid contributors a penny or two per word.[18] Because name recognition counted as little for writers as it did for the magazines themselves, moreover, pulpsters often worked under multiple pseudonyms, and they tended to brag less about their reputation or status than about the sales or the sheer bulk of the sensational product they generated. As a result, the pulps created an unusual literary marketplace — one intensely competitive and brutally labor-intensive, but also proudly democratic. Pulpsters bragged that their magazines ran on "laissez-faire principles" and that their reputations counted for nothing; "skill and craftsmanship" ruled, and the doors were always open to beginners and "apprentices." Their writers were not celebrities, artists, or authorities; they were competitors in the arena of sensational fiction, engaged in ongoing combat and dialogue with each other and with their readers. Their self-contained world seemed, in one writer's revealing description, an egalitarian "publishing fraternity."[19]

Since they were able to draw on almost no other form of marketing, pulp magazines frequently sought to remind their readers of the qualities that distinguished them from the larger world of mass entertainment: their "sturdy independence," "voluntary circulation," the "precious contact" they seemed to foster between reader and writer, and above all their atmosphere of communal intimacy. "Are you with us?" *Black Mask* frequently asked its audience, "will you tell your friend Bill about [the magazine] — and maybe Hank and Pete also? There are hundreds of thousands of men in these United States that would have exactly the same opinion of *The Black Mask* that you have — if they only knew about it."[20] At a time when mass-market magazines like the *Saturday Evening Post* and the *Ladies' Home Journal* boasted circulations in the millions, the editors at *Black Mask* imagined at their most euphoric that they might reach several hundred thousand readers. Compensation for that comparatively small readership, though, came in the atmosphere of fraternal intimacy. Only in the world of the pulps, the magazines' adherents suggested, would readers and writers still address each other as Bill, Hank, and Pete, and only in such a limited world would "elaborate promotion schemes" still have less significance than word-of-mouth.[21]

Such sentiments ran strongly through *Black Mask*'s Klan debate. The stories that favored the Invisible Empire in the magazine's special issue avoided statements of racial antagonism or political dogma, but they stressed the fraternal vision at the emotional core of both Klan politics and pulp publishing. Turning on the conflict between true fellowship and dangerous individualism, these stories portray the Klan as a group that seems at first secretive and repressive and that is then revealed to be the very voice of the people. In Herman Peterson's "Call Out the Klan," for example, Bruce Martin, a Northerner who has moved to the Blue Ridge Mountains, first describes the KKK as "a bunch of would-be reformers, . . . [who] think they know how all of us should live." His distaste for the group seems borne out when hooded figures kidnap his fiancée, but Martin soon discovers that these were fake Klansmen and that he must rely on the true vigilante force to recover his beloved. His arrogance properly rebuked, the contrite protagonist learns to see the "organization in a different light." "That is the real Klan," a sympathetic sheriff informs him, a local brotherhood that "aims ever to do good — even with violence."[22]

Peterson's imperative title underscored the thinking that appeared most often in support for the Klan in *Black Mask*'s debate. The Invisible Empire expressed a tacit general will, members and allies suggested, and in the midst of crisis that force could be summoned to unify the community. The Klan sympathizers among *Black Mask*'s readers echoed Peterson's vision of redemptive fellowship. They spoke frequently of "ideal Americanism," emphasizing the way its qualities appeared especially in the fellowship exemplified by Klan members — "fraternity men," "a pretty good bunch of fellows," "very fine men," or the "honorable citizens in every community." In this "best argument in favor of the Klan," one such Klansman explained, the Invisible Empire was "not a far-away and mysterious organization that we know nothing of, but its members are you and I and Bill and the rest of decent, law-abiding fellows in the community." Moreover, the most enthusiastic letters in *Black Mask*'s debate described not just the KKK and its ideal America as intimate communities; they attributed the same qualities to *Black Mask*'s Klan Forum. Praising the magazine's ability to avoid the "ignorant and biased denunciations" promulgated by "controlled newspapers," these readers suggested that *Black Mask* itself had fostered a vital fellowship analogous to the Klan's redemptive mission. Sheltering Klan sympathizers from the scorn directed at them by national elites, the magazine had encouraged its readers "to address" each other "as brothers" and thus empowered "real Americans who have been afraid to speak freely during recent years."[23]

Like Peterson, too, *Black Mask*'s pro-Klan readers tended to imagine the group's vision of communal fellowship as an engine of violent social transformation. They celebrated the Klan for its ability to "make and enforce laws — written or unwritten," for its role in the nation's "moral awakening," and for its part in pressing social crisis toward a moment of chiliastic decision: "When the Night Hawk rides at the zero hour, Americans . . . will stand back to back against those who would subjugate our great country." But *Black Mask*'s Klan sympathizers also responded to this vision of apocalyptic community by bringing out the nativist subtext that writers like Peterson preferred to leave in the deep background. Klan sympathizers thus reminded the magazine that there were foreign "elements" and "rabid anti-Americans already among us," and they pointed out that the Klan was determined to see that "America remains a white man's country," guided by "the same Protestant spirit in which the God-fearing Christian forefathers founded it."[24] As such readers emphasized, the Klan's vision of national community rested on a profoundly nativist sense of national identity. It was the authority of a common white, Protestant heritage, Klan leaders always stressed, that was to provide the glue of "binding obligation." Once translated into a political program, moreover, that assumption became a thoroughly racial conception of American citizenship. A "republic is possible only to men of homogeneous race," Klan leaders contended, and they justified that conviction by explaining that the mores of American life and the very principles of democratic government were the result of a unique cultural history — "the many-times distilled product" of a particularly white Protestant "experience." Rather than universal or even legal principles, then, the rights and obligations of citizenship were the emanation of "racial instincts." They belonged to only those people whose genealogy equipped them for their proper use. As one spokesman explained in *Black Mask*, the Klan's vision of inheritance had "exploded" the "theory of the melting pot." People "whose history is entirely different from ours . . . can never become American." The "very ideas and ideals" inscribed in their past "prevent them from being good citizens."[25]

According to Klan leaders and racial ideologues, then, the evils of moral decline and of economic and political oligarchy were merely the symptoms of a more fundamental disease. Crisis gripped the nation because "strangers" had introduced corruption into the body politic. For just that reason, though, the defense of "100 percent Americanism" would be the catalyst for a renewed communal enterprise. Inspired by a "new idealism," members of a homogenous American race would assume the inherited rights and obligations of "good citizenship." Once these "real Americans" dispatched the aliens in their midst and recognized that they were themselves "links in a vital chain, charged with high duties," the purified nation would become again the fraternal republic it had been in a fantasized past. Indeed, so powerful in *Black Mask*'s debate was the Klan's language of racial community that many of those readers who attacked the KKK accepted the very terms proposed by Klan sympathizers to praise the organization. Few attempted to defend individual freedom or the "liberalism" that the Klan sought to subject to racial boundaries. Rather, like the Klan, they tended to describe America as a familial nation joined by mutual obligation and common inheritance, and they objected mainly to the narrowness of the Klan's criteria for membership. "My dear Klansman," one typical reader pleaded, "you do not understand us at all . . . ; those of us who are 'practical' Catholics will stand the acid test when you are really and truly looking for 100 per cent Americans."[26]

BOOKED FOR THE CITY

The authors of hard-boiled crime fiction shared with the Klan some of the basic features of the group's diagnosis of social crisis. Dashiell Hammett, for example, described the post-World War I United States as utterly cut off from "an earlier and simpler world — the world B.C. . . . before credit and the crisis of 1918." Carroll John Daly similarly pictured a society that had declined from a virtuous republican history, as his hero Race Williams suggests in one story when he rebukes a corrupt union organizer, Abe Nation, with the sardonic remark, "You're an honest man, too, Abe." The allusion to Lincoln describes in brief the decline of the "Nation" — from the republican glories of the past to the corrupt society of the present.

Such intimations were common, too, in *Black Mask* throughout the twenties and early thirties. The magazine's occasional editorials attacked weakness in "citizens[hip]" and "moral responsibility," blaming the displacement of "the smaller communities" by "huge centers of population." They railed against mass culture, with its "slush and lush of degraded sex appeal," and complained as well about the elite power of "newspapers, ministers, and lawyers" whose "mission . . . is to kid us into accepting things as they are." Speaking by contrast for "the people themselves," *Black Mask*'s editor, Joseph Shaw, suggested that once "the public fully understands . . . that it is the ultimate victim of . . . plunderers," the country might return to a local, precorporate economic order of "merchant-employer[s]."[27]

The hard-boiled fiction created by Daly and Hammett suggested a deep skepticism about such a historical regression, though, and that skepticism can be traced in good part to the doubtfulness these writers implied about the ideal of native community that supported the Klan's version of republicanism. Indeed, it is only in the context of such appeals to native community that the characteristics of the hard-boiled hero take on their full import. Unlike *Black Mask*'s ambivalent critics of the Klan, for example, the hard-boiled protagonist created by Carroll John Daly for his entry in the magazine's special issue delighted in combating the Klan on precisely the ground its sympathizers held most dear. If Klansmen celebrated orderly community and envisioned a coherent local culture defined by ethnic exclusivity, moral authoritarianism, and "exalted ritual," Daly's Race Williams would confront them with an appropriate set of negative virtues: disorderliness, egocentric calculation, and disenchantment. Their effect in "Knights of the Open Palm," the story that first presented the influential private detective, would be not merely to defeat the Klan but to undermine the basic premises of Klan philosophy and at the same time to clarify the outlines of the hard-boiled protagonist. "I was booked for the city," Williams announces at the end of his tale, and the remark refers not only to his destination but to the fate of the private detective. Klansmen and racial ideologues might indict "modern urban industrial life" for being "disgenic" — fatal to the coherence of white, Protestant heritage. The hard-boiled genre Daly helped create belongs to the city, and, as in Daly's rendition of the Klan, it has tended throughout its history to depict malevolent projects for control being subverted by the disintegrative forces of urban life.²⁸

The premise of Daly's mockery of the Klan thus reversed the image of the Invisible Empire advanced by *Black Mask*'s pro-Klan stories. "Knights of the Open Palm" is set in the rural village of Clinton, where the Klan has used the façade of moral reform to subvert the rule of law and impose its own arbitrary authority. The story's setting thereby mimics the structure of *Black Mask*'s pseudo-debate on the Invisible Empire. Depicting Clinton as "about half and half; the authorities didn't side with the Klan nor did they come out against it; everybody was just sitting tight to see which way things was going to break," Daly renders the town as a correlative to *Black Mask*'s special issue and indicts the magazine's editors as ineffectual fence-sitters. But the Klan's control of Clinton also makes Daly's understanding of the Invisible Empire apparent. Having been summoned to the village in order to rescue a boy kidnapped by the Klan, Race Williams reveals the KKK to be a "half-baked organization" that preys on the weak and foments "religious and racial hatred." In Daly's story, then, it is the Invisible Empire that exemplifies those evils of modern political life that Herman Peterson attributed to a false image of the Klan. In Clinton, a local doctor points out, "the people fear the Klan," and it is the KKK, another sympathetic character notes, that uses the pretense of popular representation to engage in "money-making graft." For Daly, in short, the Klan is responsible for the corruption of popular rule that actual Klansmen indicted in their attacks on economic and political elites. Race Williams, by contrast, is the figure who uses violence to do good and who becomes as a result the genuine voice of the people.²⁹

That development is ironic. For to the extent that Race Williams comes to speak for the people, he does so by speaking *against* the community values that the Klan claims to represent. For example, Williams has little interest in Clinton itself, and unlike the heroes of "Call Out the Klan," he does not unite the people of the town in the struggle to defeat social parasites. The contrast vital to his story is simply the inverse of Peterson's — not one between social cohesion and dissension but between a repressive organization that seeks to

regulate popular life and a force of disruption that aims to undermine the coherence of local culture itself. Apart from the contest
between good and evil, then, Williams's struggle with the Klan implies a battle more fundamental to the hard-boiled genre — one between fluency and social control. The Klan, as Williams sees it, aspires to the status of a "closed corporation," and in various ways, he
points out, it seeks to restrict the dangers of "conversation": the boy
imprisoned by the Klan has been kidnapped because he intended to
testify that he saw Klansmen tar and feather an innocent woman; the
woman herself was punished because she sold alcohol for medicinal
purposes while working in the family drugstore; law enforcement in
turn is impotent against such abuses because the Klan terrifies jurors
into submission. In all of these cases, the KKK works to stymie the
ordinary civic avenues of exchange and communication. To stress
the point still further, Daly has the Klansmen warn Williams on his
arrival in town to "be careful of that tongue of yours," and Daly
makes it clear that Race's loose talk is equivalent to his more obvious
weapon, violence. Of his Klan opponent, Williams says, "he was
speaking my language now — this gun business." The association
would hold true through the remainder of Daly's pulp career; gunfire
and rhetorical power are virtually identical forces. ("Yep, it's my gun
what speaks," Race likes to point out.) And each is described as
being magically fatal to the Klan because it confronts the Invisible
Empire's hermetic ideal with the urban qualities the hard-boiled hero
embodies — action, circulation, and exchange.[30]

It makes perfect sense in this light, that Race Williams defeats the
Invisible Empire in "Knights of the Open Palm" through two associated methods. He outshoots the sluggish Klansmen, and he relies
on his knowledge of Klan arcana to insinuate himself into their
organization. Because it dramatizes Williams's ability to rupture the
boundaries of local culture, it is the second weapon that turns out to
be most significant. Having learned the Klan's "signs and symbols,"
Race can discover the Klansmen's plans and lull them into a false
sense of security. More important, his very access to the Klan's arcana undermines the group's inflated self-image. If, for Klansmen,
"mystic words" and "exalted ritual" served as the aesthetic expression of a utopian racial community, the fact that Williams is able to

crack and ridicule this invented dialect automatically tends to disenchant Klan mythology by demonstrating that secret codes are beyond political control. (The journalist who published the book from
which Daly in fact learned Klan terminology was charged by one
Black Mask reader with the revealing crime of treason.) Equally
significant, though, is the fact that Williams comes to his knowledge
of the code from his informant in "Mike Clancy's gin mill." Where
Klansmen sought to use arcana on behalf of racial community and
against "far away and mysterious organization," Race bewilders the
Invisible Empire precisely because he excels at manipulating the
obscure networks of the city—trading money, information, and
threats between the two shadowy organizations of "the dicks and
the crooks."[31]

That Race Williams's basic mission is to use such exchange to
desacralize the Klan's "spiritual philosophy" becomes apparent at a
dramatic highpoint of Daly's tale. Confronting the most evil member
of Clinton's klavern, Williams defeats the man in a gesture that sums
up the methodology of Daly's story: "I make a grab and pull off the
big lad's hood. I just wanted to get a look at his map and one look
was enough—you could a picked him in a straw hat at Coney Island.
He had a chin like one of the Smith Brothers or both of them—all
whiskers and all hair and eyebrows."[32]

The oppositions here are clear enough. Race Williams represents
the multiethnic, Eastern, urban world of Coney Island. His opponent matches the Victorian figures of the Smith Brothers. But even
more important than this contrast is the action that Williams performs to defeat his enemy. Just as he undermines Klan jargon by
demonstrating its permeability, here Race turns Klan regalia into
absurd frippery, robbing the Klansman of its psychic protection and,
more drastically, stripping the Invisible Empire of the mythical authority its costume was meant to represent—the group's claim to
represent the spiritual community of the white race. Confronted
with the corrosive energies of the city represented by Williams, such
claims are shown to be merely narrow forms of self-interest and
foolish longings for outmoded kinds of social control.

The most significant feature of Race Williams's opposition to the
Klan, though, is not merely that he reveals Clinton's Klansmen to be

motivated by personal desire rather than community spirit, but that he claims to be impelled himself by such apparent vices. The "cash transaction was all that interested me," he brags in a remark that sums up the hard-boiled character's penchant for denying any motivation but self-interest. Of course, such claims almost always must seem partly untrue; it is important that the hard-boiled hero prove his heroism by some gesture of self-sacrifice. But the defense of self-interest is important in itself because it establishes Williams's claim not to be bound by the demands of collective identity or communal obligation. In Daly's description, everyone is motivated by personal interests, and in this way he avoids making his attack on the Klan the story of a battle between cultures or the tale of a conflict between the false and true representatives of Clinton's communal identity. Thus, his central quality, Race Williams suggests, is his unwillingness to be suckered by the childish snares of group identity: "Of course, I'm like all Americans — a born joiner. It just comes to us like children playing; we want to be in on the fancy names and trick grips. But it wouldn't work with me. . . . No, I like to play the game alone. And that's why I ain't never fallen for the lure of being a joiner."[33]

In effect, Daly simply reverses the terms of KKK ideology. Klan leaders during the twenties imagined the nation torn between a natural "republic" and invidious "liberalism." The former was the legitimate political expression of "men of homogenous race." The latter was a kind of "national, racial, and spiritual treason" and had to be kept within the "fixed bounds" of "American racial instincts" — precisely because, by giving reign to "strangers" and "denatured intellectuals," liberal freedoms tended to weaken the "chain" of common inheritance.[34] Daly sees much the same conflict, but he inverts the values attached to these political impulses. More significantly, he alters their racial associations, trumping the Klan by going it a notch lower on an imaginary ladder of national origins. Now it is the republican virtues of civic association, the habits of "joiners" exemplified by the Klansmen, that seem artificial and childish — a matter of "fancy names and trick grips." The true spirit of the race embodied by Daly's hero stands for a radical version of the liberal individualism that the Klan hoped to control. Thus, having infiltrated a Klan meeting and marveling at its absurdity, Williams says,

"I felt as white as my robe in comparison with most of that gang," and the remark sums up the implications of the protagonist's name. Race Williams represents the true essence of whiteness. The nature of that quality is to scoff at the Klan's fraternal bonds and to pursue an uncompromising individual liberty.

As if to confirm the impact of such an approach, several Klan readers attempted to trace Daly's anti-Klan sentiments to the influence of an Irish-Catholic heritage, claiming for instance that the story was "worthy of his name."[35] But Daly shunted such criticism aside, first by implying that Race Williams represented the genuine version of the American inheritance that the Klan sought to possess, and second by suggesting that such an inheritance could not be tied to any particular group affiliation. The meaningful distinction, his story assumes, is not between "old stock" Americans and new, but between the fictions of collective identity and the immutable truth of personal self-interest. His hero opposes the Klan not because he is impelled to do so by group identity, but because, in his most fundamental nature, he is "booked for the city."

In one sense, then, Daly falls squarely within the discourse inhabited by the Klan and by a substantial part of political opinion during the twenties. Seeking to legitimate a particular set of values, he invents a source for them more profound than the accidents of social organization — the font of race. On the other hand, though, it is easy to see how Daly's way of using this notion might work to undermine the KKK's nativist thinking and ultimately to discount the significance that the Klan and its sympathizers sought to give to racial inheritance in the twenties. What "Knights of the Open Palm" attempts to portray is something like an antinativist racialism, or a racially legitimated opposition to ethnic separatism.[36] In Daly's story, "Race" is a primitive source of vitality, but it is one that refuses to belong to any community in particular; and its natural political expression therefore comes in the commitment to the open features of "liberalism" and "modern urban industrial life." Race itself has become "disgenic."

Of course, except for its opposition to nativism, there was nothing inherently progressive in such radical individualism. The contrast between individual freedom and closed institutions emphasized by

"Knights of the Open Palm" could be put to deeply conservative purposes—as Daly demonstrated in the stories that followed his attack on the Klan. His second Race Williams story, "$3,000 to the Good," set the hard-boiled protagonist in conflict with the greedy union official Abe *Nation*, and a story that followed soon after similarly cast the detective against a corrupt liberal senator who uses the radio to "embrac[e] the whole *nation*—the poor and the laborers—the great middle class." For the politically unsubtle Daly, in other words, labor unions and liberal politicians assume the same status as the Klan. Each represents a corrupt form of political solidarity. Each aspires to a spurious *national* status. And each can exercise no claim on the radical independence of Race.[37]

Thus, while Race Williams's refusal to be a joiner undermined the Klan's vision of native community, the potential endpoint of such a commitment was a radical skepticism about all forms of social organization—one that would invalidate not just Klannish fantasies of community, but every idea of civic obligation or human solidarity. Such implications were beyond Daly's ken. Race Williams took too much pleasure in action (or "*Action! Action!*" as one story put it) to worry too much about its ultimate implications. It would take Dashiell Hammett, a far more perceptive writer, to explore the disturbing possibilities of the hard-boiled hero's radical autonomy. Following Daly's lead, Hammett created in the anonymous Continental Op a hard-boiled protagonist who refused to be constrained by the claims of inheritance, by the demands of community or law, or by the restrictions of conventional morality. The result in Hammett's short stories from the twenties and in his first novel, *Red Harvest*, was a version of antiheroism that stressed some of the uglier features of Race Williams's self-interest. Again, though, it will be helpful to clarify this direction by first fleshing out some of the alternatives against which it contended.

JUNGLE SHADOWS

Race Williams did battle against the Klan in only his first story, finding more mundane opponents to humiliate in Daly's subsequent fiction. But throughout the mid-twenties, during *Black Mask*'s Klan debate and for several years after the magazine ceased making explicit reference to the group, hard-boiled fiction engaged in an implicit contest in the magazine with a variety of thriller narrative that echoed the main tenets of Klan ideology. These were exotic stories of foreign adventure — tales of white men beset by tropical dangers — that drew on the recent Tarzan vogue (and that echoed the miscegenist themes of H. P. Lovecraft's contemporary pulp gothic stories). Their particular variation of imperial adventure was already a prominent feature of pulp fiction in general at the time when Daly and Hammett began publishing. For several years, it had been appearing in the pulps, especially in *Black Mask*'s prestigious competitor *Argosy*. But foreign-adventure fiction gained ground in *Black Mask* only in 1923, around the same time that the hard-boiled crime story began to develop in the magazine. As the Klan debate unfolded in *Black Mask*'s back pages, this exotica quickly became a staple of the front section, and over the next few years the stories created by Daly, Hammett, and their imitators fought for readers against this latter-day version of Klannish fantasy.

Like Race Williams's battle with the KKK, the contest pitted hard-boiled fiction against an ideological vision it simultaneously resembled and derided. As *Black Mask*'s editors pointed out, both hard-boiled crime fiction and its exotic competitor targeted the "he-man [reader] with good red blood flowing in his veins"; both, too, liked to think of their characters as "human quarry"; and both focused their attention on "the border" of "the civilized state." But the foreign-adventure genre displayed a particular sympathy with the vision of nativist community that Race Williams had struggled to defeat in "Knights of the Open Palm." The common thinking was apparent in an advertisement that *Black Mask* ran for Herman Peterson's "One Dried Head." This new serial, the magazine announced, would feature "pirates, and black dwarfs with poisoned arrows, a stunning white girl and a new radio-equipped ship." Only a few months earlier, Peterson had published "Call Out the Klan" for *Black Mask*'s special issue. This new fiction retold that story by infusing its concerns with the romance of the exotic. The Invisible Empire's anxiety about local control and native community became here the melodrama of racial conflict that was always implicit in Klan rhetoric: black dwarfs compete with white technology for ownership of the "stunning white girl."[38]

As they did with the Klan, both Carroll John Daly and Dashiell Hammett mocked the elaborate fantasy and the dreams of order central to foreign-adventure fiction.[39] But the exotica proved to be far more persistent in *Black Mask*'s pages than the Klan had been — perhaps because the patent fiction of foreign adventure did not appear to be directly connected to any political program and perhaps because, by pushing the national frontier out to distant locations, these stories created images of racial solidarity that drew no explicit lines among "old stock" and recently arrived Americans. Nevertheless, tales like Peterson's "One Dried Head" closely approximated the themes of Klannish nativism, a commonality that can be seen especially in the way in which this fiction revised the traditions of the imperialist adventure story. The exotic fiction that began to appear in *Black Mask* around the time of its Klan debate plainly drew on the conventions of foreign exploration and racial conflict that had provided rich material for a previous generation of adventure writers. Ivan Ignatieff's "Jungle Shadows" even named its narrator Marlow in a backhanded compliment to Conrad. But, in an important sense, these tales seemed less like imperial fantasy than *anti*-imperial fantasy. Their most striking theme was not a sense of civilizing mission or of regeneration through racial conflict, but an utter terror at an impending loss of purity.

Thus, much like the Klan of the twenties, this new genre of adventure fiction expressed a yearning to reestablish crumbling cultural barriers and a longing to return from tainted lands to hermetic local community. Ignatieff's Marlow explicitly rebukes the "illusions" of imperialism, warning his listeners that merely to enter the jungle is to begin to lose the prestige of racial definition, and the stories that accompanied his bore out the warning. The heroes of these tales awake in strange lands to discover themselves prey to the miscegenist schemes of ruthless natives. They strive to live up to "old standards and ideals" — to remain "white enough" — to escape the threat of mixture, or they destroy themselves and their beautiful daughters to avoid falling prey to darker creatures. But in nearly every case, simply touching foreign soil creates the likelihood of degeneration and mixture. In Philip Fisher's "Fungus Isle," for example, sailors shipwrecked on a Pacific atoll discover that their skins literally darken as they succumb to the advance of a tropical disease. There is no escape so long as they remain on the island — or, by implication, abroad at all. "Cleanness" can be had only at home.[40]

At the center of this exotic fiction, then, lay a recurrent battle between insidious miscegenation and an imperiled, domestic homogeneity. That crucial preoccupation was typically developed through two related subthemes, each of which makes the close sympathy between this fiction and Klan ideology still more evident. First, the exotic stories that competed with hard-boiled crime fiction in *Black Mask* typically presented themselves as tales of fraternal bonding, thereby echoing the dynamics of "Call Out the Klan." In the struggle to defeat foreign corruption, a group of men unites itself into a harmonious brotherhood. Second, that brotherhood confronts not just external difference but internal dissent, usually in the form of veiled class antagonism. Insofar as the heroes are victorious against aliens, then, they also triumph over the bacillus infecting the community, banishing strangers and turning the tension among true brothers from a potential weakness into a source of mutual strength.

Consider, for example, John Ayotte's aptly named "White Tents" — the story of an army mapping mission in the Hawaiian forest. Isolated from civilization, Ayotte's platoon is suddenly confronted by subversion when an enlisted man named Nordstrom goes mad and slaughters several of his fellow soldiers in their sleep. The platoon's leader, Colonel Mortimer Edwards, must then join his shaken lower officers on a mission to capture the killer. Strengthened by military discipline and inspired by their battle against evil, the soldiers trace their enemy to a jungle "gorge," where he appears as a "maniac leer[ing] across the chasm." In the story's climactic scene, the soldiers banish this corruption, working together to flush their prey and send him screaming into the canyon below.

Like "Fungus Isle," Ayotte's story does not speak directly about race, but it draws on such firmly established conventions of jungle adventure and racial degeneration that there can be little doubt of the tale's subtext. For Colonel Edwards, the Hawaiian jungle is a "queer place" where "reason" is displaced by "superstitious, prehistoric fears," and it is the presence of these primeval energies that accounts for Nordstrom's decline and that transforms his rebellion against military hierarchy into a racial struggle. Across the chasm, Nordstrom is no longer a white soldier, who might be driven by some sense of class resentment. He has become "a wild man of the forest," alien by his very nature to the civilization represented by the army. Furthermore, in Ayotte's description, the effort to defeat this primal evil amounts to a replay of the recent European conflict that racial ideologues during the twenties described as the advent of nativist struggle. According to Hiram Evans, "it was the World War that gave us our first hint of the real cause of our troubles," because it revealed that ostensibly American citizens, "whom we had allowed to share our heritage and prosperity, and whom we had assumed had become part of us, were in fact not wholly so." As Colonel Edwards stalks Nordstrom, his mind jumps back to "Soisson . . . the crash of artillery, the intermittent hammering of machine guns," and then turns to a vision of his "country home" where two women wait: "They were mother and daughter, . . . and they both rushed to greet him." The association works to teach Colonel Edwards the same nativist lesson that the Great War conveyed to Hiram Evans: the subversion of ethnic aliens endangers the purity of a chaste, familial world. Once again, the community exemplified by the army is imperiled by a racially defined internal enemy. And once more, the community regains the fraternal intimacy and orderly form attractive to Klansmen by joining together to destroy that corruption. By plunging its enemy into the jungle gorge, then, Ayotte's symbolically rich mapping expedition reestablishes a racialized "border" to "the civilized state" — granting it the coherent status that Evans called the "integrity" of "unity in nationhood." It is no wonder that in the moment the maniac is "smashed to jelly," the Colonel himself "faint[s] dead away." For at the jungle chasm, Edwards purifies his world in a single moment of violence by destroying the double who inverts the values that he himself embodies.[41]

Just in case Ayotte's vision of nativist community was not clear enough, the editors of *Black Mask* introduced "White Tents" by reinforcing the expulsive logic at the heart of the fiction: "If you don't get a thrill and a shiver out of the old Colonel's adventures," they told their readers, "you're not human and *Black Mask* can't include you in its big family." Neither Carroll John Daly nor Dashiell Hammett, however, appeared to have much interest in that racially defined family. Neither cared much for Ayotte's brand of fiction, and the stories both men published at the time showed little interest in the vision of family and clan that Ayotte shared with his editors. In Hammett's fiction, in particular, family turns out to be a distinctly compromised ideal, either fictive or predatory. Fathers destroy their sons and mothers abuse their daughters; children betray their parents; siblings exploit each other; and in all of Hammett's oeuvre, there are perhaps one or two minor instances of domestic affiliation that do not appear ultimately murderous. In a small way, the pattern shows a presumption that tends to hold true throughout Hammett's work and that of many of his followers. In hard-boiled crime fiction, the bonds of inheritance typically exercise little benevolent authority. Most importantly, they fail to fulfill the mission that the KKK and their sympathizers attributed to the twin ideals of family and race. At least for Daly and Hammett, blood cannot provide the "vital chain" or "fixed bounds" that racial ideologues during the twenties hoped would foster the development of a fraternal republic.[42]

Rather than the orderly community envisioned by Hiram Evans and Colonel Edwards, then, hard-boiled fiction tends to portray disorderly society. More to the point, it typically treats the themes raised by *Black Mask*'s exotica in a sharply different manner than that of writers like Peterson or Ayotte. Consider, for example, a passage from Hammett's "Zigzags of Treachery," published just a few months after "White Tents":

> The night traffic of Kearney Street went up and down past me: Filipino boys in their too-dapper clothes, bound for the inevitable black-jack game; gaudy women still heavy-eyed from their day's sleep; plain clothes men on their way to headquarters to report before going off duty; Chinese going to or from Chinatown; sailors in pairs, looking for action of any sort; hungry people making for the Italian and French restaurants; worried people going to the bail bond broker's office on the

corner to arrange for the release of friends and relatives whom the police had nabbed; Italians on their homeward journey from work; odds and ends of furtive-looking citizens on various shady errands.[43]

In contrast to the exotica that was running in *Black Mask* at the same time, hard-boiled crime fiction moved the border away from distant locations and, in the guise of places like Kearney Street, set it at the interior of American society. Like the Hawaiian jungle, such places were, in every sense, on the edge of the domestic rectitude that the Klan sought to defend, but Hammett's street replaces "far-away and mysterious" aliens with intimate cosmopolitanism. Throughout the remainder of its career, hard-boiled crime fiction would remain fascinated by this kind of urbanity. Its crucial underworld setting is always, as Raymond Chandler would describe it, a "mixed" region that nevertheless has its own language, customs, and mysterious affiliations. The band of criminals in *The Maltese Falcon*, to choose a minor instance, is made up of Casper Gutman, apparently a Jew, Joel Cairo, a "Levantine," and Wilmer Cook, whose hometown of New York is described by Sam Spade in anti-Catholic tones as "Rome-ville." When the novel's femme fatale admits to being part of this world, she also drops those aliases, Miss Wonderly and Miss *Le-Blanc*, that indicate a hyperbolic bid for respectability and white-ness. Once a player in Hammett's criminal milieu, she becomes Brigid O'Shaughnessy, a name that is correspondingly ethno-empha-tic. It's probably not a coincidence that Brigid shares a first name with the patron saint of Ireland and a last with a prominent San Francisco machine politician. She is familiarly ethnic in a manner shared by the idiosyncratic underworld figures that appear through-out the genre — outside of or before the law in ways that can make her alternatively enticing, endearing, or terrifying.[44]

The genre is filled with such ethnicizing gestures, and it so consis-tently makes reference to stereotypical images that on the whole no one could accuse it of being enlightened or of doing much to combat ethnocentrism. But the difference between the ethnic imagery here and that in foreign-adventure fiction is fundamental. Dapper Fili-pinos are a favorite caricature of hard-boiled crime fiction, for in-stance, but they are not, as they are in Ignatieff's "Jungle Shadows," "a race unapproachable."[45] Put simply, where the border is a "chasm" in the foreign-adventure story, it is a sieve in the fiction of Hammett, Daly, and their successors, and the ultimate effect of this rendition is to undermine the effort central to Klan ideology — to fashion orderly community by making race and nation coterminous. On the mixed ground of Kearney Street, the "native Americans" and "honorable citizens" at the heart of the Klan's vision of a "wonderful nation" are bound to give way to a civic sense far less confident and virtuous. We are left with Hammett's "odds and ends of furtive-looking citizens."[46]

Like Daly's "Knights of the Open Palm," then, the passage from "Zigzags of Treachery" and its analogs throughout Hammett's fiction inhabit the same broad discourse about the "disgenic" features of "modern urban industrial life" that inspired Klan leaders, racial theorists, and foreign-adventure fiction during the twenties. Like Daly as well, though, Hammett seeks to put that rhetoric to uses that the Invisible Empire and its allies would reject. Most fundamentally, like Daly, Hammett dismisses the sacralized features of "the community's sense of justice" and thus declines to racialize the opposition between law and crime. This contention may seem unlikely at first, given the consistency with which hard-boiled crime fiction makes reference to ethnic stereotypes, but those conventional markings nearly always fail to rise to the level of racial distinction. Unlike "White Tents" or "Jungle Shadows," the hard-boiled genre typically neglects to resolve social decay by casting it as a conflict between cultures or races. *The Maltese Falcon*'s cosmopolitan gang of criminals may make this point most immediately since their crucial feature — that they are so cosmopolitan — works to underscore the fact that their association is based not on inheritance, but on shared criminal interests. Nor is there in Hammett's fiction anything like a unified community to which such cosmopolitanism might be opposed. Rather, Hammett consistently underlines the fictive stature and the basic unreliability of the social demarcations upon which the Klan and foreign-adventure writers intuitively relied.

A brief story like "Creeping Siamese" makes the case for this perspective most polemically. In it, Hammett's narrator, the Continental Op, confronts a pair of murderers who have invented the exotic racial threat referred to in its title in order to cover their own greed-inspired crimes. Even after he has elicited confessions from these criminals and taken one into custody, though, the Op blanches when they pass a group of Malaysian sailors on the street. He knows that if the criminal spots these "brown men," the murderer, however improbably, could identify one of them "as his Siamese, and God knows what a jury would make of it." In this one brief anecdote, then, Hammett uncovers the scapegoating fantasies of foreign-adventure fiction and its Klannish analogues. Race, the story implies, is an empty but potent social fiction.[47]

Typically, though, Hammett makes this point in more subtle ways. Another story from this period, for example, "Dead Yellow Women," knowingly plays with its audience's expectations about cultural distinction, at first seeming to confirm and then undermining its racialist presuppositions. As the story's deliberately sensational title suggests, the tale begins with murdered Asian women and an exotic interest in the mysterious world of Chinatown. The function of the title, however, is exactly to mislead in this direction, and the story ultimately disqualifies its own Orientalist premises. Chinatown turns out to be not so inscrutable as the story first implies, and the reasons for crime, rather than being exotic or connected to ethnic identity, involve the mundane pursuit of profit and advantage. Hammett's narrator marks the effect of these presuppositions in the description of a minor character named Loop Pigatti, whose underworld tavern appears often in Hammett's early fiction. Pigatti, Hammett's narrator explains, runs "a dive down on Pacific Street, where Chinatown fringes into the Latin Quarter. Loop is a tough citizen, who runs a tough hole, and who minds his own business, which is making his dive show a profit. Everybody looks alike to Loop. Whether you're a yegg, stool-pigeon, detective, or settlement worker, you get an even break out of Loop and nothing else."

Such is the egalitarianism of Hammett's underworld — a fantasy of a purely profit-driven society, in which the only meaningful social forces stem from the pursuit of individual interest. In such a milieu, Hammett implies, ethnic distinctions become ultimately insubstantial. And even his narrator's way of phrasing this description solicits and defies our expectations about race while confirming the basic point. Everyone looks alike to Pigatti because he sees them all through the lens of calculation, and Hammett sets us up to believe that this lack of discrimination refers to ethnicity by setting the dive between Chinatown and the Latin Quarter. But so removed is Pigatti, and Hammett's narrator, from such considerations that ethnicity itself never even enters the calculus. To the extent that Pigatti can see any differences that he may then decide to ignore, those distinctions have nothing to do with culture or heritage, but are matters of legality and illegality. What counts for him is not the border between ethnic groups, but those occupational or class positions (yegg, detective, settlement worker) that situate people in relation to the underworld.

Throughout Hammett's fiction, much the same holds true. Commerce and self-interest dissolve those ethnic boundaries that the Klan sought to cast as metaphysical principles, and when race is summoned, it tends to be a cover for the profit motive. Thus, "Dead Yellow Women" at first traces its crimes to the Chinese nationalist effort to throw off the "alien race" of the Japanese. But the real issue soon turns out to be the use of this nationalist vision as a cover for opium smuggling, rum-running, and "the coolie traffic." Likewise, when the Op's client, an assimilated Chinese American woman, suddenly appears in a Chinatown hideout in traditional garb, announcing, "I am here where I belong. . . . I have come back to my people," Hammett's protagonist knows to suspect that she is the dupe of less elevated purposes. He dismisses her explanation with the analysis that invocations of heritage tend to get throughout Hammett's work: "That was a lot of bunk."[48]

Although descriptions of places like Kearney Street or Loop Pigatti's tavern may seem to suggest our current discussions of "hybridity," then, Hammett's fiction usually implies a more radical skepticism about racial or cultural inheritance than contemporary preoccupations with "borderlands" allows.[49] The point of "Dead Yellow Women" or "Creeping Siamese" is not to summon more complex models of racial identity than the Klan had imagined, but to suggest the emptiness of race altogether. Thus, throughout hard-boiled crime fiction, the heavy ethnic coding common to the genre tends to be mutable and various because it is typically employed in the service of a fantasy about class and commerce rather than, as in *Black Mask*'s exotica and in Klan rhetoric, one of racial solidarity. For

Hammett especially, ethnic codes serve to mark a criminal milieu that amounts to a kind of class fraction or a professional subculture, and as Brigid O'Shaughnessy's mobility and multiple names suggest, it is always possible to assimilate to or disassimilate from such a world (a prospect that is the opposite of the way the Klan sought to "explode" the "theory of the melting pot").

To return to the quoted passage from "Zigzags of Treachery," this is the comic import of Hammett's inclusion of "hungry people making for the Italian and French restaurants" among the Chinese going to and from Chinatown and the Italians coming home from work. The apparent category confusion here is the whole point of hard-boiled fiction's use of ethnicity. For Hammett's narrator, who sees the world through the same lens as Loop Pigatti, the common feature that groups all of these people together, along with "gaudy women," cruising sailors, and "plain clothes men," is simply the fact that they pass through the same neighborhood at the same time. That is, something related to geography, work, and class. Insofar as ethnicity is seen in these terms—as a fact of political economy and not a feature of racial identity—people going to eat Italian and French in this neighborhood become ethnicized themselves. As part of Hammett's catalog of an urban region, they occupy the same category as the Italians and Chinese on the same street—which is to say that wherever hard-boiled crime fiction stresses the idea of class or place, it will not give an account of ethnicity that looks coherent by the standards of the Klan.

BODIES PILED UP

For the Klan as for *Black Mask*'s exotic fiction, race and "obligation" promised to overcome the disintegrative effects of the market and the disenchantments of modernity. For the hard-boiled crime fiction created by Daly and Hammett, interest consistently trumps race and honor. The contrast marks both the common ground inhabited by these two styles of thought and the fundamentally divergent ways that they departed from it. One way to see how crucial this dynamic became to the whole development of hard-boiled crime fiction is to note its centrality to later texts in the hard-boiled tradition that seem far from the origins of the genre and even more distant from the concerns of the Ku Klux Klan. The detectiveless stories of murderous lovers favored by writers like James M. Cain, Cornell Woolrich, and Jim Thompson, for example, are of another period and style than the early stories of Carroll John Daly and Dashiell Hammett. But, as the stories of Daly and, more thoroughly, of Hammett tend to do, these later texts typically show the noble demands of honor being unravelled by the mundane force of interest.

Indeed, the crux of novels like Cain's *The Postman Always Rings Twice* and *Double Indemnity* is basically a variation on the Prisoner's Dilemma — the hypothetical used by theorists of Rational Choice specifically to bring out the conflict between individual calculation and social goods. The suspense of the novels boils down to the moment when the lovers are forced to choose between mutual commitment and personal safety, and the effect of the inevitable choice for the latter is that the lovers are transformed from allies into self-destructive antagonists. What is more, for the hard-boiled writers as for the Klan, that destructive necessity is understood as the loss of a noble demeanor, and of particularity itself, to the absence of discrimination associated with consumerism and mass society. Great lovers are, of course, traditionally cast as aristocrats, and what writers like Cain portray in the inevitable defeat of their criminal protagonists is the way that such pretense cannot be maintained in the face of the individual calculation demanded by the market and by bureaucratic institutions. Lovers who feel forced to betray each other in these stories opt for a destructive egalitarianism — the vice of a leveling democracy, in which each viciously reciprocates the injury done to the other — over the aristocratic liberty that previously distinguished the pair from all other people.

That, after all, is what Cora of Cain's *Postman* means when she tells her lover: "We were up so high, Frank. . . . We had more than any two people in the world. And then we fell down. . . . we had all that love and we just cracked up under it. It's a big airplane engine. . . . But when you put it in a Ford, it just shakes to pieces. That's what we are, Frank, a couple of Fords." Cora's rhetoric is grandiloquent but apt. If great love is aristocratic, its symbolic defeat is accomplished by the twentieth century's most potent symbol of mass-market democracy — the Ford. In the workings of Cain's plot, Cora and Frank are defeated more specifically by the criminal justice system and the insurance industry. But by the terms of Cain's novel, these symbolic and narrative evils are indistinguishable. Consumerism, the courts, and the insurance industry conspire together to construe individual behavior in the light of social norms and group activity. And for Cain's protagonists, as for the Klan, the result is not merely to defeat the pretense to distinction, but to dissolve the racial prestige that is itself imagined as a kind of nobility. *Postman*'s prime figure of commerce and commonality is Cora's husband, "the Greek," who owns the novel's crucial insurance policies as well as the "roadside sandwich joint" ("like a million others in California") that provides its main setting. As the restaurant's sign makes clear, Nick Papadakis is a version of Hammett's Loop Pigatti — a figure for whom commerce has the capacity to mediate and dissolve ethnic distinctions: "It had a Greek flag and an American flag, and hands shaking hands, and Satisfaction Guaranteed . . . all in red, white, and blue Neon letters."[50] For Cain, in other words, it is not sufficient to suggest, as his novel relentlessly does, that the mass market cheapens or that consumerism levels the differences among people even as it encourages the individual desire for distinction. The seriousness of those processes is registered in the fact that they undermine racial identity. Becoming part of this world makes Cora "feel she wasn't white."[51]

The pathos of Cain's novel, then, is in one sense comparable to that evoked by the Klansmen of *Black Mask*'s debate. Love, for Cora and Frank, aspires to a type of community so essentially private that it is ethnically pure, outside the law, and, like the Klan's jargon, beyond ordinary communication.[52] Its loss means that, rather than being joined by spiritual bonds, their relations are mediated by precisely those institutions of mass society — the market, the law, the insurance industry — that are symbolized by the Postman of the novel's title.[53] There is no escape in Cain's novel from the banalities of bureaucratic institutions; they always ring twice. The difference between the presumptions of hard-boiled fiction and that of Klannish thinking, though, is exactly in the way Cora associates these matters with race. The reason she can feel more or less white, the reason she is married to Nick Papadakis in the first place and then plots to kill him, is summed up in her remarks to Frank about the Ford. What matters to her is being "up so high," and what drives her is the desire "not [to be] a bum . . . to *be* something."[54] Cora, like Cain's later creation, Mildred Pierce, is intensely ambitious, and she is dismayed at being the helpmeet of an immigrant running a diner. In this sense, though, feeling less white for her is indistinguishable from feeling cheap and unsuccessful. She is less concerned about miscegenation, the key theme of *Black Mask*'s exotic fiction, than she is about class mobility.

Rather than foreign corruption, then, "the Greek" stands in *Postman* for a type of triviality that Cain describes as typical of *American* culture. Nick epitomizes a "whole goddam country that lives selling hot dogs to each other." That he is Greek simply marks the fact that he is somewhere near the bottom rung of a ladder whose acme is thought of as "white." Though perhaps not much less ugly, then, this way of invoking ethnicity differs from that of the Klan or of the fiction of foreign adventure. In Cain's novel, "Greek" and "white" are part of the same continuum; for the Klan and the writers of pulp exotica, the foreign and the domestic are, or should be, ontologically discrete. Furthermore, both Klansmen and pulp exotica writers imagine that once this discontinuity is recognized and celebrated, the special bonds of ethnic identity will overcome class antagonism and status anxiety. In Cain's novel, though, ethnicity is essentially the same as class position. If Cora feels less white when she feels cheap, she can counter that feeling, she suggests, by moving up in the world.[55]

In short, though they may turn to ethnic allusions for their symbolic resonance, hard-boiled crime writers like Daly, Hammett, and Cain consistently suggest that inheritance lacks the profound significance that racial theorists sought to give it during the twenties. The social realities of class, of institutions, and of interest always undercut the "high idealism" of race. That fact might be taken as a significant influence on hard-boiled crime fiction's much-celebrated moral ambivalence. Rather than seeing the instability in the genre's images of ethnicity as a product of the relative enlightenment or tolerance of the story's protagonists, in other words, we might see the indecisiveness or amoralism of those figures as stemming in part from the absence of the meaningful racial distinctions that anchored nativist re-formism during the twenties.[56] Klan rhetoric and foreign-adventure stories bore ugly ideological content, but they were deeply moralistic genres, committed to mutual obligation and "high idealism." Each found it easy, therefore, to envision a just and coherent society. In-deed, they invoked "sacred" and "fundamental laws" — legal princi-ples that "bound" because they expressed "racial instincts" — and they imagined that the restoration of those laws would remake polit-ical institutions so that the state might become again "the organized virtue of the community."[57] Because they lacked that inspiring sense of latent cultural heritage, Daly and Hammett also lacked the Klan's compelling moral vision, and thus they conceived of laws and politi-cal institutions not as temporarily sullied expressions of the commu-nal will, but as inherently bureaucratic forms that exercised little emotional authority.

In effect, hard-boiled crime fiction seemed more cynical about the law than did Klan ideology, less idealistic about citizenship and re-form, because it was unwilling or unable to imagine that governing institutions could be redeemed by the triumph of racial community. And one key result of this refusal came in the genre's account of vigilantism. Both Klan ideologues and the authors of hard-boiled crime fiction wrote as if extralegal action was a natural response to social corruption. Their ideas about what vigilantism could accom-plish, however, were nearly direct inversions of each other. And the irony of the contrast was that, while Daly and Hammett defended a variety of "liberalism" against the Klan's nativist republicanism, for that very reason the vigilantism depicted by them tended to expand into fantasies of violence that far surpassed anything in either Klan rhetoric or foreign-adventure fiction. By the terms of its own ideol-ogy, the Invisible Empire during the twenties was a nonviolent, civic organization whose members would act to enforce "fundamental laws" only in those extraordinary situations where there was no other way "to take care of their communities." Klan leaders during the twenties stressed the exceptional nature of popular justice, and they always preferred to focus on the group's less objectionable pub-lic appearances. Similarly, stories like "White Tents" or "Call Out the Klan" were remarkable for the fact that they included only isolated moments of conflict and rarely more than a violent death or two. By contrast, from its beginnings, hard-boiled crime fiction seemed driven to produce a surplus of corpses, and the fiction proceeded as if it had set out to substantiate, and revel in, the Klan's fear of the disintegrative features of modern life; without communal bonds, social action tends inevitably toward the condition indicated by the title of an early Hammett story — "Bodies Piled Up."[58]

The difference between these two directions, then — toward limited or extreme images of violence — struck to the heart of the ideological dispute between hard-boiled crime fiction and nativist fantasy. Klan rhetoric and foreign-adventure stories envisioned limited violence because they both thought of vigilantism as an inherently local remedy for an ailing social body. Violent conflict was necessary, they suggested, but only to awaken the community and to restore "integrity" to racial boundaries. The shedding of blood would function, therefore, in a nearly sacramental manner — to seal the borders of a contained and harmonious world. In hard-boiled crime fiction, by contrast, racial distinctions are illusory and social boundaries irrevocably permeable. Rather than restoring justice in a single transformative moment, then, violence tends to leak out of control. "Murder succeeds murder," as *Black Mask* pointed out at the time; the hard-boiled protagonist is always threatened with the possibility of going "blood simple"; and as one reader complained trenchantly at the height of the fiction's golden age, the resulting "chain murder plot is never satisfactorily ended."[59] For Klan ideology and its fictional analogs, violence was the unifying voice of a common people. For the hard-boiled writers, by contrast, it became the expression of personal liberty and the emblem of a society too various and complex to be submitted to dreams of moral control.

Throughout the twenties, then, hard-boiled fiction and Hammett's stories in particular offered narratives of amoralism and irresolution both as a representation of the conditions of modernity and as an alternative to the forms of moral coherence that Klansmen and their sympathizers sought to impose on "urban industrial life." The culmination of this tendency, and the clearest expression of its implications, came in *Red Harvest* — Dashiell Hammett's first full-length book and his initial departure from the pulp magazines. It was in

Hammett's novel that the vision of moral reform and orderly community advanced by the Klan and its allies was subjected to the most withering skepticism ever mustered in *Black Mask*. As the title suggests, though, *Red Harvest* was also fittingly the novel that best portrayed the way in which hard-boiled fiction's alternative commitment to radical individualism and moral neutrality could issue in extreme violence. Hammett's novel has sometimes been celebrated for the way that it dismantles the detective story. (Barely a third of the way through its narrative, the Op solves the murder with which the book begins; more than a dozen deaths follow, and the book leaves no suggestion that justice has been achieved or a coherent community restored.) But in order to fully appreciate Hammett's ingenuity and his novel's account of violence run amok, we need to recognize that *Red Harvest* is not only a deconstruction of the detective story but the logical conclusion of the critique of Klannish fantasy that hard-boiled fiction began in "Knights of the Open Palm." Creating a parodic version of the Klan's myth of civic redemption, Hammett's novel depicts what might happen if the Klannish idea of popular reform were carried to extremes at the same time that Klan ideology was stripped of the vision of native community that underwrote its political ambitions.[60]

Red Harvest begins, therefore, from the premises of populist reformism that the Klan first introduced into *Black Mask*'s pages in 1923. The Continental Op sets out to clean up the "crime and political corruption" that dominates the Western mining city of Personville — known in "thieves' word[s]" as Poisonville — a city that exemplifies the vice, autocracy, and oligarchy that the Klan and its allies feared were taking over the United States in the twenties. Indeed, the title of the first installment of Hammett's novel when it appeared as a serial in *Black Mask* in the fall of 1927 drew directly on a moral rhetoric analogous to the Klan's in order to establish the authority of this vigilante campaign. "The Cleansing of Poisonville," like the Klan's vision of an "organized crusade" to "reform and cleanse" political institutions, promised a story in which corruption is routed, democracy and social health restored. As Hammett's editor indicated when he introduced the story as a tale of "civic politics" portraying "a city whose administrators have gone mad with power and lust of wealth," the novel suggested an image of populist uprising: the poison of "mysterious organization," would be vanquished and a corrupt elite of urban "administrators" rebuked, so that the personal features of community could triumph. But *Red Harvest* soon undermines the Op's determination to "clear the burg of vice." Nineteen slayings after beginning his version of a "reform campaign," Hammett's Continental Op has succeeded only in bringing martial law to the city, in ensuring his own censure, and in preparing Personville for a fresh round of abuse. "You'll have your city back, all nice and clean," he points out to the autocratic mining owner who seeks to rule the town, "and ready to go to the dogs again."[61]

Not only does *Red Harvest* cast doubt on the project of reform, though. It also regards with deep skepticism the popular authority that Klannish thinkers relied on. Hammett never even pretends to offer an account of healthy popular community. Only criminals cross the Op's field of view, as if Personville had no inhabitants except thieves and corrupt officials. And to the extent that any just order can be maintained in the city at all, the Op suggests that it will be the product of national "press associations" and the "white collar soldiers" of the National Guard — representatives of precisely those national elites and state bureaucracies that the Klan sought to abjure with the virtues of local community. Moreover, unlike the Klansmen who wrote to *Black Mask* and the protagonists of the exotic fiction that appeared in the magazine, the Op makes no claim to act as the voice of the people. His most compelling motivation, he admits, is personal vengeance, and a vengeance to be taken on the town as a whole: "I don't like the way Poisonville has treated me. I've got my chance now, and I'm going to even up." Like Race Williams in Clinton, in other words, the Op is avowedly motivated by private interests. But Hammett's protagonist takes the hard-boiled hero's assertion of personal motivation to far greater and far more disturbing lengths than Race Williams ever approaches. The Op becomes so intoxicated by vengeance and the pursuit of righteous violence that he abuses people who have treated him decently, encourages the indiscriminate murder of both Poisonville's kingpins and its insignificant, small-time hoods, and even betrays the working-class men he might claim to represent. As Thomas Roberts points out, "*every-*

body who trust[s] the Op loses." It is apparent, too, from the dubious reactions of his fellow detectives that even by the undemanding moral terms of vigilante justice, the Op's campaign has degenerated into a pathological search for personal gratification. Thus, where both the Klan and foreign-adventure fiction envisioned a native community joined by the moral leadership of disciplined men, Hammett portrays the absence of fellowship and the willful aims of a rogue vigilante. If *Red Harvest* is a novel of populist reformism, in other words, it is one in which reformism leads to no reform and populism summons no people.[62]

That tendency to undermine its own apparent presumptions works throughout Hammett's novel. At the heart of the Op's campaign is a struggle against gangsters and bootleggers that echoes the themes of nativist reformism of the 1920s. As a city subjected to the rule of crooks and tycoons, Personville resembles that "border" of the "civilized state" that inspired *Black Mask*'s adventure fiction. In fact, like the Hawaiian jungle of "White Tents," it is a stateless milieu that demands a heroic effort to reestablish civil order. Moreover, as in the nativist thinking of the period, the forces of corruption are exemplified by bootleggers, gangsters, and corrupt police who suggest the era's common associations between crime and ethnic "strangers." The major forces in the city's battle for power include the bootlegger Pete the Finn, the gambler Max Thaler — whose "dark" and slim appearance calls up the period's conventional anti-Semitism — and the Irish police chief, Noonan. Their numbers are rounded out by a host of lesser characters given comparable ethnic identifications: MacSwain, O'Marra, Riordan, and a gang of "swarthy foreign-looking men." As he did in his shorter works and in later novels as well, Hammett draws on such conventional associations to fashion a fantastically cosmopolitan underworld. But, once again, he denies the tendency to conceive of crime and corruption as a conflict between native and foreign cultures. Personville's criminal world draws no racial distinctions. Its members associate along commercial lines rather than ethnic ones, and this criminal world includes "old stock" Americans as well as new arrivals. Likewise, the Op's associates (Mickey Linehan and Dick Foley) are ethnically indistinct from the city's criminals. Most important, in contrast to stories like "White

Tents," the novel offers no picture of white, Protestant virtue, nor any hint of an ethnically homogenous community victimized by criminal strangers. Where Klansmen sought to describe criminals and "grafting politicians" as "all un-American," Hammett's fiction thus points to the temptation of such judgments and simultaneously suggests their ultimate uselessness.[63]

As if to confirm that unreliability, Hammett alludes to the emptiness of racial distinctions in the novel's very setting. *Red Harvest*'s Personville is a city "smoked" into "a uniform dinginess," whose sky and citizens are "a faded gray," whose Industrial Workers of the World (IWW) leader is a "gray man" wearing "rumpled gray clothes" and whose "face was grayish too, even the thick lips." The police chief has a face "gray, flabby, damp like fresh putty." His plain-clothesman wears a "gray overcoat" with a "gray hat." Even the story's femme fatale is "gray-stockinged" and lives in a gray house.[64] That monochromatic palette indicates not so much that Hammett aims for moral subtleties in this story — that, as it is often said, he reveals shades of gray. There is *only* gray here, an indiscernible haze of uniform dinginess. Just as Loop Pigatti can see no distinctions among his clients, the Op recognizes no differences among the IWW organizer, the chief of police, and the prostitute. They are equally corrupt because equally a part of Personville's criminal market, and as the Op begins to manipulate and to become caught up in this market, he quickly finds himself equally indistinguishable — very "much like a native." It is as though all of Personville suffered the transformation threatened by Fungus Isle, but without leaving that divide between the darkness of the exotic and the "cleanness" of the familiar that the foreign-adventure story preserved when it allowed its sailors to escape.

Indeed, it is exactly because the sharp racial and moral distinctions crucial to the Klan and to foreign-adventure fiction have disappeared that vigilante violence, once begun, has no clear stopping place in Hammett's novel. "Everybody's killing everybody," Personville's police chief complains in a perfect summation of the way all distinctions of identity and even the most relative political and moral differences have evaporated. In such a context, the obvious subsequent question — "Where's it going to end?" — is not merely rhetorical. In the

Op's anarchy, no one has a monopoly on violence, and no one can have expectations about where it will cease. It is in this context as well that the city's double name, Personville/Poisonville, makes most sense. The infection that spreads through Hammett's city is one that reduces citizens to indistinguishable reflections of each other — a single, violent, Hobbesian person. Hence, too, the site of the murder that begins the novel's wave of destruction: Hurricane Street. That name seems at first inappropriate to a Western mining city, but it turns out to foreshadow the manner in which violence in such a world increases in fury, "boil[ing] out under the lid" until it assumes the force of a natural disaster. Lacking the defining chasm of "White Tents," mayhem extends in Personville until every combatant is dead or too weary to continue. Hammett's city thus mimics exactly the dystopia that racist ideologue Lothrop Stoddard feared a "denationalizing element" would make of American culture. Without the "will to national unity," the "solidarity of ideals and culture" that creates a sense of common racial destiny, America becomes a "no-man's land": "non-descript," "Nothing-in-Particular," a "hellish bedlam."[65]

In such a milieu, Colonel Edwards's project to remap the cultural boundaries of American citizenship becomes absurd, and Hammett indicates the otiose nature of such an ambition in a remarkable sequence at the heart of the novel. As he realizes that he is succumbing to his own violence, the Op falls into a laudanum-inspired, two-part dream. In the first part of the dream, he wanders through a boundless megalopolis, walking "half the streets in the United States": "Gay Street and Mount Royal Avenue in Baltimore, Colfax Avenue in Denver, Aetna Road and St. Clair Avenue in Cleveland, McKinney Avenue in Dallas, Lemartine and Cornell and Amory streets in Boston, Berry Boulevard in Louisville, Lexington Avenue in New York." He is in pursuit of a nameless woman, a paradigmatic example of the genre's uncontainable femme fatale, and her displacement of exotic fiction's "stunning white girl" corresponds with the dissolution of the geographic and ideological legibility that white womanhood sanctified in both Klan discourse and in the Klannish fiction of foreign adventure. Just as he can see no secure boundaries between natives and strangers, the Op is unable to imagine the reassuring domestic figures that Colonel Edwards turns to in "White

Tents." Left only with the femme fatale, he envisions the nation as an unmappable and indistinct urban landscape.

In the second part of the dream, however, the uncontrolled spaces of its first part are replaced by a dramatically coherent civic terrain. The Op finds himself atop a tall building before "millions of up-turned faces in the plaza, miles down" attempting to crush the skull of a convenient, "small brown man" wearing "an immense sombrero." The image, as Hammett said of a similar scene of mass politics in an earlier story, is "spectacular, theatrical," and it brings up much the same implications as do "Dead Yellow Women" and "Creeping Siamese." It points to the social force of race at the same time that it emphasizes its fictive nature. The options presented by the Op's dream, then, are stark and exemplary. There is either the open city that expands indefinitely, or there is the protofascistic image of a mass society unified by the theatrics of racism. Even the coherence of this latter option is treacherous, though. For, preparing to kill the "little brown man" he unaccountably hates in front of the waiting mass below, the Op finds himself plunging "off the edge of the roof with him." At the moment when the scapegoat is due to be sacrificed in a ceremony of civic bonding — when, analogously, Colonel Edwards's chasm would be sealed by the descent of *one* of these figures — Hammett's protagonist loses distinction from his imaginary enemy and falls with him into the open divide. As with all the other differences in Personville that build upon this fundamental difference, racial opposition has ceased to be meaningful.[66]

LITTLE ONES AND BIG ONES

Like "Knights of the Open Palm," then, *Red Harvest* dramatized hard-boiled fiction's founding conflict with the nativist reformism exemplified by the Klan. As in Daly's fiction, it portrayed the hard-boiled protagonist as an inversion of nativist heroes like Colonel Edwards. The Continental Op and Race Williams are less the guardians of "borders" and "standards" than "middlem[e]n" whose traffic undermines cultural distinctions. Like Daly's story, therefore, *Red Harvest* casts the hard-boiled genre itself as a negative version of Klan ideology — an enemy brother of a sort, both beholden to and repelled by nativist ideas of race and order. Thus, if the choice first defined by *Black Mask*'s Klan debate lay between the two options presented so starkly by *Red Harvest* — between an incoherent city, stripped of traditional ideals, and an authoritarian community unified by racism — the fiction that followed Daly and Hammett's would tend most often toward the direction of shattered ideals. Indeed, the hard-boiled genre would reach the period of its greatest prestige during the thirties and early forties, when the fantasy of the vital multiethnic city first depicted by Daly and Hammett, and the fiction's tendency to avoid the battle between natives and strangers in favor of its own mythology of class antagonism, would accord well with the New Deal populism that supplanted the nativist spirit of the twenties. The significant conflicts of these stories came not between Americans and wild men of the forests, but between "little ones" and "big ones," struggling individuals and "great industrial institutions."[67]

Not to say that hard-boiled fiction never engaged in racial fantasy, that it never envisioned a blood fellowship of the type imagined by the Klan, or that it never sought to root a vision of justice and social cohesion in a dream of common inheritance. Precisely because hard-boiled populism so closely resembled its nativist opponents, such invocations of race would always remain compelling possibilities for the genre. And especially during the fifties, when New Deal populism began to lose authority and black urbanization and white flight pointed to the end of the white, working-class city beloved by the genre, hard-boiled writers like Raymond Chandler and Mickey Spillane would re-create a vision of republican virtue and racial conflict that closely echoed features of Klan fantasy. That was always a minority position in the genre, though. And in the best examples of the fiction, the characteristics of the hard-boiled hero fashioned by Daly and Hammett flourished precisely because they offered modes of action and affiliation that had nothing to do with inheritance. In fact, long after the twenties, hard-boiled fiction's emphasis on urban exchange and on the ubiquity of self-interest continued to appeal to some writers exactly because such attitudes encouraged a doubtfulness about the fictions of race that did not depend on any appeal to good intentions. Daly and Hammett dismissed the Klan's vision of racial community, not because they imagined a society built upon tolerance or benevolent universalism, but because they assumed that all people were driven by a self-interest that made dreams of racial obligation absurd. The attraction of such a presumption is perhaps best described by their successor Chester Himes, who returned questions of racial conflict and community to the genre during the fifties and who shared his predecessors' suspicion of the fantasies of racial brotherhood. "Human beings," Himes claimed, echoing the skepticism that Daly and Hammett first directed against the Klan during the 1920s, "all human beings, of whatever race or nationality or religious belief or ideology . . . will do anything and everything."[68]

In fact, it was in large part because hard-boiled crime fiction began from that premise that the fortunes of the genre would be closely aligned with the progress of the New Deal during the thirties and forties. However spurious the intentions of *Black Mask*'s editors were when they began the magazine's Klan Forum, the debate they set off turned on just the problem that would lie at the heart of the New Deal—the paradox inherent in the idea of liberal democracy. Klansmen and their supporters in the twenties recognized that the growth of industrial capitalism had ratcheted up the classic tension between liberty and equality into outright antagonism. A rapidly urbanizing mass society made it evident that the United States was not a society of equals nor a nation of self-governing local communities, and the Invisible Empire was willing to take drastic steps in response. If it was necessary to subject personal and economic freedom to racial community in order to foster responsible citizenship, then so be it—the Klan chose a commitment to equality (for white men, at least) over a defense of liberty.

The fiction created by Daly and Hammett began from the opposite choice, but that direction left the genre's writers with a central, unresolved problem: how to imagine a decent society in a country that had few compelling sources of solidarity and only the most rudimentary language of mutual obligation. During the thirties and early forties, long after the death of the Klan, New Deal politicians and intellectuals would likewise worry over some of the problems that the Klan had raised in the early twenties. These New Deal efforts, too, would often hinge on the attempt to re-create a sense of communal citizenship, or on the need to rethink the meaning of liberty in an industrial society; and, as was true in a smaller way for Daly and Hammett, those problems would seem all the more serious because New Deal liberals could not turn to visions of racial fraternity to imagine fantastic solutions for their dilemmas. In many respects, they faced a society that resembled the distended and disordered landscape in the first part of the Continental Op's dream.

Indeed, six years after the publication of *Red Harvest*, the legal scholar Felix Cohen relied on imagery much like Hammett's in order to mount a defense of the New Deal. "To the extent that any social relationship is exempt from governmental control it presents what Hobbes calls a state of nature," Cohen argued, "a war of all against all." That war was especially apparent in the realm of "industrial relations," Cohen claimed, and he called on Hobbes to insist that its violence was always latent even "before actual hostilities break out."[69] For Cohen as for Hammett, in other words, industrial oligarchy left the country in a state of undeclared civil war and always on the verge of bursting into terrible violence. The solution that he suggested was close to the one Hammett hinted at when the Op promised to bring the National Guard to Personville: to extend the federal government's control over the economy and to abandon the outmoded constitutional orthodoxy that protected capital from government regulation. It was a position closely aligned with the early New Deal's emphasis on "planning" and centralized political authority and one dependent on a related "realist" critique of traditional liberal dogma. The language of that critique, as we will see in chapter 2, ran strongly through Hammett's fiction as well.

2.

"MYSTIC RIGMAROLE"

Dashiell Hammett and the Realist Critique of Liberalism

[During the twenties, progressives] became hard-boiled
about radicalism. . . . we were forced to recognize economic
determinism and the strength of social habit. We turned . . . to
exposition of the losses, wastes, and absurdities of the existing state
of affairs, without assuming that we could do anything much about
it. . . . All the time we indicated . . . what seemed to us the unifying
idea behind our point of view — that the chief fault of the existing
disorder was lack of planning and control in the general interest.
. . . We may eventually have the sort of radical movement . . .
which exists not merely on paper and in the minds of a few ideal-
ists, but has its solid roots in economic and political organizations
of powerful groups with common interests.
— George Soule, "Hard-Boiled Radicalism,"
The New Republic, 1931

"We don't get along, do we?" he said after he had taken a
drink, "and it's a shame because I think we could do each other
a lot of good." — Dashiell Hammett, "Tulip"[1]

In the second chapter of Dashiell Hammett's *The Maltese Falcon*, Sam Spade is summoned to the scene of his partner's murder. The brief but striking passage that follows sums up much of what made Hammett's fiction distinctive and points simultaneously to a central problem of the hard-boiled genre that his novel exemplifies:

> A few yards from where Spade had dismissed the taxicab a small group of men stood looking up an alley. Two women stood with a man on the other side of Bush Street, looking at the alley. There were faces at windows.
>
> Spade crossed the sidewalk between iron-railed hatchways that opened above bare ugly stairs, went to the parapet, and, resting his hands on the damp coping, looked down into Stockton Street.
>
> An automobile popped out of the tunnel beneath him with a roaring swish, as if it had been blown out, and ran away. Not far from the tunnel's mouth a man was hunkered on his heels before a billboard that held advertisements of a moving picture and a gasoline across the front of a gap between two store-buildings. The hunkered man's head was bent almost to the sidewalk so he could look under the billboard. A hand flat on the paving, a hand clenched on the billboard's green frame, held him in this grotesque position. Two other men stood awkwardly together at one end of the billboard, peeping through a few inches of space between it and the building at that end. The building at the other end had a blank grey sidewall, and the shadows of men moving among lights.[2]

It is a typical portrait of the fantastic city Hammett favored — full of intense sensation, yet affectless and lacking in any impression of community or order — and its spectral image would become a commonplace of the fiction that followed in the hard-boiled genre. Concealed in the scene as well, though, is an allegorical image of the fiction's most basic narrative dynamics. The policeman who hunkers grotesquely before the billboard is a mirror to Miles Archer, Hammett's dead partner, whose corpse lies in the alley behind the advertisements because he lacked the necessary shrewdness and distance to escape the murderous Brigid O'Shaughnessy. In that sense, the policeman is a counterpart as well to all the inadequate detectives who stumble through the modern mystery story. Like C. Auguste Dupin's Paris

Prefecture or Sherlock Holmes's Scotland Yard, the awkward cop exemplifies the ordinary lack of insight that prevents the police from gaining the perspective available to the inspired detective. Just as Miles Archer is a Dr. Watson whose thickheadedness and weakness for feminine beauty result not just in embarrassment but in his death, the twisted cop is an extreme, physical emblem of the limitations of Holmes's Inspector Lestrade. Laboring literally to see past the distracting signs of mundane commercial culture, the policeman personifies "the exceptionally knotty problem" that Hammett claimed confronted all real detectives. He is surrounded by "altogether too many" clues and is so entrapped by what we might call webs of signification that, in Hammett's subtle parody of Plato, he comes to play the part of the chained soul who sees nothing but the shadows of real events. The implication of the scene is clear; not to be able to sort out the welter of information in an urbanized world, to fall prey to the false enticements and deceptive pleasures generated by a consumer economy, is to have the "small eyes" that Miles Archer shares with the police — and to end up, therefore, either crippled or dead.[3]

In the classic detective story invented by Poe and perfected by Conan Doyle, the detective-genius stands where Sam Spade does and remedies the limitations of his less perceptive counterparts. Pressed into service by helpless clients and hapless police, he sees through the confusion that surrounds every other character and from his unique vantage establishes the right reading of signs. If the events of the murder narrative typically present an impression of ordinary life as an overwhelming proliferation of clues, it is the detective-genius who restores a sense of wholeness, order, and moral confidence — not just by discovering a criminal, but by proving the patterns of meaning that organize everyday life. Separating false appearance from true, trivial data from significance, he makes a structure out of apparently random signs, turns information into culture, and transforms a potentially disordered world into a community bound by webs of shared meaning.[4]

In Hammett's passage, however, this dynamic has been significantly changed. Sam Spade is not brought to the scene as an eccentric genius; the police summon him as a potential suspect, and, though he looks down on the grotesquely bent policeman from a symbolically significant height, he will turn shortly from this eminence to be questioned by the police. His position as privileged observer, in other words, is short-lived and contingent, and the passage in which he looks upon the murder scene thus accurately predicts the tone and structure of the novel's ending. There Spade identifies Brigid O'Shaughnessy as the murderer, abandons her as his lover, and turns her over to the police, but he must do all these things at least in part in order to be free from arrest himself. In both the novel's opening and its conclusion, then, Spade exemplifies a superiority and freedom that is registered against a figure (the bent cop, Brigid) who is, by contrast, imprisoned. But in both cases as well, Spade is himself more or less at the mercy of the police and thus unlike the traditional detective-genius, whose freedom is the result of his personal ability to discern and thereby escape the patterns that confuse other people. In effect, the law demands Sam Spade's independence so that it can have Brigid's arrest, and once again the implication seems clear. In the world of Hammett's fiction, one can experience freedom only at the cost of someone else's limitation, and autonomy itself becomes therefore a kind of compulsion: whatever feeling Spade may have for Brigid — and it is part of the strength of Hammett's novel to suggest that he experiences more than a fleeting attraction — he *must* arrest her and his own desire in order to remain free. "I won't [love you]," he tells Brigid, "because all of me wants to."[5] Hammett's protagonist, one might say, is constrained to freedom in direct proportion to the way the grotesquely twisted policeman is constrained to his limited perspective or that Brigid is bound over to the court. And, as Sam Spade's resigned attitude at the novel's conclusion and as the flat endings characteristic of so much of the hard-boiled genre suggest, little seems redemptive or consolatory about such a situation. Like Spade, Hammett's protagonists are typically forced into an unhomely alienation so that they may avoid a lethal imprisonment. There appears to be no happy middle ground.

Indeed, if this opening passage does allude to Plato in order to comment obscurely on the resolution to Hammett's novel, closer attention makes its implications seem still more ominous. For, despite the fact that Sam Spade looks upon the scene from the eminent vantage of the detective and philosopher, he is also the person who watches the shadows moving on the cave wall. It is the grotesquely bent policeman meanwhile who appears to see the true evidence behind the façade. Through the rest of the novel Spade will struggle to discover those facts himself, but this opening image casts that effort in an unusual light by actually inverting Plato to suggest that it is the chained soul who sees the truth and the free intelligence that is trapped by delusion. That implication haunts Hammett's writing and points to the radical revision he brought to the mystery genre. The classic detective story traditionally introduces violent disruption so that the conventions and meaning of everyday life can be refound and reassented to, becoming in this way a mythic image of the re-creation of the social contract. As he suggested in *The Thin Man*, though, when he had Nick Charles remark that "murder doesn't round out anybody's life," Hammett's fiction challenges the basic features of that story. In his world, free consent seems impossible, pattern and convention rarely feel reassuring, and the detective's capacity to see them appears less a way of rediscovering the ordinary than of remaining irretrievably alien to it. Those innovations, more-over, not only remade the detective genre, they both echoed and commented revealingly on a central strain of reformist thought that ran through the New Deal era.

TRUE MAGIC AND LEGERDEMAIN

The revisions that Hammett brought to the detective story genre corresponded closely to the dynamics of his literary career, echoing his unusual experience in the literary field of the interwar years and dramatizing the strategies he brought to the era's publishing market. Even during Hammett's lifetime and during an era of literary super-stars, that career was a legendary success. Hammett was the ex-Pinkerton who, although he had never completed high school, could quote James, Conrad, and Anatole France and who had made the pulp crime story into a form of some literary credibility. He was the first of the *Black Mask* writers to move from the pulps to the highly regarded publishing house of Alfred A. Knopf, the first to gain se-rious recognition from contemporary intellectuals, and the first to set out consciously to make something avowedly literary out of the detective story. By the same token, he was also the first writer to claim that such an effort would be inherently problematic, and the first to make hay of the notion that bringing the detective story artistic legitimacy would involve not just an effort to polish and improve it, but a struggle to transform its basic features.

There had long been, of course, pop writers of considerable gifts and authors of literary repute who earned vast popular success, just as there were many figures who were unconcerned about the divide between mass entertainment and serious art. Hammett's career developed, though, during a period in which the values of an emerging literary intelligentsia emphasized the antagonism between commercial success and artistic legitimacy and in which, at the same time, the popular arts were brimming with a creative energy that constantly challenged the legitimacy of such a divide.[6] The period during the mid- to later twenties in which Hammett came of age is now often thought of as an era of little magazines and literary celebrity, but these were in fact only the most evident features of a booming publishing market and a literary world in the process of rapid growth and diversification. Over the course of his career, Hammett would straddle a number of that world's developing subfields. His first success came in the era's flourishing pulp magazine industry, which had expanded dramatically in the years following World War I to become a vibrant and virtually self-sufficient literary arena by selling entertainment to a growing working-class readership. As chapter 1 noted, though, those pulp magazines were both linked to and overshadowed by the massive commercial and cultural presence of the era's "big slick" magazines. Powered by the exponential growth of advertising and consumer capitalism throughout the twenties, those magazines built vast circulations and competed with high prices for a population of celebrity authors that they had themselves helped bring into existence. At the same time, a group of upstart book publishers emerged to challenge the dominance of the nineteenth century houses like Scribners, Harper's, and Ticknor & Fields. Led by Knopf, who had begun the assault in 1915, and by a group of imitators like the flamboyant Boni & Livwright that sprang up in the twenties to follow Knopf's lead, these new publishers challenged the authority of the old-line houses by dedicating themselves to literary excellence and cultural innovation rather than to the genteel stewardship that had been the central value of nineteenth-century publishing. Many of the writers published by those newer houses — and by both big slick magazines and avant-garde periodicals — could dedicate themselves to the values of intellectual autonomy in turn because they found new sources of support outside the publishing market, in the development of philanthropic and scholarly foundations, in the expansion of university employment, and in the emergence of a network of private patronage dedicated to the avant-garde. The result of these combined forces was a period of now legendary literary ferment — "a new and brilliant world for books," as Hammett's lover Lillian Hellman later put it, recalling her own youthful experience at Boni & Livwright.[7]

In his famous move from *Black Mask* to Knopf, Hammett drew heavily on the values cultivated by the emerging literary intelligentsia of the twenties and used them self-consciously to reflect back upon the work he had done in the popular commercial genres nourished by the pulps. What made that experience distinctive was that Hammett cast himself as addressing an elite readership at odds both with the cultural stewardship of literary tradition and with the prominence of the commercial mass media, and he therefore placed himself in an unusual role. His experience in the pulps and his background as a Pinkerton agent gave Hammett the authority of an outsider and enabled him to claim knowledge of a public beyond the one familiar to the educated readership that became his primary audience. At the same time, Hammett would suggest that such experience was valuable only insofar as it could be given the clarity that he associated with new styles of cultural leadership. Indeed, when he described himself as bringing the detective story to aesthetic credibility, he would look upon the popular fiction he exploited both as a literary resource and as a dangerous force of seduction and confinement.

The growing importance of the distinction between art and commercial entertainment thus became for Hammett at once galling and enabling. During the heady period in which his career developed, literary modernism encouraged both recondite sophistication and broad tolerance for the once unseemly features of urban popular culture. Especially in *Smart Set*, the archly clever magazine edited by H. L. Mencken and George Jean Nathan where Hammett published his first brief writing, the two forms seemed part of a single movement of cultural rebellion. Alone or in combination, each could be pitched against the Victorian moralism of what Hammett called "the world B.C." — before credit and the crisis of 1918. Against the "thou-shalts and thou-shalt-nots" that he associated with such a past, and against the "dream world" of mainstream mass media, Hammett would marshal the energies of both low and high culture — speaking in the same breath of the Barnes collection of fine art and prizefights, hobo lore and the theory of relativity, the "St. Louis Blues" and Flaubert. Such invocations were consciously mobilized against both cultural snobbery and populist anti-intellectualism, but in either direction Hammett's concerns were Menckenian. He was consistently preoccupied with the distortions and dangers of what he later referred to as "popular belief," and he suggested that it was up to a vanguard of adventurous artists and intellectuals to overcome the baleful effects of "common sense."[8]

While Hammett may have sought recognition for his own efforts, then, he was, unlike his editors and peers in the pulps, far from culturally egalitarian. As he warned one of his first editors, he was "hard to get along with where fiction's concerned." Indeed, he disdained his own pulp work, referring to it dismissively as "blackmasking," and he had little but scorn for most examples of detective fiction generally, refusing to treat it as a variety of entertainment with its own critical standards. "Literature," he claimed, "is good to the extent that it is art, and bad to the extent that it isn't."[9] Unlike some of his followers, moreover, Hammett was never much of a populist, and he saw little sign of vitality, or creativity, or rootedness in vernacular literacy. Underworld slang, he claimed, was little more than "jargon" — "a conscious, artificial growth, designed more to confuse outsiders than for any other purpose." Where a later writer like Raymond Chandler would become enamored of "the American vernacular" for the way it seemed to present an alternative to sterile, literary sophistication, Hammett saw in slang only "meaningless" distortion. He was willing to concede that such language was at moments "singularly expressive," but those were the occasions when a critical intelligence was able to separate out the gold from the dross and to do so, moreover, by seeing the places where criminal slang betrayed not its users' inventiveness but their impoverishment.[10]

In short, though he later became famous — or infamous, as the case may be — for his socialist politics, Hammett was also an elitist, and he envisioned the pursuit of literary autonomy as a way to elude and objectify the forms of imprisonment implicit in vernacular expression. Where Chandler imagined himself caught up in a constant effort to escape "the literary life" and thus came to view his imaginary underworld as a rich and vital milieu, always being taken over by routinization, Hammett's perspective was nearly the reverse. The effort to grasp and evade the confusions of contemporary society, he suggested, was constantly being compounded by stereotypes, folklore, common sense, and superstition — all the mystifications of popular belief. Thus, in an early essay about copywriting titled emphatically "The Advertisement IS Literature," Hammett called on the authority of Conrad and Anatole France to note that the "language of the man in the street is seldom either clear or simple" and that the "favorite words of the plain man are those which enable him to talk without thinking." The "simplicity and clarity" for which copywriters should strive, by contrast, were "the most elusive and difficult of literary accomplishments."[11]

At the same time, Hammett never had any patience for "the spinster environment" of academic expertise or the "serious thoughts" of cultural pretense, and he derided their high-minded removal from the demands of ordinary life. The authorial stance he developed from this combination of attitudes was much like the description of him proffered by a bunkmate during World War II, when Hammett served as a volunteer enlisted man in the Aleutians: "just like anybody else except he's got more sense." Hammett quoted that remark with a hint of self-mockery, but also with evident approval, perhaps because it corresponded so closely with the intellectual ideal he pursued from his first literary efforts during the early twenties: to be broad-minded and nonacademic and in that sense a man of the people, but at the same time to be able to see with greater precision and breadth than the ordinary citizen. The writer, he later suggested — again, only half facetiously — should be someone who could "make sense of . . . [things] for folks," especially in those cases where the folks could not. Some of the "fancier yarns come from people who are trying" to tell the truth but who are "out of the habit," Nick Charles says in *The Thin Man*, significantly expanding on the traditional domain of the detective story. The difficulties with which the detective must contend in Charles's description are no longer conscious deceit alone, but unwitting self-deception and popular confusion. It was up to the writer, as it was to the detective, Hammett implied, to find the "clear or simple" truth hidden in the tangled language of the man on the street.[12]

In fact, although he left little evidence about either his motivations or his actions during this period, it seems likely that similar thoughts underlay the turn to leftist politics that Hammett made during the thirties and early forties, after he had all but abandoned his literary career. If the dynamism of Popular Front politics during this period stemmed, as several historians have suggested, from the determination of artists and writers to serve as "cultural representatives" — the "organic intellectuals" who would speak to and for a newly emerging popular formation — that goal accorded well with the idea of the work of the writer that Hammett had developed by the mid-twenties.[13] Indeed, it may be that the broadly democratic politics of the Popular Front appealed to Hammett as much for the way they legitimized that vision as for any particular social transformations they anticipated. Thus, Hammett worked with left and liberal magazines and newspapers like *Equality* and *PM* that aimed to popularize progressive politics as well as avant-garde literature. (Hammett prepared a review of *Finnegans Wake* for the dummy issue of *PM*). He explained to the Third American Writers Congress in 1939 that the "contemporary novelist's job is to take pieces of life and arrange them on paper," and during the war he sought to continue this mission, editing a newspaper for soldiers stationed in the Aleutians. It was a job that Hammett took seriously, and he explained it in much the same terms that he had used to describe advertising some twenty years before. It was the newspaper's role, Hammett explained, to cut through the ignorance and misinformation fostered by the "dream world" of mass media and to use entertainment in the service of civic pedagogy: "we want to produce a soldier who . . . knows more, not less, than he ever knew about his world in civilian life." That aim would be made easier, he suggested in the same half-mocking manner that he used to describe his effort to "make sense of . . . things for the folks," by the fact that "we have our public penned up on an island where they can't get away from us." Here as before, it was the work of the writer to edify a recalcitrant people and to impose clarity upon popular confusion.[14]

That sense of intellectual mission, with its combination of populist sympathy and cultural elitism, not only underwrote Hammett's politics; it determined the shape of his literary career. In particular, it helps to explain the central enigma of that career — the way a brief, three-year period of remarkable creativity, in which Hammett wrote his four important novels (*Red Harvest, The Dain Curse, The Maltese Falcon,* and *The Glass Key*) gave way to nearly three decades of silence and frustrated ambition. As a young writer, Hammett was emboldened by the idea of bringing artistic achievement to pulp fiction, but when that combination no longer seemed novel or significant or even plausible, he no longer had a subject, apart from his own inability to write and thus descended into a long period of what his lover Lillian Hellman called "angry privacy."

There was little hint of that creative silence when Hammett first left the pulps and sent his fiction to Knopf in the late twenties. In his first correspondence with his publishers, Hammett was eager to please, but also overweeningly ambitious, and he cast his literary goals in much the same manner that he had used previously to describe the difficulties of copywriting. In 1928, Hammett thus explained to Blanche Knopf: "I'm one of the few — if there are any more — people moderately literate who take the detective story seriously. I don't mean that I necessarily take my own or anybody else's seriously — but the detective story as a form. Some day somebody's going to make "literature" of it (Ford's *Good Soldier* wouldn't have needed much altering to have been a detective story), and I'm selfish enough to have my own hopes."[15]

Such remarks made large claims for Hammett's work. But they also asked their readers to regard it in a particular fashion: to consider just how far the writer had met his hopes to make "literature" of the detective story. To what extent was it art, to what extent simply bad writing? The effect of Hammett's ambitious pronouncements, in other words, was the opposite of the egalitarian result one might expect. They did not say, as Chandler later would, that the question of whether something was "art" or "literature" was unimportant. Rather, Hammett suggested that this was the *only* question, and he asked his readers to scrutinize his writing to wonder how far he had come toward reaching his own high standards. In order to cast himself as the rare figure who could make literature out of the pulp detective story, then, Hammett needed to presume not only that the effort would be meaningful, but that it would be so challenging as to seem all but impossible. Pulp writing or "blackmasking" was, Hammett thus implied, a kind of vernacular, analogous to criminal slang and to the thoughtless speech of the man on the street. It demanded a writer who was able to find the "expressive" material hidden within the meaningless and artificial growth of everyday communication. If that effort were to be significant, though, it had to be constantly threatened by the very confusions that the writer sought to overcome and by the constant threat of backsliding.

While Hammett might initially defend the literary merits of his own novels against cultural prejudice, then, he could do so only with great diffidence. For it would always be unclear just how far they deserved to be taken seriously as literature and how far, by contrast, they were the equivalent of meaningless jargon. A slightly later pair of letters to his publishers, sums up that reluctance and the whole direction of Hammett's career as a novelist. Having delivered his first three books to Knopf in just over a year, Hammett asked editor Harry Block: "How soon will you want, or can you use, another book? I've quite a flock of them outlined or begun": a horror novel (to be given the brilliant title, *AEAEA*), a "pure-plot" detective story, a "political murder mystery," an "underworld mystery," and a story of a gunman along the lines of *Little Caesar*. To this catalog, he added, moreover, a proposal for a book collecting the stories and novellettes he had done for *Black Mask*. Though he said he wanted to edit and rewrite this material — to winnow out its expressive core, as it were — Hammett was confident that these stories contained a wealth of good material to be salvaged: "a more complete and true picture of a detective at work than has been given anywhere else."[16]

One month later, however, that plan and the ambitious attitude behind it had been abandoned. Having reread the stories, Hammett said, he had decided that they would never be anything better than "fair" and thus were not worth the effort. Likewise, the novels he outlined in the letter to Block would never be attempted. After finishing *The Glass Key* and then writing the less ambitious *The Thin Man* a few years later, Hammett would publish only a handful of stories and one further, very minor novella, *Woman in the Dark*. Though he had spoken confidently in 1931 of "try[ing] . . . [his] luck with another genre," and although Alfred and Blanche Knopf would continue for years to beg him to send them any material he wished, Hammett quickly abandoned his literary ambitions and put the bulk of his energy into other pursuits — first, drinking and movie-industry hackwork, and then political activities and editorial efforts with Lillian Hellman on her plays. From the portrait of Nick Charles in *The Thin Man* on, too, the writing Hammett did attempt — unfinished stories, novels, plays, film treatments, and the screenplay for Hellman's *Watch on the Rhine* — would be populated with protagonists who had surrendered their ambitions and who were wryly self-lacerating about their failures. And though he guarded his privacy angrily, as Hellman noted, Hammett occasionally spoke the same way about himself. "What little imagination I've got is used up," he claimed during the fifties, and in a similar vein during the same period, he left the unfinished autobiographical novel "Tulip" hanging with the sentiment "if you are tired you ought to rest . . . and not try to fool yourself and your customers with colored bubbles."[17]

The remarkable thing about this resignation, however, is not so much that it seemed to come over Hammett at the very peak of his career, but that he had predicted it from his very first efforts to become a writer. During the early twenties, long before he had achieved his literary reputation or even a name in the pulps, Hammett wrote a brief story titled "Magic." The tale is an allegory of the discipline and entrancing powers of "Art," but it features a weary spiritualist who denounces rather than praises his legerdemain to an apprentice and who predicts the way the apprentice's career will follow suit: "In this nonsense you've learned you'll find the satisfaction a man has in doing what — however silly — he can do skillfully. . . . You'll have your skill, and your craftsman's pride in that skill, and the money it brings you and presently you'll be middle-aged and old." The story suggests that Hammett had fallen early for the glamour of a certain type of literary despair. For "Magic" is both a hymn to and a complaint against artistic professionalism (and is thus an early example of a theme that would become central to Hammett's detective fiction). The magician has dedicated his life to an ascetic pursuit of spiritual mastery intended to grant him power over other men; in this sense, he resembles a more sedentary version of the Continental Op or Sam Spade. To "the extent one becomes a magician," he warns his apprentice, "one ceases to be a man" and is denied worldly pleasures like love or wealth or comfort. But, as in *The Maltese Falcon*, the pursuit of such inhuman mastery results less in freedom or power than in constraint. The magician discovers that he is locked into a "mystic rigmarole" that mocks the "True Magic" after which he had once yearned, and, in this light, his commitment to ritual and craft seems less an extraordinary spiritual pursuit than an ordinary form of routinization. The magician may cease to be a complete man because of his strict dedication to learning, but that is nothing special. The "same thing," the protagonist notes, "might hold true of sailors and jewelers and bankers."[18]

Several years before he bragged to Blanche Knopf about making "literature" out of the detective story, in other words, Hammett had already envisioned something very much along the lines of a negative version of that transformation — one in which such an effort might seem less like an achievement than a trivialization of the ambition itself. That possibility was built into Hammett's theory of literature, and it is a reminder that, although they differed sharply on political ideals and aesthetic tastes, Hammett and Chandler shared a fundamental problem. The fact that each imagined that great civic importance lay in the effort to redeem the detective story meant that their ideas about writing were likely to flip-flop between arrogance and abjection. Their work could seem either a remarkable transcendence of limits or, as in "Magic," a kind of empty "legerdemain." In Chandler's case, the result was nostalgia for an ephemeral popular vitality and for the evanescent promise of a "public taste." For Hammett, by contrast, the central anxiety focused on the loss of intellectual purchase and the peril of useless specialization. Beneath the boast that he would make "literature" out of the detective story, or that he would discover clarity in thoughtless popular speech, lay the inevitable suspicion that, like the magician, he would discover that he was not the master of popular delusion but its victim. The anxiety is apparent in the dilemmas of his most famous protagonists. If Chandler's Philip Marlowe is always yearning after a fading brotherhood and pining for Moose Malloy or Terry Lennox, Hammett characters like the Continental Op and Sam Spade must struggle against the temptation to give way to popular seduction. The central issue of *Red Harvest*, for example, is the threat that the Op will go "blood simple" — that he will become so caught up in the "meaningless" world of "thieves' word[s]" that there will be no distinction between detective and criminal. He is rescued from that possibility only by his willingness to submit to the procedural demands of his boss, the Old Man — a discipline as formal and empty as the magician's "mystic rigmarole." Likewise, the crux of *The Maltese Falcon* comes in Sam Spade's unwillingness to "play the sap" for Brigid, but again, the only counter to criminal desire is the thin glue of professional obligation.[19]

Like "Magic" and like the murder scene in *The Maltese Falcon*, these stories pitch empty autonomy against ordinary constraint without either resolving the conflict or finding one pole more welcoming than the other. They suggest, as well, a more jaundiced view of the writer's ambitions than Hammett's boasting initially implied. If, for example, Ford Maddox Ford had really written a concealed detective story in *The Good Soldier*, as Hammett suggested in his letter to Blanche Knopf, what would be the point of working to make the detective story "literature"? Wouldn't the ambitious pulp writer actually be showing that, rather than an achievement surpassing popular confusion, "literature" was merely a glorified form of pulp fiction? By the same reasoning, the claim that advertising *was* literature might not just emphasize the difficulty of copywriting, but strip literature of some of its burnish. If both copywriters and artists (like magicians and bankers) must train themselves to achieve simplicity and clarity, then one might wonder whether there was anything special about literature to begin with — if it, too, were not merely a subtle variety of commercial seduction. The "chief goal" of

advertising and literature, Hammett admitted, was the same pragmatic ambition: to "secur[e] the maximum desired effect on the
reader." By this description, literature might seem less like a means
of clarifying the seductive confusions of everyday life than a way of
multiplying them.[20]

FROM CONTRACT TO ADMINISTRATION

Translated into the narrative terms of the detective story, those questions would become the central problems of the novels that Hammett wrote during the late twenties and early thirties. If the classic
detective story is about the effort to make order out of confusion,
Hammett's fiction both emphasized the appeal of that vision and the
unlikelihood of its realization. More specifically, his novels and stories fundamentally altered the role of the detective — whose job had
been to make sense of things for folks. In Hammett's rendition, the
ways that the detective pursued that end and the chances of his
success were sharply changed.

In this manner, however, Hammett's novels not only thematized
the problems at the heart of his literary career. Doing so, they also
echoed contemporaneous changes in the definition of the civic-
minded intellectual. During the years in which Hammett matured as
a writer, the rapid professionalization of higher education and the
growing vision of an administrative national state combined to bring
about profound changes in the ways that a burgeoning intellectual
class thought about its work and its relation to political life. Each
encouraged ever greater emphasis on the importance of technical
expertise and ever less faith in the value of popular understanding;
together, they produced a basic transformation in elite conceptions
of civic life — a shift, as Michael Sandel puts it, "from contract to
administration."[21] The central presupposition of late-nineteenth-
century American legal and political theory had been the notion that
society cohered by the free and reasoned consent of autonomous
individuals. In the English jurist Sir Henry Maine's influential formulation, modern societies had progressed "from status to contract."
American intellectuals during the interwar era, by contrast, saw far

more irrational habit than rational agreement in their world, and far more unequal power among groups than egalitarian freedom in individuals. In light of that perception, a broad range of thinkers argued that it became the mission of experts and officials to see society not as an aggregation of individuals but as a whole whose shared needs they might identify and protect. "There is amid the welter of self-serving groups, clamoring and struggling over [politics]," the legal scholar Karl Llewellyn claimed, "the recurrent emergence of some wholeness, some sense of responsibility which outruns enlightened self-interest, and results in action apparently headed (often purposefully) for the common good." It was the job of the expert and the administrative official, Llewellyn and many of his contemporaries assumed, to recognize the common good that rose above individual interest and to guide society in the purposeful movement toward its achievement.[22]

This was the transition that George Soule spoke of when he referred in 1931 to the development of a new, "hard-boiled radicalism." Speaking from the pulpit of the *New Republic* — a principal voice of centralized planning throughout the twenties and early thirties — Soule argued for a managerial revision of liberal ideology and explained the way in which that vision differed from the Progressive Era reformism whose tradition he sought to carry on. During the first decades of the century, Soule explained, Progressives like Herbert Croly (and their political allies like Teddy Roosevelt) had been able to find hope in a vague image of evolutionary progress and democratic renewal. Imagining a redemptive spirit of collective unity springing up in the midst of the nation, they sometimes had acted as if it were enough to invoke what Croly called "the promise of American life" and to "declai[m] against . . . [injustice and inefficiency] on grounds of abstract principle" alone. Industrial concentration and mass communications had already begun to create a tightly integrated economy, Croly and his peers argued; once guided by prophetic leadership and a sense of national mission, Americans would naturally grow together to realize their collective bonds and to create the powerful national state that could express and guide that common body.[23] Their neoprogressive heirs altered that perspective — on the one hand, by lowering hopes for a natural evolution toward political change; on the other, by giving a corresponding emphasis to the role of a small, highly trained vanguard. The experience of World War I and their sojourn in the wilderness of the twenties had forced neoprogressives to become less dewy-eyed about the prospects for collective redemption, Soule claimed, and more aware of the resistance to reform that would be put up, not just by capitalists and reactionaries, but by the inertia of "social habit." Given the massive power of big business and the decline of Progressive causes like state-building and organized labor, it no longer seemed to many intellectuals as though society were tending naturally toward the benevolent collectivism envisioned by Croly and many of his contemporaries. Given, too, the fervor stirred up by wartime propaganda and the hysteria of postwar nativism, the cultural renewal that Progressives once envisioned in collectivism no longer appeared an inevitably good thing. Instead of simply denouncing "the profit motive or the lack of public ownership of the means of production," then, hard-boiled radicals needed to master the "technical skill" and the specialized knowledge vital to an industrial economy — "economic science, scientific management, politics, and other social disciplines." Only by turning from moral exhortation to "scientific analysis," Soule argued, could neoprogressive reformers hope to replace the "hunches and bosses" of a disordered society with the reliable methods of "administration and management."[24]

In effect, Soule's "hard-boiled radicalism" called for a planned society led by a technocratic elite — a vision that echoed not only through leading journals of liberal opinion like the *New Republic* and the *Nation*, but throughout the professional social sciences on whose authority Soule's argument drew. All through the twenties the leading figures in those fields had sought to replace the vague evolutionary vistas and the language of democratic renewal that had been prominent before the war with a new emphasis on science and technical expertise. In sociology, protofunctionalists like William Ogburn insisted that their discipline involved more than a moral critique of modern society — that it was a scientific pursuit that could "taboo . . . ethics and values" and "crush out emotion" by emphasizing the centrality of "hard, dull, tedious, and routine tasks." Leading political scientists likewise embraced an avowed ethical neutrality, stressing the crucial role of organization in political life and down-playing the importance of particular goals or values.[25] Perhaps the most illuminating comparison to Hammett's work came, though, in the world of legal scholarship, where a new generation of "realist" critics rose in the late twenties and early thirties to attack the "classi-cal" legal orthodoxy of the nineteenth century. Like their contem-poraries among neoprogressive journalists and professional social scientists, legal realists drew on styles of critical scholarship that had been prominent before the war (especially the antiformalism of Oliver Wendell Holmes Jr. and the sociological jurisprudence of Roscoe Pound) and gave those traditions a fresh, technocratic em-phasis. Theirs was a newly scientific perspective, legal thinkers like Jerome Frank, Karl Llewellyn, and Thurman Arnold argued — one well-suited to the demands of an emerging administrative state. By their account, law was not primarily the system of ethical princi-ples that their "classical" predecessors had imagined, but a body of "tools" or "engines" to be used, like the methods of sociology and political science, by the "sober technicians" of a professional elite. "What . . . officials do about disputes," Llewellyn famously claimed, "is . . . the law itself."[26]

In each of these fields, then, the invocation of scientific expertise was inseparable from a desire prominent among liberal reformers and New Deal policy makers throughout the late twenties and early thirties: a yearning to replace an outmoded liberal contractualism, which seemed only to create a chaotic and unjust society, with the more efficient methods of planning and administration.[27] Once tech-nical intelligence had been freed from "the thick prismatic lenses of principles and ideals," Thurman Arnold argued, it could pursue im-portant "practical results." Realists and neoprogressives thus cast themselves as contestants in a pitched battle with the dead hand of worn-out ideologies; they were champions of "the functional ap-proach" against the "transcendental nonsense" of nineteenth-century dogma. By the same token, however, they tended to see themselves as embattled by popular delusion. No matter how sincerely they were dedicated to serving "the general interest," the era's technocrats re-mained, by virtue of their most basic presumptions, tacit antidem-ocrats, and their arguments rang with disdain for what journalist

Stuart Chase called "the new illiteracy" of the popular citizen.[28] By the terms of their own unacknowledged dogma, society was divided between a small cadre of "technicians" or "fact-minded" experts and the inert mass of ordinary people. Overwhelmed by the complexity of an industrial and urbanized world, those people had given their faith to myth, fable, fantasy, and folklore — all the irrational and confining forces of "social habit." The nation's intellectual elite needed, therefore, not only to create the bureaucratic structures necessary to manage a complex society, but to carefully manipulate the public into accepting what was good for them. It was up to "our priesthood," Arnold argued — "the spinners of our national dreams whom we call our intellectuals, and who are composed of our lawyers, our economists, and our editors" — to fashion "the creed and mythologies" that would foster popular consent to political change. Only in that way would it be possible "to create intellectual order out of the tangled folklore of the time."[29]

Dashiell Hammett belonged to that generation of intellectuals who dismissed contract for administration, and his fiction rewrote the detective story — which had been, after all, a parable of the social compact — to follow suit. The stories of urban corruption and underworld crime that Hammett helped to make the staple fare of *Black Mask* in the twenties picked up on a central theme of the various managerialist critiques of democracy: the ways in which the era's oft-touted "crime wave" challenged the capacity of traditional political institutions to govern a metropolitan society.[30] The brief portraits of mass society that Hammett offered in novels like *Red Harvest* and his recurrent depiction of disembodied urban spaces, where civic engagement and public community seem impossible (like the locale rendered in the second chapter of *The Maltese Falcon*), echoed the managerialist dismissal of popular democracy.[31] More fundamentally still, his attitude toward his genre itself echoed the perspective that realist thinkers took toward the "transcendental nonsense" of liberal orthodoxy. Disdaining the pulp "blackmasking" with which he began his career and pointing out the patent unreality of most examples of detective fiction in general, Hammett committed himself to working within a tradition that struck him as mainly absurd. Like the legal realists — who sought to use the law as a tool and simultaneously to strip it of its conventional claims to neutrality or disinterest — Hammett needed to rely on that tradition and to point out at the same time how fantastic it tended to be; he thus bathed the detective story in much the same "cynical acid" with which his realist contemporaries doused legal institutions.[32] This is the attitude that Nick Charles sums up when he notes that murder doesn't round out anyone's life. Holding up the classic detective story's parable of so-cial contract to withering scorn, Hammett cast it in much the same role that realists attributed to classical legal thought. It was a com-forting but implausible fantasy that could neither be believed nor wholly dismissed.

Indeed, Hammett even drafted a brief, unpublished essay that showed both how close he was to the era's realists and neoprogres-sives and the crucial places where they parted ways. In "The Bound-aries of Science and Philosophy," written around the same time that he composed "Magic," Hammett laid out the elements of his own homespun epistemological theory and his version of the arguments that were transforming the professional social sciences during the twenties. Drawing on Einstein's recently published work of popu-lar explanation, *The Meaning of Relativity*, Hammett argued that knowledge is irrevocably divided between empirical experience and theoretical explanation — or "science" and "philosophy." "Science" is made up of "percepts," or "defined, limited difference[s]" in an observer's experience — in short, quantifiable sensory evidence. "Phi-losophy" depends on "perception," which is more nearly "meta-physical" or conceptual. Perception, Hammett claims, is not a form of sensation, but a way of accounting for the limits of sensation and of extending thought beyond the inevitable "discontinuities" of sci-entific evidence. The two dimensions of knowledge are thus bound together in a complementary, yet antagonistic, relation, and neither the metaphysical principles of "philosophy" nor the empirical facts of "science" can claim to be foundational. "Philosophy" needs the empirical evidence of "science" to avoid becoming empty generaliza-tion, while "science" needs the theoretical refinement of "philoso-phy" to keep from breaking up into endless nominalism. Each is reliant upon the other, yet each is given to imperial incursions on the territory of its counterpart. "Science cannot define, cannot limit, itself. Definitions of science must be philosophical definitions. Science cannot know what it cannot know." And vice versa: "Philosophy, like science, cannot define, cannot limit, itself." It "cannot know that there is anything it does not know." Each must be restrained, therefore, by constant resistance from its opposite. "The validity of science and philosophy depends upon this difference between them, just as the validity of scientific and philosophical data depends on differences."[33]

What Hammett's essay did not mention is that most of these arguments were commonplaces of the intellectual discourse of his day. Allusions to recent breakthroughs in physics and geometry were a standard tactic of the era's realists and neoprogressives, and those writers used such references in much the shaky way that Hammett did — to support the radical empiricist claim that an irreparable divide fell between metaphysical theory and empirical fact. They tended to claim further that the conventional tenets of liberal democracy epitomized the dangers of empty theory and that the increasing complexity of scientific knowledge proved that society must be governed by a small intellectual elite.[34] Here, though, Hammett's essay suggested a different conclusion. Realists and neoprogressives cast themselves as the avatars of science and the enemies of philosophy. Like Thurman Arnold and William Ogburn, they imagined that it would be easy to throw off the thick lenses of principles and values in order to turn to the useful tools of technical expertise. Though only implicitly, Hammett's essay pointed to a key blind spot in that perspective. By his account, although science might pretend otherwise, it depended on the antagonism of philosophy to give it shape and direction. Indeed, Hammett implied that a high price would have to be paid in blindness, arrogance, and self-defeat for forgetting that fact. It was that cost his detective fiction would go on to dramatize.

TANGLED FOLKLORE AND INTELLECTUAL ORDER

The tales that Hammett produced when he brought the premises of "Boundaries" to the detective story sometimes seemed as if they had been written with the ideas of the era's various "realist" thinkers directly in mind. When, for example, the Continental Op concludes *Red Harvest* by telling us that he spent a week in a hotel room drafting reports justifying, and pasting over, his actions in Personville, he echoes an argument that contemporary realists claimed was true of all features of the law: that in the real world judges and officials first made pragmatic decisions and then created the "formal justifications" that would appear to legitimize those actions. Officers of the law operated by "hunches," the legal scholar Jerome Frank famously argued, and then "work[ed] back from conclusions to principles." The "rules" that they claimed to follow were "incidental, the decisions [we]re the thing."[35] Hammett's Op makes the same point. "It's right enough for the Agency to have rules and regulations," he acknowledges, "but when you're out on a job you've got to do it the best way you can." His "reports" are "something to hide the details under."[36]

Like the realists as well, Hammett implicitly joined that description to a particular view of the relation between law and society—one that saw legal codes as inevitably impermanent efforts to manage an urban society in a state of constant flux. People attributed rationality, stability, and predictability to the law, Frank argued, because of their need to gain some sense of "permanence and fixity." They longed for a "Father-as-Infallible-Judge" to order their worlds, and they found him in a false vision of the law as a divinely sanctioned code of morality.[37] Hammett virtually anticipated the point. The Op "labor[s] and sweat[s]" over his reports in an attempt to deceive his boss—the rarely glimpsed, coldly authoritative Old Man. In Hammett's rendition, that literary effort is the same kind of specious formalism that Frank saw in legal reasoning—an effort to make sense of the decisions already made by the Op and to reconcile him with a comfortingly austere patriarch. His reports thus stand in much the same relation to the rest of the novel that realists like Frank saw between formal law and unpredictable social action. In the novel's famous opening passage, the Op recounts how he first fell in to Personville's violent underworld: "I first heard Personville called Poisonville by a red-haired mucker named Hickey Dewey in the Big Ship in Butte. He also called his shirt a shoit. . . . Later I heard men who could manage their r's give it the same pronunciation. I still didn't see anything in it but the meaningless sort of humor that used to make richardsnary the thieves' word for dictionary. A few years later I went to Personville and learned better" (3).

Juxtaposed to the novel's conclusion, this opening passage illuminates *Red Harvest*'s underlying binary structure. For, given the events that follow in the course of the narrative, it reads as if the name Poisonville had been poured into the porch of the Op's ear. Poisonville is a vernacular terrain — a city characterized by oral communication, reciprocal interaction, and, as Frank might put it, a complete absence of "permanence and fixity." (Indeed, the city looks like a melodramatic rendering of the pulp arena of anonymous combat that Hammett described himself trying to escape by making literature of the detective story.) Its infectious violence starts to affect the Op as soon as he begins to take part in its various modes of informal exchange. All those features are exemplified, moreover, by the figure who stands at the center of Poisonville's criminal kingdom and who sets off its wave of violence, the prostitute Dinah Brand — a woman who not only oozes sexual vitality, but whose "thoroughly mercenary, frankly greedy" attitude makes her a nearly literal figure of an untamable, speculative market. The Op can rescue himself from this bewildering carnival of desire and violence only by submitting to the labor of writing and the stern visage of patriarchal authority. Replacing the vernacular word and democratic exchange with formal writing and hierarchical authority, the Op literally takes himself out of Poisonville and saves himself from going fully "blood simple."

It seems no coincidence, then, that the Op struggles to draft his reports in "the Roosevelt Hotel" — a reference to Teddy, of course, and not Franklin. For in its rendition of a strong antagonism between law and society, the formal and the vernacular, Hammett's novel both invokes and parodies the Progressive Era reformism exemplified in popular myth by Teddy Roosevelt (and associated as well with Roosevelt's opponent Woodrow Wilson — also tellingly alluded to in the novel's original murder victim, Donald Willson). If Progressive reformers once hoped they could "clear the burg of vice and corruption," Hammett suggested along with neoprogressive George Soule that they had turned out to be sadly mistaken. Indeed, *Red Harvest* is emphatically a post-Progressive novel and wears the same chastened air that Soule's essay does. In Hammett's rendition, Poisonville is the place where Progressive, along with Klannish, fancies come to die. Not only has "civic refor[m]" literally been murdered, "organized labor" is a "used firecracker" — crushed by the post-World War I recession and by the thugs hired by the city's autocrat (13, 9). Less explicitly, Hammett's novel implies that the Progressive hope for reconciling formal learning and popular life through a sense of collective national mission is a fantasy. Donald Willson pursues that ambition when he returns from Paris, gives up poetry, and throws himself into reformist journalism, and the results for him are not promising. The opening and closing passages of the novel emphasize the point. In Hammett's version of the neoprogressive social theory that came to the fore after World War I, the vernacular terrain of thieves' words and the formal regimen of writing and patriarchal authority seem inevitably at odds.

It was not simply, then, that Hammett revised the detective story by making it more veristic, or more violent, or more American. Rather, drawing on the same instrumentalist assumptions that underlay much of the era's reformist thought, he transformed the ideological implications of his genre — pointing it away from a mythology of contract and toward a focus on the attractions and perils of administration. In his rendition, the detective story would no longer be about the way that social consensus was threatened and re-created, but about the way in which people could be shaped, molded, and manipulated by the very institutions and beliefs that once seemed transcendent and disinterested.

Nearly every aspect of Hammett's fiction reflected that transformation. The classic mystery story often cast its ordinary characters as bewildered or exploited until the intervention of the detective genius — who freed them from their momentary confusion and allowed them to resume their ordinary lives, with a fresh appreciation for their very ordinariness. In keeping with the premises of realist thought, Hammett's fiction offered an intensified portrait of both the confusion of ordinary people and the work consequently required of the detective hero. His novels and stories are packed with characters who resemble the ordinary citizen envisioned by the realists — prisoners of fantasy and delusion, "held by the parts . . . [they are] playing" and ensnared in delusional visions of themselves and their world. What is more, Hammett began like the realists from the presumption that such conditions were not anomalous, but exemplary. "Thinking's a dizzy business," the Continental Op explains in *The Dain Curse*: "a matter of catching as many of those foggy glimpses as you can and fitting them together the best you can. That's why people hang on so tight to their beliefs and opinions; because, compared to the haphazard way in which they're arrived at, even the goofiest opinion seems wonderfully clear, sane, and self-evident. And if you let it get away from you, then you've got to dive back into the foggy muddle to wangle yourself out another to take its place" (181).[38]

As Steven Marcus noted some time ago, the Op's pragmatist-inspired emphasis on the instrumental use of concepts — his assumption that ideas are, as Llewellyn put it, "thinking tools" (which some people will use and others will be used by) rather than mirrors of reality — also remade the work of the detective. For, it meant that the hero didn't simply clear away lies to discover the truth; he set out to shape events and the way in which people understood them.[39] Much as the realists sought to change conceptions of the law from its classical image as a set of transcendental principles to an acknowledgment that it was a kit of tools for the task of social engineering, Hammett's detectives replace the eccentric genius of the classic detective story with the professional craftsman. His heroes are not "omnipresent, omniscient" revealers of the truth who "restor[e] moral certainty to the world," as the classic, "Heroic Detective" is sometimes said to be.[40] They are agents with ends in mind, and they pursue those ends by setting out to deceive, beguile, manipulate, and confuse other people. "My way of learning," Sam Spade points out, "is to heave a wild and unpredictable monkey-wrench into the machinery" (*MF* 86). His counterpart, the Continental Op, acknowledges that his work is to construct narratives "with the object of putting people in jail, and I get paid for it" (*DC* 22).[41]

In this manner, Hammett's detectives echo the antiformalist impulse that was a hallmark of contemporaneous social criticism — the yearning to free technical intelligence from "principles and ideals" so that it might pursue "practical results." For Hammett, as for realists and neoprogressives as well, that effort hinges on the intellectual's abilities to grasp and control the myths and habits that constrain other people. This is the gist of the scene from *The Dain Curse* in which the Op acknowledges that he creates narratives to put people in jail. The Op's partner in that conversation, Owen Fitzstephen, is a decadent novelist who fabricates a story of a family curse in order to deceive and control his young niece Gabrielle — inventing fictions to make her, in effect, "his property" (227). Over the course of the novel, the Op first becomes aware that someone has manipulated Gabrielle and then ultimately discovers that Fitzstephen is the author of the "literary grift" that ensnares her (18). The resulting narrative — which is organized around a series of conversations between Fitzstephen and the Op, becomes a baroque meditation on the intractable power of narrative itself. Cast as antagonistic creator and critic, Fitzstephen and the Op struggle back and forth over the whole length of the book — as if the two sides of Hammett's authorial persona, the pulpster and the ironic modernist, were doing battle.[42] The Op disproves one fantastic tale or specious theory after another, only to see a successor rise in its place, and so potent do these stories prove that Hammett likens their power not just to curses and hauntings, but to religion, love, and ultimately morphine addiction. It appears, in short, nearly impossible to free Gabrielle of the fables that imprison her, the more so because she would rather believe that she is cursed and evil than that she may have been duped, or worse, that she may be just an ordinary person in an unpredictable world.

It turns out, then, that the Op can only free Gabrielle of her various dependencies by creating a new story for her to embrace. In an effort to give her the strength to break her morphine habit, and by implication her belief in the curse that she thinks haunts her, the Op implies that he has fallen in love with her, thus replacing Gabrielle's conviction of her evil power with an idea of her healthy attractiveness. Then, having broken her of one bad habit, he fittingly turns her over to her murdered husband's family, who "had simply seemed to pick her up as was their right" (231). Hammett's point is clear. Although the fable she adopts may be benevolent or destructive, Gabrielle must believe in some mythic image of herself, and though she will belong to someone who makes her happy or someone who makes her miserable, she will need to be the property of someone. By extension, when Fitzstephen suggests to the Op early in the novel that they do the same kind of work — fabricate stories to manipulate other people — the meaning of their conversation echoes the contrast implicit in Thurman Arnold's description of "our priesthood." Like Arnold, the Op wants to make "intellectual order" out of "tangled mythology," but because people must have folklore, the salient distinction is no longer between true and false stories, but between useful inventions of the kind that the Op means to wield and parasitic fantasies of the type that selfish aristocrats like Owen Fitzstephen create. The battle between them is implicitly not one between the honest and the deceptive, but between good and evil priests.

What such a perspective left tellingly unanswered, though, was why one story was preferable to another — why it was better, say, for Gabrielle to belong to her husband's family than to her uncle, or why the Op should struggle to make Personville the property of Elihu Willson rather than the territory of the criminal gangs with whom Willson competes. Hammett began *Red Harvest* much as neoprogressives did in their effort to invent a hard-boiled radicalism, by dismissing the naïve moralism of reformers like Donald Willson in order to embrace the ostensibly value-free pragmatic expertise represented by the Continental Op. But where realists and neoprogressives imagined that they could simply step away from the entanglements of ethics and philosophy, Hammett's fiction suggested — along the lines predicted by "The Boundaries of Science and Philosophy" — that they might remain unconsciously beholden to the very metaphysical principles they sought to dismiss. Though the Continental Op sets out to ignore the written code of rules and regulations, for example, he turns out to seriously need them. However empty his reports are, it appears to be only the fact that he must submit himself to the regime of formal justification that removes the Op from Personville's bewildering and ultimately lethal vernacular exchange. The irony that results is a key feature of Hammett's fiction. The Op is as violent, cruel, and self-interested as anyone in Personville, Hammett implies; all that distinguishes him from the criminals he betrays and kills is his purely formal adherence to laws that have been stripped of any ethical content.

In this manner, Hammett highlighted the problem basic to realist thought. Seeking to reduce conflicts over law and politics to value-free questions of efficiency and technical expertise, realists and neo-progressives denied themselves the means to explain why anyone should agree with their aims and left themselves in a perilously ungrounded position.[43] "It is not necessarily true," Thurman Arnold argued, "that the only choice is between naive faith in principle and cynical denial of the validity of principle." He had, he acknowledged in the final paragraph of his major work, *The Folklore of Capitalism*, "no doubt as to the practical desirability of a society where principles and ideals are more important than individuals." There was, however, nothing "peculiarly sacred about the logical content of these principles," Arnold claimed. They were valuable because they made society "more secure spiritually and hence more tolerant," but it would be a mistake to believe "that organizations must be molded to them, instead of the principles being molded to organizational needs." For Arnold, in other words, the smooth functioning of society depended on the fact that people remained devoted to certain beliefs that seemed more significant than their interests. What those beliefs entailed, however, mattered less than the fact that they existed in some form. Indeed, if such principles were not to calcify into rigid dogma, people would need to remember that at bottom their principles were merely the expression of organizational needs and could therefore be changed for more useful ideals. Social order depended, in short, on beliefs that seemed to transcend individual interests but were in fact the product of such interests. In order for those principles to operate effectively, then, their adherents would need both to have faith in their importance and have the sense not to take their own convictions too seriously. In effect, Arnold called for a society of noncredulous believers — a stance, he suggested, that could truly be maintained only by an intellectual elite. Felix Cohen made a similar point more concisely. "A realistic advocate," he argued, "will at least not be fooled by his own words."[44]

Hammett's fiction focused on how hard such a role would be to maintain. His noncredulous believers are always at risk of falling beneath some myth or, worse, of believing in their own transcendence. Something along these lines is the ultimate irony in *The Dain Curse*, in the final defeat suffered by Owen Fitzstephen. Through most of the book, Fitzstephen looks like a realist nightmare — an evil priest whose skillful fictions the Op, like Gabrielle, must struggle to resist. In the novel's conclusion, though, that situation is dramatically inverted. Having had his machinations revealed, Fitzstephen plans to escape justice by pleading insanity, or as he puts it in the language of fin de siècle decadence, "authorial degeneracy" (220). As Fitzstephen describes this condition to the Op, it reflects his continued belief that he is a great artificer, capable of deftly manipulating the popular mind. But the Op undermines this confidence with the brilliant tactic of agreeing with the author's avowedly false self-description. Fitzstephen is in fact insane, the Op suggests, and thus "legally . . . entitled to beat the jump if ever anybody was" (221). In effect, he renarrates Fitzstephen's fable, reading it symptomatically, so that Fitzstephen becomes, as Gabrielle previously was, not the author, but merely the vessel of his own tales of degeneracy.

Ironically, since Fitzstephen is Gabrielle's uncle and himself a Dain, such a reversal gives new credibility to the notion of the Dain curse that the Op has spent so much time and effort discrediting; for it suggests that the stories of a violent legacy of familial degeneration have merely passed to Fitzstephen rather than to Gabrielle. Indeed, the situations of these two Dain descendants have simply been inverted. Earlier, Fitzstephen had gained his own sense of mastery by creating stories that convinced Gabrielle she was the victim of a congenital mental disease. In the novel's conclusion, Gabrielle comes to believe that she is healthy and sane — in good part through the very sensible operation of repressing her recollection of the things she did when she believed she was not. She "can't make [her]self believe that all that actually happened to [her]," she says (231). Fitzstephen, on the other hand, who believed he was supremely rational because he could circulate tales of insanity, must now fear that he is crazy for the same reason. Toward the beginning of his novel, Hammett has Fitzstephen condemn "the hypothesis of an unconscious or subconscious mind as a snare and a delusion" — a conviction that Hammett's narrative suggests must itself be the product of repression (33). For, with the book's conclusion, Fitzstephen discovers precisely that he is ensnared by the power of unconscious motivations. Gabrielle, by contrast, who had always believed in the ultimate reality of obscure psychic forces, becomes healthy when she simply denies that there is any knowledge that she hides from herself. As her uncle did before her, she creates her autonomy by unconsciously repressing the snare of the unconscious. One Dain, it seems, must always be degenerate and trapped so that the other may feel sane and free

In this manner, Hammett parodied the realists' confidence that they could manipulate the creeds that held other people and skewered it with an acute observation: a realist could be certain of his own fact-mindedness only by comparing himself with someone less clear-sighted. What Owen Fitzstephen dramatizes is the danger inherent in that situation (a danger inherent in all styles of antiformalist critique); a realist who seems fact-minded to himself might discover to his surprise that he is someone else's example of the absurdly credulous dupe.

That peril, moreover, is not limited to the villains in Hammett's fiction. In an introduction he later wrote for *The Maltese Falcon*, Hammett made it clear that the trap was open for his protagonists as well. Describing the models he had drawn on to create his characters, Hammett claimed that Sam Spade was intended to exemplify the "dream man" of the private detective — "a hard and shifty fellow" who wanted to be "able to get the best of anybody he comes in contact with, whether criminal, innocent by-stander or client." Through much of the novel, Hammett makes that fantasy seem plausible. Surrounded by guile, deception, and erotic temptation, Spade maintains the chaste professional autonomy first exemplified by Hammett's magician — an effort that culminates in the climactic passage where Sam Spade counts off his seven reasons for turning Brigid over to the police. The crucial moment in the novel, however, follows that passage when Spade discovers to his apparent chagrin that he cannot convince his secretary Effie that he has made a just decision. "I know you're right," she says, "But don't touch me now" (217).

That moment is important because it indicates the extent to which Hammett had revised the mystery story and the costs that Hammett saw in that revision. Almost invariably, the classic detective novel ends in some ritual of consensus, a scene of public reconciliation that emphasizes the genre's dedication to the social contract. Hammett's

novels typically refuse that resolution and emphasize the unlikelihood of mutual agreement or common understanding. What is particularly telling about the conclusion to *The Maltese Falcon*, though,
is that it suggests that no one really wants to get the best of everyone
all the time. Even those figures like Sam Spade who are determined to
manipulate rather than be manipulated sooner or later find themselves longing for someone who will simply agree with them. When
they do, Effie suggests, their very skill at manipulation will make that
reconciliation unlikely.

Hammett underlines that failure, too, by sending in another angel
of devastation in the novel's final lines. In a revealing subplot, Sam
Spade has spent much of the novel trying to evade the clutches of Iva
Archer—the widow of his murdered partner and Spade's former
lover who, despite his obvious indifference, refuses to acknowledge
that the detective does not care for her. In the book's last scene, Iva
makes an ominous return. Having already indicated her disapproval
of Spade, Effie, speaking in "a small flat voice," announces Iva's
arrival: "Spade, looking down at his desk, nodded almost impercep-
tibly . . . and shivered. 'Well, send her in' " (217). Here again, Hammett's subversion of his own hero seems clear. If in the novel's climactic passage Spade was able to fight off the enticements of fantasy
and desire in order to turn Brigid over to the police, this scene suggests how brief his mastery must be. He ends surrounded by much
the same forces that seemed defeated—as if, like the fictions engi-
neered by Owen Fitzstephen, the seductions of emotion and belief
crop up again every time they appear to be finished.[45]

That implication not only undercut Sam Spade's heroic stance, it
commented ironically on the presumptions of the era's realist critics.
In the description of those writers, the political life of the twentieth-
century United States would be divided by necessity between a mas-
terful priesthood and a supine citizenry. Hammett's fiction echoes
that vision and casts it in conventionally gendered terms. (He notes
fittingly, for example, that Effie's perception of Spade is based on
what she has read in the newspapers; she exemplifies, in other words,
the problems of popular citizenship and emotional manipulation
that the novel raised with the billboards of its opening murder scene.)
Like the Continental Op in *The Dain Curse*, Sam Spade stands sur-

rounded by forces of emotion, desire, and credulity that in Hammett's rendering are distinctly feminine. Indeed, when Effie sends Iva into Spade's office, it seems as though they are virtually in league against him and, more importantly, that his power to resist is spent. However sternly the realist priesthood sought to control popular delusion, Hammett implies, its victories, by virtue of the very stance it took up, were bound to be fleeting.

THE POLITICS OF LOVE

Hammett never got much beyond these problems. Indeed, the autobiographical novel he left unfinished in the fifties returned to them yet again. Telling the story of the conflict between Pop, a failed writer who has withdrawn to the mountains to contemplate his defeat, and Tulip—the working-class counterpart who pursues him there—Hammett emphasized once more the failed marriage of intellectual authority and popular credulity. Tulip is the voice of "experience," and he disdains the writer's intellectualism. ("Things get dull when you reason the bejesus out of 'em. . . . Couldn't you just write things down the way they happen?") Pop, on the other hand, exemplifies "erudit[ion]." He has a fondness for arcane knowledge and difficult problems—Rosicrucianism, theoretical physics, mathematics—and he suggests that no "feeling can be very strong if it has to be shielded from reason." The debate between the two makes up the major part of Hammett's fragmentary narrative, and it restages the dilemma that bothered Hammett throughout his career. The working-class Tulip needs Pop for much the same reason that Gabrielle Leggett needs the Continental Op. An analog to the representative man-on-the-street of Hammett's remarks on advertising and to the countless helpless figures who roam through Hammett's fiction (his name indicating his apt feminization), Tulip finds it impossible to think clearly without the benefit of the symbolic order that the writer can provide. He thus plagues Pop to write his story because he believes that "a somewhat consecutive . . . course of events—no matter how dissimilar they may seem—gives life . . . form." Pop, on the other hand, appears to lack just those features of "experience" and appetite that characterize Tulip. So arcane and involuted have his efforts become that his idea of literary ambition is to write a "story on a Möbius band, designed to be read from any point in it on around to that point again." His own name appears to indicate the diminishment of patriarchal authority, as if to parody the paternal civic role Hammett once sought to defend. Throughout his fiction Hammett's protagonists—the Magician, the Continental Op, Sam Spade, Nick Charles—take a pedagogical stance toward the benighted people they mean to help, an attitude Hammett echoed when he described his own politics. Here Pop is confronted in Tulip by a virtual child he finds himself unable to instruct or to flee.[46]

In Hammett's earlier fiction, the antagonism between these kinds of characters constituted a vital and unresolved problem. In this last work, as Tulip points out in the remark quoted as an epigraph to this chapter, the meeting of mental and manual labor has become a dialogue of the deaf, and as if to indicate how fatal that situation was to Hammett's ambitions, the manuscript trails off with a remarkable statement of literary skepticism. Explaining both why he feels no connection to Tulip and why he can no longer write, Pop remarks: "[T]he first time I met him I had a wary feeling that he might come to represent a side of me. His being a side of me was all right, of course, since everybody is in some degree an aspect of everybody else or how would anybody understand anything about anybody else. But representations seemed to me—at least they seem now, . . . devices of the old and tired . . . to ease up like conscious symbolism, or graven images." Concluding that realization with the acknowledgment that "if you are tired you ought to rest," Hammett abandoned both the novel and his literary career.[47] By the terms Pop set out, of course, no other option was possible. The writer who rejects representation and symbolism, will no longer have any material with which to work. But the striking language of resignation in this passage can be interpreted along political as well as literary lines—since without representation there can be no future for either the writer or the civic expert that Hammett and his neoprogressive contemporaries championed. Like Pop, the realists of the interwar era distrusted representation. By their account, the world was full of enticing and misleading fables, and they suggested as a consequence that a traditional devotion to the ideals of representative democracy had to be abandoned. Fact-minded experts could best serve the public not by looking for the ambiguous will of the people, but by ignoring the unreliable mechanisms of popular representation to pursue their own sense of the general interest. Ultimately, neoprogressives assumed along with George Soule that their projects for social reform would find "solid roots" in "common interests." Once the irrationalities of the unregulated marketplace had been tamed, technical experts and illiterate citizens could discover their mutual place in the national community. "We shall have," Soule promised, "a warm and active bond with our fellows."[48] Like the conclusion to *The Maltese Falcon*, though, "Tulip" pointed to the difficulty that the managerialist would face trying to rediscover consensual relations in a world that seemed to run by administration. In Pop's description, seeing the artifice and malleability of representation — realizing that "anything can be symbolic of anything else" — makes it appear so abstract and unreal that it becomes possible to imagine oneself connected at once to everyone and to no one in particular (340). Technical expertise appears to kill political association.

The richest exploration of that problem came, however, not in "Tulip" but in a much earlier work — *The Glass Key* (1932), Hammett's fourth novel and his last earnest effort to make literature of the detective story. According to his biographer Richard Layman, *The Glass Key* was Hammett's favorite among his books.[49] That may have been so because, more than any other, *The Glass Key* integrates the mystery plot into a complex novelistic fabric (it is the only one of Hammett's books in which the protagonist has never been a detective). But *The Glass Key* is also impressive for the way it makes a distinct narrative problem out of Hammett's aesthetic ambitions. In *The Glass Key*, the problem of cultural reconciliation becomes for the first time an explicit topic of Hammett's fiction. For the first time as well, Hammett suggests clearly what the political stakes of that problem might be.

At its most immediate, *The Glass Key* is the story of a doomed friendship. By implication, though, the novel is also a skeptical rendition of the aims of Hammett's realist and neoprogressive contemporaries. For it hinges on the brief allegiance between Paul Madvig, the political boss of a small Eastern city (presumed by Hammett's biographers to be Baltimore), and the novel's protagonist, Ned Beaumont — a professional political adviser. Madvig is a child of his city's working-class wards and a product of its rough-and-tumble machine politics. He represents, and appears to dominate, the city's blue-collar ethnic voters. Beaumont is a political hired gun, a strategist and a hard-boiled intellectual who travels from one city to the next plying his trade. Over the course of the novel, Beaumont makes increasingly desperate efforts to enable Madvig to hold onto his power — which is under assault not only from a rival machine but from the reformist forces of "women's clubs" and "respectable citizens" — and to preserve the two men's friendship (63, 64). Both efforts are doomed. When the novel ends, Madvig's machine is headed for a terrible defeat in the municipal elections. More important, his alliance with Beaumont is dead. In the novel's final scene, Beaumont informs Madvig with brutal directness that he is leaving town with Janet Henry, the aristocratic woman whom Madvig loves.

Though its presence only becomes fully clear in this final scene, the strange love triangle among Beaumont, Madvig, and Janet Henry provides the *The Glass Key*'s fundamental armature, and it reveals more clearly than any other feature of the novel Hammett's underlying concerns. What makes it seem both strange and, for most of the narrative, implausibly vague is that its bottom leg is thoroughly dispassionate. Although they leave together in the novel's conclusion, neither Janet Henry nor Beaumont appears to care strongly for the other. Henry seems most driven by the revulsion she feels for Madvig, and by the embarrassment it causes her. Beaumont, with the trademark laconic attitude of the Hammett protagonist, never says anything more impassioned to Henry than "You're all right" (210). Indeed, the novel's final lines show him not, as one might expect, looking at the woman with whom he's about to begin an affair, but "staring fixedly" at the door through which Madvig departs (214). By emphasizing the inevitable failure of Madvig and Beaumont's alliance, that grim resolution underlines the novel's central point: that the conscious personal decisions and political calculations that people make prove ultimately insignificant. Madvig may respect

Beaumont's intelligence, but he cannot resist his attraction to the aristocratic milieu that Janet Henry represents, a world that both spurns and exploits him. By the same token, though Ned Beaumont, like George Soule's technocrat, may long for "solid roots" in a powerful political organization, he seems all but doomed to an alliance with the world of inherited privilege that he dislikes. That Beaumont and Henry become lovers without passion only underscores Hammett's key implication. Everywhere in *The Glass Key*, fatality outweighs personal choice.

In this manner, Hammett's love triangle not only exploits the pathos of male bonding, it offers an implicit meditation on the hiatus that characterized American political life while Hammett wrote in the early winter of 1930—after the Crash and the evident demise of the 1920s' boom, but before the Hoover administration had been thoroughly discredited by its failure to pull the economy out of recession. That administration had come to power in 1928, when Al Smith and the Democratic Party went down to defeat in an election decided in large part by nativist hostility to the ethnic, working-class voters represented by urban machines like Paul Madvig's. Hammett's novel draws a local parallel to that development, and closing with Madvig's determination to "clean house and pu[t] together an organization that will stay put," it presciently envisions the reconstitution of the political landscape that would begin with the return to power of the Democratic Party in 1932. In the meantime, *The Glass Key* suggests, political life is moribund. One of the book's striking features, Layman notes, is that for "a novel in which political power plays so great a part, *The Glass Key* is remarkably apolitical."[50] It depicts no stirring ideology or strong belief and seems to be about abstract power alone. Linking that sterile condition to the dissolution of the friendship of Beaumont and Madvig, Hammett's novel implicitly attributes the Democratic Party's failure to offer a compelling alternative to the missed connection between a national professional elite and the world of local, working-class party organizations.

As the complaints of neoprogressives like George Soule suggest, that failure had been a central topic of civic concern all through the twenties. During those years, political commentators, especially those at liberal journals like the *New Republic* and the *Nation*, worried over the symptoms of an ailing democracy — declining levels of voter participation, growing signs of vast political ignorance or apathy, and a widening divide between the nation's political officials and its popular citizenry. Those complaints led many to join writers like Soule in doubting the civic achievements of Progressive Era reform. As Michael Schudson points out, a central feature of that reformism had been the attempt to install a "new model of citizenship" — one that would dismantle the key role played by party affiliation and community life in the nineteenth century so as to replace it with a new emphasis on "principles and issues." Seeing "interest" rather than "sentiment" as the core of politics, Progressives had called for "a citizenship of intelligence" rather than one of passionate party loyalty. By the twenties, the problem with that ambition had begun to seem apparent. It was simply not possible, most neoprogressives assumed, to create a whole nation of intelligent voters.[51] It would be necessary therefore, some argued, not to destroy parties and political machines, as Progressives had hoped to do, but to accept their inevitability and to treat them in the same manner that realists hoped to use creeds and laws — as tools to be employed by "a competent, practical, opportunistic governing class."[52]

The Glass Key places itself at the crux of this situation. Paul Madvig epitomizes the urban machine that Progressive reformers had hoped to destroy. Not only does he operate by patronage and graft, he is driven by the loyalties and passions that seemed inimical to a citizenship of intelligence, and he sees politics not as a matter of interest and issues but as a form of tribal war. He does not understand public image, Madvig acknowledges, but he does "know fighting, . . . going in with both hands working" (65). It is fitting, then, that Madvig is under assault by "the respectable citizens" and that he is defended by Ned Beaumont, the coolly pragmatic strategist who, unlike the city's reformers, accepts that there must be political "insiders" and "outsiders" (64, 63). Focusing on the tense relations between that dispassionate adviser and Madvig's untutored political battler, Hammett highlights the neoprogressive's central anxieties about the relation between expertise and popular citizenship and about the related problem of the place of the ethnic, working-class voter in American political life. "Brains or no brains," Beaumont says in a near parody of neoprogressive thinking, those voters are "used to being taken care of" (11). *The Glass Key* implies that it is up to the alliance of the expert and the machine boss to see that they are taken into account, and then goes on to point to the failure of that alliance.

In fact, in less direct ways hard-boiled crime fiction had been concerned with these issues for some time, and Hammett's novel both drew on and revised some of the key conventions that the *Black Mask* school of crime writing had generated during the twenties. Having rejected the KKK's nativist republicanism, the magazine's writers were faced with the implicit task of addressing the problems of political corruption, urban disorientation, and ethnic diversity that Klan propaganda emphasized. Those problems accordingly became central themes of the emerging hard-boiled genre during the later 1920s. Perhaps because of their implicit commitment to urban freedom, moreover, and because of their tacit opposition to the Klan's racism and moral authoritarianism, the hard-boiled response to the problems of the twentieth-century city looked in certain respects very much like some of the central ideas of the era's neoprogressive reformers and social scientists.

At the core of that response lay a fable of civic maturation and an obsession with the problem of the genre's mythic underworld. In the hard-boiled stories that ran in *Black Mask* during the late twenties and early thirties, that hidden terrain became a re-creation of the primitive frontier — a landscape that was at once open and intimately knowable. Life in the hard-boiled underworld is "glittering, blatant, and intensely alive," but every character in its realm is also, like Chandler's Philip Marlowe, an "important public character"; he or she is known, has an established reputation and a consistent standing in a closed society. The appeal of such a world must have come in part from the fact that, while it heightens the excitement of the city, dramatizing the novel features of an urbanizing society, it also somehow exists outside mass culture. The hard-boiled underworld emphasizes flash, style, and liberty, but it depends as well on intimate social activities and intense face-to-face encounters of the type that writers in the twenties often feared were disappearing from society. As the fiction describes these milieux, though, they usually appear not just as marginal realms, but as outmoded stages in a process of historical development—before rather than outside a complex, urbanized culture. The hard-boiled underworld is typically antique or atavistic, its inhabitants colorful and immature natives. Like the "red-haired mucker named Hickey Dewey," who opens *Red Harvest*, or Tulip, the criminals of hard-boiled fiction often seem virtual children, driven by undisciplined desires and incapable of adapting themselves to the demands of a routinized world. This was the implicit point of Hammett's claim that he had "never known a man capable of turning out first-rate work in a trade, profession or an art, who was a professional criminal."[53] The denizens of the hard-boiled underworld are primitives, charming or terrifying, and their societies are historical throwbacks. Like *Red Harvest*'s Poisonville, they are always on the verge of being wiped out by "white-collar soldiers."

Hard-boiled crime fiction during the late twenties and early thirties turned time and again to the tension between this imaginary landscape and the mundane world of bourgeois civil society, typically placing its heroes in an uncomfortable position between the two and asking them to choose between the affective force of clan loyalty and the abstract principles of the law. In Carroll John Daly's paradigmatic version of this story, *The Snarl of the Beast* (1927), for example, Race Williams confronts two linked evils: a gang of vicious criminals headed by the Beast of the title and a corrupt, aristocratic family haunted by a tradition of internecine violence. Each of these paired antagonists stands for a problem of the modern city. The Beast exemplifies the "teeming tenements of the Lower East Side" where his gang is headquartered—a cosmopolitan region where "a dozen languages fill the air like a cheap radio set." The Davison family represents an irresponsible patrician elite. Daly conflates these two problematic faces of the city through a complicated plot, but he also suggests that they are joined by a more substantial logic: each stands for the repudiation of civic responsibility. So, when Race Williams wanders through the "forest . . . impenetrable" of the Lower East Side, he notes that its darkness is the result of the kind of landlord who ignores "tenement house laws"—a "wealthy, drunken man at his club, perhaps, who couldn't tell offhand the number, or even the street the disreputable building he owned was on." The "struggling mass" of the tenement district and the aristocratic family are thus joined as models of incomplete citizenship, both of them contributing to the stygian unknowability of the city. Each of them follows tribal passions rather than the dictates of good citizenship, and in different ways — through a compulsion to animal violence or through an obsession with lineage — each elevates "blood" over the rule of law.[54]

Though Daly's plotting and diction were melodramatic in the extreme, *The Snarl of the Beast* plainly anticipates Hammett's far more subtle novel. The Beast's criminal "organization" and the decadent Davison family play much the same roles as do Paul Madvig's political machine and *The Glass Key*'s patrician family. Like the Davisons, the Henrys represent a gentry that is especially dangerous for being in decline. Senator Henry, Beaumont points out, is "one of the few aristocrats left in American politics" — a status, we eventually discover, that drives him, like Daly's villains, to murder (9). Madvig's machine, much like the Beast's gang, is less a bureaucratic organization than a patriarchal clan, bound together by the thirst for warfare. Even the love triangle in *The Glass Key* is forecast by Daly. After he has defeated both the Davison family and the Beast's organization, Race Williams's victory is completed when he saves Milly — an honest working-class girl drawn into prostitution by her love for the detective's client Danny Davison, the last decadent member of his family. Rescuing Milly from violence and sexual exploitation, Race also bestows on her the Davison fortune, which in a display of civic virtue she donates to charity. Like the detective, in other words, Milly makes public wealth out of private luxury. Her innocent flirtation with Race and the intimation that they may have a future together thus become an image of free, consensual union — to be held in contrast to the slavish dependence that once bound Milly to Danny and to the irrational tribal loyalties that run all through the book. *The Glass Key* re-creates that story. When Ned Beaumont agrees to take Janet Henry away with him, he warns her both that people will accuse her of deserting her father and that she will be leaving behind her family's wealth and position. Janet acknowledges both results, and much as Milly donates the Davison fortune to charity, willingly turns the family home over to "our creditors" (211). In both novels, heterosexual agreement signals the victory of abstract public bonds (of charity or debt) over the closed world of familial inheritance.[55]

Even more striking than the parallel between Daly's and Hammett's novels, though, is the formal similarity that each shares with some of the prominent social science of their day. Throughout the twenties, the dominant liberal response to the ethnic diversity and seeming disorder of the nation's metropolitan centers came in the developmental models of assimilation popularized by the Chicago School of sociology—in the work of William Thomas and, especially, Robert Park. Each saw the city in terms close to those that ran through *Black Mask* during the period. Like the fiction of Daly and his peers, Park's highly influential vision cast the twentieth-century metropolis in a deeply ambivalent light. On the one hand, it was an environment distinguished by confusing "mobility" and consequent "social disorganization." "The telegraph, telephone, newspaper, and radio" had "converted the world into one vast whispering gallery." Alongside the railroad and, more seriously, the automobile, the new mass media had acted to transform "human geography," breaking through "the isolation which once separated races and people." At first glance, too, the effects of that intense communication were highly negative, producing the conditions that Daly's novel rendered in melodramatic terms. The "breaking down of local attachment and the weakening of the restraints and inhibitions of the primary group" gave rise, Park argued, not only to the anomie emphasized by European sociology but to the crime wave that contemporary American observers feared. The stronger and more extensive the urban environment grew, the more one saw an "increase of vice and crime."[56] On the other hand, the seeming evils of the metropolis could also be forces of progress. By "destroying the cultures of tribe and folk," the city enabled the replacement of inherited and conservative "primary groups" by consciously chosen, progressive "secondary groups." Substituting "the freedom of the cities" for "local loyalties," the urban environment not only produced crime and vice, it broke the "sacred order of tribal custom" and made room for "the rational organization which we call civilization."[57]

Park's ambivalent vision of the twentieth-century city echoed through the social discourse of the interwar era. It formed the background for John Dewey's argument that "the great society" of a distended metropolitan civilization might be replaced by a "great community" of mutual interaction, as it did for Lewis Mumford's claim that the city enabled a transition "from habit to choice": a "transfer of emphasis from the uniformities and common acceptances of the primary group to the . . . purposive association, and the rational ends of the secondary group."[58] In a still stronger form, similar thinking undergirded the era's realist and neoprogressive discourse. For, like Park, Dewey, and Mumford, writers like George Soule and Thurman Arnold saw the twentieth-century U.S. as a land partly freed from the constraints of tradition and poised, therefore, between habit and choice. On the one hand, American society could no longer depend on the customary beliefs of nineteenth-century tradition; on the other, it had not yet reconciled itself to the demands of modernity and remained beholden to outworn creeds and mythologies. It was that indeterminate state, Soule and Arnold each argued, that made the leadership of a new intellectual priesthood necessary.[59] In the meantime, all of these writers agreed, American society seemed trapped in an unresolved condition. Drawing on the legacy of civic republicanism to warn against the dangers of license and corruption, they argued that "urban freedoms" had broken the hold of custom, but that these freedoms also had dissolved the restraints that tradition usually placed on desire and destructive passion. Though posed in different ways, the question for all was whether reason could defeat power and cruelty.

As *The Snarl of the Beast* suggests, hard-boiled crime fiction was equally preoccupied with the problem of replacing clan and custom by law and civil society. But the authors of *Black Mask*'s pulp stories enjoyed one great advantage over their contemporaries in the social sciences and social criticism: they could imagine mythic resolutions for the problems they raised. If the hard-boiled story tended to see metropolitan society much as Park or Soule did—as stranded between the inherited coherence of custom and the consciously intended structure of civilization—it typically found some dramatic means to counter that impression, usually in a moment of violent conflict that both clarified and dispatched the problems at issue. Here, too, *The Snarl of the Beast* is particularly revealing. For the method Daly uses to resolve his narrative turns out to provide both a paradigmatic example of the genre's central conventions and a revealing contrast to the idiosyncratic turn that Hammett gave them.

All through *The Snarl of the Beast*, Race Williams is frustrated by the obscurity and the boundless disorder of the city and by the irrational passions that seem to drive its citizens. Those difficulties are highlighted by the detective's problems in getting to the root of the crimes he is investigating and by his troubles with his client, Danny—who like many subsequent such figures in the genre is needy, manipulative, and treacherous. In the novel's climactic passage, however, all of those problems are resolved. Race is lured by Danny to a trap in an abandoned house in "the wilderness, on the very edge of the city," where the detective suitably confronts the embodiment of the "primary" and primitive forces opposed to civic responsibility (206). As he sneaks through the abandoned house, Race comes across a scene of terrible sexual cruelty. The Beast has kidnapped and bound both Danny and Milly, and in an effort to force Danny to reveal his family's secret wealth, he now prepares to torture the girl with "a sharp pointed knife—almost like a stiletto, but a bit thicker" (213). In the novel's pivotal scene, the detective pauses to watch this horrific tableau and then rushes in to confront and defeat his enemy.

It would be difficult to overstate how central scenes of this type were to the developing hard-boiled crime story. Some version of Daly's pornographic scenario became a nearly obligatory feature of the genre, one reproduced in countless lurid magazine covers and sometimes in the more subtle narrative tableaux of the genre's best writers. Time and again, the hero watches in some degree of paralysis as an evil figure prepares to torture a helpless woman, usually in an all but explicitly sexual manner.[60] The reasons for the centrality of that convention were more than simply prurient, however. For the tableau of cruelty and submission that Daly's scene exemplifies also served as a tacit allegory of the genre's central tension—the conflict between civic responsibility and unrestrained, irrational desire. Sociologists like Park feared that the American city would become a place, not where civilization reigned, but where the decay of tradition gave free reign to the most destructive passions and dangerous impulses. *The Snarl of the Beast* provides a graphic image of that civic decline and threatens its hero with the prospect that it might extend to him. As Race watches the Beast prepare to torture Milly, there is, of course, a suggestion that he, along with the reader, is held captive by a secret pleasure in sadistic abuse. More significantly, though, the detective's momentary paralysis aligns him with the helpless girl herself, whose vulnerability at the hands of the Beast takes the degradation that she experiences as a "girl of the night" to the furthest possible extreme. Most tellingly of all, it closely identifies the paralyzed watcher with the pathetic Danny, whose decadence is registered in the fact that he cannot bear to see Milly suffer and dies from the strain. In short, the scene offers a complex tableau of degradation. In each of the analogies with which Race Williams is implicitly presented, he can see a version of himself reduced to a bestial, or infantilized, or pathetically feminized condition, and in each of them Daly suggests some nightmarish version of the "primary" forces that threaten to submerge the civic realm of the city. When Race rushes in to combat the Beast, therefore, he not only struggles with a cartoonish metaphor for the raging id, he battles it in the name of public responsibility and must risk his own standing in the process. "Through blood I looked at blood," Williams remarks just before he defeats his enemy.[61]

In that allegorical manner, *The Snarl of the Beast*—like Robert Park's sociology and Thurman Arnold's political advocacy—championed the victory to be wrested over the obscurity of the city and the "primary" forces that account for its illegibility. Hammett's *The Glass Key* takes up similar problems and, though with far greater deftness, approaches them with the same conventions that Daly used. The implications of their stories differ sharply, however. Point by point, Hammett's novel dims the picture of civic triumph that ran through the rhetoric of his contemporaries and undercuts the very ground for optimism that they found.

That difference begins with the portrait of Hammett's protagonist. Like nearly all detective heroes and, like the era's realists and neoprogressives in particular, Ned Beaumont takes up Park's civilizing mission. His task is to displace irrational bonds with rational agreement. Like the hard-boiled detective in particular, moreover, Beaumont is distinguished by his willingness to suffer on behalf of his clients. In both roles he is ineffective, but in neither case, Hammett emphasizes, because he is anything less than a sterling example of the qualities he is meant to represent. As we will see more fully, Beaumont undergoes extraordinary physical trials on behalf of Madvig. Indeed, like countless similar figures from Depression era fiction — from Steinbeck's Jim Casey to Faulkner's Joe Christmas — Beaumont's bodily suffering renders him a Christlike martyr for the community he hopes to serve. (Falling into a coma after a brutal beating, Beaumont awakens in a hospital on "the third day" and is greeted by Madvig's exclamation: "Christ, I'm glad to see you alive again" [94, 95].) A seemingly perfect reconciliation of sentiment and intellect, Beaumont is also coolly rational in pursuing carefully chosen ends. In the novel's opening passage, we watch him stand before a gambling table — another central image of Depression era literature — where he loses badly at craps. The next scene, however, shows Beaumont on the phone to his bookie. Drawing on his knowledge of the conditions at a local track and a prediction of rain, he places a bet that will more than recoup his losses and thereby establishes a central feature of his character. In much the same terms that the era's neoprogressives used to speak of themselves, Hammett casts his protagonist as a pragmatic intellectual — a figure who, by calculating probabilities, can master the contingent features of an uncertain world.

All the more striking, then, that neither sentiment nor intelligence serve Beaumont particularly well. Throughout the novel, he meets one person after the next who has rushed to some hasty or ill-considered judgment and attempts in various ways to point out the errors they have made. In almost every case, he fails miserably. The reason, Hammett makes clear, is that neither people's minds nor their feelings can be easily changed or manipulated. If the classic detective story is a narrative of disconfirmation — or "disambiguation," as Steven Marcus puts it — where false stories and misleading evidence are disproved so that a "clarity of explanation" can be established, *The Glass Key* suggests that the task is all but hopeless.[62] No matter how clear the evidence he presents or how compelling a story he tells, Beaumont has an almost insuperably difficult time convincing others to share his point of view. "There was nothing," the narrator notes of one such character after Hammett's protagonist lays out a chain of compelling evidence, "to indicate that she had been at all convinced by Ned Beaumont's argument" (109). In most of these examples, moreover, Hammett emphasizes that his protagonist fails because of the ineradicable powers of love and desire. Madvig's daughter, Opal, mounts an anonymous public relations campaign to have her father arrested for murder because she believes mistakenly that he has killed her lover and cannot be convinced otherwise. Janet Henry shares Opal's view and defends it without any doubt although her strongest evidence for that belief is her distaste for Madvig himself. "You don't hate him because you think he killed your brother," Beaumont points out to her. "You think he killed your brother because you hate him" — an accurate charge she simply shrugs off (146). Most tellingly, Madvig himself will not act to clear his name because he fears that the effort might interfere with his plans to win Janet Henry's hand. If not for its grim tone, Hammett's novel would seem a comedy of mistaken beliefs, misguided desires, and pathologically inflexible passions.

It is that quality in particular that makes *The Glass Key* a revealing comparison, not just to Daly's *Snarl of the Beast*, but to the whole tradition of detective fiction writing that preceded it. For Daly, as for his realist and neoprogressive contemporaries, the irrational forces of love and desire exemplify the most dangerous features of the contemporary metropolis. Freed of the restraints of tradition, those forces threaten to turn the city into a chaotic realm where passion trumps responsibility and personal desire outweighs the rule of law. The aristocrat's clannishness, the Beast's criminal passions and his desire to exact revenge on the Davison family that spurned him, Milly's economic enslavement to the degrading work of prostitution — all in Daly's rendition represent a city where liberal freedoms lead only to the destruction of civic order. But, like most detective stories, *The Snarl of the Beast* also suggests that those irrational forces can be defeated so that decent citizens like Milly and Race can meet again on the ground of free consent. There, it seems, the moderate affection of bourgeois marriage can triumph over the self-destructive passion of sexual possession. It is also at that point, however, that Hammett parts company with his peers. In the world of *The Glass Key*, no affection is moderate, and irrationality, destructiveness, and cruelty appear the very essence of love.

So, although the hard-boiled crime story often seems a genre dominated by cynical calculation, where rational self-interest is pursued to extreme ends, in this particular example Hammett suggests the opposite. Over and again he portrays parasitic and self-destructive relations where passion outweighs interest. There is, for example, the minor figure of a newspaper editor who shoots himself when his young wife flirts with Beaumont — an event that suddenly transforms her infidelity to passionate grief. There is Beaumont's own exceptional dedication to Madvig, a dedication that not only withstands Beaumont's physical suffering but Madvig's cruelty and indifference and one that seems as driven by desire as any other example in the book. (Waking in the hospital, Beaumont announces, "I don't want any [doctors]. . . . I want Paul Madvig" [95].) But the best example may be the murder narrative at the center of the novel. Near the beginning of the book, Beaumont comes across the corpse of Taylor Henry, Janet's brother and the son of Madvig's political ally, Senator Henry. Near the novel's conclusion, Beaumont reveals that the Senator himself killed his son and that he did so because, needing the votes that Madvig's machine could deliver, he would not allow his son to interfere in their arrangement. Like Daly's Davison family, then, the Henrys become the model of a corrupt and self-destructive aristocracy. As an image of the Democratic Party elite, they suggest, moreover, a patrician class that exploits and betrays the party's immigrant, working-class constituency — an apt portrait of the relations between the party's Southern oligarchs and its Northern urban voters in the twenties. The most significant feature of this story, though, is the fact that before he was killed, Taylor had set out to thrash Madvig with a walking stick for kissing his sister. Here, as everywhere else in Hammett's novel, love and the passions of clan loyalty outweigh the negotiation and compromise of politics.

This theme gets its most dramatic rendition in an extended depiction of cruelty and violence at the novel's center—a passage that echoes the climactic scene of *The Snarl of the Beast*, but also tellingly alters and displaces it. If Ned Beaumont is a Christ figure, it is because he is willing to endure terrible suffering for Paul Madvig. As one of his tormenters points out, he is "a God-damned massacrist," and he proves his fidelity when he is kidnapped by Madvig's rival and tortured for whatever political "dirt" he might have on his boss (185). Like Daly's climactic tableau, the scene is redolent not just of violence but of erotic cruelty:

> Ned Beaumont mumbled something about Fedink [a former lover] and sat up. He was in a narrow bed without sheets or bedclothes of any sort. The bare mattress was blood-stained. His face was swollen and bruised and blood-smeared. . . .
>
> O'Rory said: ". . . Now listen to what I tell you. You're going to give me the dope on Paul. . . . Maybe you think you won't but you will. I'll have you worked on from now till you do. Do you understand me?"
>
> Ned Beaumont smiled. The condition of his face made the smile horrible. He said: "I won't."
>
> O'Rory stepped back and said: "Work on him."
>
> While Rusty hesitated, the apish Jeff knocked aside Ned Beaumont's upraised hand and pushed him down on the bed. "I got something to try." He scooped up Ned Beaumont's legs and tumbled them on the bed. He leaned over Ned Beaumont, his hands busy on Ned Beaumont's body.
>
> Ned Beaumont's body and arms and legs jerked convulsively and three times he groaned. After that he lay still. (88, 90)

Although we never learn the exact nature of the apish's Jeff's methods, we do know that the torture Beaumont suffers is more than enough to hospitalize him and that it is marked in strongly sexual terms. Jeff calls Beaumont his "sweetheart" and asks as he tortures him, "Don't you like it, Baby?" (186, 88). Nor are these erotic suggestions incidental. They indicate a central feature of Hammett's novel—one that comes out most strongly in contrast with the more conventional narrative modes apparent in *The Snarl of the Beast*. For Daly, the sexual violence practiced by the Beast represents the exceptional face of the dangerous, but still rare, forces of irrational desire that threaten the city. By the same token, the peril that Race confronts and overcomes when he witnesses that torture is the danger represented by the bound bodies of Milly and Danny and by his own paralysis: the threat of feminization and of the defeat of will by submission. Once Race overcomes those dangers, he can replace violence with consent and irrationality with the homosocial bonds of a civic order. Thus, as soon as Race defeats the Beast, the police enter the scene. Once Race's enemies, and now his allies, they are the official forces destined to bring the vigilante and the girl of the night back into the geographic and legal limits of the city.

What is significant about Hammett's passage, by contrast, is that it both invokes and dismisses this story. Raising, like Daly, the threat of erotic cruelty and effeminate submission, Hammett neglects to offer Daly's civic alternative. Thus, where Daly's scene is pivotal and marks the climax of the novel, Ned Beaumont's suffering seems deliberately anticlimactic and resolves nothing. More tellingly, of course, where Daly's hero witnesses a terrible image of humiliation and is threatened with such degradation himself, Beaumont literally undergoes something like the tortures that the Beast plans for Milly. That difference is fundamental. For it indicates that the distinction that is vital to Daly — the contrast between consensual relations and those of domination and submission — has disappeared.[63] *The Snarl of the Beast* hinges on the contrast between a civic world, marked by mutual agreement and homosocial order, and a world of destructive and irrational passions symbolized by sexual cruelty. In Hammett's rendition the two worlds are reduced to a single entity. Hence, the fact that the phrase Paul Madvig uses to describe politics — "going in with both hands working" — turns out to be nearly identical to the one that Madvig's rival uses to order Beaumont's torture: "Work on him." Politics and torture, fraternal affection and sexual cruelty, the civic and the irrational — in *The Glass Key*, these are not alternatives but stages on a single continuum.

Thus, it is fitting that later in the novel Beaumont's torturer, Jeff, will turn on his boss, Shad O'Rory, killing O'Rory with his bare hands. Like Senator Henry and his son, Taylor, those two men exemplify the truth of politics in Hammett's novel: that it is driven by irrational passions and organized by hierarchical relations of violence and cruelty. Though the Senator and his son are far more genteel than O'Rory and Jeff, in one key respect the two pairs of men seem nearly identical. Senator Henry beats his son to death with a cane, for speaking "as no son should speak to a father" (207). Jeff strangles the patriarchal ruler of his gang after O'Rory makes a failed attempt to silence him. Each of these pairs presents an implicit analogy to the friendship between Beaumont and Madvig, so that it is a telling moment when Beaumont and Madvig themselves come perilously close to blows. Physical violence between them is narrowly avoided when Beaumont first backs down and then Madvig quickly apologizes; placed in context, however, with the novel's other political killings, it nonetheless makes a resonant suggestion. Like all the other allegiances in the novel, Beaumont and Madvig's friendship turns out to rest on an implicit hierarchy and on the always latent promise of violence. Thus, once their bond has been challenged, and once the threat of conflict has been explicitly raised, the friendship between the two men is, as Beaumont acknowledges with tears in his eyes, "done for good" (197). Since even relations that seem consensual turn out to be matters of dominance, Beaumont has only two choices. He can, like Jeff and Taylor Henry, battle the leader of his clan until one of them is dead; or he can leave town, abandon his friendship with Madvig, and give up the realm of politics and passion altogether.

DONE FOR GOOD

Hammett emphasizes the grim tone of his novel by having Beaumont make the latter choice, but that decision is less important than the fact that either option subverts the perspective of Hammett's realist and neoprogressive contemporaries — and, more broadly, the whole tradition of the detective story that Hammett once sought merely to revise. In the classic guise of novels like *A Study in Scarlet*, the detective story functioned as a parable of liberalism by suggesting that, although people were sometimes driven by irrational forces and selfish desires, they could also enter into freely chosen agreements. Both the hard-boiled stories of writers like Carroll John Daly and the social theory of interwar realists and neoprogressives sought to make that picture more complex. Compulsion, irrationality, and coercion extended far wider than was once thought, they suggested, and the realm of rational deliberation and consent was far narrower, far more fragile and unstable than nineteenth-century liberals imagined. For that very reason, realists argued and Daly suggested, American society called out for the strong leadership of a civilizing elite. In Thurman Arnold's extreme version of this view, it would be up to an "opportunistic governing class" to make rational use of the irrational forces of custom and myth and to thereby guide the nation's less intelligent citizens to tacit consent in a new, more civil order—much as Race Williams rescues Milly from the servitude of prostitution or the Continental Op manipulates Gabrielle Leggett into domestic happiness.

The Glass Key accepted that realist diagnosis of contemporary society but cast doubt on the realist cure. It was true, Hammett's novel suggested, that people were controlled by myth and habit, driven by irrational fears and passions, and impelled by selfish desires that they did not themselves understand. The public world of politics, like the private sphere of love, ran not on consent and reason, but on cruelty and dominance. But if that were true, Hammett's novel implicitly asked, what would make a realist like Thurman Arnold, or one like Ned Beaumont, believe that he could rationally control it? If at the core of politics, as of love, lies unreasoning instinct, then the realist project to rationalize civic life could only fail. It would mean trying to strip politics of what made it political, and love of what made it compelling. Thus, it is fitting that when Ned Beaumont leaves town with Janet Henry, the two of them do so without any sign of strong feeling. They choose not love, but inertia, Hammett suggests, and leaving the realm of politics and emotion behind, they head off for the deracinated realm inhabited by Hammett's failed intellectuals.

That conclusion points to a central implication of Hammett's fiction. The novels he wrote during the late twenties and early thirties—on the cusp of the New Deal—rewrote the detective story, moving the genre away from its fables of social contract and turning it toward a literature of social administration. *The Glass Key* emphasized a reaction to that transition that ran, though less strongly, through all of its predecessors among Hammett's other novels: that the commitment to planning and expertise demanded a high price in alienation and in the weakening of political association. Among some New Deal policy makers, critics, and political theorists in the later thirties, similar realizations encouraged a hostility to centralization and a search for ways to reinvigorate political participation and popular community. In the world of the hard-boiled crime novel, the arid irony that Raymond Chandler saw in Hammett's fiction inspired him to a new revision of the genre. The novels that Chandler began to publish during the later thirties remade the detective novel again, so that it became not a fable of social contract, or a vision of expert administration, but an elegiac parable of sentimental affiliation.

3.

THE PULP WRITER AS VANISHING AMERICAN

Raymond Chandler's Decentralist Imagination

We face a dilemma; there is no reason to conceal its proportions. . . .
We need a strong central government. . . . But I have deep
apprehension . . . unless we learn how many of those central
powers can be decentralized in their administration. . . . We who
believe devoutly in the democratic process should be the first to urge
the use of methods that will keep the administration of national
functions from becoming so concentrated at the national capital,
so distant from the everyday life of ordinary people, as to wither
and deaden the average citizen's sense of participation and
partnership in government affairs. *For in this citizen participation
lies the vitality of a democracy.* — David Lilienthal,
TVA — Democracy on the March, 1944

[The pulp writer belongs to] the long list of vanishing Americans.
— Fletcher Pratt, *American Mercury,* 1939[1]

The organizing principle of Raymond Chandler's fiction remained
almost unvaryingly constant over the twenty-five years that he wrote
detective stories. From the early pulp tales he published in *Black
Mask* in the thirties through the long novels he wrote in the late
forties and the fifties, Chandler returned time and again to a vision of
male fellowship and showed the way it was undermined by the vari-

ous evils of the modern world. The way he told that story changed significantly over the course of his career, but each of the novels for which Chandler is best remembered — *The Big Sleep, Farewell, My Lovely, The Long Goodbye* — depicts the deep feeling between Philip Marlowe and some idealized brother figure; and each shows that brotherhood falling prey to corruption and exploitation.

In only one novel did Chandler temper that vision of sentimental loss with a more optimistic conclusion. *The Lady in the Lake* (1943) ends with Philip Marlowe atop a dam in the San Gabriel Mountains, watching as a team of soldiers at its base removes the body of the novel's villain from his smashed car. On the crown of the dam, Marlowe stands surrounded by a folksy local sheriff and by a capable U.S. Army soldier, who, guarding the dam against wartime sabotage, shot the villain as he attempted to flee across it. That group of men presents a telling mirror image to the one of those at its base. *The Lady in the Lake* focuses on the story of a corrupt police detective, gone bad because of vicious circumstance and the influence of an evil woman. John Degarmo could have been a good cop, Chandler implies, but driven by love for the femme fatale Muriel Chess and seduced by the rampant corruption of the Bay City police force he became first a thug and then a depraved killer. In the novel's lachrymose final line, Marlowe looks down on his mangled body and thinks that the corpse is "something that had been a man."[2] The group of figures who stand atop the dam present a converse image. They are disciplined, professional, and, though mutually reinforcing, each autonomous — the epitome of the fraternity that Chandler valued. In a there-but-for-the-grace-of-god-go-I kind of story, *The Lady in the Lake* suggests that Marlowe's body is not crushed, that he remains a man, because, rather than falling amid corrupt confederates and evil women, he became part of a fellowship of decent men.

What was it about this book in particular that prompted Chandler to draft such a resolute and comparatively optimistic conclusion? *The Lady in the Lake* is Chandler's wartime novel, and it is energized throughout by the problem of popular commitment to wartime aims. But the novel's geography itself appears to have influenced Chandler's conclusion. *The Lady in the Lake* is the only one of his works whose critical scenes take place outside metropolitan Los

Angeles, and the dam that appears at several crucial points in the story seems particularly important to Chandler, providing a strongly marked formal structure to close his narrative. Much of the novel's action concerns Marlowe's countless travels across the Los Angeles Basin, especially his westward trips into the dangerous terrain of Bay City — Chandler's rendition of a corrupt Santa Monica and the place of origin of both Degarmo and the murderous Muriel Chess. At the dam, that movement is ended by reversal. Marlowe travels east and upward into the San Gabriel Mountains, moving away from L.A.'s corrupt coastline to assume a rare, stationary perspective on the novel's landscape. Replacing the confusing horizontality of urban Los Angeles with a stable, vertical structure, Chandler's dam becomes an architectural rendering of the way his novel works to contain dangerous movement and corrosive desire.

But the dam is important for more than its formal role alone. As Chandler surely knew, when he relied on it to close off his narrative, he was also calling on one of the most potent social symbols of the era — the clearest image of the transformations that had reshaped the Western landscape over the previous decade. Made famous especially by the massive engineering feat of the Hoover Dam and reinforced by the Colorado River Project, the Bonneville and Grand Coulee Dams on the Columbia River in Washington, the Shasta Dam in Northern California, and the Hansen Dam that rerouted the Los Angeles River during the late thirties, the dam as heroic public works project was the most dramatic emblem of the New Deal in the West. In most other respects, the New Deal had not taken strong hold in California; the influence of the federal government had been largely held off by militant conservatives and homegrown populists throughout the thirties. But, like the rest of the nation, California saw an enormous infusion of federal dollars for public works during the Depression. The era's massive construction projects thus became the main face of political change in the region, rare symbols in historian Kevin Starr's phrase "of shared value and public life." As Chandler's friend J. B. Priestly put it in one starry-eyed description, the Hoover Dam seemed to predict "the soul of America under socialism."[3]

The particular site to which *The Lady in the Lake* alludes was probably not itself a New Deal project, but the qualities that Chandler associates with this structure closely match the values his contemporaries attributed to the era's giant public works projects.[4] For their champions, the Hoover Dam and its lesser analogs were "common denominator[s]" — state-sponsored re-creations of the West's mythic frontier, where democratic fellowship triumphed over inherited privilege. Chandler's novel speaks in similar terms. Banishing not only the femme fatale and the corrupt cop, but the arrogant rich as well, it unites representatives of the federal government, local community, and private enterprise in defense of the common good. Chandler's contemporaries marveled that New Deal public works could bring together "laboring stiff[s]" and men who spoke in "college jargon." The dam in *The Lady in the Lake* likewise joins Marlowe's cultivated sensibility to the rural wisdom of the backwoods sheriff and the disciplined toughness of the federal soldier. Like the rural village that surrounds the lake, those men constitute Chandler's brief image of democratic community.[5]

In this manner, Chandler's novel drew not only on the rhetoric of the New Deal, but on a particular side of the New Deal — a "decentralist" vision that came to the fore especially in the later thirties when Chandler first began publishing as a novelist. This was the aspect of New Deal reform that had descended from Wilson's New Freedom, from Brandeis's complaints against monopoly power, and from widespread hostility to the power of Wall Street and the House of Morgan. It was also the sole aspect of the New Deal that truly succeeded in the West, where it drew on a long-cultivated frustration with Eastern power and where the private firms who benefited by the era's public works contracts threw their weight behind the Roosevelt administration, endorsing the way the New Deal reshaped both public financing and labor relations.[6]

In the popular journalism of the day, those Western industrialists became the public face of a new, New Deal capitalism — politically liberal, supportive of strong government, and open to organized labor. The dams, aqueducts, bridges, and highways they built throughout California during the thirties, and the military production industries they created in the forties, became a mythic image of the success of the decentralist New Deal — physical emblems of the partnership of federal financing, local planning, and private enterprise. In the decades following World War II, that picture would alter sharply as the memory of Brandeis was displaced by the celebration of Keynes and as Southern California was transformed by postwar development. By the fifties, the rise of corporate giants like Kaiser and Bechtel would come to exemplify an unexpected legacy of the New Deal — the alliance of big business and big government that Dwight Eisenhower warned against in his attack on the military-industrial complex. During the late thirties and early forties, however, California's version of corporate consolidation appeared to be only a distant possibility. The region's industrial giants still cast themselves as scrappy local entrepreneurs; their reliance on public dollars seemed an example of the way that federal spending could break the stranglehold of Wall Street to foster local opportunity and regional community.[7]

The Lady in the Lake stands almost literally at the hinge of these two visions of California. The men who guard Chandler's dam and the placid rural community that surrounds it look like a nearly exact rendition of the benefits the era's antimonopolists hoped the New Deal would foster: "decentralized administration, regional development, and the encouragement of small, integrated communities."[8] Tellingly, though, this is a brief image in Chandler's fiction, soon to be replaced by vociferous denunciations of postwar mass society. It seems, in short, that Chandler could imagine the fellowship of decent men forming only during wartime and that he could envision it flourishing only far from his true subject — the dystopian world of Los Angeles.[9] One way to understand Chandler's fiction and the trajectory of his career, then, is to see the dam at the conclusion of *The Lady in the Lake*, and the decentralist New Deal to which it alludes, as the absent center of Chandler's literary imagination — the unifying structure that seems always missing from his Los Angeles and the analog for the unrealized common denominator that Chandler referred to as "public taste." The fellowship that Chandler imagines briefly at the dam is a rare glimpse of a fleeting desideratum. In his early novels such fellowship of decent men is all but overwhelmed by the monopolistic elite of California's old landholding oligarchy. In his later fiction it is swamped by postwar consumerism.

Throughout his fiction, though, a decentralist utopia of male cama-raderie provides the vantage from which Chandler casts his critical vision of L.A.

1.

A FASCINATING NEW LANGUAGE
Chandler's Early Career

It is not surprising that Chandler would envision a decentralist uto-pia. The Los Angeles depicted by this fiction was a city built by decen-tralization and premised, as the director of city planning explained during the twenties, on the virtues of "the small unit."[10] At once dedi-cated to an ideology of individual freedom and ruled with an iron hand by a tiny coalition of leading families, interwar L.A. was a city that aspired to centerlessness but that turned out in fact to be gov-erned by concentrated power. Chandler had been soaking up the at-mosphere of that city for nearly two decades before he began writing detective stories. For more than half that time, he had worked as an executive in the booming oil business, an industry likewise divided between an ideology of small-scale free enterprise and the reality of monopolistic concentration. He absorbed there both the Brandeisian distaste for centralized power, which was a standard perspective among Western industrialists, and an awareness of the ways in which that ideology was often compromised by its adherents. His dislike for "organization" and "middlemen" would only be sharpened by his experience working as a screenwriter during the forties.[11]

But Chandler's disenchanted version of the decentralist ethos was not just a reflection of the politics and economics of Los Angeles. It also drew significantly from Chandler's years in the pulp industry, an experience that may have done more than anything else to shape his particular aesthetic values and his peculiar narrative methods. By the mid-thirties, when he began publishing in *Black Mask*, populist dis-dain for economic concentration had become a key feature of pulp industry ideology; pulp writers and editors frequently congratulated themselves for being independent craftsmen and entrepreneurs who were dwarfed by their competitors in the mainstream mass media.

For Chandler, that ethos was closely associated with personal and aesthetic transformation, and it would remain a crucial feature of his literary attitudes long after he left the industry.

In this respect, Chandler's experience with the pulps and the attitudes he took from them differed significantly from those of his most famous predecessor. When Dashiell Hammett began writing for *Black Mask* in 1922, he was an ambitious young man working in a new and poorly defined industry. He looked at *Black Mask* as a stepping stone to more serious literary pursuits, and he viewed the pulps in general, as most of his contemporaries did, with Menckenian disdain. When Chandler began writing for *Black Mask* in 1933 he was already middle-aged. He had been fired for alcoholism from his position with the Dabney Oil Syndicate in 1932 and faced the lowest depth of the Depression with few prospects. Looking to the pulps to reinvent himself as a writer — because "the literary standard was flexible, and there was a chance to get 'paid while learning' " — he was, moreover, returning to a career at which he had already failed. As a young man, Chandler had made an unsuccessful attempt to work as a journalist in Edwardian London. Taking up a more humble version of that ambition twenty years down the road, he could ill afford the swaggering confidence that Hammett brought to *Black Mask*, and he consequently recognized far different qualities in pulp writing. By Chandler's account, the pulp world was not the morass of cheap fantasy that Hammett saw, but a vital world of vernacular creativity. *Black Mask*, he would later claim, had been a "rough school" — a place where he had been lucky enough to forget the "arty and intellectual" tendencies that marred his youthful literary efforts.[12]

So, while both Hammett and Chandler used their experience writing for the pulps as an avenue to greater opportunity and prestige, their attitude toward that experience, and the literary problems they made of it, were almost polar opposites. For Hammett, "blackmasking" was a degraded form of labor and the pulps an extreme version of the popular confusion evident throughout the cultural landscape. The problem he faced in trying to "make literature" of that material was the need to exploit pulp fantasy while remaining free of its seduction — a tension registered in the recurrent story he told of the battle between dangerous mystification and potentially sterile expertise. Chandler, by contrast, saw the pulp world much as its champions did, speaking of them in later years with something akin to filial piety. Though unsophisticated, the magazines were "honest and forthright," he argued. Against "the pseudo-literate pretentiousness" of middlebrow journalism and the shallow withdrawal of the "literary life" — each of which seemed to Chandler reprehensibly "feminine" — they remained a masculine world of vital competition. In building on the techniques he had learned among the pulps, then, Chandler's task would be less to escape the perils of pop fantasy than to glory in the magazines' "fascinating new language." All he wanted to do as a novelist, he later claimed, was to see what that language might do as "a means of expression which might remain on the level of unintellectual thinking" even as he gave it "the power to say things which are usually only said with a literary air."[13]

Thus, for precisely the reasons that Hammett dismissed the "jargon" of the criminal underworld, Chandler praised the language of the pulps. As a kind of "vernacular" expression, pulp language seemed to him less a form of mystification than a repository of neglected popular virtues. In pulp fiction he discovered the "hard vulgarity," the "strident wit," and the "utterly unexpected range of sensitivity" hidden in "the American mind."[14] In this sense, moreover, Chandler's attitudes corresponded with the shifting status of the pulp industry and with the broader currents of cultural belief characteristic of American literature during the thirties. When Hammett wrote for *Black Mask* and later for Knopf during the twenties, the pulps were a reviled form of publication and the urban, working-class audience to which they were targeted appeared outside the mainstream of American life. By the mid-thirties, though, attitudes had shifted dramatically under the pressure of the Depression. Precisely that urban, ethnic working class, which only a short time before had seemed alien rather than American, came to look like one of the exemplary faces of American popular identity, and throughout cultural life both artists and audiences expressed fresh interest in previously marginalized forms of pop and folk culture. Everywhere in the worlds of American art and literature, the idea of cultural eminence itself lost prestige to be replaced by appeals to the authority of the democratic and popular.[15] Thus, the features of pulp fiction, which had once seemed provincial and subterranean, were by the later thirties quickly coming to seem exemplary of American culture. Indeed, the years Chandler worked in the industry, 1933 to 1939, were the halcyon days of the pulps and the golden age of *Black Mask* especially. By the time Chandler published his first novel with Knopf, hard-boiled crime fiction in particular had received both critical recognition and vast popular acclaim through the work of Hammett and James M. Cain (as well as that of lesser writers like Raoul Whitfield). When he departed *Black Mask* for Knopf in 1939, then, Chandler must have seemed, to himself and to his audience, less an escapee from a narrow world than the emissary of a vital and yet still underrecognized popular terrain.

That changed environment meant that Chandler's ambitions faced a question that, although perhaps equally difficult, was decidedly unlike the one that had concerned Hammett — not, can pulp fiction be made into "literature," but, would its particular virtues survive the transition? Having seen Hammett's example, Chandler had no doubt that the hard-boiled crime story could admit of serious literary accomplishment; "an art which is capable of" *The Maltese Falcon*, he claimed, was capable of "anything."[16] But, given his tendency to imagine an inherent tension between the "vernacular" and the "literary" — one that came down to a contrast between spontaneous natural invention and arid formalism — he had to wonder whether the honesty he admired in pulp fiction could continue to flourish outside the pulps themselves. The fundamental problem of his fiction became the effort to preserve a demotic energy that appeared both vital and necessarily evanescent. The legitimacy of his fiction and the legitimacy of public culture generally, Chandler implied, depended on its fragile vernacular spirit. Chandler's critics often charge him with being an "aesthete" and an "elitist" — a decadent stylist whose "implied programme for superior living" reflected a "disengagement with the difficult compromises of reality."[17] But, while such comments ironically echo exactly what Chandler hated about both "the literary life" and the mainstream mass media — and while they may capture what he feared could be true of his own writing — they misconstrue Chandler's motivations. In the history of hard-boiled crime fiction, it was Hammett who was the committed elitist, and the question that dogged his work was whether that elitism could be maintained in the face of its own implausibility. Chandler, by contrast, was a sentimental populist, and the core preoccupation of his work was the effort to hold onto an ever-fading democratic legitimacy.

In his essays and letters Chandler constructed a critical theory to explain this ambition. Turning to the pulps for an unrealized vision of cultural democracy, he indicted the institutional divisions that fragmented American literature and imagined his own work as a harbinger of the "public taste" that might bridge high and low culture, popular readership and intellectual expertise.[18] Everything about his fiction both reflects that grandiose aim and Chandler's awareness that it must inevitably fail. The weirdly disparate diction of the novels brings together the vernacular dialogue of pulp narrative and a hyperliterary interior monologue — only to emphasize the lack of resolution between the two. The loosely constructed plots similarly hold off the synthesis of *histoire* and *discourse* at which detective fiction typically excels. Letting "scene outrank the plot" and "fact" escape the "simplicity of fiction," they reflect a desire to cede pride of place to an ephemeral "felt experience" that Chandler imagined always being overtaken by the formal and institutional.[19] Likewise, the thematic focus of Chandler's entire oeuvre — his obsession with the lost brother — turns on the constant disappearance of vernacular legitimacy and the fading virtues of the open frontier. In each feature, Chandler's fiction gestures toward the "common denominator" of popular community and complains at its frustration.

The thinking common to all these features can be seen best perhaps by comparison to Ross Macdonald, the writer most often called Chandler's successor (and the figure whose own effort to give the detective story a literary finish repelled Chandler). For Macdonald, whose career began significantly after the pulp era was all but finished, detective-story writing starts, as it does for his predecessor — with "the shocking realization of . . . limitations" and with a resulting sense of schism. "My ambition split into two parts which I have spent most of my life trying to put back together again." The vast difference between the two writers, Macdonald makes clear, is that for him crime fiction is capable of such restoration. "Chandler described a good plot as one that made for good scenes, as if the parts were greater than the whole. I see plot as a vehicle of meaning. . . . Which means that the structure must be single and *intended*." Not only does such a redemptive vision rely on a faith in the unifying force of imaginative literature about which Chandler was deeply skeptical; it links such faith to the particular image of a consistent public taste that Chandler's entire career rebuked. For Macdonald, literature overcame "schizophrenic pain" in the motion with which he "possess[ed]" his "birthplace" and was "possessed by its language." That recovery of an implicitly national community depended precisely on the dream of a common literature that Chandler invoked only at his most utopian. For Macdonald, cultural hierarchy, and by extension class stratification, simply cannot persist in the face of common language: "popular culture is not and need not be at odds with high culture. . . . There is a two-way connection between the very greatest work and the anonymous imaginings of a people . . . [and that connection] holds a civilization together like nothing else can."[20] If Chandler's plotting and style seem less singly intended than Macdonald's, that is because for him the idea of common taste and a classless people, though no less desirable, was a far less convincing likelihood.

THE COMMUNITY OF EXPERIENCE AND THE LABOR OF OTHERS

By focusing on the frustrations that prevented a "public taste" rather than celebrating its latent reality, Chandler mimicked the issues at the center of New Deal decentralism. His fascination with an evanescent vernacular spirit mirrored the demand for popular representation that echoed throughout the American thirties. Praising the TVA for the way it stimulated regional development, Sherwood Anderson summed up the key feature of that thinking—the desire to replace political bureaucracy with local participation. "Government has again grown near to life," Anderson announced. "It may be the politicians remain a race apart but the politicians are no longer the government." For most of Anderson's contemporaries, however, popular democracy seemed less an achievement than an open question. As David Lilienthal, the director of the TVA and the Roosevelt administration's most prominent champion of decentralization, explained: "grassroots democracy" remained an as yet unfulfilled promise of the New Deal. Its realization would require not only "widespread and intimate participation of the people" in the decisions governing their lives, but "some drastic changes in the prevailing relations between experts and the people, both in industry and the government." Only by "awakening in the whole people a sense of . . . common moral purpose," Lilienthal argued, could that commitment to mutual participation succeed.[21]

The most influential theoretical statement of that belief, and the version closest to Chandler's thinking, can be seen in the various attempts that John Dewey made throughout the era to defend the importance of participatory democracy. In *Liberalism and Social Action* and a body of related writings from the later thirties, Dewey used the occasion of the New Deal to expand on ideas he had been developing since the turn of the century, seeking to redefine liberalism so as to defend it against its corruption by monopoly capitalism and bureaucratic government. In this respect, although he positioned himself to the left of the New Deal (and to the right of socialist politics), Dewey provided the best theoretical articulation of the demand for popular citizenship that ran through much of the rhetoric of the thirties. That effort hinged on the notion that classical liberalism had been antiquated by the intense organization of urban, industrial life. Though traditional liberal theory once might have suited a decentralized economy, Dewey argued that in the twentieth century it had become little more than a defense of the evils of industrial capitalism — where "power rests finally in the hands of finance capital, no matter what claims are made for government of, by, and for all the people." In order to save liberalism from that distortion, then, it would be necessary to make it more democratic. Citizens would need to discover that true individualism did not mean an antisocial hostility to the common good, but rather the opportunity for self-development that came with participation in "associated life." By the same token, political and economic institutions would need to be reformed so that "all those who are affected by social institutions . . . have a share in producing and managing them."[22]

In a limited sense, of course, the ideal of literary democracy central to the ideology of pulp publishing closely echoed Dewey's language of public deliberation, and thus Chandler's elaboration of that ideology came in some ways to resemble Dewey's vision. Indeed, where Hammett's urge to clarify popular mystification chimed with the rhetoric of the era's realists and neoprogressives, Chandler's social vision and his aesthetics might best be called Deweyan. Unlike Hammett, Chandler saw art not as an effort to escape delusion, but as an attempt to rediscover what Dewey called the "community of experience." (No word was more important to Chandler, or to Dewey, than "experience"; Dewey's major aesthetic statement, published in 1934, was *Art as Experience*.) For Dewey, pursuing that end was the very opposite of the "museum conception" of art — in which a narrow "special culture" comes to replace the "common" knowledge that at its best the experience of art tutors. Chandler's desire to reassert the value of "public taste" and his determination to protect the hope of a democratic literature against its debasement by both "the literary life" and mass culture echoed that view almost note for note.[23] Such, in fact, was the gist of his renowned essay "The Simple Art of Murder," in which Chandler attempted to substantiate, against both the "critics' jargon" and his own doubts, his conviction that "there is no such thing as serious literature." At its best, he claimed the "realistic mystery" proved that there were no inherent distinctions among high culture and popular entertainment, the "literature of expression" and the "literature of escape." "There are no vital and significant forms of art," Chandler argued at his most millenarian, "there is only art" — the good and the less good. The achievement of the hard-boiled crime story pointed to that truth, Chandler suggested, since it proved that "important writing" could be done in popular genres. All that prevented our full realization of the fact was the hidebound prejudice of the cultural elite, on the one hand, and the banal commercial production of mass media on the other.[24]

At the center of Chandler's critical theory, in short, lay a Deweyan appeal to the promise of cultural democracy — a promise that in fact was always being traduced by bureaucratic professionalism and the rule of the market. And recognizing those Deweyan strains in Chandler's criticism helps to explain two of the most persistent themes of his

fiction: the vision of popular fellowship and its inversion — the omnipresent condition of parasitism and exploitation. Time and again,
Chandler's most villainous figures are the decadent elite of the non-
producing class — people who, in Dewey's analogous terms, "act
vicariously through control of the bodies and labor of others."[25] For
Chandler, as for Dewey, such people are distasteful not merely because they may be exploitative, but because the very idea of profit
without labor and, more basically still, of social alienation is tendentiously evil. Because it reflects the drive for specialization over the
values of common experience, of the separation of "intelligence"
from "force," the very idea of management represents the broken
promise of popular community. For Chandler, as for Dewey, the
division of mental and manual labor is the root of the corruption of
culture, and the reason for the significance of its redemption.

Consider, for example, "Try the Girl," the 1937 *Black Mask* story
that, along with a handful of other pulp novelettes, became the basis
for *Farewell, My Lovely* and that made a revealing allegory out of
Chandler's literary concerns. Like Chandler's second novel, "Try the
Girl" features the efforts of the detective-protagonist to intercede
between a charismatic ex-con and the singer whose love he would
like to regain. (The principal characters here are Ted Carmady, Steve
Skalla, and Little Beulah/Vivian Baring, rather than Philip Marlowe,
Moose Malloy, and Velma Valento/Helen Grayle.) "Try the Girl"
thus contains in outline several of the elements that would be essential to the success of *Farewell, My Lovely*. The story begins, just as
the novel later would, with the protagonist stumbling across the gi-
gantic and enormously colorful Skalla on the racially mixed ground
of Central Avenue. There, in search of Little Beulah, Skalla manhan-
dles the detective and then murders a black bar owner. But those
actions only serve to redouble the detective's growing sympathy for
the naïve ex-con, and the entire ensuing narrative builds upon that
unaccountable affection. As in *Farewell, My Lovely*, it leads the
detective to aid the ex-con in his quest and encourages him to battle
the whole corrupt network of Los Angeles society in the effort. Like
Farewell, My Lovely, then, "Try the Girl" amounts to a homosocial
romance. It uses the pursuit of a distant woman to spur the more
important and far deeper sympathy between the protagonist and his

counterpart from the lower orders. In this early version of the story, though, that plot has an unusually definite outline and it establishes a clearly resolved, though wildly implausible ending. It thus serves to illuminate the concerns that, although more complex, would remain at stake in Chandler's later novel, and in doing so it casts some revealing light on the nature of Chandler's enduring preoccupations.

The most striking difference between "Try the Girl" and *Farewell, My Lovely*, and perhaps the weakest aspect of the short story, is that in the pulp story the woman does not turn out to be a villain. Like Helen Grayle, Vivian Baring is a singer who has shed a tawdry past (and perhaps the subtle hint of a background in the racially mixed world of jazz) to move up in life. As Velma Valento later would, Beulah has changed her name and left Central Avenue for a career as a radio singer. She is the star of KLBL's Jumbo Candy Bar program, "A Street in Our Town," a radio show on the brink of distribution by a national network. Unlike her successor, though, Vivian does not marry a rich and fragile old man. As we learn only in the story's conclusion, she remains faithful to Skalla's memory, and in the final scenes we see her sit by his bedside, "holding one of his huge, limp fingers" as he dies.[26] The story's two villains, rather, are Dave Marineau, the manager of KLBL, and his wife. As Chandler's complex narrative unfolds, we eventually learn that Marineau has been using his knowledge of Vivian's past in an attempt to blackmail her into an affair, even as he tries to suppress knowledge of her background for the sake of public relations. Encouraged by Skalla's release from jail, Marineau seeks to force his attentions upon Vivian, who, determined to protect herself, shoots the manager to death. In the story's climax, Carmady, Skalla, and Marineau's wife, who has long suspected her husband of having an affair with Baring, all arrive at Vivian's apartment. There Skalla attempts to take the blame for Marineau's death, and in response Marineau's wife shoots him several times in the belly, assuming for herself the murderous role that Helen Grayle would play later in *Farewell, My Lovely*.

Unlike *Farewell, My Lovely*, then, "Try the Girl" is not the story of the tension between a treacherous woman and a faithful man. Rather, its underlying concern is the conflict between vernacular legitimacy and falsely formalized representation that occupied the heart of Chandler's critical thinking. What matters to Chandler, in short, is the moral contrast between the predatory mass media represented by Marineau and the honest and forthright popular vitality that belongs to Skalla. Like Moose Malloy, the recently released Skalla resembles a "hunky immigrant" longing to enter the promise of American life; even more than Malloy, he represents in that role the urban, ethnic working class that had recently emerged as the prime element of the New Deal coalition. In his first appearance, Skalla wears "a front-door handkerchief the color of the Irish flag," and as an ex-vaudeville bouncer and "an old circus man" to boot, he summons up an image of the vibrant world of commercial entertainment that catered to the working class between the wars (137, 170). Marineau, by contrast, stands for everything that Chandler most feared and despised in the mass media. He aims to both repress and exploit Vivian's background in the world that Skalla represents, and he seeks to replace its genuine vitality with a false image of American identity—the pseudo-homespun atmosphere suggested by a radio program called "A Street in Our Town."[27]

By placing Vivian Baring between these men, Chandler turned his critical theories into populist agon. Like the vernacular Chandler celebrated, Skalla is a charismatic but inherently doomed source of legitimacy. A Rip Van Winkle figure (literally "a giant"), he represents an outmoded, heroic age of grand actions and simple pleasures (137). Marineau, on the other hand, is a skilled and unscrupulous manipulator of public relations and corrupt cops. The implicit question that Chandler's story raises, then—one apparent in its last image, where the singer grasps the finger of the dying Skalla—is whether Vivian Baring will be able to defeat the evils represented by Marineau in the effort to preserve and make use of the authentic energy embodied by her lost lover. Put in more abstract terms, the question is whether the vitality of the ethnic, working-class city can somehow find representation in "A Street in Our Town." That will be the difference, Chandler implies, between a cheap commercial façade and a genuine popular voice. Vivian is not just the star of that show; she is also its writer, and when she grasps Skalla's "huge, limp finger," she makes an obvious attempt to take possession of the masculine energy he represents in order to communicate it to the feminized world that

Chandler perceived in the mainstream mass media. The pathos of the story thus stems only in part from the fact that Vivian and Skalla now belong to worlds so divided by class that "he didn't know her from the Queen of Siam" (181). The more significant counterpart to that fact is the unresolved question of whether their mutual love can bridge that divide so as to form the image of redemptive "public taste."

The most striking feature of "Try the Girl" is the bizarre means that Chandler uses to arrive at a vaguely optimistic answer to this question. It is a device that weirdly literalizes the story's title. In order to protect Vivian from police suspicion and to suggest that she was roughed up by Marineau, Carmady grabs Vivian and beats her until her face is badly bruised. This is far from a merely pragmatic gesture, though. Indeed, Carmady, who was manhandled by Skalla in the story's first scene, and who fell in love with the giant as a result, now serves as a go-between in Skalla's love affair with Vivian. Bragging of his sympathy with Skalla ("if nobody else in the world thinks" Skalla is a "nice guy," Carmady claims that he does), the detective almost literally communicates to Vivian the physical suffering he previously received:

> Her eyes flamed at first and then turned to black stone, I tore her coat off, tore her up plenty, put hard fingers into her arms and neck and used my knuckles on her mouth. I let her go, panting. She reeled away from me, but didn't quite fall. . . . (178)
>
> I hadn't even kissed her. I could have done that, at least. She wouldn't have minded any more than the rest of the knocking about I gave her. (180)

To contemporary readers, this passage may look nearly pornographic.[28] To Chandler, though, the barely concealed rape fantasy implicit in it contained a tacit image of mystic communication and high idealism. When Carmady beats Vivian, Chandler implies, he does so not just to shield her from suspicion, but as a means of communicating to her the disappearing spirit of Steve Skalla — a spirit Carmady is privileged to possess because he was the last person to speak to the ex-con and, as importantly, because he was bruised himself by the giant. That Skalla's finger is limp when Vivian holds it means obviously that she can receive the energy he represents in no other way than through the mediation of the detective. Violent abuse becomes, therefore, his means of conveying Skalla's desire to her — and, much as in the analogous rape scene from *Serenade*, of rescuing Vivian from the debased commercial relations personified by Marineau. As in Cain's novel, sexual assault grants an otherwise unavailable popular legitimacy. Ugly as it is, then, the title "Try the Girl" turns out to be startlingly exact, and more significant than the *cherchez la femme* that is its most obvious meaning. Vivian Baring proves that she is worthy of Skalla's legacy when she undergoes a trial by ordeal, and when she shows (as her name suggests) that she is willing and able to bear the violence with which it must be communicated. The detective proves, meanwhile, that he is capable of preserving and transmitting that vital wealth.

COUNTERPUBLICITY

"Try the Girl" represents, then, an extraordinary translation of Chandler's cultural criticism into narrative terms — an allegory of what the story itself refers to as "counterpublicity" (154). If the masculine popular energy exemplified by pulp fiction were to survive in the world of the mainstream mass media, Chandler's story suggested, it would have to do so by subterfuge and a kind of chiliastic violence. That expectation would become suitably more complex and less optimistic when Chandler moved beyond pulp stories and began to construct full-length novels for clothbound publication, but it remained the key to his critical sensibility through the remainder of his career.

For that reason, "Try the Girl" also provides a clear statement of the particular role that Chandler imagined for his detective protagonist. Unlike Hammett's heroes, the Chandler detective would not work to disenchant the popular delusions that held other characters in thrall. Nor would he, like the hero of the "classic" detective story, gradually piece together the puzzle at the heart of the story. Chandler's distaste for that illusion of ratiocination was notorious and another element in his lack of interest in strong plotting. Rather,

Philip Marlowe and his avatars function in a manner suggested by Chandler's emphasis on the redemptive power of sentiment. Like Carmady in "Try the Girl," who absorbs and passes on Skalla's love and longing, they serve as emotion collectors. Moving through the fragmented landscape of Los Angeles, they absorb the injuries and attitudes of a host of minor characters so that eventually the city can be drawn together into a landscape unified by common feeling. The most obvious emblem of that emotion is physical injury and suffering. Thus, at the conclusion to "Try the Girl," all of the story's virtuous characters—Skalla, Vivian, and Carmady—share the fact that they have undergone some measure of physical torment. But such evident pain is only the most dramatic image of redemptive feeling. The protagonist's job is to elicit such sentiment wherever it is latent so that it can be brought to an otherwise unavailable focus. Think, for example, of Philip Marlowe in *Farewell, My Lovely*, struggling up through the Montecito in order to speak to the gangster-king Laird Brunette on behalf of Moose Malloy, or the analogous scene where Marlowe goes to city hall and presents Malloy's case to the police, or the many similar moments in Chandler's other novels where the detective intercedes with the powerful on behalf of the neglected and ignored. His role in those passages is like that of an unannounced courtier, demanding that attention and respect be paid to ordinary suffering. The detective in this view is the person who salvages the demotic and mundane features of everyday life (those examples of "felt experience" that are analogous to the rich empirical evidence of "scene" and "fact") so that they can be brought to an otherwise suppressed representation.

In these respects, Chandler echoed the appeal to popular community at the core of New Deal decentralism and retooled the detective story to follow suit. If Hammett revised the parables of social contract at the heart of the genre to emphasize the importance of administration, Chandler pushed its conventions in the opposite direction—searching for stronger images of popular community than mere consensual ones and hoping to find them in sentimental affiliation. By contrast to Hammett's fiction, a story like "Try the Girl" thus imagines that "the people"—however narrowly they are represented by Steve Skalla, and however improbable and mystical the process — might be given representation in the mass media and that they might receive the sympathy not only of a Carmady or a Marlowe, but the pity of the police and local elite. In Chandler's fiction, everything turns on that extension of feeling; for it is the emblem of the way a common public can be formed over social division.

Consider, for example, the bare outlines of the novel that Chandler built upon "Try the Girl." In *Farewell, My Lovely*, Philip Marlowe draws the disparate features of Los Angeles into something that looks like a New Deal coalition. His travels take him from a hotel clerk in Watts; to Jesse Florian, an impoverished and alcoholic widow; to Anne Riordan, the spunky daughter of an honest cop; to Red Norgaard, the operator of a boat taxi — a collection that, along with Moose Malloy, links African Americans, the urban poor, the white ethnics of the working class, and honest middle Americans in a community of sympathy. The original version of the story in "Try the Girl" even has the private eye pause to "wonder what it felt to be" a humble bartender, "mixing [drinks] . . . all day and never [getting] to drink one" (175). Like an idealized version of the welfare state, in other words, Marlowe feels the pain of working stiffs and those who have been neglected by an unjust society, thus tying the fragmented landscape of Los Angeles into a more or less coherent narrative of victimization. The only figures excluded from the compassion he elicits are those who prey on this latent image of the people: religious charlatans, gangsters, gigolos, corrupt cops, and the idle rich. In this light, the parodic version of the Statue of Liberty that appears in the novel's opening passage comes to serve a crucial hortatory function, one further underlined by the novel's rendition of the Native American Second Planting — the "primitive man" who has been corrupted by con artists and "the slimy dirt of cities" until he has become a "Hollywood Indian" (85). Just as Marlowe fulfills the purposes to which the decent state should aspire, those tarnished American icons invoke ideals of national character both to reveal their corruption and to demand the redemption of an authentic culture. By the time Moose Malloy is sacrificed in the final scenes of the book, all of these concerns have been focused on him, and he dies bearing not the sins of the people, but their common sufferings and their need for representation.

Chandler's detective works, in short, to emphasize the political virtue of empathy — or, as Chandler might have put it, of "unintellectual thinking." Much as Chandler imagined himself building on the vernacular language of the pulps so as to create a public taste capable of overcoming the constraints of literary tradition, the detective works to expand mundane affiliations and common emotions in order to create a popular coalition that might surpass the limits of corrupt institutions. Nowhere is this effort more apparent than in what may be among the most controversial and misread features of Chandler's fiction — his use of racial stereotypes. In particular, the scenes that open *Farewell, My Lovely* have resulted in some stern denunciations of Chandler. The "dead alien silence of another race" that Marlowe and Moose Malloy encounter when they enter Florian's in search of Velma Valento appears to confirm Chandler's reflex racism (5). That Marlowe bonds with his white brother Malloy against this alien presence and that his feeling for the ex-con becomes deeper after Malloy kills the bar's black owner would seem to seal the point. It is only because of their common membership in the white race, and because of their essential foreignness to the "dinge joint" around them, that Marlowe and Malloy can recognize their mutual interests. By contrast, the black residents of Central Avenue barely seem to exist (4). "Marlowe never sees them in autonomous terms, as people struggling with their own problems," one representative critic notes, "let alone in simple social terms as a class faced with repressive forces of various sorts, economic and ideological." The residents of Chandler's Watts are there only to provide "an emblem of the inscrutability of black society to the white detective."[29]

But, much like the interpretations of Chandler's style that dismiss him for being a snob and an aesthete, such arguments misinterpret exactly the features of Chandler's fiction that they rightly identify as significant. Just as Chandler sought to resist the narrow aestheticism with which his critics would subsequently charge him, the opening of *Farewell, My Lovely* aimed to illuminate and to cut against precisely the racism for which Chandler was later castigated. That concern becomes apparent when Chandler introduces a bigot far more indifferent than Marlowe to the residents of Central Avenue — the exhausted bureaucrat Captain Nulty, who is unmoved by "shine killing" and who can only be inspired by "pix" and "space" in newspapers that care nothing for African Americans (11). By contrast, Marlowe looks positively sympathetic to the black victims of crime.[30] More importantly, he must open himself to such sympathy — and thus ignore his initial reaction to the "alien silence" he first perceives in Florian's — if he is to perform his job successfully. Chandler emphasizes this point in a famous passage by sending Marlowe to gather information from a desk clerk at a Central Avenue hotel. Trading a drink for information, Marlowe engages with the clerk in a scene of Geertzian "thick" interaction: nods, gestures, glances are heavily laden with the subtly expressed content that enables Marlowe to continue his investigation. The implication of this complex conversation is that Marlowe is both more sensitive than the racist police and press and more ethnographically skilled at negotiating an urban terrain to which they are effectively blind. Moreover, the conversation depends on Marlowe's willingness to treat the people of Central Avenue with sympathy and, as the clerk notes, with a modicum of "dignity" (16). That small extension of feeling is what enables him to communicate with the residents of Central Avenue at all, and the contrast between this relative empathy and the callousness of Nulty indicts the L.A. police for being the representative of a state unwilling or unable to extend itself to the care of all of its citizens.

Rather than "alien," then, the residents of Watts become for Marlowe exemplary of a city underserved by its bureaucracy and inadequately represented by its media. Like the micrologue of Central Avenue, the whole of Los Angeles is an arcane and hermetic text, always resistant to interpretation but also open to the patient and sensitive observer.[31] Indeed, the crucial fact the desk clerk brings to Marlowe's attention is that the high price of neon signs means that Florian's had the same name under its previous, white owner. Not only must Marlowe open himself to his interlocutor in order to read the sign correctly, then, but the double movement of interpretation, with its demand for openness and empathy, is portrayed as undermining prejudice and mediating racial difference. The residents of Central Avenue thus assume in Chandler's novel a role that, for Chandler, is relatively analogous to that of Moose Malloy. They are neglected victims whose mute presence demands an interpreter to bring them within the realm of social concern. This representation of

African Americans as silent figures wise with unexpressed suffering brings with it a host of ugly caricatures, and it is, of course, heavily paternalistic in a manner that was typical of many of the portraits of suffering that sought to justify an expanded state during the Depression.[32] But, however unattractive it may be, such paternalism is not racially exclusive. It assumes that the marginal are the most dramatic representatives of otherwise obscure, common experiences. And, although it may well be vulnerable to liberal kitsch and far from immune to shoddy uses, it is an imaginative mode whose political orientation differs sharply from the invocation of "alien" experience with which *Farewell, My Lovely* begins. The point is proven, ironically, by the fact that Chandler shamelessly transfers the novel's compassion away from the citizens of Watts to Moose Malloy. As outsiders, Malloy and the people on Central Avenue look to Marlowe less like antagonists than mutual victims of privation and neglect. Both are ignored or mistreated by the government that should protect them, and their violent conflict thus becomes, as Chandler's first version of the story outrageously puts it, "more or less self-defense on both sides" ("Try the Girl," 179). Marlowe's fleeting interest in the black victims of crime can be altered easily to passionate feeling for their victimizer, therefore, and the people of Watts, having served to raise concern and dramatize neglect, are free to disappear from the novel's focus.

The point, in other words, is not that Chandler's fiction is devoid of racial insensitivity; *Farewell, My Lovely* reeks of prejudice, and it provides an excellent example of the way that a certain variety of paternalistic sympathy can turn quickly to exploitation. In addition, by casting white brotherhood against alien silence, the opening passage of *Farewell, My Lovely* certainly points to the symbolic potency of racial division. When he had Moose Malloy react with confusion and then fury to the "dinge joint" that has replaced his past, Chandler presciently identified the way that racism would flourish in the postwar years as the white-working class city and the New Deal coalition built upon it gave way before black urbanization. Los Angeles was ahead of the curve in this development, as in all other features of postwar life, but in the late thirties, the intense racial battles over the character of the city were still some ways off and in

Chandler's early fiction they remain only a suggestion. As we will see in greater detail, Chandler would prove fully capable in later years of drawing on the virulent language of racial community. But in "Try the Girl" and *Farewell, My Lovely*, those possibilities are yet undeveloped. With the exception of a few moments analogous to their opening passages—*The Big Sleep*'s depiction of Lash Canino, for example, who changes from a man in "a belted brown suede raincoat" to, simply, "the brown man" as he becomes more purely evil (112, 113)—the earlier novels would remain largely unaware of the symbolic power of racial definition, and bigotry would be incidental rather than fundamental to their social vision.

Here, too, Chandler echoes the broad political atmosphere of the New Deal era, which, as historians have noted, placed greater emphasis on matters of class standing and economic reform than on culture and ethnicity and which used such matters to emphasize the potential sympathy between the middle class and the disadvantaged.[33] To depict a city divided by class, by bigotry, and by corrupt institutions in this vein was less to celebrate social antagonism than to complain against the abuse of public spirit and to use it to invoke broader forms of political association. It was only when that political environment shifted in the late forties and early fifties that Chandler would rediscover the possibilities he had left undeveloped on Central Avenue and return for an organizing social vision to an idealized image of racial community.

WORKING-CLASS BODIES AND UPPER-CLASS CONTAINERS

The most striking change in "Try the Girl" as it became *Farewell, My Lovely* was the way that, in turning his heroine into a femme fatale, Chandler sharply lessened the populist optimism of his earlier work. Where in the earlier story Vivian Baring cements the bonds among honest men and carries the spirit of the white ethnic to the nation, *Farewell, My Lovely* depicts noble male affiliation falling prey to a ruthless woman, and it suggests that Moose Malloy's memory will survive only in the reveries of Philip Marlowe. That would be the story that Chandler would tell for the remainder of his career, and the pride of place it gave to the faithless woman would always be the central structuring principle of his novels. Even when he turned in the later 1940s from the class-oriented populism of the New Deal to a racialized idea of national consciousness, Chandler's virulent antifeminism would remain consistent. It is important to recognize, though, that his first novels developed that misogynist parable mainly in the economistic terms that the Depression placed at the center of political focus. Velma Valento/Helen Grayle, for instance, is a femme fatale very much in the grain of Brigid O'Shaughnessy/Miss Leblanc or Cora Papadakis/Chambers. All are women for whom the shedding of ethnic associations signals a dangerous class mobility. Indeed, Velma/Helen's assumed name points to the novel's primary concerns; she is a woman who allows herself to be spirited from one camp to another and who is therefore saddled with the responsibility for destroying both. What happens to her is exemplary of the conviction prominent in the late thirties that the rich prey on the common good and seek to wall off natural resources, as Marlowe complains, in "containers just for the upper classes" (72). As in the long tradition of antimonopolist rhetoric from which the thinking stems, she serves as a figure for the unseemly way in which decrepit financiers like the ancient Judge Grayle can rely on wealth to replenish their dwindling vitality.

Like the novel's relative indifference to race, that image of Velma as what Marlowe calls "frozen capital" chimed significantly with the public rhetoric of the late thirties (139). During the final years of the decade, especially, as the Depression continued beyond the reformist programs of the first and second New Deals, a widely shared economic theory arose to explain the persistence of low growth and mass unemployment. According to this description of "economic maturity" or "secular stagnation," the era of American investment had drawn to a close with the completion of the nation's industrial development. "Our industrial plant is built," FDR declared, echoing this argument. "Our last frontier has long since been reached." With that end to the "age of capital investment," economists explained, there would be fewer rewards to distribute, and thus as some adherents argued, more need for both public investment and an active system of social welfare. According to this chastened vision of what Jim Thompson later called an "economy . . . of scarcity," a powerful national state would be necessary precisely because the private sector could no longer be relied on to generate the investment needed to return the economy to even those levels it had achieved in the twenties. Likewise, since economic expansion could no longer guarantee "equality of opportunity," the federal government would need to protect the weak from the strong—monopolists, financiers, and "economic royalists," who were decadent in this view not simply because they limited competition and accrued undue power, but because they unjustly appropriated scarce resources. The work of the New Deal, FDR explained, would require not "producing more goods," but "administering resources . . . already in hand."[34]

The sensibility that contributed to such remarks can be seen operating all through Chandler's early novels. Nearly everything about them reflects an ethical contrast between the small and honest, on the one hand, and the large and corrupt, on the other—between a righteous sense of limits and the irresponsible habits of waste. The "fiscal system" in Chandler's early fiction is closed and limited; the world is "small, shut in, black"; the promise of beauty a matter of "false hopes." The evil of the decadent is equivalent to the fact that in their world "anything could happen except work," and the virtue of the poor and forgotten is that they recognize the democracy in poverty and powerlessness. "What did it matter where you lay once you were dead," Marlowe asks at the end of The Big Sleep. "In a dirty sump or in a marble tower on top of a high hill?" (The Big Sleep 76, 121, 116, 139; Farewell, My Lovely 30, 72). The "secular stagnation" that New Deal theorists perceived throughout the American economy appears in these novels in the image of diseased and dying kings like Judge Grayle or General Sternwood of The Big Sleep, just as it does in the exhausted oil well where Rusty Regan is buried in that first novel.

Even the tone and narrative structure of Chandler's early work reflects the continuing influence of those Depression era styles of thought that would have to be discarded before the focus on race became useful. Spare and reworked from pulp stories as those texts are, they correspond fittingly with Chandler's literary investment in the minor and the general air of privation that pervades Marlowe's prewar life. Indeed, their very mode of construction echoes the theory of "economic maturity" that New Deal policy makers used to legitimize a redistributive state. "Cannibalized" from the literary capital that Chandler built up in his years of writing for the pulps, his novels draw on an inherently limited fund of wealth. "I won't discard anything," Chandler claimed in order to justify the way he pirated his *Black Mask* stories to fashion the oddly shaped novels. And that literary commitment to salvage assumed, as did FDR when he spoke of managing resources already in hand, that the building of productive capacities was part of the past. The responsibility of the present was to preserve and manage precious resources — a demand that appears in the novels in the urge to memorialize the wealth of "scene" and "experience" that seems always on the verge of disappearing.[35]

The moral importance of scarcity and its intimate connection to Chandler's obsession with parasitism is clearer still in Chandler's first novel, *The Big Sleep*. From its initial publication, Chandler's debut novel was touted as a startling portrait of Los Angeles in the late 1930s. But few of Chandler's critics have seen much in the way of a cogent structure or underlying symbolic order to the novel. Like the city it depicts, *The Big Sleep* has always appeared a labyrinthine and immensely tangled text, and even Chandler recognized that it lacked the mythically resonant story at the heart of *Farewell, My Lovely*. At its core, however, *The Big Sleep* contains a narrative as definite as that in Chandler's second book and one that relies on similar moral terms. Like *Farewell, My Lovely*, *The Big Sleep* is an allegory of economic predation in which the vernacular energy of the white ethnic falls prey to the economic elite. "To hell with the rich. They made me sick," Marlowe notes at one point, and Chandler's novel suggests that the image is literally intended.[36] At its heart, *The Big Sleep* is a gothic tale of the way that the wealthy survive by leeching the vitality of the forthright and honest.

   The representative of that popular energy in this novel is, of course, Rusty Regan — the "earthy," "vulgar," and "very real" ex-bootlegger who has married the aristocratic Vivian Sternwood and whose disappearance from the Sternwood mansion provides the excuse for Philip Marlowe's investigations (12). Although we learn in the novel's climax that Regan was murdered by Vivian's degenerate younger sister,

Carmen, and that he is buried in an abandoned oil sump, for most of the novel all of the characters assume that Regan has run off with Mona Mars, the wife of the gangster Eddie Mars. Thus, at one point, Captain Gregory of missing persons predicts Mars and Regan's return, and in doing so he points to the novel's central metaphor: "They're in a strange town and they've got new names, but they've got the same old appetites. They got to get back in the fiscal system" (76). Those are the basic terms of Chandler's novel: the contrast between the "earthy and vulgar" matter of bodily appetites and an immaterial "fiscal system." Much like the conflict between the mass media and the urban, ethnic working-class in "Try the Girl" or the analogous tension between the spontaneous "vernacular" and the formalized "literary" register of Chandler's aesthetic theory, it is a comparison that pits bodily energy against a parasitic, abstract economy. Indeed, in a kind of pseudo-Marxism, Chandler paints capital as a vampiric force driven to steal the labor power of honest workingmen.

Every aspect of Chandler's novel refers back to that central image. At the heart of its "fiscal system," for instance, lies the Sternwood riches — wealth that, taken from now drying oil wells, depends on a nearly exhausted source of primitive accumulation. Like those wells, too, the novel's patriarch, General Sternwood, is the almost lifeless "survival of a rather gaudy life" — a man whose "thin bloodless hands" signify the skeletal remains of nearly depleted natural resources (6, 7). Implicit in both sets of images is a vision of economic production as sheer natural exploitation; the Sternwood wealth depends on the ability to extract vitality from inherently limited natural resources. And the remainder of Chandler's novel follows in this vein. From Arthur Geiger's pornography ring to Eddie Mars's gambling clubs, the Los Angeles of *The Big Sleep* does not have an economy so much as a closed system of blackmail in which characters flourish, as Vivian Sternwood says of Mars, by "bleed[ing]" other people "white" (138). That Mars allows Vivian to win at his gambling tables and then steals her money back again makes the point in brief. There is an inherently limited stock of money to go around in *The Big Sleep*, and all of the characters compete to get a piece of it.

Thus, in Chandler's world, wealth stems less from production than from predation, and in keeping with that presumption the novel multiplies outrageous stories of vampirism. The most obvious image of such parasitism occurs in the central example of Carmen Sternwood, who (again in a literalized metaphor) turns the men she encounters into "saps," draining them so thoroughly of vitality that, with the exception of Marlowe, each becomes a corpse (88). Carmen is literally a "predatory" figure; her "small sharp teeth" are equipped for vampiric purposes, and when she has dispensed with Rusty Regan, he is a depleted natural resource — a "horrible decayed thing" fittingly abandoned in one of the Sternwoods' exhausted oil wells (138). When, by contrast, Carmen is denied the chance to satisfy her appetites — as when Marlowe resists her offers — the reason for her violence becomes clear. She grows "aged, deteriorated" so that she begins to sound like a creature resembling her father (4, 93, 133). Without male vitality to suck dry, in other words, Carmen herself begins to decay and to approach the condition of the family wells.

Carmen is a classic and ludicrously exaggerated example of the female vampire, but, though more subtly, Chandler suggests similar qualities in her sister and her father. Like Carmen, Vivian Sternwood shares the attributes of the vampiric woman. Her face is "taut, pale"; her "dark parted hair was part of the darkness of the night"; her lips are "red and harsh." She "click[s] her teeth" ominously when she is annoyed; slowly tears a handkerchief to pieces with her teeth when she is angry, and threatens to cut Marlowe's throat, "just to see what ran out of it" (87, 89, 93). Like Carmen, too, she leeches men of vitality. Once dead, "Rusty didn't mean anything" to her, she admits, and another suitor is glimpsed tellingly passed out in his car (138). In a key image that runs all through Chandler's novel, Vivian's room, like her pale face, is startlingly composed only in shades of white, so that it "looks bled out" (11). As with Carmen's face of "scraped bone" and her father's "bloodless hands," the colorlessness of Vivian's face and surroundings — in a famed image, "as artificial as a wooden leg" — emphasize her vampiric associations (95).

Neither of these women "has any more moral sense than a cat," General Sternwood says of his daughters. But the striking aspect of Chandler's novel is the way he extends these classic features of the femme fatale to the General himself. "Neither have I," Sternwood acknowledges, and the admission makes it clear just how thoroughly the General, like his daughters, is a figure in the tradition of the succubus (9). The General admits as much when he says of Rusty in the beginning of the novel that Regan "was the breath of life to me — while he lasted" (7). Like his daughters, in short, General Sternwood, who "look[s] a lot more like a dead man than most dead men look," treats Regan as he does his oil wells — a natural source of wealth that can replenish his own dwindling resources until it is itself exhausted (130). Thus, despite the fact that on its surface the novel looks like a story of male loyalty in which Marlowe proves his allegiance to the dying general in the face of the temptations of the Sternwood daughters, there is a subtle antagonism running between the detective and his client all through the novel. The reason for that undercurrent of hostility, Chandler implies, runs deeper than personal feeling to reflect the brute facts of economic exploitation. However much Marlowe may prefer the General to his daughters, the logic of Chandler's plot ultimately casts the old man as a feminized sexual predator (a "sentimental old goat") analogous to the vampiric women who surround him. Trapped in the bower of his orchids, the General resembles the predatory female beasts of turn-of-the-century fantasy. He needs to lure guileless young men like Regan and Marlowe to join him in corruption. The plants in the General's hothouse have famously "the flesh of men" and the "rotten sweetness of a prostitute," and they thus put in botanical terms exactly what the General wants from Regan — to buy his young flesh (7). Marlowe makes the point more clearly later when he asks the Sternwoods' butler: "What did this Regan fellow have that bored into [the General] so?" The butler replies, "Youth . . . and the soldier's eye." Like his daughters — and not incidentally like Vivian Baring — General Sternwood yearns in virtually erotic terms to receive the violent masculine energy of an authentic lower order. It may not be a coincidence, then, that in their final conversation Marlowe leaves the General much as he does Carmen when she propositions him: "lax on the bed, his eyes closed and dark-lidded, his mouth tight and bloodless" (130). As the Sternwood's butler points out, Marlowe has the same "soldier's eye" as Regan did, and much like Carmen, the General recognizes the same vitality in the detective that he once saw in the bootlegger. Thus, when Marlowe refuses the General's commands and, more importantly, his money, Chandler's protagonist acts as he did with Carmen. In implicit contrast to Regan, he refuses to trade his body for money.

Like *Farewell, My Lovely*, then, *The Big Sleep* creates a myth of economic predation well-suited to the antimonopolistic rhetoric of the late thirties. The only way to avoid the vampirism that kills Regan, Chandler suggests, is to live the life of Marlowe, struggling as far as is humanly possible to stay out of the clutches of the "fiscal system." The pathos of Chandler's novel depends in this light on the fact that it is a survivor's tale. Having escaped the parasitic Sternwoods, Marlowe can only look back with sorrow and longing on the fraternal figure who failed to resist so assiduously and who paid for his weakness with his life. Rusty Regan is in this sense a direct analog to Moose Malloy. Each is an example of the mythic figure that FDR famously identified as the "forgotten man" — the populist emblem of the ordinary worker exploited by a "highly centralized economic system."[37] "Try the Girl" had suggested that by means of heroic commitment and mystic violence the spirit of that figure could be rescued and communicated to a national culture badly in need of its virtues. In *The Big Sleep* and in *Farewell, My Lovely*, that hope has largely disappeared. The task of the detective is merely to struggle to remember the decent and rapidly disappearing men everyone else is determined to exploit and forget.

In his next two novels, *The High Window* and *The Lady in the Lake*, Chandler would continue to work such themes, sometimes in far less interesting or subtle ways than in *The Big Sleep*. But, although Chandler had published four novels in the years between 1939 and 1944, over the next five years he would produce little apart from essays and critical screeds directed against Hollywood and contemporary mass culture. By 1949 when he finally released his fifth novel, American society had been substantially altered by postwar expansion. The New Deal rhetoric that had formed such an important part of the background of Chandler's early novels had long been displaced by wartime boosterism, the return to prominence of the conservative right, and the lowered expectations of Harry Truman's

Fair Deal. In keeping with these developments, Chandler's fiction would change dramatically as well. Although it retained some of its most familiar attributes — including, of course, the central presence of Philip Marlowe — the world Chandler's fiction addressed and the manner in which it conceived and criticized that society differed remarkably from what had come before.[38]

2.

CULTURAL ALCHEMY
Chandler's Later Career

The depth at which Chandler's literary convictions mattered to his novelistic vision can be seen most clearly in what may have been his most devastating piece of literary criticism — a portrait of a successful popular writer, Roger Wade, that Chandler created for his most traditionally novelistic book, *The Long Goodbye*. "All writers are punks and I am one of the punkest," Wade tells Philip Marlowe, and the novel bears his estimation out by making Wade responsible for twelve "sex-and-swordplay historical novels" that "sell brutally" despite, or because of, the fact that they are "all lies." A "mercenary hack" by his wife's description and his own estimation, Wade embodies everything Chandler disliked about middlebrow mass culture (250, 93, 306). He vends a false image of gentility to a public whose yearning for distinction only confirms and hastens the mutual debasement of author and audience, and Chandler makes him pay for those sins by depicting Wade as a bitterly unhappy man who falls into pathetic vulnerability at the feet of his wife and his houseboy. It seems plausible, in this light, to take Roger Wade for a version of what Chandler feared might become of his own writing were he to surrender his critical beliefs and give way to the temptations of mainstream success. That association becomes still more forceful in a remarkable passage of "stream-of-consciousness" raving that Chandler quotes from Wade's private writing:

The moon's four days off the full and there's a square patch of moonlight on the wall and it's looking at me like a big blind milky eye, a wall

eye. Joke. Goddam silly simile. Writers. Everything has to be like something else. My head is as fluffy as whipped cream but not as sweet. More
similes. I could just vomit thinking about the lousy racket. I could vomit
anyway. I probably will. Don't push me. Give me time. The worms in
my solar plexus crawl and crawl and crawl. I would be better off in bed
but there would be a dark animal underneath the bed and the dark
animal would crawl around rustling and hump himself and bump the
underside of the bed, then I would let out a yell that wouldn't make any
sound except to me (203).

Wade's rant continues on for several pages, a clever parody of
Chandler's own penchant for silly similes that also includes the main
clues to the novel's mystery. More importantly, the passage also far-
cically re-creates the tragic theory of culture that Chandler laid out
in his essays and letters. Wade's ravings are the private side to the
false public created by his popular success, and the particular way
that Chandler characterizes these texts expands brilliantly on his
indictment of "literary life" and mass culture. Rendering the popular
novelist's diaries as "stream-of-consciousness" expressionism makes
modernist experiment merely the private side of middlebrow fiction — the "miasma of failure" that mirrors "the cheap gaudiness of
popular success."[39] In this light, modernism — whose full canoniza-
tion as the party line of American intellectual life coincided with
Chandler's career — becomes the anticommercial façade of a literary
culture dominated by the market. Stream-of-consciousness narrative
becomes the kind of writing one does when one is bragging disin-
genuously about not taking any money for one's work.

For Chandler that dialectic indicated a tragic impoverishment of
contemporary culture. In hopeful moments, as in "The Simple Art of
Murder" and "Try the Girl," he sketched a utopian vision of its
transcendence. Such a prospect was rooted, though, in the cultural
politics of the New Deal era, and in the later years of Chandler's career it fell upon hard times. The portrait of Roger Wade from 1953's
The Long Goodbye reflects its decline, envisioning a segmented cultural marketplace in which a sterile literary sophistication survives
only as the effete dependent of a voracious consumer society.

The two impressive novels that Chandler wrote toward the end of his career, *The Little Sister* and *The Long Goodbye*, develop that critical vision in extreme detail. With wistful regret and paranoid comprehensiveness, they record the broad cultural transformation of American society described by contemporary intellectuals, somewhat overconfidently, as the evolution from a "class" to a "mass" society.[40] For Chandler as for many of his peers, the surprising economic growth of the postwar years and the changes it wrought — the end of chronic mass unemployment, the apparently unstoppable expansion of a new suburban middle class, the now indisputable authority of mass entertainment and mass consumerism — all seemed marks of a dramatic alteration of American society. Nearly overnight, the United States had come to seem to Chandler less a society riven by hierarchical class antagonism than one built on a shallow, comfort-driven, and market-oriented consensus ("a democracy of cupidity" rather than "a democracy of fraternity," as Richard Hofstadter put it harshly at the time). That transition might be described in the light of what James M. Cain called in 1947 the "terrifying concept" of "the wish that comes true."[41] For, if Chandler's early novels bridled at economic injustice, inadequate government, and cultural division, postwar California seemed to offer a booming economy, an expansive state apparatus, and, most importantly, the vision of a culture unified by the mass consumer market.[42]

One place that transformation seemed particularly evident was in the decline of the pulp industry — the "rough school" where Chandler earned his credibility, whose "honest and forthright" qualities he hoped would counter the evils of mass-market banality, but which was now experiencing a slow but irreversible decline. During the war, inflation and government-ordered paper restrictions delivered a crippling blow to the pulps' narrow profit margins. At the same time, those restrictions had almost no effect on the pulps' competitors in the mass market magazines and in the rapidly developing paperback industry. Because they used different paper stocks than the pulps, were far more deeply capitalized, and had more efficient systems of distribution and more stable sources of profit, the "big slick" magazines and paperback books were able to exploit a rapidly growing market during and after the war. Pulp publishing, by contrast, shrank progressively. As Fletcher Pratt foresaw as early as 1939 —

the year, coincidentally, in which Chandler released his first novel and Pocket Books began publishing mass-market paperbacks in the United States — the pulp industry was doomed to extinction, and its paradigmatic laborer, "the million-word-a-year-man," was fated to join "the growing list of vanishing Americans."[43]

Thus, the cultural antagonism that had been key to Chandler's critical sensibilities seemed in the late forties and early fifties to be quickly evaporating. Mass-market magazines and the growing paperback industry lacked the sharp sense of hierarchy and segregation that had underwritten the pulp ideology. Several of the paperback firms that flourished after the war sprang from pulp publishing, and along with their competitors in the industry, they quickly absorbed pulp writers and genres and transformed them to suit the new regime. The transition between the era of the pulps and that of the paperbacks, however, was but one aspect of changes that occurred throughout the American economy during and after World War II as a booming consumer economy altered many of the central assumptions of the late thirties and early forties. It was in this period that Keynesian economics and interest-group pluralism displaced the New Deal's vision of the regulatory state and that the moral investment in the "forgotten man" gave way before faith in a "relegitimize[d] capitalism."[44] Most important for hard-boiled crime fiction was the changing social significance of labor and class. The success of industrial unionism and the postwar détente between organized labor and big business, along with postwar affluence generally, seemed in the late forties and fifties to signal the fulfillment of "the great middle class" predicted by Carroll John Daly in 1924. As Ira Katznelson explains, it now appeared that "an American society based on class division had been supplanted by an interest-group society of voluntary associations," in which labor would no longer function symbolically or in fact as "political opposition" but as one interest group among others. Like the pulp writer, the laborer could be said in one sense to have "become American" and also to be, for that very reason, a "vanishing American." The working-class "reading public" that Fletcher Pratt claimed for the pulps appeared to have been integrated, as Katznelson says, by "the language of partnership, negotiation, and the law" into a society of abundance, but to have been stripped by the same process of a specific class identity.[45]

Much as *The Big Sleep* built its baroque narrative vision atop the Depression era belief in an economy of scarcity, Chandler's late novels constructed an entire mythology around a critical response to the "democracy of cupidity" of postwar mass society. The result was a thorough reorientation of Chandler's aesthetic and political presuppositions. The atmosphere of privation and limits that shaped his narrative methods and his sympathy for Moose Malloy in *Farewell, My Lovely* or Rusty Regan in *The Big Sleep* has disappeared from the later novels. The plutocrats who rule over their fictional worlds, for instance—Jules Oppenheimer, the movie tycoon of *The Little Sister*, and Harlan Potter, *The Long Goodbye*'s newspaper baron— are not fading patriarchs as were Judge Grayle and General Sternwood, but the vibrant totems of a consumerist society and an emerging information age. Their riches and power, like the economic abundance of the postwar era, appear to expand indefinitely, precisely because, as Marlowe complains, wealth no longer has the industrial base associated with the Sternwood money—"some individual bony structure under the muck."[46]

Along with that bony structure, the late fiction has dispensed with the political vocabulary that energized the earlier novels. Unlike the social geography of *Farewell, My Lovely* and *The Big Sleep*, which tended to divide rather sharply between scenes of exorbitant wealth and grim decline, the landscape of the later novels is dominated by a distressing middle ground. *The Long Goodbye*, for example, makes heavy weather out of the Carne Organization, a corporate detective agency that crosses the Pinkertons with *The Man in the Gray Flannel Suit* and that promises to squeeze small-time operators like Marlowe out of business. But the novel also offers the analogous example of Doctor Verringer, a quack who administers an "art colony" in the desert and who is overrun by suburban development. And there is the still more telling example of the book's primary setting, the "subdivider's dream" of Idle Valley. "Paradise Incorporated, and also Highly Restricted," the development has displaced the illegal casino that operated in that location in *The High Window*, establishing a sham aristocracy where there was once an outpost of the hard-boiled demimonde (116, 248). Between this false privacy of suburbia and the false public of Harlan Potter's mass culture moves Philip Marlowe, but even he shows signs of the deterioration that embitters Chandler. He has traded the kitchenette apartment and Murphy bed that in earlier novels signified urban transience for a furnished house "on a dead-end street" in Laurel Canyon (6). The transition, as with Verringer's colony and Idle Valley's casino, signals the decline of those counterpublic realms that had been vital to hard-boiled crime fiction. "Avenues of escape are closed," as Hannah Arendt worried at the time, "because society has incorporated all strata of the population."[47]

Such an incorporated geography presents obvious difficulties to a writer like Chandler. For it suggests that social ills can no longer be traced to scarcity and class conflict. The sour-grapes wisdom that concludes *The Big Sleep* — that all people are equal in death — becomes unconvincing when the rich no longer seem like parasitic exceptions to common experience but merely prominent examples of universal abundance. Likewise, as *The Little Sister*'s jaundiced account of Manhattan, Kansas, makes clear, the honest folk of the Midwest can no longer serve, as they did in *The High Window*, for a moral contrast to the idle rich and the corrupt city. An inflationary economy has robbed the early novels' class-oriented populism of force by making class itself seem immaterial, and an omnipresent mass media similarly undermines the divide between country and city, leaving the "homely" image of rural folk itself an "unreal" product of mass fantasy. Hollywood, Marlowe complains: "will make a radiant glamour queen out of a drab little wench who ought to be ironing a truck driver's shirts, a he-man hero with shining eyes and brilliant smile reeking of sexual charm out of some overgrown kid who was meant to go to work with a lunchbox, . . . [and] might even take a small-town prig . . . and make an ice-pick murderer out of him . . . , elevating his simple meanness into the classic sadism of the multiple killer" (*Little Sister* 237, 158).

The problem with postwar mass culture, in short, is not merely that the media is manipulative or that it distorts popular will, but that it artificially inflates values so that the vital class friction at the center of *The Big Sleep* or *Farewell, My Lovely* dissipates into a general absence of distinction. In Marlowe's philippics that tendency is itself ludicrously expanded until it seems not just tacky but — as in the above rendition of Orrin Quest — murderous. Long sermons are delivered in *The Little Sister* and *The Long Goodbye* about movies, radio, and newspapers, about cheap food, tacky housing, flashy cars, and empty homes, all of which serve to make the California landscape seem not merely ugly or even corrupt but malevolent. And those very meditations, themselves abundant and ripely developed in the postwar novels, dramatize the transition to the late Chandler from his earlier work. No longer tied like the early texts to the paltry capital, the "bony structure," that Chandler had developed in the pulp industry, books like *The Little Sister* and *The Long Goodbye* mimic the inflationary economy they denounce, expanding to double the average length of the early novels and gaining a density of texture far out of keeping with the limited range of *The Big Sleep* or *Farewell, My Lovely*. Indeed, liberated from the self-conscious awkwardness of the early novels and the aesthetic and economic principles with which their methods were associated, Chandler's writing threatens to fulfill a critical evaluation he always distrusted — that he had elevated detective fiction toward "serious" literature — and approaches perilously near to that middlebrow fiction of earnest importance and "decent expression" he detested. "Too literary," along with its variations, is an insult repeated several times in this period, and it refers to a gaffe as egregious as the brash nouveau riche mansions that Marlowe detests (*Long Goodbye* 247, 368). Both are forms of overreaching.

The problem thus implicitly raised for Chandler as author matches the one he projects onto the landscape of Los Angeles: how to reconcile vast new wealth and the sense that class and cultural hierarchy are no longer binding with moral and aesthetic theories premised on schism and limitation. The resulting dilemma becomes the subject of *The Long Goodbye*, Chandler's last successful book, his most accomplished work by traditional novelistic standards, and by far the most mournful and sentimental of all his stories. Far more than *Farewell, My Lovely* even, it reads like a paean to the end of male fellowship and a memorial to the passing of Chandler's literary ambitions.

At the center of the novel is once again Marlowe's intimate relationship with an idealized brother figure — this time Terry Lennox, a
genteel and charismatic drunk Marlowe stumbles upon in L.A. and
feels unaccountably driven to help. Rather than a bounder from the
lower orders like Moose Malloy or Rusty Regan, though, Lennox is
an example of what *The Little Sister* called "prewar stock" — a figure of such unusual grace and nobility that, although American, he
seems to Marlowe almost English in contrast to the shallow landscape that surrounds him (158). When Marlowe first encounters
him, Lennox is kept in a marriage of convenience by Sylvia Potter,
the vulgar and trampy daughter of the newspaper baron. But Sylvia
is brutally murdered shortly thereafter, and Lennox naturally becomes the main suspect in his wife's death. When Lennox comes to
Marlowe for assistance, the detective reflexively springs to the rescue
and helps his brother escape to a new identity in Mexico (a first
intimation of the way Chandler's novel will describe moral decline as
a kind of corruption in national and, implicitly, racial identity). For
this act, Marlowe is briefly but cruelly imprisoned by the Los Angeles police. He "k[eeps] faith" with Lennox, though, refusing to
submit his friendship to the inspection of police or press and suffering vilification as a result.

In what seems at first to be an unrelated subplot, the novel then
turns to the story of Eileen Wade, an Idle Valley neighbor of the
Lennoxes and a woman of remarkable beauty, who hires Marlowe
to care for her husband. Roger Wade is a successful pop novelist, but
also a terrible drunk, tortured by guilt and driven to self-destruction,
and Eileen hopes that Marlowe can protect her as well as her husband from his drunken rages. It is a mission Marlowe seems to fail
when Wade soon dies, an apparent gunshot suicide. But in the novel's climactic scenes, Marlowe reveals that Wade has been murdered,
and he ties the two plots together. Eileen Wade, the detective explains, is the novel's femme fatale and the root of its evil. She was
Lennox's lover and wife in wartime London, when he served in the
British army under the name Paul Marston (the initials indicating his
twinship with Chandler's protagonist). But she believed her husband
killed in battle, and she returned to the United States to a second
marriage with Wade. When she comes across her first love in post-

war L.A., then, she is shocked to see him alive, but she is even more disturbed to find him a shadow of his former self, "a friend of gamblers, the husband of a rich whore" (329). The strain between her memory of an ideal past and the reality of a corrupt present soon drives her to homicidal rage, and she first murders Sylvia, managing to implicate both Lennox and Wade in the crime, and then kills Wade in a way that throws suspicion on Marlowe. After she is confronted with her crimes, Eileen committs suicide, bringing the novel's cycle of destruction to a finish.

In its broad outlines, then, Chandler's novel is a story of decline and fall achieving a sense of destruction and a body count approaching that of Renaissance tragedy—a quality Chandler underscores with characteristic allusions to Shakespeare and Christopher Marlowe. The ideal beauty that the detective first perceives in the paired figures of Lennox and Eileen turns out to be a hollow remnant in the first case and a murderous sham in the second. Their once aristocratic love (much as in the transition at the heart of *The Postman Always Rings Twice*) is replaced by their banal and predatory second marriages. More importantly, the vision of fellowship with which the novel begins turns out in retrospect to be a prefatory narrative contrasted to the bulk of the book's action. Here the intimate bonds between Marlowe and Lennox are replaced by the awkward alliance between the detective and Wade, a professional relationship that comes to stand for a host of market-driven or bureaucratic connections. Brotherhood is replaced by impersonal relations—between cops and citizens, doctors and patients, drug dealers and addicts, householders and domestic servants, racketeers and gamblers—whose weak affective force seems depraved in contrast to the initial vision of ideal fellowship. "This is just a job to me," Marlowe tells Wade, contrasting his professional service to one man with his personal fealty to another. And the situation makes both Marlowe and Wade feel like "bastard[s]" (148, 150). Lacking brotherhood, they also lack the legitimacy that made Marlowe's earlier friendship seem unselfish and redeeming.

In one sense, then, Marlowe's brotherhood with Lennox re-creates his earlier relationship with Moose Malloy. The ideal brother in both cases is a remnant from a heroic age whose last echoes are rapidly fading. And in both novels, Chandler thus seizes on a figure who might indict the ordinary order of Los Angeles by confronting it with an image of class opposition. Malloy and Lennox are each striking, and nearly solitary in the fictional universe of their novels, for not being bourgeois. The white working-class world at the moral heart of *Farewell, My Lovely* having seemed to vanish in the postwar era, Chandler no longer looks to forgotten men and working stiffs when he is seeking an honest alternative to his corrupt society. Fading aristocrats, however, can be summoned readily to serve a similar purpose.

In another sense, though, the change in the status between Moose Malloy and Terry Lennox indicates some fundamental alterations in Chandler's thinking, a transition that can be seen most clearly in the central motif of a $5,000 bill that Lennox sends to Marlowe from Mexico. Encapsulated in this bill are all the dilemmas about which the novel worries. On the one hand, it is a mark of Lennox's central qualities — his "manners," "breeding," and generosity. On the other, its extraordinary denomination sums up Lennox's own decadent wealth and the dangerous abundance of the postwar world. Regarded as payment, moreover, the bill threatens to turn Lennox and Marlowe into client and professional — little more than a minor version of the mass-marketed services offered by the Carne Organization. Worse still, it might attach the taint of bribery to Lennox's generosity. Either way, though, it promises to disenchant the crucial bonds between Marlowe and Lennox, fulfilling what Dwight Macdonald referred to at this time as the "Gresham's Law in cultural . . . circulation" — a kind of "cultural alchemy" that turned everything into "the same soft currency."[48]

Marlowe negates such dismal possibilities, however, and transforms the bill into a mark of fellowship with a simple gesture. He refuses to exchange it, instead keeping the bill locked in his safe and removing it occasionally only for sentimental purposes. Instead of its monetary value, then, he emphasizes the bill's rarity — "only about a thousand in circulation" — and refers to it consistently as a "portrait of Madison" (85). The description is orphic as far as the novel's other characters are concerned, but that obscurity just serves Marlowe's purposes. Money, as *The Postman Always Rings Twice* and the stories of Hammett and Daly emphasized, makes intimate relations public and indistinct. But no one aside from Marlowe knows what a "portrait of Madison" means, and no one else can approximate or understand his bond with Lennox. Redeeming money by turning it into art, Marlowe simultaneously stumbles onto a tenet of the Klannish thinking that Hammett and Daly worked so diligently to undermine thirty years before: idealized brotherhood resists the disintegrative force of the market. The only way to ensure that Lennox survives as an aristocratic ideal—that he maintains, as the Klan sought to do in a different manner, the force of breeding against a nondescript democracy—is to be certain that his money is no good. If, by the terms of Dwight Macdonald's version of Gresham's Law, bad money drives out good culture, here the commitment to good culture is imagined to invert the process.

Fittingly, then, Marlowe's reaction to Lennox's bill not only departs from the attitudes of his hard-boiled predecessors; it reverses the implications of Chandler's own early fiction. In *Farewell, My Lovely*, "frozen capital" was a sign of the parasitic vices of the rich, and its ability to win them a "special brand of sunshine . . . just for the upper classes" was a mark of unjust wealth (72). In *The Long Goodbye*, Marlowe freezes his own capital, and he discovers accordingly that it "had a nice glow around it. It created a little sunshine all its own" (85). The reversal points to a shift in Chandler's perception of the balance between the popular and the private. In the early novels, Marlowe typically regarded private wealth as an incursion on public rights, and he stood implicitly for an emerging popular coalition against its abuses. If he defended his "small, private notions" against the police, it was so he could use them on behalf of vulnerable figures like Moose Malloy or Merle Davis. In the later novels, though, "the people" cannot be conceived in the manner that the pulp magazines and Depression politics encouraged. No longer a latent force for reform, they have become a "damn fool public," and the "little guy" is less a sympathetic victim of organized interests than the hopeless prey of his own desires (*Long Goodbye* 243, 351).[49] The point for Marlowe is no longer to stand with the people against the powerful, but to find every way possible to resist mass ignorance. "All a man named Marlowe wanted from it was out" (220). Private sunshine accordingly begins to look less like a vice than the last virtue.

Along with this disenchanted sense of the people comes, therefore, a suitable shift in attitude toward the police and the state for which they stand. In the early novels, because they represented frustration with a sclerotic government, cops were at worst inadequate or corrupt. At best, an effective individual or two — a Captain Gregory or Lieutenant Breeze — might work alongside the detective. In the later novels, though, Chandler is no longer concerned with inefficient or inadequate institutions. Like many of his contemporaries, he is fascinated by what seem like echoes and portents of the newly conceived problem of totalitarianism. Thus, Marlowe is not just harassed or ignored by the cops. He is brutally questioned and imprisoned by police who are not so much corrupt as unremittingly hostile to the detective's claims to private enterprise and individual freedom. Marlowe himself, therefore, is no longer the vanguard of a renascent state. Instead, he struggles desperately to preserve the "private citizen" against what seems like an omnivorous drive toward incorporation — a movement pressed by an imperial public, an omnipresent media, and an invasive government (352).

Harlan Potter, with his chain of newspapers and his publicity machine, and the police, with their brutal procedures, represent the last two of these dangers, and each of them seeks to make life hell for Philip Marlowe. But it is the first — the indistinct mass public — that is the most threatening of all Chandler's problems and that is therefore fittingly represented by his most consistent sign of evil, the femme fatale. No longer emblems of the parasitism that leeched working-class vitality in Chandler's earlier work, lethal women like Sylvia Lennox and, more significantly, Eileen Wade now embody the feminization of the public that Chandler feared from mass culture. Seeking to feed off Terry Lennox's aristocratic grace, they commodify and dissipate nobility exactly as Marlowe refused to do. A "dream girl" and "a beautiful nothing," Eileen Wade is thus ultimately repulsive to Marlowe less because she is a double murderer than because she parallels and degrades his own attitudes. Like him, she longs to preserve an aristocratic ideal against a corrosive market.

But unlike Marlowe she is willing to use fake war memorabilia and commercially vended "British luxuries" to do so, "build[ing] another kind of memory" out of the past, "a false one" (324, 325, 300, 302).

Embodying all the qualities that Chandler most feared in the "formal" mystery and the "slick" magazine, then, Eileen Wade becomes the very expression of middlebrow culture as Chandler perceived it — genteel, delusional, and emasculating. That she is a killer besides amounts in Marlowe's estimation to little more than a side effect of these vices. For the truly significant danger that the femme fatale represents is the dystopic vision of mass culture that haunts "The Simple Art of Murder." To Eileen Wade, Terry Lennox is ultimately little more than a masturbatory fantasy, a "figure she could have maybe just invented . . . to have a toy to play with" (185). And she thus inverts Marlowe's homosocial romance, replacing its "democracy of fraternity" and its underlying vision of a redemptive "public taste" with a highly literal version of a "democracy of cupidity." An inversion of Chandler's critical theories, she raises the disturbing possibility that all ideal bonds are but masturbatory fantasies — that there might be no such thing as a "democracy of fraternity" to contrast to the vulgarities of the market, and that the force of mass culture might be so potent that, as Lennox admits in the novel's final scene, an "act is all there is. There isn't anything else" (378).

THE CITIZEN'S LAW AND THE REVOLT OF THE WHITES

Thus, where *Farewell, My Lovely* was the product of a broadly New Deal sensibility, *The Long Goodbye* offers an elaborate indictment of mass society and its dangers, problems that struck to the heart of Chandler's aesthetic theories and shadowed his literary ambitions with cartoonish counterparts. Why, one might wonder, though, should that have led Chandler to racial themes that were at worst incipient in his earlier novels? As a great many of his contemporaries demonstrated — writers like Hofstadter, Arendt, and the New York intellectuals whose work Chandler knew and, if skeptically, read — it was possible to develop a stinging critique of mass culture without any particular emphasis on race. Closer attention to *The Long*

Goodbye, however, reveals that Chandler's sense of the dangers of mass media and middlebrow culture led him not just to his standard armature of misogyny, but to a language of racial corruption that was carefully intertwined with his antifeminist motifs, and it suggests that, in comparison to the various caricatures and stereotypes in his prewar and wartime fiction, this language was far from an incidental part of his understanding.

One clue to the origins of that thinking might be seen in the triumphal rhetoric employed by the era's spokesmen for the achievements of "people's capitalism." Henry Luce, the postwar decades' prime representative of mass-market publishing and a figure not incidentally echoed in *The Long Goodbye*'s Harlan Potter and nastily parodied in Kenneth Fearing's brilliant 1946 thriller *The Big Clock*, took the country's vast economic power for a portent of the American Century. "America," Luce claimed in his vision of imperial mission, "must become the elder brother of the nations in the brotherhood of man." For those writers, though, who sought to position themselves against Luce and the image of America he seemed to represent, the pious internationalism of the statement indicated everything that was wrong with mass culture. If, as countless critics of the period argued, commercial entertainment leveled hierarchy, its furthest extent would come in the triumph of global banality — "an international sodality of man on his lowest level," in which "differences between backward and advanced countries become attenuated." True art, Clement Greenberg had influentially contended, sought to create "something valid solely on its own terms."[50] By that description, mass-marketed kitsch and postwar internationalism had a basic quality in common. Each lowered cultural barriers and, in the resulting borderless diffusion, made things subject to terms that seemed improper to themselves.

A writer like Chandler, then, who sought to imagine a "public taste" *against* the mass media, might naturally conceive it as the product of a conflict between a coherent and a dissipated national culture — especially if the writer felt inclined to cast matters in melodramatic terms, as Chandler avowedly did. Thus, the editors of *Partisan Review* introduced their forum on "Our Country and Our Culture" in 1952 with a cold war counterpart to the Stalinist vision of "socialism in one country." Intellectuals, they claimed, "now realize that their values, if they are to be realized at all, are to be realized in America and in relation to the actuality of American life." The most powerful weapon against both international socialism and the imperial dissemination of culture represented by figures like Luce had become a republican image of national cohesion — an ironic echo of the way that, three decades earlier, the Klan had employed a vision of a fraternal republic as an answer to the corrosive effects of modernity. And, much as with the Klan, the more defensive that image became, the more likely it was to be intensified by an implicitly racial language of common heritage. Even a writer with the impeccable leftist credentials of Kenneth Fearing, when he fantasized about the omnipotence of mass media might describe it, therefore, with the bizarre and ugly image of "a Black Republic" — a dangerously lulling world of "warmth, . . . ease, and above all . . . simplicity" — and might imagine a citizen's uprising against this inversion of a desirable national culture as "a revolt of the whites determined not to be sold down the river into" the slavery of mass-mediated banality.[51]

The appeal of racial thinking turns out to be, then, as direct and as far-reaching as the motif of *The Long Goodbye*'s $5,000 bill. In Chandler's earlier novels, race could seem relatively impotent because the writer remained preoccupied with a class-based image of social coherence whose ideological tendencies pointed away from ethnic autonomy. When that image lost its appeal, though, Chandler still required a way to imagine a unity of "public taste" that would seem more elevated than the mass-market fantasy he figured in Eileen Wade. He needed, moreover, a source of popular vitality and personal connection that could be contrasted to the weak affective bonds engineered by a bureaucratic state and a shallow mass media. For Chandler, as for many who followed him, the ties of culture or inheritance presented an obvious solution to these demands. It was an answer, though, that required the writer to reverse his sense of the relation between bureaucracy and race, much as he changed his attitude toward frozen capital and private sunshine. Thus, in *Farewell, My Lovely* the thick texture of ordinary communication pointed *away* from racial difference and contrasted the vitally "mixed" world of the streets to the bland, surface homogeneity of the press and the police.

In Chandler's late novels, the bureaucratic methods of the state, the force of law, and the publicity of the media appear more "thin," less politically deep and binding than ever. But now it is the police that seem multiethnic and the people who are ideally homogenous. The bonds of race thus become the key symbol of that underlying, thick social glue that bureaucratic arrangements hope to approximate but, in Chandler's view, progressively impoverish. Like the artistic over-tones of the $5,000 bill, cultural inheritance becomes the rich surplus that eludes rationalization and opposes the market.

Thus, when it seeks to dramatize the perils of mass society and cultural decline, *The Long Goodbye* complements its antifeminism with images of national-racial corruption — nearly all of which focus on the dangers presented by a permeable border with Mexico. This was the symbolic terrain, energized by the postwar explosion of anxiety about "wetbacks," that Orson Welles put to such effective use five years later in *Touch of Evil*. Chandler's vision, though, is nearly the reverse of Welles's advocacy of tolerance and interna-tional cooperation.[52] In a telling aside, Marlowe refers to the smug-gling of stolen cars between the United States and Mexico as "part of the good-neighbor policy, as the hoodlums see it" (43). But through-out the novel, Chandler suggests that only a hoodlum could see value in the international trade championed by Luce and the Democrats' Latin American diplomacy. Indeed, for Chandler, internationalism seems to produce hoodlums simply by fostering ethnic integration. Most prominently, there is the gangster Mendy Menendez who ha-rasses and later seeks to kill Marlowe. But Roger Wade's servant Candy — a Chilean immigrant, casually described by everyone but himself as Mexican — plays a similar role, warning Marlowe that although he speaks English, "I think Spanish. Sometimes I think with a knife" (185). Even the officer who presides over the oppressive L.A. police, Captain Hernandez, is pointedly Hispanic. The most dramatic example, though, concerns, suitably, the debasement of Terry Lennox and the aristocratic ideal he once embodied. It is only in the final pages that Lennox returns to the novel and we discover that he did not die in his escape to Mexico as we had been led to believe. Instead, Lennox has sought to abandon his past by using makeup and plastic surgery to transform himself into Señor Maioranos, a Mexican citizen. Though for Lennox the change is at first "just an act," for Marlowe it is immediately far more than cosmetic. For it indicates the way he and Lennox are now "two other fellows" than they once were, and it thus seems so drastic as to amount to a transformation in racial identity. Referring to American citizens, Marlowe is careful to draw a distinction between "Real Gringoes" and "just transplanted Mexicans"—a crucial division since it allows him to think of Mendy and Candy as solely temporary visitors to the north. By the same absolute logic, when Lennox abandons the United States for Mexico, he does not just switch citizenship, he becomes an entirely different person—"less Nordic"—and he suffers a symbolic death more drastic than any literal one could be. As Marlowe informs Lennox, becoming Señor Maioranos means "you're not here any more. You're long gone" (372, 375, 377, 378).

For Marlowe, then, ethnic corruption is the physical and spiritual expression of Lennox's "moral defeatis[m]" (377). By extension, it sums up the disappearance of all the noble qualities that Chandler believes did not survive into the postwar world. As such, though, the surgery that makes Lennox look less Nordic merely completes a process of degeneration that began when he served in the British army during World War II. It was then, after being badly injured, that Lennox began to become a mere imitation of the noble virtues he had previously embodied. But right from the beginning, the decline that cuts him off from "any kind of ethics or scruples" appears as a loss of racial prestige, since the worst effect of the war is not that Lennox is injured or psychically battered. It is that his heroism creates "a sort of bond" between Lennox and his foxhole mates—the racketeers Randy Starr and, most importantly, Mendy Menendez, both of whom become powerful crime bosses after the war (377, 20). For Chandler, the wealth and prominence of these men indicates the quality of the postwar order—the "price" in "organized crime . . . we pay for organization" (352). But, beyond this manifest corruption, the fact that Lennox's wartime experience makes him willing to associate with such criminals reflects the decay of the "Nordic" ideal. Like Candy and Maioranos, the "very dark" Menendez (who "probably started out as a pimp in a Mexican whorehouse") marks a decline in moral stature as a progress toward Mexico (74, 76).[53] Far more than crime—from which, however, it is barely distinct in Chandler's novel—the price of bureaucracy becomes a disturbingly integrated society.

What Chandler does with *The Long Goodbye*, in effect, is to take his contemporaries' fears about the democratizing effects of an international mass market and turn it into a noxious racial fantasy. Like formerly isolationist politicians in the postwar years, he confronts the unhappy realization that no nation "can immunize itself by its own exclusive action," and makes that awareness into a massive sense of affront and corruption.[54] The real problem with mass society as *The Long Goodbye* portrays it, though, is not merely that it threatens to incorporate racial difference. It is that such incorporation is imagined to be lethal to a fantasized fellowship among those who are already members of a shared culture. It is the war, after all—the source of mass "organization" in Chandler's mythology—that comes between Chandler's two ideal figures, Lennox and Eileen Wade, and that thoroughly debases both of them. Likewise, Marlowe and Mendy Menendez come into conflict when they both seek to care for Terry Lennox, and Candy similarly challenges the detective because he resents the services that Marlowe performs for Roger Wade. In each of these last two examples, a homosocial bond that is cast as natural and disinterested is contrasted to one that appears artificial, transethnic, and predatory by contrast. The logic underlying the contrast is nicely summed up in a brief exchange between Marlowe and a cabbie that takes place early in the book, as the detective, attempting to rescue a drunken Lennox from the police, hustles him into a taxi. The sympathetic driver tells Marlowe:

> "I been down and out myself. In Frisco. Nobody picked me up in no taxi either. There's one stony-hearted town."
> "San Francisco," I said mechanically.
> "I call it Frisco," he said. "The hell with them minority groups." (11)

The bonds among the three men in this scene are a direct contrast to those sealed among Lennox, Starr, and Menendez in the wartime foxhole. Although they sketch a social hierarchy—from the aristocratic Lennox, to petit bourgeois Marlowe, to working-class cabbie—the men are united by a mutual care that is the opposite of the cop's hostility, of the "stony-hearted" indifference associated with San Francisco, and of the exploitative relations between Lennox and Mendy or between Wade and Candy. Indeed, it is the fact that three men in the cab are fellows without being socially equivalent that is the main issue; for, rather than the false democracy of mass culture, they represent a brief example of Hofstadter's contrasting "fraternity" — a "stable society," in Clement Greenberg's analogous description, that had the capacity "to hold in solution the contradictions of its classes."[55] Most significantly, the sign of that solution, the common language that reaches across class difference, is the vernacular that simultaneously links these men and displays their indifference to "them minority groups." Amazingly, the passage makes it sound as if such minorities were in some way responsible for the coldness of urban life, and, indeed, that is very much the implication that runs throughout the novel. Moments of generosity and good faith, like that between the cabbie and Marlowe, or more significantly between Marlowe and Lennox, are only the fragments of a true fellowship that has been obscured by the likes of Mendy and Candy and by the supervention of Señor Maioranos, whose very name points back to the "better years" that his new identity abandons.

In fact, Chandler suggests clearly that the idealized fellowship glimpsed in Marlowe's bond with Lennox depends heavily on racial, or at the least deeply antiliberal, thinking. For, Marlowe notes, it requires judging people not "by what they do," but by "what they are" (95). Indeed, to such a perspective — as Candy suggests when he claims that "think[ing] Spanish" means "think[ing] with a knife" — the liberal presumption that people are to be judged by their actions and not their identities is so alien that the two conditions become ultimately indistinguishable. People simply do what they are — their behavior the necessary expression of an underlying identity. That is why Lennox cannot describe his Mexican persona as "just an act." It is the fact of his moral decline that lets him pull off the performance in the first place. He has already become Mexican in Marlowe's eyes, and, since surgery merely confirms the transformation, his performance is unwittingly sincere when he would prefer it were ironic. For the same reason, though, Mendy Menendez can brag about having "a place in Bel-Air that cost ninety grand . . . , a lovely platinum-blond wife and two kids in private school back east, . . . two Cadillacs, a Chrysler station wagon, and an MG," and his performance will always be just "hamming" (76). He can spend however much he likes, but by the terms of Chandler's opposition, those will be merely the things he does, and thus just an example of over-acting. Candy's insubordination and touchy sense of honor are similarly for Marlowe merely an effort "to upstage" the detective (171). No matter how heartfelt or accurate their statements may be, no matter how earnest their actions, they will be automatically insincere. Neither will ever be a "Real Gringo."

It is the police, of course, who are assumed to judge people, too quickly and harshly, by what they do — who are oblivious above all to the natural merit of Terry Lennox and slow to recognize the evil of Mendy Menendez or the deceit of Candy. The point is worth noting; for it suggests that although Chandler liked to portray the cops as authoritarian brutes, what he really objects to is the fact that, beholden to the demands of a liberal concept of law and the constraints of procedural justice, they are prevented from seeming like the outgrowth of an organic community. The police are not evil because they are brutal or because they are on the take; such signs of corruption are merely expressions of an underlying failure to live up to the fellowship embodied by Lennox and Marlowe. Even presumably honest cops are seen, therefore, with distaste. These are the implications of the elegiac concluding line of the novel: that "no way has yet been invented to say goodbye to [the cops]" (379). The abstract and abusive force of the law simply outlives the vernacular bonds of true fellowship. And in this sense, the ineradicable presence of the police stands for a continuum of disappointments: the inescapability of bureaucracy, the unavailability of justice, and the inability of Chandler's novels to fulfill the chief mission of the detective story — to naturalize the law within an image of coherent community.

It seems almost predictable, then, that the novel's most powerful cop, Captain Hernandez, is also its only Hispanic character apart from Mendy and Candy (with the exception of "a big mean-looking Mexican," who also turns out significantly to be a member of the police force). For, in this way, Hernandez exemplifies the basic problem of Chandler's postwar world. As Friedrich Schiller put it in the brief for a coherent culture that is the locus classicus for all appeals to "public taste" of Chandler's sort, he stands for "the State [that] remains eternally alien to its citizens because nowhere does feeling discover it."[56] That this man reeks of integrity, efficiency, and sheer decency does little to counter the fact that there can be "no feelings at all" between him and Marlowe (345, 273). Instead, it just emphasizes the gulf between the men. His admirable qualities, which in Chandler's later novels are presumed to be one set of attributes of an expanding government bureaucracy, exemplify the coldness that displaces the ideal brother who is "just . . . not here anymore" (378).

The converse of Chandler's theorem about the inescapability of the police, therefore, is the extraordinary maxim spoken by the D.A., Sewell Endicott, in Chandler's previous novel, *The Little Sister*. "The citizen is the law," Endicott claims, and although that sentiment is proffered, nominally, in a complaint against vigilantism—to suggest that even Marlowe "owe[s] a certain obligation to the law"—it has an effect opposite from its apparent intentions (227). Rather than criticizing him, the phrase turns the vigilante into a hero by making him the person who seeks to restore an original continuity between a people and its laws. What Marlowe presumes, and even Endicott allows, is that so long as there is no such direct and immediate equivalence between citizen and law, legal institutions are deprived of legitimacy and become a purely formal bureaucracy: "laws [are] for other lawyers to dissect in front of other lawyers called judges so that other judges can say the first judges were wrong" (*The Long Goodbye* 315). And, for Chandler (as for our contemporary right-wing secessionists), no one owes any obligation to such institutions: "We think of the law as an enemy. We're a nation of cop-haters."[57] Indeed, what the fellowship among the three men in *The Long Goodbye*'s cab suggests, as does the more significant friendship between Marlowe and Lennox, is that to the extent there are the remnants of a spiritual fraternity in Chandler's novels, it can be recognized precisely in shared antagonism to the law and to the state it represents. Marlowe, Lennox, and the cabbie are the elements of a nation *because* they are cop-haters and, by the same token, disdainers of "minority groups."

For the later Chandler, then, laws are inauthentic documents or culturally impoverished expressions — the equivalent, in short, of the meaningless literature that Chandler indicted in his letters and essays for lacking roots in the life of a people. The "formal" mystery, the "apparatus of intellectualism" and the black-letter law, like the police, are all foreign and decadent because they are not equivalent to the citizen. From this perspective, the failures of a culture become not just aesthetic errors but racial ones as well. Thus, it is eminently fitting that Chandler's defeated "big writer man," Roger Wade — the representative of both middlebrow entertainment and modernist experiment — should become for Chandler the character who more than any other represents slavish submission to feminized gentility and ethnic corruption. Passed out on the floor of his suburban mansion, at the feet of the woman who will eventually kill him and the servant who presumes to act as his equal, Wade is the representative of a hopelessly decadent culture. Whether he is a dishonest writer and a terrible drunk because, as one character implies, he has been defeated by his wife and humiliated by his servant, or whether he is their victim because literary corruption has sapped him of will finally cannot be decided. For Chandler, the two examples of decline, like the legal conditions of doing and being, are ultimately indistinguishable. As writer and patriarch, Wade his been reduced to domestic and implicitly erotic servility to the subservient figures he no longer has the strength to keep in their places. "We used to call them servants," Wade says of Candy, "Now we call them domestic help. I wonder how long it will be before we have to give them breakfast in bed" (245).

The point is made in an equally striking way in the transformation of Eileen Wade, a metamorphosis that matches the dramatic racial change in Terry Lennox. When Eileen first appears in Chandler's novel, a nearly transcendent image of beauty, she calls forth from Marlowe a famous catalog of blondes, an anatomy that seeks to frame the impossible ideal that Eileen conveys to the detective. The list ranges from "the metallic ones who are as blonde as a Zulu under the bleach" to "the small perky blonde" who practices judo and reads the *Saturday Review* to the "languid" blonde who "is reading *The Waste Land* or Dante in the original." It is a catalog in other words that ranges from low- through middle- to highbrow, a cultural hierarchy that is transcended and held in place by the "exquisitely pure" figure of Eileen—"unclassifiable, as remote and clear as mountain water, as elusive as its color" (89–90). At this moment in Marlowe's perception, Eileen is the regal figure who anchors cultural values, who thus ensures that "idealism" and "contempt" are meaningful terms, and that cultural aspiration is a noble project. That her remote color is simultaneously a racial ideal can be seen in the way that Marlowe thinks of her when he imagines her in danger: "she was running down a moonlit road barefoot and a big buck Negro was chasing her" (189). In this incarnation, in short, she is another version of "the stunning white girl" crucial to the Klan and to the fiction of foreign adventure in the twenties. When, however, she turns out to be a false idol, propped up by commercial gimmicks and cheap fantasy, she threatens to undermine the entire hierarchy she seemed to order. No longer the unclassifiable beauty, she has become the figure of artifice who subsumes races—the "Zulu under the bleach."

Later novels like *The Long Goodbye*, then, aptly developed Chandler's aesthetic theories. They evoked a nostalgic image of a fraternally unified culture, and they depicted that brotherhood as falling victim to a society robbed of its cultural integrity and falsely joined by the market, mass media, and bureaucratic government. Moreover, Chandler's very way of fashioning this myth reinforced his presumptions. His novels made common cause with the complaints of the most prominent intellectuals of the day—sometimes eliciting the qualified approval of those critics—and distanced his work from a booming popular culture that celebrated all the developments that Chandler most feared: suburbanization, mass consumerism, middlebrow culture, a bureaucratic state, and the mediation of ethnic and racial division. In this sense, the situation dramatized by Chandler's postwar novels amounted to an ironic reprise of the dilemmas faced by Dashiell Hammett and Carroll John Daly during the twenties. All of these writers found themselves divided between a populist language they despised and an elite way of dismissing it that seemed untenable. For Hammett and Daly, the urban intellectuals' disdain for the Klan's parochialism depended on a prestige and institutional security impossible to imagine. Chandler was drawn similarly to the mandarinism of his day, and he shared the distaste of writers like Arendt, Hofstadter, Greenberg, and Dwight Macdonald for the democracy of cupidity he saw all around him. Unlike many of his contemporaries, though, he could not place his faith in the spiritual rigors and saving virtues of modernism — a form of renunciation that struck him as little more than effete withdrawal. Lacking another critical vocabulary, he seized upon the nationalist intimations in the writings of his contemporaries and turned to a despairing version of the racialized republic that his hard-boiled predecessors had rejected.

Chandler's late novels would not be detective fiction at all, however, if they did not offer some kind of symbolic resolution to the disintegration they bemoan in the likes of Terry Lennox and Eileen Wade, and in order to grasp the force and the deep motivation of the logic that underlies these texts it may be useful to turn in conclusion to the way that *The Long Goodbye* ties up its loose ends. By its finish, the novel's principal characters are all actually or symbolically destroyed — Roger and Eileen Wade both dead, and Terry Lennox effectively banished. Along with these departures, though, Chandler rounds out the conclusion by deporting Mendy Menendez to Mexico and similarly dispatching Candy in an exchange that reinforces the novel's dedication to a homogenous national culture. Having explained that Eileen Wade killed her husband, Marlowe must then convince Candy not to vengefully stab his employer. "Be smart and go back where you came from," he advises. "This job here is dead." The ambiguity of Candy's reply is revealing: " 'Lot's of jobs,' he said quietly. Then he reached out and dropped the knife into my hand. 'For you I do this' " (315). The vague pronoun makes it sound as if Candy agrees both to give up his knife *and* return to Chile, and by Chandler's terms the gestures are equivalent. In Idle Valley, or perhaps in any American locale, Candy is automatically a threat, a Mendy Menendez in the making, because employers like Roger Wade lack the virility to restrain his aggression. His very presence implies the knife he frequently displays. Returning to his background, Candy willingly gives up everything that made him dangerous, and he is transformed into the amiable role of "peasant" (297). Even the gentlest Latin American becomes a "hoodlum" in the

United States, the conclusion implies, and can be rescued from criminality only by banishment.

It is an exchange parallel to this one, however, that is among the most telling in Chandler's novel. Very near to the end of the book, Marlowe bids an effective farewell to the world of Idle Valley and Harlan Potter in a conversation with Potter's black chauffeur, Amos. A "graduate of Howard University," Amos startles Marlowe with perfect syntax, refined diction, and a knowledge of T. S. Eliot. Yet, though this scene may be intended to seem unbigoted, it is actually far more patronizing than those on *Farewell, My Lovely*'s Central Avenue and much more disturbing in its implications. Where in *Farewell, My Lovely*, Marlowe comes for information to the desk clerk at the Hotel Sans Souci, here Amos is tutored by Marlowe about Eliot, and the most striking feature of their conversation, aside from its subject, is the way it highlights the gulf between the men by combining Marlowe's vernacular with Amos's stiff and remarkable deference:

> "In the room the women come and go/Talking of Michael Angelo." Does that suggest anything to you, sir?"
>
> "Yeah — it suggests to me that the guy didn't know very much about women."
>
> "My sentiments exactly, sir. Nonetheless I admire T. S. Eliot very much."
>
> "Did you say 'nonetheless'?"
>
> "Why, yes I did. Mr. Marlowe. Is that incorrect?"
>
> "No, but don't say it in front of a millionaire. He might think you were giving him the hotfoot."
>
> He smiled sadly. "I shouldn't dream of it." (356–57)

On the surface, Chandler's dialogue creates a bond between the men by establishing their common opposition to the high-handed ways of millionaires and their shared condescension to high modernism. But the further implication of their exchange, much as in Marlowe's final conversation with Candy, is that once Marlowe leaves the corrupt world of Idle Valley, he and Amos will no longer have anything to do with each other. Black and white meet in Chandler's later novels not on the "mixed" streets of Los Angeles, but in the limousines of millionaires. As in the exchange with Candy and the departure scene with Linda Loring that immediately follows — where the detective refuses Harlan Potter's remaining daughter — the conversation between the two men is thus one of the novel's many farewells, a series of conversations in which characters explicitly or by implication agree to live in separate worlds. Like Marlowe and Candy, Marlowe and Amos agree in effect to speak different languages, just as the three men in Chandler's cab share a vernacular at odds with cops and minority groups. Indeed, that Amos's speech is hypercorrect while Marlowe's is exaggeratedly casual only emphasizes the notion that they speak virtually different tongues. Amos's careful diction and his spotless manners dimly recall the courtly ideal represented by Terry Lennox, but unlike Lennox his breeding does not make him Marlowe's brother and equal. Instead, as with the final image of Candy, he is reassuring because he rejects the false democracy of mass culture in an elaborate performance of deference and distance. He knows enough to know his place and to accept it graciously.

It is especially fitting in light of Chandler's social vision, then, that the two men's departure turns on the poetry of T. S. Eliot. For, in essence, their solitary point of connection is their agreement that modernist poetry is, like empty laws and cheap fiction, a deracinated language (a charge given special force, in a book where women are the chief evil, by the fact that Eliot does not know much about women). In a complete reversal of Marlowe's conversation with *Farewell, My Lovely*'s desk clerk, Marlowe and Amos's common knowledge turns out to be useless information, no knowledge at all. Much as in Roger Wade's stream-of-consciousness diaries, modernism here is the obverse face of mass culture — the empty literature produced by a corrupt society and a sign of the false democracy the virtuous man rejects. Its only usefulness is to point by contrast to the remnants of the "public taste" it has helped to displace.

That the scene is also one of the novel's many departures points to the implications of such an understanding for Chandler's genre. As its best, critics have pointed out, detective fiction offers a myth of social integrity by mimicking a sacrificial economy — identifying scapegoats and banishing them from a restored community. In rejecting the racialized social coherence of the Klan, writers like Hammett and Daly challenged that myth, fashioning a detective fiction whose most striking feature was its own relative incoherence. In his late novels, Chandler leans heavily in the opposite direction, dismissing one character after another to strand the protagonist in a chaste, but ultimately empty privacy—a "self-sufficient, self-satisfied, self-confident, untouchable bastard" (363). A novel like *Red Harvest* takes the detective story to one limit of its coherence, failing to establish the image of unified community because it cannot find a useful scapegoat. *The Long Goodbye* is similarly unable to create a substantial sense of solidarity, but for a contrary reason. Chandler finds, in effect, too many scapegoats, banishing every feature of the postwar world and leaving Marlowe no one to feel communal with. The detective story, as he would soon acknowledge, had seemed to reach the end of its useful life.

4.

LETDOWN ARTISTS

Paperback Noir and the Procedural Republic

[T]he government's responsibility [for the postwar economy] will be important; at the very least, it will have to apply the Keynesian medicine. Americans who are determined to preserve capitalism should welcome [the Keynesian] way out because it does not interfere with the individual's choice of goods, his freedom to invest as and when he pleases, and his prerogative to choose his occupation; it merely proposes to keep the economy at a high and stable level by appropriate monetary and fiscal policy. — Seymour Harris, *Saving American Capitalism*, 1948

You don't want to write, Springer. Not really. I read your novel. You don't have anything to say. You don't know anything about people and you don't want to learn. — Charles Willeford, *The Black Mask of Brother Springer*[1]

By the late 1950s, Raymond Chandler acknowledged that the hard-boiled detective story had run its course. Countless imitations had led the private eye into lifeless caricature. Worse still, those writers who managed to be innovative with the genre, and who had achieved surprising success as a result, split it off into two disappointing directions. Both surrendered to the spirit of the age as Chandler saw it and abandoned the tension between literary art and popular expression that he thought crucial to his own fiction. The virtues of Philip Marlowe had fallen prey, on the one hand, to Mickey Spillane's lowbrow "mixture of violence and outright pornography" and, on the other, to the literary pretense of Ross Macdonald. Faced with these inadequate options, Chandler suggested, the crime story could advance only by abandoning the detective form for "the novel of pure suspense."[2]

Although he was not referring directly to such figures, Chandler might have been describing the way that writers like David Goodis, Jim Thompson, and Charles Willeford brought the hard-boiled crime story to a new stage in its development during the "paperback revolution" of the 50s. Publishing mainly in the trashy "paperback original" lines put out by Gold Medal, Lion, and Beacon, these writers remade the hard-boiled crime story by abandoning the detective protagonist and his ambivalent struggle to balance cops and crooks, law and desire, state and citizen. Dispensing with "th[at] tired old private-eye stuff," as Jim Thompson put it, they seized instead on the possibilities suggested by James M. Cain's thrillers and built their stories around self-destructive criminal protagonists. Elements of the fiction that began in *Black Mask* and the pulp magazines of the twenties and thirties survived to suggest a common lineage — especially the confrontational vernacular of the first-person narrator. But the new, paperback version of the hard-boiled story focused on those features of the genre that seemed most grotesque or cruel or uncanny and, extending them to new extremes, remade the hard-boiled story into a drama of psychopathology. No longer "a halfway house between the dicks and the crooks," as Carroll John Daly once bragged, the genre's typical protagonist became a freak, a loser, or a sociopath. The plots built around him became suitably episodic and often bizarrely expressionist, and the tone of the fiction settled into a monochromy of "sullen despair" and "hopeless frustration." In the resonant description offered by David Goodis, the typical protagonist of this new style of pulp fiction was the "letdown artist" — an expert in the "harmony of error."[3]

The roots of these transformations in hard-boiled fiction lay in significant changes in the genre's publishing contexts and especially in subtle, yet profound alterations in the meaning of the genre's most highly charged value — popular voice. If writers like Hammett and

Chandler thought of themselves as engaged in a complex and unlikely effort to mediate the popular and the literate, what they meant
by "popular" was at least always fairly clear. Indeed, it corresponded
closely with the most salient common representations of "the people" during the thirties and early forties — mainly the urban, ethnic,
working class that made up the core of the New Deal constituency.
By the 1950s, however, the place of that class in the nation's political
and cultural order had shifted dramatically and "the popular" was
no longer such a cogent notion. The economic and political settle-
ments that shaped the postwar decades made the once oppositional
"CIO working class" the center of national culture.[4] No longer a
marginalized population, that bloc had emerged from the war looking like prototypical Americans, and their most prominent markings
of geography, ethnicity, and economic status appeared to be fading
rapidly into the image of a new, suburbanizing middle class. The
United States no longer seemed a society where the battle between
"little ones" and "big ones" would make intuitive sense. Instead, it
appeared to have submerged the most significant political disputes of
the New Deal years in the anti-ideological agreement that state-
fueled, but privately managed, economic growth could meliorate
social conflict. In Charles Willeford's brilliant description, the political landscape of the Eisenhower era looked "half-Republican and
half-Socialist."[5]

Because of its peculiar publishing history, hard-boiled crime fiction
was well-placed to explore these wide-reaching transformations in
the nation's political discourse. During the twenties and thirties, the
segmented structure of the literary marketplace lent credibility to the
hard-boiled writers' criticisms of a hierarchically divided literary
culture. But that situation changed significantly following the death
of the pulp industry in the fifties and its displacement by the dynamic
forces of the paperback revolution. Previously, pulpsters could think
of themselves as inhabiting a subterranean literary democracy, and
those rare figures like Hammett and Chandler who moved from the
pulps to clothbound publication could describe themselves as literary migrants traveling from low to high culture. With the death of
the pulps and the rise of the paperbacks, though, the very notion of
literary hierarchy seemed to many at least momentarily in doubt.

Both the champions and the many critics of the paperback revolution agreed that mass-market publication had "taken the classics away from the protective custody of the pedants" and created an unprecedented "melange of serious literature and trash." The question was whether this erosion of literary barriers represented an admirable democratization of culture — "good reading for the millions," as the slogan of New American Library put it — or a "general degeneration [of culture] from the 19th century standards."[6] From either perspective, the paperback revolution seemed as fatal to cultural hierarchy as the era's general prosperity did to the class-oriented politics of the thirties.

PUTTING GOVERNMENT IN ITS PLACE

No writers did more to exemplify the shift in cultural attitudes that accompanied these changes than Mickey Spillane and Ross Macdonald. The remarkable success each of them experienced in the postwar decades would have been inconceivable apart from the structural transformation of the publishing industry that their books represented. More specifically, the diverse alterations they wreaked on the tradition of the hard-boiled crime story corresponded closely with the era's reorientation of the literary marketplace. Both Spillane and Macdonald drew on the narrative rhetoric of the hard-boiled genre while retooling it significantly to fit the demands of the growing postwar reading public. In the process, each author refined and simplified the fiction so that it became more potent, even as it lost the conflicts that had previously lent it vitality. In the work of both Spillane and Macdonald, these developments looked like unambiguous signs of literary democracy. The ambivalent meditations on artistic authority, popular legitimacy, and mass entertainment that characterized the work of Hammett and Chandler are absent from this fiction. What has replaced them is a pair of complementary tales of cultural victory. One of these stories speaks of triumph from below, the other of condescension from above, but each reconciles the tensions exacerbated by earlier hard-boiled novelists. In a manner exemplified by their unprecedented sales figures, Spillane's and Macdonald's novels amount to celebrations of postwar mass culture posing as critiques of its limitations.

Significantly, the basic stories that both Spillane and Macdonald created during the fifties began as narratives of the returning military man, a feature that emphasized each novelist's derivation, and departure, from the cultural politics of the New Deal. In depicting the reentry of soldiers and sailors to postwar life, each writer focused on the shifting relations among state, society, and representative figures of the common man, and each thereby created an allegory of the transformation of the New Deal into the Fair Deal and the "corporate commonwealth" of the Eisenhower era. In their novels, the rhetoric of the New Deal seems at once fulfilled and transformed — especially by the way that the "developmental" and reformist politics of the thirties had disappeared in the era's relegitimation of capitalism and its emphasis on the natural harmony of social welfare and economic expansion.[7] In Spillane and Macdonald's world, the common man comes into his own. But he needs little assistance from government, and he has no need to fear corporate power. He needs only to be strong in the pursuit of the opportunity ostensibly open to all. The lesson that Spillane found in his success — that "anybody can be a Winner . . . all you have to do is make sure you're not a Loser" — is in different ways the moral that each writer teaches.[8]

In Spillane's case, this is a story of the enfranchisement of the enlisted man — an apotheosis of the ordinary Joe in which hard-boiled fiction's traditional distrust of plutocrats becomes a dismissal of cultural elites. That story could not be clearer than it is in Spillane's first and paradigmatic book, *I, The Jury*. The novel's very title celebrates the triumph of personal will over the social apparatus of the law, and its narrative reasserts that victory in the conflict between Spillane's protagonist, Mike Hammer, and the novel's villain, Charlotte Manning. Manning, we eventually learn, is a ruthless heroin dealer and, more significantly, the murderer of Hammer's best friend and wartime foxhole mate. A familiar example of the emasculating woman, Manning's name indicates her unwillingness to accept the feminine "instinct" for submission, and her method for murder, seducing men and then shooting them in the gut, reflects her determination to reverse the natural hierarchy of sexual authority. In the novel's conclusion, that inversion is itself reversed, a transformation accomplished when Mike Hammer shoots Charlotte as she stands unclothed before him. In a nasty image of sexual gratification, the wound creates "an ugly swelling in her naked belly" from which a "thin trickle of blood well[s] out."[9]

Charlotte Manning's evil does not stop, however, with either her illegal commercial activities or her predatory desires (which are, in any case, interchangeable images of emasculation). She is also an exemplary figure of the postwar era's emerging therapeutic bureaucracy. A Park Avenue psychiatrist specializing in "mass psychology," Manning draws power not just from her seductive beauty, but from her ability to "study people, observe their behavior and determine what lies underneath." She is, in short, not just a femme fatale, but a representative of the social-scientific elite, professionally skilled at exploiting "the frailty of men"; she is thus one example of the many intellectual charlatans whose authority is easily vanquished by Mike Hammer's popular righteousness. "The people have their justice," Hammer claims. "They get it through guys like me once in a while," and that victory follows from the sheer popular virility that Hammer represents. As Manning acknowledges admiringly, Hammer can "make life obey the rules he set[s] down." His "body is huge, . . . [his] mind is the same. No repressions."[10] She, in short, is all manipulative intelligence; he, pure corporeal energy. Only one of the two, Spillane's narrative implies, can survive.

The defeat of Manning and of the various kinds of seduction she represents — of female sexuality, drugs, and psychiatric expertise — is analogous, then, to Hammer's dismissal of every restraint that resists the huge force of his body, "the tedious process of the law" especially. As Hammer explains, "the people" and the justice they desire are distinct from the corrupt "society" represented by the legal system. Having raised the specter of the bureaucratic apparatus of postwar mass society, then, *I, The Jury* summarily dispatches it, hinting briefly at the prospect of failure in order to emphasize the hero's victory. In the process, the novel defines the narrative scenario that Spillane would retell over the course of his next six stunningly successful novels and the first draft of a plausible vision of the postwar United States. In Spillane's telling, the American people become a

bristling militarist fraternity, invigorated by its own ruthlessness toward internal as well as external enemies. But Hammer's defeat of
Manning also predicts Spillane's victory over cultural authority in
general, a triumph unimaginable to his hard-boiled predecessors. In
later comments, Spillane suggested that the critics who carped about
the pornographic violence of his fiction and who worried about the
vast size of his readership could only be "frustrated writers" who
"resent success." Such comments cast literary expertise in the same
role as Charlotte Manning. Like "mass psychology" and "the tedious process of the law," it amounted to little more than a bankrupt
and ultimately doomed attempt to deceive a public that knew what it
liked.[11]

Thus, Spillane's novels fulfilled one side of hard-boiled crime fiction's traditional aspirations — depicting the triumph of vernacular
will — while leeching those ambitions of the very complications that
made them interesting. A similar claim can be made for the work of
Ross Macdonald, which likewise descends from one side of hard-
boiled crime fiction's conflicted aesthetic and which thereby complements Spillane's fundamental narrative nearly point for point.
Where Spillane tells of the cultural victory of the enlisted man, Macdonald's story is one of the enfranchisement of another representative man of the postwar era — the "G.I. Bill intellectual." With the
exception of the protagonist of his first book, *Blue City*, the returning heroes of Macdonald's novels are, like Macdonald himself as
well as his most important protagonist Lew Archer, not enlisted men
but former junior officers. Characteristically ensigns, lieutenants,
and captains recovering from the psychological trauma of war, they
face return to postwar society via the mediating institutions of psychotherapy and higher education. Their mission, emblematized by
the work of the detective, is to plumb the mysteries of "the human
mind" — to embrace and ultimately to control a Niebuhrian "tragic
inner life." Macdonald's novels are thus paeans to the spiritually
ennobling force of culture and the social benefits of education. (Significantly, Macdonald, along with James M. Cain, is one of the two
major hard-boiled writers discussed in this book to receive a college
degree, and the only one to have gone on to graduate work in English

literature.) "Social mobility," Archer notes with only surface irony, "is my stock in trade."[12]

Thus, where Spillane's depiction of postwar society imagines a macho fraternity overcoming the inadequacies of law and bureaucracy, Macdonald's vision is Arnoldian, invoking the spiritual democracy to be fostered by high culture. Colleges and universities not only provide the main settings for several of his novels; they serve as Macdonald's primary symbol for the postwar agencies of social welfare. And the significant questions raised by his fiction, therefore, are not, as in Spillane, whether an illegitimate bureaucracy will restrain a vigilant popular will, but whether higher education can fulfill its democratizing promise. Do learning and literature truly serve "constructive purposes," his most accomplished novels ask? Do they aid in the formation of that "character or personality" that grants meaning to the individual life? Or will college provide only shallow cultivation, teaching not depth but sophistication and turning out not men of culture but "treacherous little hustlers," who have learned nothing but "how to cheat people"?[13]

The presumption, of course, is that education can make people of character. Indeed, the many pathetic victims and criminals who litter the pages of Macdonald's fiction, along with the seedy neighborhoods or the tacky suburban homes they inhabit, give testimony to the importance of the insight and depth that higher learning is presumed to provide. What is wrong with such people, Macdonald typically suggests, is not that they are constrained by socioeconomic forces or that they are driven by greed or the desire for power — the causal factors that weighed most heavily in the previous generation of hard-boiled fiction — but that they have failed to understand themselves. They are prisoners, Archer says, of "half-realities."[14]

Such a perspective rests on an assumption alien to writers like Hammett and Chandler, one legitimated for Macdonald's generation by the agencies of cultural diffusion represented by both higher education and the paperback industry. For Macdonald, as for many of his contemporaries, not only did high culture and psychotherapy suggest an invaluable spiritual discipline; they were presumed to be available to, and to work in the same fashion for, all people. Nor was culture merely a democratically owned property; it seemed a democratic force that worked subtly to overcome differences and thus to unify the whole nation, forging a "connection between the very greatest work and the anonymous imaginings of a people . . . hold[ing] a civilization together like nothing else can."

Thus, in a nice inversion of Spillane, Macdonald echoes the earlier hard-boiled writer's appeal to a unified "public taste" while simply dispensing with the conflicts those earlier writers envisioned. Indeed, for Macdonald, the antagonism that mattered most to his hard-boiled predecessors seems like little more than sentimentality. Looking back on the populist rhetoric of the thirties, Lew Archer is struck by its seeming obsolescence. In the prosperous postwar years, a defense of "the rights of the working class" or a description of the nation as divided "between the rich people and the poor people" seems sadly antiquated—the belief of "a previous century." Like many of the era's G.I. Bill intellectuals, moreover, Macdonald suggests that the rhetoric of class conflict is not only unsuitable to postwar society, but a trivial misapprehension of fundamental human values to begin with. "The leading fallacy of our times, underlying fascism and communism and even most of the liberalisms," one of his earliest protagonists proclaims, "is the belief that political man is man in his highest function, that political forms are the salvation of the individual soul. . . . I simply want government to know its place. . . . The end has got to be determined by non-political values."[15] Such proper ends are determined, Macdonald ultimately makes clear, neither by governmental authority nor by the collectivist language of class politics, but by a commitment to knowledge of the "individual soul" and a defense of the "inner life."

If Spillane might be said to reconstruct New Deal populism in the image of cold war militarism, Macdonald offers a complementary and similarly plausible view of the postwar order. Lew Archer and his analogs in Macdonald's fiction represent the voice of what would soon be called the liberal elite—the champions of mass higher education, urban renewal, and the "rights-based" liberalism that would flower in the Great Society programs of the Johnson administration. The role is encapsulated in the persona of one of Macdonald's earliest protagonists, the probation officer Howard Cross. As his name indicates, Cross is not just a social service bureaucrat. As Archer will later be, he is the thriller hero as man of sorrows. He "feel[s] the weight of lives pressing" on him, and he mourns the squalor, moral and environmental, in which the victims he seeks to represent must live. Traveling through the rapidly declining ethnic working-class city, once the prime terrain of the hard-boiled novel and now ravaged by postwar suburbanization, Macdonald's hero sees not the vital public world of his hard-boiled predecessors, but a landscape of moral decline — "a limbo of side streets" whose "blight . . . creeps outward from the centers of cities."[16] For a writer like the early Chandler, urban geography provoked anger at inequity and social corruption. For Macdonald, inner-city blight exemplifies psychological illness and moral failure, and there is little reason for anger at such things. All that his protagonist can do is to extend the compassion that might aid the weak, the ignorant, and the suffering to take advantage of their opportunities.

The uncertainty that troubled Macdonald's hard-boiled predecessors has disappeared as thoroughly from this vision as from Spillane's. Macdonald celebrates the spiritual value of education and great literature without any of the ambivalence that characterized the attitudes of Hammett and Chandler. Spillane glories in popular vitality without showing any awareness of the confusion or weakness that the earlier hard-boiled writers discovered in the vernacular. Each writer, too, dispenses with the problems of politics and government by imagining a unified national community that would have been inconceivable to their predecessors. For Hammett, as for Chandler, there was "no way . . . to say goodbye" to the police. Because a coherent "public taste" was unimaginable, the law would remain forever bureaucratic and the community necessarily divided against itself. For Spillane and Macdonald, such problems have all but disappeared. Each puts government in "its place" — Spillane by allowing the fraternity of vigilant men to trump bureaucracy and civil liberties, Macdonald by elevating "the good life" of the cultivated self over the shallow "life of society."[17]

In a manner that coincides with these one-sided developments of the genre, each writer, too, flattens the emotional range characteristic of previous hard-boiled fiction. For Spillane, there appears to be but one meaningful emotion, righteous fury. "I hate hard," Mike Hammer announces. And though Macdonald rightly earns credit for the nuance of his characterization, his fiction, too, tends to circle around the single prominent emotion felt by his protagonists — pity. Since everything in Macdonald's fiction hinges on the need to educate the "individual soul," the worst villains encountered by Howard Cross or Lew Archer are neither Spillane's internal subversives, nor the parasitic oligarchy that characterized hard-boiled crime fiction during the thirties, but people who have failed to come to grips with the inner self. Rich and poor alike, they are life's losers — people dogged by failings in the moral insight and personal will that grant Macdonald's heroes a potent sense of identity. Rarely are such "Mr. Nobod[ies]" truly bad people in Macdonald's eyes; they are merely too weak to discover their own failings and have gone therefore "hollow or soft inside."[18] Ironically, these figures are much like the weak men who fall prey to Charlotte Manning in *I, The Jury* or who are seduced by communism, bohemianism, or psychotherapy in Spillane's subsequent fiction. They have failed to thrive in a world brimming with potential, and they draw attention, therefore, to the protagonist's own hard-won success.

THE INTOLERABLE SELF

The most interesting developments in hard-boiled crime fiction during the late forties and through the fifties shared little with either Spillane or Macdonald, and they depicted neither the unrepressed body of Spillane's fiction, nor the cultivated sensibility of Macdonald's. These were stories, rather, that claimed to speak from the perspective of the losers and Mr. Nobodies of the world, and they offered an aesthetic sensibility and a vision of postwar society sharply at odds with those of their paperback contemporaries.

In large part, those differences can be traced to the unusual position that writers like Jim Thompson and Charles Willeford occupied in the literary field of their day. The social vision and the aesthetic sensibility that ran through Macdonald's fiction, like the vision and sensibility that characterized Spillane's, were inseparable from the writer's particular success with the new form of the paperback novel. Everything about Macdonald's fiction, for example, spoke of those vast hopes for cultural democracy exemplified by New American Library's motto "good reading for the millions." Like NAL and those champions of the paperback who celebrated its diffusion of great literature, Macdonald anticipated the extension of high culture to people in need of its spiritual guidance. By contrast, Spillane might be taken as a representative of the spirit that saw the paperbacks as a means to wrest cultural authority from "the protective custody of the pedants." His fiction celebrates the way that the mass-entertainment market defeats cultural authority and gives power to the popular consumer.[19] These are two parables of the democratization of culture, and each corresponds to, while parodying, an aspect of the conflicted ambitions traditional to hard-boiled crime fiction.

The inventors of paperback noir — Thompson and Willeford especially — had an entirely different experience of the postwar literary marketplace, a difference that can be seen in the writers' publishing histories alone. Macdonald could be said to have reversed the trajectory followed by Hammett and Chandler. In what would become one paradigm of the postwar popular novelist, he first published his work with Knopf and then experienced his greatest sales in paperback reprints of the novels. The movement of his books, from elite prestige to popular circulation, thus mirrored Macdonald's understanding of the dissemination of knowledge as well as the sentiments of his protagonist. All worked in a top-down fashion. By contrast, Spillane's unprecedented success outlined another paradigm of popular authorship in the postwar decades. He was the first mainstream, mass-market novelist who defined himself primarily as a paperback writer, and the experience legitimated a sensibility nearly the opposite of Macdonald's. Huge paperback sales allowed him to disdain the prestige of clothbound publication and the cultural authority he associated with it.[20]

Writers like Thompson and Willeford could claim neither of these advantages. They published neither prestigious clothbound books nor the mass-marketed paperbacks at the vanguard of the new industry. Rather, they were among the first generation of authors to write for the niche market of the "paperback original" — cheaply

manufactured, sensational, and nominally formulaic books produced by low-budget houses. "We all at once discovered we were
what many of us had secretly wanted to be," their contemporary,
D. B. Newton, reported of the experience, "novelists, instead of mere
pulp-paper hacks."[21] But, like the bemused Newton, they also discovered, that that status did not deliver the redemption it may have
seemed to promise. Although Thompson and Willeford enjoyed
large and steady sales, they had neither the mass authority accrued
by Spillane, nor the cultural approbation enjoyed by Macdonald.
Furthermore, they could no longer draw on the populist vision of
literary hierarchy that had been traditional to the pulps. Indeed, the
very success of the paperback revolution served to cast the literary
marketplace in much the same terms that characterized the broader
social discourse of the era. The United States that had emerged victorious from its war with fascism, and that seemed in the rhetoric of
the cold war to be embroiled in fresh battle with another species of
totalitarianism, no longer appeared a society divided along the class
lines of the Depression. And political theorists and social critics consequently developed a new "pluralist" view of American democracy
that rapidly became liberal dogma during the later 1940s and the
1950s. In this view, industrial society should no longer be thought of
as tendentiously oligarchic, and state action should no longer be
imagined necessary to curb the influence of monopolistic power.
Rather, American democracy, in Robert Dahl's paradigmatic formulation, was naturally "polyarchal" — dominated neither by majority,
nor by minority rule, but by "minorities rule." Political power was
therefore simultaneously egalitarian and elitist. At any given time, a
handful of influential figures directed the actions of government, but
because democratic institutions depended on open and fair competition, their rule would always be challenged by newcomers, who
might emerge from any segment of society. "Power in America,"
sociologist David Riesman concurred, appeared "situational and
mercurial." It resisted all "attempts to locate it."[22]

Thus, the political theology of postwar liberalism cut against the
most basic presuppositions of earlier hard-boiled crime fiction. And
the literary marketplace of the period worked to redouble that influ-

ence by emphasizing the apparent dispersal of power and meritocratic opportunity that the era's intellectuals saw throughout American society. As the paperback industry expanded during the forties
and fifties to develop various submarkets and audiences, it appeared
to be arranged ever more completely along the horizontal lines
sketched by diverse reading publics rather than by the vertical ladder
once imagined by pulpsters. And as the literary universe appeared to
lose its tacit class structure, the possibilities for the hard-boiled writer
altered. Where previous figures like Hammett and Chandler could
imagine themselves trapped between legitimate literature and popular sensation, and could see themselves as exemplary figures for that
very reason, writers like Thompson and Willeford confronted a contrary situation. They were neither high nor low. Indeed, those very
categories seemed to be rapidly disappearing. In Clement Greenberg's representative description of the postwar cultural landscape,
"all hierarchical distinctions" appeared to have been "exhausted and
invalidated." The "polyarchy" of the postwar political order seemed
to be echoed by a "polyphonic" culture in which "no area or order of
experience" could be "intrinsically superior, on any final scale of
values, to any other."[23]

So although the paperbacks in some ways gave writers like Thompson and Willeford a much larger audience than even the most successful pulpster had enjoyed (Chandler's publishers considered themselves extremely fortunate when *The Big Sleep* sold 10,000 copies;
Thompson's novels of the 1950s regularly went through printing
runs of 200,000 or more) and a readership that was probably much
more widely distributed as a matter of education, income, and geography than the pulp audience had ever been, these writers' very success cast doubt on the ideas of popular representation and literary
ambition that had been important to earlier hard-boiled authors.[24]
They could no longer claim, as pulpsters once had, to speak for an
autonomous publishing fraternity, nor to be the victims of an unfair
cultural hierarchy, and the result was a vision of literary culture that
differed sharply from that of their contemporaries. If Mickey Spillane
cast himself as the avatar of popular will, allying himself with those
who praised the paperback revolution for the blow it dealt to snob-

bery, and if Ross Macdonald embodied the vision of the paperbacks as the agent of cultural dissemination, the creators of paperback noir saw the literary marketplace as its critics did in their most apocalyptic vein — as a "melange of serious literature and trash" that undermined meaningful distinctions and the very idea of public discourse. "Polyphony" in this light meant not democracy, but confusion.

The stories these authors told reflected that perception. They depicted a disembodied social universe and protagonists whose failures came to seem ever more private and impervious to the language of social reform, who were forced to suffer what Thompson called "the cruelest punishment of all — the unending necessity to live in . . . [an] intolerable self."[25] For the creators of paperback noir, the postwar world looked not like the realization of mass democracy, but a system of bureaucratic institutions and individual alienation. Where Spillane and Macdonald saw the triumph of the common man and the victory of "the people" or "the inner life" over politics, Thompson and Willeford mourned the loss of public culture. They found no people to celebrate and an inner life that was not a refuge but a prison.

ALMOST LIKE WRITING

For Jim Thompson, the connection between the confusion of the literary marketplace and the decline of the New Deal was direct and very nearly explicit. Thompson's novels often dramatized the mélange of literary codes produced by the paperback revolution. Like the celebrated *A Hell of a Woman* — which featured a preface likening Thompson to Joyce and Faulkner along with a lurid cover and blurb, and which concluded with an experimental divided narrative — they drew simultaneously on the conventions of high modernism and trash genre to make a mockery of literary distinctions.[26] But the invocation of cultural prestige in Thompson's novels tends not to signify the developed sensibility enjoyed by Macdonald's Lew Archer. When Thompson alludes to modernist aesthetics, he does so not to display his protagonist's learning but his disorientation, and, throughout his fiction the mixture of traditionally high and low literary voices suggests not an egalitarian national spirit, but the disappearance of meaningful perspective.

In this respect, Thompson's novels echo the dynamics of his literary biography — a career that began in the cheapest fractions of the pulp industry, turned crucially for a short time during the thirties to social documentary and political engagement, and returned in the fifties to crime narrative. It was during this last period that Thompson wrote the nearly two dozen paperback novels for which he is now remembered, and his particular abilities with sadomasochistic fantasy flowered in the form. For Thompson, though, as Robert Polito's biography has shown, this was a story in which the writer's skill and success were inseparable from a larger sense of failure and political disappointment — making him not only different from his contemporaries Spillane and Macdonald, but unlike his hard-boiled predecessors as well. Dashiell Hammett and Raymond Chandler each believed that they had ultimately failed to fulfill, or had been prevented from, realizing their talent. But they had little doubt that they were closest to making good on their potential when they wrote the novels by which they are now canonized. Thompson, by contrast, looked at his best fiction as a mark of a concession in his abilities and more broadly as a sign of the disappointing political atmosphere of the postwar U.S. Thus, when an editor at New American Library noted in an internal memo prompted by Thompson's own desperate correspondence, that Thompson was "originally a novelist of considerable promise" but had "turned some years ago to the mystery field, and more particularly to what might properly be called the 'psychological crime' story," he echoed the tale that Thompson had constructed to explain both the political history of American literature and his own career. Each, Thompson implied, involved a descent into criminal psychology from a once admirable but now irrevocably lost public-spiritedness.[27]

At its most gothic Thompson's crime fiction invoked just this association. The conclusion to his 1952 breakthrough novel, *The Killer Inside Me*, for example, finds Thompson's protagonist — the sadistic killer and folksy deputy sheriff Lou Ford — speaking to us from beyond the grave. Ford has just been blown to pieces in an apocalyptic shoot-out, and he ends his narration by envisioning a heavenly community of the misfits who populate Thompson's fiction:

> "Yeah, I reckon that's all unless our kind gets another chance in the Next Place. Our Kind. Us people.
>
> All of us that started the game with a crooked cue, that wanted so much and got so little, that meant so good and did so bad. All us folks. . . . All of us."[28]

Only six years before, in his second novel, *Heed the Thunder*, Thompson had concluded with a similar passage of populist sentimentality, invoking "the real people, the people of the land." In a classic example of Popular Front rhetoric, this peroration apostrophizes "the hunky land, the Rooshan land, the German land, the Dutch and Swede land, the Protestant and Catholic and Jewish land: the American land." But Thompson then concludes his novel by predicting the disappearance of this vision of common popular nationality. The land, the book's last sentence warns, "was slipping . . . surely, . . . swiftly into the black abyss of the night."[29] By the time Thompson wrote *The Killer Inside Me* that descent seemed complete. If *Heed the Thunder* pointed elegiacally to a Depression era language of populist democracy, *The Killer Inside Me* employs the same rhetoric but turns it on its head. The folksy tone remains, and carries all through the narration of Thompson's murderous protagonist, but it is now a means of cruelty in Ford's hands. (Thompson's most renowned invention may be the way that Lou Ford wields cliché maliciously, to injure the sensibilities of his tolerant listeners.) Likewise, the force that binds "all of us" is no longer our basic goodness, but instead our meanness, crookedness, and covetousness. For Thompson, that journey from one image of popular community to another would seem a fitting way to describe a postwar landscape in which the most prevalent ideas of democracy seemed to depend less on the ideals of public welfare than on the virtues of self-interest.

His first novel, *Now and On Earth*, predicted this very transition. The autobiographical story of Thompson's work in the wartime aircraft factories of San Diego, *Now and On Earth* mourns the decline of the thirties' language of collectivism and its displacement by surveillance and competitive individualism. Though itself closer in both form and spirit to proletarian literature than to the crime fiction at which Thompson would later excel, the novel makes it clear why the thriller narrative would be suitable to such an environment. For the most salient characteristic of the world Thompson portrays is that it has replaced the vocabulary of common responsibility with the alienating language of competition and meritocracy. Explaining war industry employment systems, for instance, the narrator, James Dillon, complains about "the newspaper talk to the effect that the aircraft plants have made the WPA and other relief agencies unnecessary. Nothing could be further from the truth. You find no dispossessed sharecroppers or barnyard mechanics here. They get no further than the office-boy in the Personnel Department." Though an occasional "misfit" like Dillon himself sneaks through, the industry hires only skilled workers and college-educated supervisors. Moreover, the plant's production demands and its system of supervision undercut any possible experience of class solidarity or common effort. "Every man is pretty much on his own here. Every man has just a little bit more to do than he can get done in eight hours, and there's no time to help another man even if you want to."[30]

In such an environment, Thompson implies, the solipsism and paranoia central to the thriller novel are common experiences. And, as if to lend credibility to that impression, the climax of the novel comes when the narrator, betrayed by a coworker, is interrogated by the FBI for his suspected communist sympathies.[31] But the novel also has a less obvious, and perhaps more significant implication. It suggests that along with populist collectivism, the writing of the New Deal and the mediatory stance of that era's public intellectual cannot survive in the new world. Like Thompson himself—who played a prominent role in the Oklahoma Writers' Project and in the Oklahoma City Communist Party until red scares and political harassment drove him from the city in 1939—James Dillon was once a project director for the WPA. As he looks back on that work now, he feels forced to concede its irrelevance. Turning out "fifteen million words for the Writers' Project . . . got me twenty-five thousand reminders ten million times a day that nothing I'd done meant anything." In the novel's present tense, the protagonist is an *ex*-writer who feels surrounded by signs of the failure of his aesthetic and political ambitions. He distrusts his fellow workers, he feels embarrassed by his wife's lowbrow sensibility and her liking for pulp entertainment, and he looks on the Popular Front culture of the thirties — exemplified by an abandoned "complete set of Carl Sandburg recordings" — as pathetically antiquated. If folk culture is lost to him, so, moreover, is the connection with literary prestige he once imagined his work as a writer might bring. Looking back on a lost romance with a lover who embodied traditional cultural eminence, Dillon refers nostalgically to the missed rapprochement that had been a central issue for both the hard-boiled crime story and New Deal populism: "Five years later I would have admitted, in the security I had then [as a director for the WPA], that she was not superficial and she would have conceded that the common streak in me was no broader than it needed to be. And each would have borrowed from the other and profited by it."[32]

This was the tension between "common" voice and literary authority that the previous varieties of hard-boiled crime fiction worked to great effect. Thompson's novel suggests that the one lost chance for the mediation of high and low came with the programs for cultural reform pursued by the New Deal. It was, then, as director of the Oklahoma Writers' Project that James Dillon would have had the standing and confidence to make use of literary sophistication, and that the devotees of genteel culture would have found reason to appreciate the virtues of popular expression. Now, though, that chance has disappeared, and its failure hangs over everything that occurs in Thompson's novel, the original example of the protagonist's many disappointments. During the thirties, Thompson had cast himself as an exemplary face of the New Deal — one whose writing could mediate disputes between capital and labor, agriculture and industry, high culture and low.[33] But, having lost the populist language of public works to the alienating world of private industry, Thompson's protagonist can turn his creative energies only to the inventory system he develops for the defense plant. The transition is a synecdoche for the way that the discipline and surveillance of meritocracy displace meaningful public expression. Bookkeeping takes the place of cultural work; routinization replaces common voice. The hero's new system, the sole outlet for his literary intelligence, becomes "almost like a piece of writing."[34]

Just what he meant by that phrase, can be understood best by referring back to one of Thompson's earliest efforts to write serious fiction. In an unpublished story titled "Sympathy" that he wrote while a student at the University of Nebraska in 1931 (and that was based on his own experience of working as a door-to-door salesman), Thompson tells of a credit agent named Miss Kublins who seeks to get a response from a long-delinquent client. Discovering that the man has not only lost several jobs but that he has been abandoned by his wife and that one year later he saw his two young children die in a fire, Kublins decides to appeal to the debtor by telling of her sympathy. "I put myself in the position of a man who loves a woman so much he must hate her," she writes. "I imagined my two innocent children were screaming in horrible, undeserved torture. . . . And in that moment when my imaginings were your realities my heart went out to you." Her letter closes by reminding the unfortunate man of his debts. "I know that you will get this money to us in some way, so that you will not hurt and disappoint a friend . . . as you have been hurt and disappointed." The story ends with a fittingly cruel irony. Two days later, Miss Kublins learns that the debtor has committed suicide, deeded his body to the state medical college, and requested that payment for the corpse should be sent to his creditors."[35]

The scenario Thompson imagined in this story anticipated and inverted the message that he would find in the WPA. In Thompson's rendition, as in that of many of his WPA colleagues, the Writers' Project exemplified the civic mission of public education — an opportunity to "counter wasteful political disagreement" by overcoming "self-deception, inhibition, and habit" — and thus an example of the benefits of state action and intellectual leadership. "Sympathy," like James Dillon's bookkeeping system, does not deny those possibilities so much as offer a less uplifting version of them. Like Thompson's work on the Writers' Project, both Dillon's bookkeeping and Miss Kublins's dunning letters are efforts to intervene in and to rationalize commercial relations. Each of these kinds of writing involves an attempt to reduce the unpredictability and inefficiency of the market, and each depends on the writer's imaginative projection—his or her ability to see, as Miss Kublins puts it, "imaginings" as "realities." The difference, of course, is that work on the Writers' Project points not just to the power of intellectually fortified management, but to the virtue of the disinterested pursuit of the public good. By removing him from the demands of the market, Thompson suggested, the WPA freed the "honest and conscientious" writer to become "a mirror" to the whole nation. The state-financed writer spoke not for employers or employees, skilled or unskilled labor, farmers or consumers; he told "the story of America."[36] What both *Now and On Earth* and, especially, "Sympathy" do, by contrast, is to remove that civic alternative to the market in order to raise the corrosive suggestion that disinterest is always finally interested, that all appeals to the civic good are driven by private ends. Each in this way appears to confirm a message that its critics have often leveled against liberalism—that it imagines a world in which there is no public realm, only private actors and in which common feeling therefore becomes falsely manipulative sentiment.

The pathos of the crime fiction that Thompson would write throughout the fifties comes in the way in which it appears to confirm that suspicion. The calculation, the brutality, the perverse fatefulness, and above all the loneliness depicted again and again by his novels all depend for their effect on the *frisson* we may experience when we discover that sympathy is really manipulation, that protestations of disinterest conceal selfish calculation, that all people are predatory, and, most importantly, that as a consequence, public action is pointless. Most Thompson heroes resemble Miss Kublins in that they possess the intelligence and sympathy in order to imagine themselves in the place of another, but, like Lou Ford, they usually use that ability to manipulate or to injure their neighbors. Like Miss Kublins again, though, they tend to discover that this ability turns on them—that rather than becoming masters of circumstance as they expected, they become its victim.

If we read Thompson's crime fiction as a lament for the state leadership and civic purpose that Thompson associated with the WPA, those qualities make perfect sense. They constitute a complaint against what Michael Sandel calls the "sense of disempowerment that afflicts citizens of the procedural republic." By procedural republic, Sandel means especially the brand of liberalism that rose to dominance in the postwar years and that, assuming government could be merely a neutral umpire among the freely chosen desires of individual citizens, denies the state the kind of higher ends that Thompson saw in the WPA. Like Thompson, Sandel mourns the way that postwar liberalism displaced the language of collective purpose and "formative" government that constituted a central feature of New Deal rhetoric. No surprise, then, that his sense of what is wrong with that situation closely matches the experience depicted by Thompson's fiction: "A loss of agency . . . results when liberty is detached from self-government and located in the will of an independent self, unencumbered by moral or communal ties it has not chosen. Such a self, liberated though it be from the burden of identities it has not chosen, entitled though it be to the range of rights assumed by the welfare state, may nonetheless find itself overwhelmed as it turns to face the world on its own resources."[37] Thompson's protagonists, like Sandel's citizens, are on their own, free to invent themselves, to deny obligations to others, to act as they like in pursuit of their own self-chosen ends, and, like Sandel, Thompson suggests that such opportunity is not really freedom but a trap.

One way to understand that perception is by seeing it in the context of a dilemma that the historian Thomas Haskell refers to as the problem of "transitivity" — a modern, secular, and particularly intense version of the problem of free will. As Haskell explains, although philosophically speaking we are always free to think of ourselves as autonomous and self-determining individuals — as "uncaused causes" — we are equally able to see ourselves as the end products of various forces that exceed our grasp, as overdetermined functions rather than undetermined agents.[38] In fact, each of these perceptions depends on the same intellectual capacities. It often seems that by gaining knowledge and understanding of our world we also gain more control over the factors that shape and influence us. But, as Haskell points out, a reverse experience is also likely: "the richer and more complex our knowledge, the greater the perceived force of circumstance in our lives, the more contingent our existence seems, and the less original and consequential we feel." That problem becomes particularly intense, moreover, in the secular world shaped by industrial capitalism. So long as people could refer their choices to the "supremely causal entity" of the divine, their concerns about salvation, or sin, or propitiation were likely to be more significant than their anxieties about personal autonomy. But in "the world of proliferating technique and technological innovation that the market fosters, every new capacity to act breeds feelings of incapacity in those who are acted upon, and every expansion of causal horizons for some renders more fragile the perceptions of intransitivity upon which the autonomy of others depends."[39]

If as I have suggested throughout this book, the classic detective story poses and resolves the crucial dilemmas of liberal societies, one way it does so is by staging Haskell's problem of transitivity. From "Murders in the Rue Morgue" — where we learn that Poe's orangutan is compelled both by its master and by its animal instincts — onward, the detective story has traditionally pointed to figures who are determined by instinct or circumstance in order to suggest that we readers are not wholly so. Indeed, as an acute essay by Joan Copjec points out, that premise is built into the very epistemology of the genre. Copjec notes that the detective story often pretends to a kind of radical empiricism; following clues, the narrative of detection repudiates theoretical abstraction and acts as if only the evidence of the senses gave reliable knowledge. But in truth, Copjec argues, what the genre shows is the necessity for some theoretical limit on empirical information. There has to be a detective who can assemble and reassemble the story's clues, and thus there has to be a transcendent (or "nonphenomenal") vantage not finally determined by circumstance.[40] The premise of the genre's crucial explanatory scenes, of course, is that we share that intimation of epistemological and moral agency. When we see that the murderer is compelled — first by his or her own passions and then by the law — we implicitly recognize our own freedom.

In this way, the classic detective story made a myth of the problem of agency, registering the problem of transitivity and then projecting it onto a criminal who absorbed and exorcised the threat. Hardboiled crime fiction's response to this story was to challenge its confidence, making its reassurance seem, as Chandler put it, "formal" rather than substantive. Stressing the complexity of industrial society, the genre tended to look at that world much as Walter Lippmann did in his contemporaneous meditation on the problem of urban crime. "Our civilization has become so extensive and complex," Lippmann claimed in a 1931 essay titled "The Underworld," "that we are for the most part mere spectators of events in which by a hidden chain of causes we are implicated."[41] From such a perspective, the confident resolutions of the classic detective story were bound to seem pat, and the major crime writers of the interwar years consequently emphasized the uncertainty of their conclusions and the discomforting awareness that the chain of causes could never be convincingly snipped off. But for the hard-boiled detective story, much as for Lippmann, that recognition usually came in the service of the intimation that, by recognizing the force of circumstance rather than denying it, we could reassert a qualified agency. This, too, was a central premise of the first two stages of the New Deal. Whether inspired by centralized planning, Brandeisian antimonopolism, or by NRA-style corporatism, New Deal reformers assumed that expanding public knowledge of the economy and society would help to restore the capacity for action of individual citizens and make the state an efficient agency of political leadership.[42]

The "New" New Deal that came to the fore during and after the war countered those assumptions. Turning away from planning and regulation, the Roosevelt administration's newly dominant Keynesians made fiscal policy and compensatory social insurance the primary responsibilities of government and cast the state in the role of broker rather than civic leader or collective voice.[43] In fact, a central premise of that transition was the limited capacity of political agency to control the national economy. As the Harvard economist Seymour Harris explained in an effort to popularize the role that fiscal policy might take in stimulating a full-employment economy, "the Keynesian medicine" could cure American capitalism without creating the *dirigiste* state that many of its champions and critics alike had seen in the New Deal. Indeed, fiscal policy assumed that the industrial economy was too complex to direct and that "planning" rested on a mistaken effort to personify collective groups. Against that tendency, Keynesianism conceived the nation not as collective body, but as "an economic unit," an abstract corporate entity defined not by a unified political will, but by its aggregate income, consumption, and investment.[44] Almost at a stroke, then, the triumph of fiscal policy during and immediately after the war did away with the traditional reform policies of planning and regulation and pushed aside advocates of social welfare and social democracy, leaving Social Security as the linchpin of America's limited welfare state.[45] In tandem with the new centrality of fiscal policy, too, Social Security gave still more emphasis to the privatization of what had only recently been cast as civic goals — taking "the form not of a broad contract between social groups but of myriad private contracts between individuals and the state."[46] Doing so, moreover, Social Security, like the newly dominant Keynesian medicine, also narrowed the range of both political and personal agency. For what the actuarial calculation basic to social insurance does, as Michael Szalay has brilliantly shown, is to encourage a particular view of society as a statistical aggregation (and a particular view of the state as insurer) and thus to foster a diminished view of both political action and personal intention. By its nature, insurance does not plan or direct, it compensates for unforeseen events, and thus by implication, it allows individuals perfect freedom and simultaneously consigns their particular choices to inconsequentiality. When people are seen primarily as members of risk pools, their personal hopes, desires, and actions turn out to be less significant than the way they exemplify probabilistic patterns.[47]

Hence the fact that, as Michael Sandel complains, the Keynesian liberalism of the postwar years might at once seem to allow for previously unimagined individual liberty and at the same time give rise to a disembodied sense of freedom — one that could turn out to feel not only abstract but illusory. Joined to the vast expansion of the postwar economy, the predominant ways of conceiving government during the later 1940s and the 1950s worked to detach people from tangible, local worlds. Those worlds may often have been oppressive, conservative, and hierarchical, but their very immediacy also fostered the perception that they might be managed or negotiated — that, as Dashiell Hammett's fiction suggested, they might be manipulated by hard and shifty fellows; or, as Chandler's implied, that they might be softened by common sentiment. Removing people from those contexts, though, both Keynesian fiscal policy and social insurance implicitly placed individuals in statistical contexts that no one could hope to control. As Hannah Arendt explained during the same period that Thompson's career as a crime novelist took off, the compensatory state highlighted the "unfortunate truth about behaviorism and the validity of its 'laws' ": "the more people there are, the more likely they are to behave and the less likely to tolerate non-behavior. Statistically, this will be shown in the leveling out of fluctuation. In reality, deeds will more and more lose their significance." The postwar welfare state dismissed public "action and speech," Arendt complained, and made a "despotism" out of "the mathematical treatment of reality."[48]

As his first effort with the paperback thriller made clear, Thompson's fiction hinged on a similar impression. *The Killer Inside Me* takes place in a west Texas oil town whose population has increased tenfold — from 4,800 to 48,000 — in the wartime and postwar boom. Now a centerless sprawl, with a weak municipal government and the ironic name Central City, Thompson's setting is a place where popular community has devolved into a harsh antagonism between smugly complacent, conventional mores and a rebellious individual freedom that appears almost by necessity pathological. As if to second Arendt's diagnosis, Thompson suggests that in such a context the rule of law inevitably becomes bureaucratic and insubstantial (the "only legal definition we have for insanity," a lawyer and the novel's voice of wisdom points out, "is the condition which necessitates the confinement of a person") and, consequently, that the stories of crime and detection that served previously as allegories of civic and political conflict can now be understood only as problems of individual identity. "They could only find the proof in me — in what I was," Lou Ford explains, an internalization of crime, he points out, that makes identity not just foundational but, by the same token, immutable: "that's all any of us ever are: what we have to be."[49] For Thompson, as for Sandel and Arendt, in other words, the displacement of local community by a procedural state results in both unconstrained individual license and the disappearance of personal agency. That perception only blossomed fully in the gothic vision of Thompson's fifties paperbacks, but it was predicted as early as "Sympathy." For what that story depicts in its conclusion is the way the proceduralism of a credit economy almost literally transforms the consumer's body into a financial asset and simultaneously subordinates creative energy to economic management. The point, as in the analogous bookkeeping system from *Now and on Earth*, is the way the personal agency prized by civic life gives way before systems of bureaucratic administration that transcend individual persons.

It makes sense, then, that Thompson's crime novels should have dispensed with the "tired old private-eye stuff" of his predecessors. What he dismissed in that innovation was the possibility that had been represented by the detective since the genre's earliest appearance: that the conflict between law and justice could be dramatized and mediated. Tossing aside the private eye, Thompson likewise suggested that in his world there was now only the formal machinery of law and no longer either the grounds or the means to consider alternatives to its workings. An outraged sense of frustration informs that view, one that becomes fully understandable only when we see it in light of the high expectations that Thompson built up for his writing when he was employed by the WPA and in the way that the disappointment of those expectations came to exemplify the problem of "transitivity" discussed by Thomas Haskell. By Haskell's account, that problem is a peculiarly secular dilemma. For the religious mind, he suggests, the notion that one's own acts and desires are not freely chosen is less a problem than evidence of one's "intimate proximity to the First Cause."[50] It might not be inaccurate in this light to say that as a young man working on the Oklahoma Writers' Project, Thompson like many of his contemporaries divinized "the American land" — casting the nation as a collective will that transcended conflicting interests, and himself, a voice of the state apparatus, as one of its prophets. Seen in that context, his later fiction depicts a world from which that god has absconded, leaving only the apparatus behind. In that world, Thompson stresses, personal will becomes insignificant, civic life disappears, and the writer, no longer a prophet, exemplifies a system he cannot alter.

THE INTEGRITY OF SELF-EXPRESSION

As if to lend weight to that impression, Thompson several times imagined an originary moment for his criminal protagonists — in each case depicting a dual pathology: the bureaucratic dissolution of civil society and the simultaneous failure of personal self-formation. Thus, in Thompson's first crime novel, *Nothing More Than Murder*, we learn that the roots of Joe Wilmot's criminality can be traced to his abandonment by an alcoholic mother. When the infant Joe is discovered by a neighbor, who will soon turn him over to a state orphanage, Joe screams for his "money" (which the neighbor tellingly mistakes for "mommy") — a worthless "mess of whisky labels." The etiology of Joe's criminal appetite, Thompson thus implies, can be traced to his desire to replace the mother who abandoned him to a bureaucratic state. More subtly, he suggests that that desire is impelled by Joe's consequent failure to understand abstract symbolic systems. The young Joe is not able to distinguish between the desire to possess money, mother, and liquor labels, much as the older Joe will be unable to understand his dissatisfaction in pursuit of ever greater possession. In an inversion of Freud's famed *fort-da* story, where the ritual of play becomes "a great cultural achievement," allowing the child to symbolically master his mother's coming and going, Joe Wilmot never grasps the logic of substitution, Thompson suggests, and thus never has a means to conceive and mediate his desires. Unable to "identify himself with something" outside himself and thus "to picture himself as being some certain thing," he remains trapped in an intolerable, and criminally imperial, self.[51] A similar suggestion is made in the later novel *A Swell Looking Babe*, when Dusty Rhodes begins his criminal career by signing his father's name to a petition supporting victims of McCarthyism — thus insuring his father's own criminal investigation and his dismissal from his job as a high school principal. Since Dusty has the same name as his father, he creates that forgery simply by leaving the "Jr." off his own signature. Effectively refusing the Oedipal economy of training and subordination, Dusty's forgery acts simply to displace his father and simultaneously allows the civic world of education to be shut down by state surveillance. In each example, Thompson traces criminality to a failure of cultural achievement and links that failure to the displacement of the civic by the oppressively bureaucratic.[52]

Thompson's contemporary, Charles Willeford, imagined a similar but still more revealing originary moment. In the paperback crime novels he wrote during the fifties, Willeford echoed Thompson's diagnosis of postwar society, but he joined that account to a more concrete and much more disquieting reaction to contemporary political developments. The tale he implicitly used to explain that reaction is accordingly far more specific than Thompson's fables of cultural failure. The story appears twice in Willeford's writing — once as a central feature of his most ambitious and significant novel from the fifties, *The Black Mass of Brother Springer*; the second time as an anecdote heard by the author himself in *I Was Looking for a Street*, Willeford's autobiographical account of his life as a homeless teenager during the Depression. In both cases, the story appears as an obscure parable, related by an older and wiser figure to the callow protagonist of Willeford's text, and in each case the tale's enigmatic features convey Willeford's central perception of the meaning of American mass culture and public life. As the narrator of the tale in *The Black Mass of Brother Springer* explains, the anecdote concerns "the one mistake" he has ever made. The event has nevertheless shaped "the course of . . . [his] entire life," and he clearly intends that Willeford's protagonist, and by extension the novel's audience, should understand that its moral significance applies to them as well.[53]

The story concerns a white adolescent boy who is approached by a young black woman in the balcony of a Midwestern movie theater. The woman offers to sell the protagonist her sexual favors, but as the two, bent over the back of the cinema's seats, are in the midst of fulfilling this transaction, the film that has been playing suddenly breaks. The house lights come up, the crowd turns to look toward the projection booth, and the interracial couple suddenly find themselves caught in flagrante delicto by representatives of the entire community — a "school teacher, two women friends of my mother, a dentist, and several boys I knew around town." The young man's ensuing public humiliation drives him out of his local world and into a life on the road and later the army.[54]

At its core, then, this ugly parable allegorizes the displacement of local community by mass society — its bathetic hero the young man who leaves the intimate village, first for the alienation of the road and later for the mass bureaucratic structures of the military. Its key feature, however, is the peril of interracial seduction that Willeford places at the center of this tale. Without that image of tacit pathology, Willeford's story raises little of the threat it is meant to convey. No other force could be dangerous or potent enough to dislodge him from a complacent intimate world, the story's narrator suggests. And, thus, the lure and peril of miscegenation becomes the key factor in his vision of the power of mass culture. That emphasis would persist so consistently throughout the author's novels that it would suggest a robust vision of postwar society, a strong reading of American culture that would inspire the paperback writer's bizarre narrative vision. For Willeford, whose literary career developed alongside the rise of mass consumerism, suburbanization, *and* the contemporaneous development of the civil rights movement, mass society could be defined by two features in particular — its celebration of comfort and domesticity and its incipient interracial public. Seeking to develop a critical account of the postwar landscape, he combined the two to suggest that mass society almost automatically feminized and racialized its citizenry.

Indeed, as I will explain more fully, this was one implication of the very title *The Black Mass of Brother Springer*, a book whose meaning hinges on the pun implicit in its title. For Willeford's novel is centrally concerned with a postwar society whose political order is "half-Republican and half-Socialist" and whose cultural life seems characterized by *Reader's Digest*, instant coffee, and the Diner's Club. The mass public shaped by these institutions, however, is crucially represented by the congregation of an African American church. It is, in short, a *black* mass public, and for the paternalist Willeford that means a social formation that is also vulnerable, superstitious, and sentimental — in a word, feminine. The same nasty implication inheres in the enigmatic parable at the heart of Willeford's novel. When its representative young man is seduced, first by the national media represented by the movies themselves, and then by the lure of inter-racial sex, Willeford suggests that mass culture turns stalwart white men into docile subjects — alienated, sexually vulnerable, and racially suspect. That conviction would lie at the heart of the several bizarre novels Willeford would publish throughout the Eisenhower era.

Like Thompson's stories of cultural failure, then, Willeford's own primal scene not only offered a window onto the writer's peculiar obsessions, it situated his work in relation to an implicit vision of the postwar United States. All of Willeford's pulp novels would be shaped by and would operate in tacit contention with the over-whelming forces he aimed to portray in his tale of racial and sex-ual humiliation. But where Thompson's parable of cultural failure turned on the decline of the thirties' left populism, Willeford's story reflected the rightward orientation of his fiction, and it looked at the developments Thompson portrayed from a reverse angle. Unlike Thompson, Willeford never worked for the WPA, and he was unable to look back on New Deal programs for the democratization of culture with the regret that Thompson expressed. During the thir-ties, Willeford was a homeless teenager who rode the rails and wan-dered from government camp to government camp — institutions he later depicted as lifeless, authoritarian, and inefficient. He escaped this poverty by joining the army, in which he served as an enlisted man and a noncommissioned officer for twenty years, and it was only on leaving the army in 1956 that he began work as a writer, turning out short paperback novels for publishers who specialized in producing sensational, digest-sized paperbacks for newsstand circu-lation. For Willeford, as for the subject of his parable of mass cul-ture, then, the main representative of the activist federal state would be the military, an emphasis that would make Thompson's obsession with the loss of collective expression seem insignificant. Thus, where novels like *Now and On Earth* or *The Killer Inside Me* mourned the loss of a public culture once nurtured by the state and its displace-ment by alienating privacy, Willeford usually told a complementary but opposed story. The problem with postwar society in his view was not that public voice has been swallowed by private satisfactions, but that the private and individual could not be maintained against a voracious mass public. At the same time, his depiction of postwar society was one that stressed the loss of the army's homosocial discipline and camaraderie. Time and again, his novels depict postwar society in the image of a terrible, castrating heterosexuality.

Willeford told that story frequently and in a number of guises — focusing especially on portraits of various alienated and frustrated artists or criminals. But the best example may be in the brief anti-detective novel that Willeford titled *Wild Wives*. Like Jim Thompson's first work, that book most clearly suggests the way in which Willeford both drew on and departed from the conventions established by his hard-boiled predecessors. The protagonist and narrator of *Wild Wives* is private detective Jake Blake — a figure whose comically exaggerated name turns out to be quite fitting. For Willeford's protagonist is a deliberately overdrawn parody of the gumshoe made familiar by the previous generation of hard-boiled crime fiction. Blake bears all the markings of the stereotypical figure. He maintains a seedy office in a cheap hotel, antagonizes the police (while maintaining an ambivalent friendship with one sympathetic cop), and generally fancies himself, like Sam Spade, a man able to get the best of anyone in any situation. But, as Willeford takes care to emphasize, Blake is a hollow echo of his predecessors. His profession itself is in rapid decline, and Jake has almost no clientele and little hope of future work. Nor does he have the virtues represented in various ways by Sam Spade or Philip Marlowe. He lacks the strength to withstand both the destructive force of female desire and the antagonistic authority of legal bureaucracy, and he has little ability to turn his friendship with the good cop to his advantage. In short, like *Nothing More than Murder* or *A Swell-Looking Babe*, *Wild Wives* serves as Willeford's deconstruction of the hard-boiled private-eye story, and it works relentlessly to demolish the hubris proudly claimed by Hammett and Chandler's heroes. Jake Blake ends his story in a jail cell, imprisoned for a murder he did not commit, and the concluding lines of his narration indicate that the law no longer seems even slightly negotiable: "The only defense I had was the fact that I was a good soldier during the war. My lawyer passed my medals around the jury box, and they were closely examined. . . . They didn't help a bit."[55] Where the previous generation of hard-boiled stories called on homosocial camaraderie to meliorate and finally to direct a bureaucratic order, Willeford makes male bonding insignificant. The good soldier is sucked into the maw of a mass society.

Like Thompson, then, Willeford charts the emergence of a postwar order by displacing homosocial redemption with heterosexual dissolution—thereby reversing the allegory of civic development that had been central to the previous generation of hard-boiled writers. If the irony of Jake Blake's story is that he grasps none of the forces of law and society that he imagines he controls, those unmasterable energies are all represented by an alluring or repulsive feminine sexuality. Jake is ensnared by a voracious and schizophrenic sexual predator named Florence Weintraub. He is enticed and annoyed by a nubile bobby soxer named Barbara Ann Allen, who first flirts with Jake and then calls on her father to punish him for his indifference. And he is provoked and finally destroyed by Barbara Ann's adolescent brother, Freddy, an effeminate homosexual who murders his older lover and frames Jake for the crime. Even the obnoxious police authority dedicated to breaking Jake's independence is represented primarily by its association with femininity and domesticity. Jake's prime antagonist, Lieutenant Pulaski, prominently displays the photographs of his wife and five children on his desk, reminding Willeford's protagonist of his alienation from a stifling domestic regime. Wherever he turns, then, Jake is surrounded by lethal femininity, and the novel's graphic opening thus serves to outline Willeford's whole point: Jake Blake sits alone in his office doing nothing until Barbara Ann enters, holds him up with a water pistol, and then refuses to leave until Jake pretends to make her his assistant. At the moment she departs, Florence Weintraub slinks in, smiles "with a set of little white teeth . . . slanted toward the center," and asks Jake to serve as her bodyguard—a mission that will turn out to be little more than a subtle form of prostitution (14). In both cases, Willeford's protagonist finds himself lured into humiliating and predatory heterosexual entanglements. Each time, he imagines himself in cool control, and he takes a delight in commanding the women who have fallen beneath his hand. With both women he discovers, however, that his will is no match for the incipiently murderous force of feminine desire.

At the heart of Willeford's fiction, in short, lies an extraordinary anxiety about voracious women, and that paranoid fantasy points to the main interest of his novels. On the surface, most of Willeford's various first-person narrators resemble Spillane's Mike Hammer. They are rude, arrogant, aggressive, domineering — all qualities most evident in their abusive attitudes toward the women they command and seduce. Like Spillane, they are determined to be winners in a world where only losers fail to exploit every advantage. Beneath this swagger, though, lurks a barely concealed terror of feminine sexuality. In the world as Willeford depicts it, a man may feel confident, but he is hopelessly deluded if he believes he can protect his autonomy by any means apart from an ascetic refusal of desire and communication. The result throughout Willeford's fiction is a hopeless commitment to asexuality — a dedication whose pathos comes from the fact that it can never be completed or finally maintained. As Richard Hudson, the filmmaker protagonist of the aptly titled book *The Woman Chaser* explains, a person who hopes to become a great artist (or to achieve the personal authenticity represented for Willeford and his generation by the great artist) must strive to replace the "sexual drive" with the "aggressive drive," seeing women not as objects of desire, but as predatory combatants determined to sap men of vitality. The title of this novel thus turns out to be a testimony not to its protagonist's bedroom victories, but to his personal and aesthetic failures — Willeford's capsule description for the reason a story that seems at first to be about a triumphant campaign of sexual conquest and artistic triumph turns out to be one of self-destruction. For the woman chaser, sexual dominance inevitably becomes submission, and arrogant control becomes confusion — a dynamic summed up by the way that Richard Hudson, setting out to seduce an ostensibly virginal young woman, suddenly finds himself the feminized object of her intentions: "I was on my back. . . . Her restless tongue, hot and hard, licked beneath my neck, at my armpit, stabbed wetly into my ear." To be a man who gives way to desire in Willeford's world is, in short, ultimately to become a woman.[56]

For Willeford, then, heterosexuality signals a terrible public submission, a seduction from noble privacy into the banal commerce that defines postwar society. And here especially, he can be usefully compared to his contemporary Jim Thompson — whose erotic anxieties are equally prominent, though significant for quite different reasons. Like Willeford's stories of humiliation, Thompson's tales of cultural failure turn on a gothic and finally prudish atmosphere of sexual hysteria, and they typically culminate in some symbol or literal image of autocastration — as in the famous double conclusion to *A Hell of a Woman*, in which the protagonist, Dolly Dillon, either deliberately mutilates himself on a broken window or is surgically amputated by his female companion. But Thompson's fantasies of impotence differ importantly from Willeford's paranoia about sexual submission, reflecting less an anxiety about the loss of autonomy than the yearning for a pre-Oedipal innocence. Along with *A Hell of a Woman*, Thompson created several visions of castration — *The Nothing Man*, for example, whose self-lacerating protagonist has literally lost his penis to a land mine in World War II, or *Savage Night*, which ends with the narrator crawling childishly around a basement and relating his progressive dismemberment at the hands of an ax-wielding femme fatale. What all these novels share is the fact that Thompson's heroes seem first to be victims of circumstance or of feminine antagonists and are then shown to have overpowering wills to self-destruction. Each thus becomes a nightmarish story of self-mutilation in which a man destroys his own potency out of a terrible yearning for the security represented by a maternal woman. Like the aptly named Dolly Dillon, who describes his self-inflicted castration as a means to be "safe . . . [from] the thing I needed to be safe from," or Charlie Bigger in *Savage Night* who imagines his death as a way to get "back to the place I'd come from," these men are willing to kill themselves in order to escape the corruption of sex and to recover the innocence of childhood. As such, though, and as the failures Thompson inevitably shows them being, they are always incipiently impotent. The literal images of castration that often conclude Thompson's novels are merely the culminating record of their absence of agency — an absence that Thompson traces to their larger cultural failure and their imprisonment in the terrible cage of the private self.[57]

Willeford's characters face an opposite dilemma. They are not impotent but hyperpotent, driven by an overwhelming urge to sexual conquest that guarantees their ultimate defeat. Even though Richard Hudson knows that he must sublimate his "sexual drive" for his "aggressive drive" if he is to become the great artist he longs to be, he finds the effort finally hopeless, and in *The Woman Chaser*'s most devastating and complex image of humiliation he ends by seducing a female Salvation Army captain in a gay bar as a jukebox plays the maudlin tune "My Buddy." The protagonist's complete defeat comes, in other words, when sexual submission reduces him to the effeminate status of Freddy Allen in *Wild Wives* and when he falls beneath the terrible "sentimentality" that Willeford sees in both mass culture and in the bureaucratic order of organized charity. "All I had lost in the struggle," Hudson notes with self-pitying irony, "was the integrity of my self-expression" (180, 188). Thus, for Richard Hudson as for Jake Blake, sexual exchange results in social corruption. Asexuality, by contrast, represents the impossible ideal of a purely individual integrity. From this perspective, strange as it may seem in the work of an unreconstructed masculinist like Willeford, the truest and most admirable man is what Willeford calls "one type of homosexual" — that is, the type who seems not seductive and feminized, but masculine and independent, utterly removed from a society dominated by women (ww 49).

That role is best represented by a revealing minor figure in *Wild Wives*: Freddy Allen's older lover and eventual victim, an art dealer with the unlikely, but telling name of Jefferson Davis. Apart from his ineffectual ally on the police force, Davis is Jake Blake's only friend, and the reasons for the sympathy between the two men are apparent. Like Blake, Davis is at heart solitary. He lives in a hotel room whose walls are entirely covered by Klee paintings and reproductions, and he wants nothing more than to escape his relationship with Freddy Allen. He exemplifies, in other words, Willeford's central value — the principle, as another character names it, of "discrimination" — and his name thus indicates the thoroughness of his ethical commitments

(56). Jefferson Davis hopes almost literally to secede from consumer society and from its effeminate representatives, and his hotel room, completely encased in abstract painting, exemplifies a sublime refusal of communication. Modernist abstraction, like masculinist homosexuality, signals a remove from the heterosexual world of the mass public. Indeed, Willeford underlines this point by giving Davis a parallel character — Florence's husband, Milton Weintraub, a prominent San Francisco architect and Willeford's version of Howard Roark, the superhero of Ayn Rand's *The Fountainhead*. Each of these men stands at the apex of an erotic "triangle" into which Jake is "sucked" — Weintraub and his wife form the two sides of one triangle, Davis and his lover Freddy, the other (59). Each is dedicated to an uncompromising aesthetic autonomy that removes him from the banalities of ordinary communication, so that Weintraub's status as the Jewish architect is likened to Jefferson Davis's identity as the homosexual art dealer (the Jew, like the gay man, representing the cultural outlaw). Both men are thereby cast as unremittingly alien to a feminized culture. Tragically, though, each allows that autonomy to be compromised because he is unable to resist erotic enticement. (Weintraub admits that he married the schizophrenic Florence because she offers him "the best sex in San Francisco" [57].) The penalty for these men, as it will be for Jake, is death. Both are murdered by the lovers who seduce them.

As Jefferson Davis, Milton Weintraub, and Richard Hudson all suggest, then, Willeford's account of sex is also a theory of art and of its relation to a mass public — an association that lies at the heart of his baroquely inventive novels. Throughout all of them, the desire to maintain sexual autonomy becomes equivalent to a desire to maintain aesthetic autonomy and ultimately to a commitment to maintain the differentiation emblematized by racial segregation. Each of these efforts for "discrimination" is pictured in Nietzschean terms that make Willeford perhaps closest to Hammett of all the hardboiled writers. The protagonists of his novels are driven by a cruel, often violent, will to separation. More importantly, though, Willeford shows that the fulfillment of that will is ultimately impossible. Struggle as they may to fashion an aristocratic alienation for themselves, Willeford's protagonists all resemble Jefferson Davis. They cannot maintain their autonomy, and they inevitably fall beneath the tide of banality that they once imagined they could control. Indeed, Willeford takes care to suggest that such an irony is an unavoidable aspect of the very pursuit of radical discrimination. If Jefferson Davis and Milton Weintraub both represent a modernist distaste for the mass public—a distaste whose culmination would come in absolute solitude—not only their erotic potency but their very professions guarantee that neither man could ever achieve such isolation. As an architect, Weintraub commands "city projects" (15). His work is inescapably public and tellingly bound up with the state agencies of social welfare. Likewise, Jefferson Davis can command the Klee paintings that insulate his room only because he is an art dealer who is thereby compelled to operate within the cultural marketplace that he would like to escape. Indeed, Davis becomes most entangled with Freddy Allen when he exchanges a Picasso drawing for the boy's sexual favors. In both cases, elite disdain for banal consumerism cannot be separated from economic dependence on the mass public. It is the very embarrassment of that dependence, Willeford implies, that leads to the yearning for autonomy in the first place and that explains its inevitable failure.

In a series of scabrous fantasies, Willeford told the story of that yearning and failure time and again throughout the fifties. But his first novel, *The High Priest of California*, may illustrate the irony at the core of this tale in Willeford's most schematic terms. His protagonist, a used-car dealer named Russell Haxby, is the paradigmatic Willeford hero of this period—an aggressive salesman, dedicated to self-gratification, to the consumerist trappings of modern life, *and* to the most challenging examples of modernist culture. " 'In the Penal Colony' . . . is the best short story ever written," Haxby thinks, but if he is not engrossed in Kafka, he is likely to be chanting "Burnt Norton" aloud to Bartók's *Miraculous Mandarin* (21). This infatuation (no other word could describe the intense emotion Willeford portrays) with difficult art is a key feature of Haxby's character; for, by Willeford's logic it indicates not the enviably rounded humanity that interest in high culture signals in Ross Macdonald, say, nor the failure of will it points to in Thompson, but a taste for raw power. Thus, a typical Willeford scenario is one in which Haxby enters a bar, beats a man unconscious for no other reason than to let off steam, and then returns home to put Berlioz's Overture to *Romeo and Juliet* on the hi-fi. Likewise, Haxby's love of Joyce, Eliot, and Kafka distinguishes him from Alyce, the woman whose seduction forms the entire plot of the novel. A Book-of-the-Month-Club subscriber, a dabbler in ceramics, and the owner of a Van Gogh reproduction, Alyce is a pathetic embodiment of middlebrow sensibility. Haxby's disdain for her taste becomes, therefore, an aesthetic justification for his obsessive aim to seduce and abandon her. It is as though Willeford set out to reverse, with brutal gusto, the elegiac themes of *The Long Goodbye*. The woman who represents mass culture here seems, at least at first, less lethal than compliant before an elitist sensibility that imposes its will with sheer nasty glee.

What makes Willeford's fiction unsettling, though, is not merely that he equates art and domination, but that he renders the association in deeply sympathetic terms. If a writer like Chandler suggested that modernist aesthetics were the product of soulless professionalism, Willeford's novels accept the diagnosis and portray a powerful yearning for that very condition. Art becomes attractive in this view for much the same reasons advanced by the champions of modernism: it is a release from the demands of sentiment and ordinary life. In Willeford's description, though, that emancipation is indistinguishable from cruelty and from the language of class and gender and, as we will see more fully, racial hierarchy. "As a writer I was above any outward show of emotion," the hero of *The Black Mass of Brother Springer* explains, adding without remorse, "and gradually . . . I was incapable of feeling any kind of emotion. . . . I shut all thoughts of my neighbors out, and lived entirely within myself" (15).

That there might be any difficulties with such a conception — some conflict between literature and domination or between the gratification of solitude and the demands of art — is a notion that comes only slowly to Willeford's protagonists. But it is nevertheless the irresolvable problem at the heart of the novels. The difficulty is exemplified by Russell Haxby's favored pastime — paraphrasing *Ulysses* into accessible, readerly prose. That unusual hobby is Willeford's weirdly brilliant image for the dilemmas of postwar modernism and for the problems faced by the era's paperback writers in particular. For

Haxby, the habit is much like his love for Bartók and Kafka; it indicates a profound love for solitude and a callous insensitivity to matters of emotion and community. In this mode, paraphrasing Joyce is a way of communing with high art against the world of used cars and middlebrow women, a solitude exemplified by the sheer uselessness of the activity.

Yet Willeford's protagonist is also suitably unable to commit to that uselessness. Though paraphrasing Joyce seems to grant him a beautiful emptiness, Haxby hopes also to make a quick buck from his hobby. He plans to sell his paraphrase of *Ulysses* to a public he thinks ready for cheap summaries of modernist masterpieces. For that very reason, though, the protagonist's effort to translate Joyce, the mark of his achievement and mastery, also becomes a sign of his failure, since Haxby discovers that it is impossible to pander to "a simple-minded audience" while remaining inhumanly apart from it (51). When it is conceived as an attribute of isolation, therefore, modernism means screwing over a feminized public, and it fits well with the used-car salesman's sense of himself as a sharpster, getting the best of everyone he encounters. But when great literature is simply a product to be vended on the market, the translator resembles the salesman who is not the master of rubes, but merely one trading partner in a vast system of exchange — "as much a feeb as any used-car buyer." In this aspect, the arrogant hero becomes himself a member of the feminized mass public, the object rather than the subject of high culture: "I sat down with my copy of *Ulysses* and reread the Penelope episode. I finished the chapter and threw the book across the room. Joyce is so damned clever that sometimes it irritates me to read *Ulysses*. The brilliantly selected words, twisting and turning, force their way into your consciousness and coil like striking snakes" (82).

Willeford's diction in this passage is directly analogous to his description of the seduction scene in *The Woman Chaser*, where Richard Hudson finds himself not the masculine predator he thought, but the vulnerable object of a woman whose tongue stabs into his ear. The echo is fitting. For here, as Haxby fittingly occupies himself with the scene of Molly Bloom's triumph, Willeford's hero learns that he is the victim rather than the master of modernist aesthetics. The scene points, too, toward the conclusion of the novel, where we realize that, having seduced the middlebrow Alyce, Haxby has been infected by the venereal disease that has reduced her husband — a man tellingly named Salvatore "Blackie" Vitale — to childish idiocy. Here, too, the pursuit of domination leads ultimately to vulnerability and to the intimation of sexual and ethnic corruption. All of these reversals finally are summed up in the implications of Willeford's title, which like *The Black Mass of Brother Springer* plays knowingly on a latent double meaning. Russell Haxby is the high priest of California in two senses: first, as the modernist mandarin who looks down with disdain upon the shallow lives and bad taste of the masses; and secondly, as the used-car salesman who, rather than triumphing over postwar mass culture, exemplifies its most fundamental qualities. What Willeford's first novel ultimately suggests is that these two definitions are not opposites, but complements, and that the first position inevitably turns toward the second.

PUBLIC VOICE AND PRIVATE MEANING

Like *The Woman Chaser* and *Wild Wives*, then, *The High Priest of California* depicts the failure of aesthetic elitism. But if Willeford's first novel suggested that Russell Haxby's mandarin isolation could not be maintained, his second, *Pick-Up*, took care to emphasize that the world of postwar mass culture made bohemian *nostalgia de la boue* seem equally implausible. Like Thompson's *Now and On Earth* and like Willeford's other paperbacks in the 1950s, *Pick-Up* is a pulp *kunstleroman* energized by a good deal of autobiographical detail. The novel is narrated by Harry Jordan, a failed painter and alcoholic, and it concerns Harry's relations with Helen Meredith, a fellow drinker from an established family whom he meets while working as a short-order cook. Like Willeford, Jordan has served in the army, where he worked as a mural painter, and he has used his G.I. Bill benefits to complete an art degree, learning about his craft as well from mass-market magazines like "*Art Digest, The American Artist*, and *The Modern Painter*." After the war and art school, Harry graduated from murals to abstract expressionism or what he calls, in the jargon of the period, "non-objective" painting. When the novel begins, though, he has already surrendered his ambitions: "I never could finish anything I started," he admits. "I'd get an idea. Block it out, start on it, and then when I'd get about halfway through I'd discover the idea was terrible." Becoming involved with Helen momentarily reawakens Harry's ambitions — apparently because she legitimates and provides a bald incentive for cultural mobility: "I tried to define what there was about her that attracted me. Class. That was it." But when his efforts to paint her as Olympia falter, Harry and Helen agree to a double suicide. Harry fails even at this task, however, and the remainder of the story concerns his prosecution for Helen's murder and the eventual dismissal of the charges against him. (It turns out that Helen has died of natural causes.) The novel's shocker, though, comes in the concluding passage when Willeford introduces a surprising element to his pseudo-autobiographical text. Although the book never alludes to race at any point until this moment, its mawkish final lines read: "I left the shelter of the awning and walked up the hill in the rain. Just a tall, lonely Negro. Walking in the rain."[58]

It's not immediately apparent what Willeford's motive for this stunt was. He may have been attempting to set himself a literary challenge of a sort — aiming to narrate from the perspective of a black artist without ever making race an explicit issue. Such a challenge would extend, of course, to the reader. The surprise ending is clearly meant to make us rerun the plot in our minds and to lead us to search out the places where race played — or, perhaps, more importantly for Willeford — failed to play a role in Harry's thoughts and experiences. And certainly there is a powerful element of fifties "White-Negro" hipsterism to Willeford's portrait of the beleaguered bohemian, although *Pick-Up* actually anticipates Mailer's formulation by several years. There is, however, a more subtle logic to the story. Harry Jordan is a product par excellence of the democratization of culture. He becomes an artist through the major institutions of postwar expanded opportunity: the military, higher education, and mass-market publications. As Harry points out, "the army gave me the opportunity to use my skill" (140). He also notes, though, that the result of this opportunity was ultimately that he "was unable to finish any picture I started," and that reversal conveys the central implication of the novel (134). The effect of democratizing institutions for Willeford is, paradoxically, not to make art more available but to make its prestige evaporate. Rather than legitimizing Harry, expanded opportunity delegitimizes his options and goals. "There were too many art students," he realizes, "who thought they were artists [but] who should have been mechanics" (42).[59] What the trajectory of Willeford's narrative defines, in this light, is the way a sense of cultural inferiority that first appears at least relatively mediable and that is understood as the product of opportunity and a matter of socioeconomic standing becomes—through the workings of the very institutions that aim to democratize culture—something that seems unchangeable. For Willeford, whose first book was a collection of poetry titled *Proletarian Laughter*, what begins as a matter of class turns ultimately into the most extreme form of difference and abjection he can imagine—that of race.

It is entirely fitting from this perspective that Harry becomes a "lonely Negro" only after he has passed through an efficient and surprisingly just legal system—after he has had his sanity positively evaluated at a criminal hospital and had the murder charges against him rightfully dismissed. Courts and hospitals in this novel are continuous with the other institutions through which Harry has passed, and they closely resemble the aircraft plant that Thompson portrayed in *Now and On Earth*. They discipline, evaluate, and individualize their subjects. It is the very fact that the institutions of democratic life work effectively, though, that convinces Harry he is a man entirely apart and a person for whom cultural ambition, just as it appears nearest to realization, is self-defeating. The racialization of Harry Jordan is thus a more literal and fittingly personal version of the black republic of mass culture that Kenneth Fearing imagines in *The Big Clock*. It likewise resembles the loss of racial prestige that Philip Marlowe implicitly warns the failed writer Roger Wade about when he suggests that entering a psychiatric hospital would be like joining a "Georgia chain-gang" (210). In all of these cases a more or less explicitly racial identity is the counterpart to a cultural failure that is measured, and perhaps produced, by the bureaucratic institutions of mass society. Like Norman Mailer, then, Willeford exploits an image of "the Negro" in order to criticize the stultification of postwar life. But for him, race is useful not because it can be imagined as a reservoir of authenticity to be drawn on against mass culture, but because mass culture seems to call up race in the same movement with which its therapeutic apparatus makes the significance of class disappear.

Harry's personal history thus directly connects the history of American art and the history of the liberal state. As his career begins, Harry very much resembles the young Jim Thompson (not to mention the young Jackson Pollock). A mural painter employed by a major government institution, he works in a genre famous for its emphasis on popular community and social reform. In the postwar setting of the novel, Harry has abandoned this collectivist vocabulary for a style of painting equally renowned for its association with individual expression and liberty.[60] As with Thompson, though, this transition from the culture of the Popular Front to that of the cold war makes high art both democratically available and simultaneously unattainable. The bureaucratic expansion of opportunity thus results in a parodic fulfillment of Chandler's avant-gardist dreams of a "public taste." For Harry, the institutions of art are all too public and democratic. They are at once omnipresent and despicable, so that art is inseparable from the disciplinary regime of prison and hospital and without any underworld or exterior. Indeed, Harry paints only twice in this novel: once, boldly, but unsuccessfully, when he is drawn on by the appeal of Helen's status; and a second time after Helen's death, when the prison and hospital officials demand routine creative activity, forcing Harry to produce drawings for therapeutic purposes that he finds it easy to sell to people fascinated by his case. Ironically, then, Harry is most in touch with "class," when he is least successful and has turned his back on the opportunities for cultural advancement that remain open to him. He is most racially abject, by contrast, when the institutions of mass culture allow him to work as a financially successful draftsman. The two conditions echo the paradoxical options that face Russell Haxby. By Willeford's description, Harry is most an artist when he refuses to paint, and most clearly an aesthetic and moral failure when he accepts the demands of the popular market and the state. But in *Pick-Up*, Willeford makes explicit the racial themes that were merely latent in his previous novel. The paradigmatic commercial hack and the preeminent subject of the therapeutic welfare bureaucracy, the novel implies, is the "lonely Negro."[61]

The most fully worked out exploration of these distasteful implications came in Willeford's last novel from the fifties and his most wildly inventive work, *The Black Mass of Brother Springer*. It was here, in his strange and ugly fantasia on the developing civil rights movement, that Willeford fashioned his most radical and deeply paradoxical account of postwar mass culture and where he expanded furthest on his tendency to conceive that landscape in racial terms. For the protagonist of *The Black Mass of Brother Springer* is, like Willeford's other heroes, a failed artist who finds it impossible to succeed professionally while preserving the inhuman autonomy he believes art should provide. Through a bizarre turn of events, though, he also becomes an unwitting civil rights leader. Much as in *Pick-Up*, then, aesthetic disappointment in *Black Mass* is closely associated with racial confusion. Indeed, for Willeford, the measure of Sam Springer's failure as a writer comes in his embroilment with an integrating public.

At the core of this scenario lies a deliberately fantastic series of events. Sam Springer, Willeford's protagonist and narrator, is an accountant with a large Ohio dairy company who promptly gives up his work and moves to Florida when his novel — *No Bed Too High* — is accepted for publication. For Singer, writing is attractive for much the same reasons that art matters to Russell Haxby and Richard Hudson. It provides the artist with a gratifying sense of elevation above the trivial world that surrounds him. "I marveled that I had ever had any fear of this little man and his little position," the protagonist exults after defying his boss. "The publication of my novel had made me superior to him, to the company, and to any and all types of employment. I was now a man of letters, a free agent, a man who could live by his pen and by his brain!" (7). Springer the novelist looks upon his neighbors and his wife in much the same terms as he regards his former boss. They are sad, pathetic, "a pitiful crew," and the more completely he pursues his ascetic dedication to writing, the more radically the writer must remove himself from their company, embracing in his pursuit of autonomy the same antieroticism praised by Richard Hudson. "I was above it," Springer explains, describing his wife's disappointment, "the thought of sex left me indifferent, uncaring — it was all so boring anyway, and messy on top of that" (14, 15).

Yet, as in his previous novels, Willeford emphasizes the difficulty that arises in the effort to maintain such purity and the underlying paradox that such a difficulty points toward — the conflict between two, seemingly incommensurate images of the writer: the "man of letters," immune to the vulgarities of the marketplace, and the "free agent," who lives by selling the products of "pen" and "brain." The more thoroughly Sam Springer pursues the first ideal, imagining himself an artist cut off from ordinary sociability, the more difficult he finds it to actually do the writing he needs to bring in his income, and the more deeply he begins to resent the demands his wife places on their dwindling resources. The only solution Springer can imagine, of course, is to render his autonomy more complete by abandoning the wife who now seems like little more than a burden to him. That effort, however, merely intensifies the paradoxical situation in which Springer finds himself and renders more dramatic the impossibility of reconciling the liberties that Springer wants to defend.

It is here that Willeford introduces the weird and brilliant device at the center of his novel. Reading the newspaper and worrying over his growing financial difficulties, Springer comes upon an article describing the sale of the Church of God's Flock Monastery. The home of a church founded by a black preacher during the thirties, the CGF Monastery is not only the world's only Protestant abbey, it is a remnant of Depression era efforts for interracial solidarity and a veiled allusion to New Deal projects for social reform. Believing that "white men and Negroes could learn to love one another," the Reverend Cosmo Bird established his order in 1936 as an experiment to bring together an equal number of white and black men, all of whom would work together clearing the Florida jungle and building the monastery (20). Like the historical analogs of the Works Progress Administration (WPA) and the Civilian Conservation Corps (CCC), however, that project depended both on financial support (in this case, the church's trust fund), and a pool of unemployed workers willing to undergo hard labor, limited circumstances, and interracial society for the sake of economic security. With the decline of the church's financial resources and the prosperity of the postwar years, the order begins to fall apart, and its campaign to meliorate racial tension falls by the wayside. Seeing the poignancy in the decline of "the monastic way of life," then, and recognizing the vast public interest in therapeutic religion exemplified by the success of Thomas Merton, Sam Springer sets out to research the monastery. He hopes to write magazine and newspaper articles, "an inspirational book," and a *Reader's Digest* story on the crumbling religious order. When he arrives at the monastery, however, he meets its departing Abbot, who offers to ordain him on the spot, and Willeford's protagonist suddenly sees the solution to all of his problems. Taking the title Right Reverend Deuteronomy Springer, he abandons his wife and home and imagines himself entering the perfect life for his career as a novelist — "no financial worries, no responsibilities, no children, no friends; just wholesome work" (11).

Thus, like the military in *Pick-Up*, the CGF Monastery exemplifies Willeford's paradoxical vision of the relation between high art and mass culture. A public institution that enables Springer to imagine a private utopia, the monastery prompts Willeford's hero to counterpoised attitudes. Becoming a minister, he seeks refuge in the cloister of art, but by hoping to sell his story to the popular media, he aims to vend the appeal of solitude on the mass market. Those aims are at once mutually dependent and incompatible, Willeford suggests, and the remainder of Sam Springer's story exacerbates their conflict. As a newly minted minister, Deuteronomy Springer is assigned to a black congregation in Jacksonville, and there Springer discovers the depth of his dilemma. Working as a preacher, he acknowledges to himself, is merely a way of avoiding "honest work" while he dedicates himself to the consolations of serious literature (27). But once he has been placed in the midst of his congregation, Springer discovers that he cannot succeed as a minister, and thereby preserve his sinecure, unless he strives to become a true pastor to his flock. Thus, although he lacks both belief and sincere feeling for his congregation, Willeford's hero comes to resemble Pascal's doubter. Adopting the lineaments of the religious life, he discovers himself becoming an effective preacher and, more significantly, a valued member of the community he represents. The paradox is illustrated by an implausible but revealing set piece that follows shortly on Springer's arrival in Jacksonville. For his first sermon, Springer decides to lecture his flock on the literary virtues of Kafka and begins to deliver a parody of a *Partisan Review*-style humanist appreciation of difficult art. Midway through the lecture, he senses the confusion of his audience, and realizing that he must change his approach or lose his position, he begins, to the relief of the congregation, to mimic the call-and-response exhortation of a revivalist preacher. Willeford's point is clear: difficulty, originality, and authorial isolation—the hallmarks of "the integrity of . . . self-expression"—give way in this transition to convention, imitation, and popular community.

The shift between these two conditions is not just a matter of literary address, though. For Willeford, their great significance lies in the fact that they are ultimately racial in nature. When he lectures on Kafka, Springer relishes his difference from his flock, and he recognizes their distance from him. In a fitting analogy, he notes at the beginning of his lecture that his believers' prayers are as "abstract" and "clean" as a painting by Mondrian, and he draws the comparison to his lecture himself. So long as he is alienated from his church, Springer notes, both the preacher's lecture and the congregation's prayers are examples of "private meaning" (57, 58). Each maintains the chaste autonomy of the modernist work of art . When he begins to call on the jargon of the sermon, though, Springer is drawn inevitably into public dialogue, and the same transition that makes his voice accessible to his listeners makes their prayers meaningful to him. Far from manipulating and deceiving his church, then, Springer begins, however unwittingly, to become an effective tribune of their needs and desires. Thus, the community created by popular genres like sermons and prayers becomes an incipiently interracial one—and by Willeford's reasoning, therefore, tendentiously African American.

The logic of that conviction is still clearer in a scene from the earlier novel *The Woman Chaser*. Striving to create a perfect and thoroughly subversive movie, Richard Hudson thinks of himself as the opposite of his deceased stepfather, a man who made a fortune by writing a popular song called "Lumpy Grits." That fatuous tune, Hudson explains, was a watered-down rip-off of "a dozen New Orleans blues numbers," stolen "a measure at a time" and combined with an inane set of lyrics. But, in what may be an allusion to Elvis Presley's recording of "Hound Dog," it became a smash hit nevertheless — a signal example of "Americana" rolling "blithely off the lips of children and grown-ups alike" (25). By contrast, the music for his movie will be authentic and purely adult, Hudson decides, and he hires a blues guitarist named Flaps Heartwell to write the score. To insure Heartwell's success, though, Hudson takes an additional step. He accompanies the guitarist into the recording studio and proceeds to taunt and intimidate the black man until he is close to tears. These methods are cruel, Hudson acknowledges, but he brags that their results are extraordinary. The music Heartwell produces is "vicious, savage, frightening, . . . barely under control" — the closest thing possible "to wiring a Jackson Pollock painting for sound" (157). The dynamic here is the reverse of that in *The Black Mass of Brother Springer*, but the point is the same. Black prayers, black music, and abstract art all seem authentic, beautiful, and *private* to Willeford's heroes so long as they are the product of racial segregation and abusive hierarchy. They become cheap and manipulative when they point toward the sentimentalism and the "hodge-podge" of market-driven interracial exchange — a form of communication, Willeford's protagonist notes presciently, that leaves an irrevocable "mark upon us" (WC 25).

That is an ugly vision. But it is also a wickedly insightful description of the modernist investment in primitive culture, and the power of Willeford's fiction comes from his willingness to push the implications of a certain intellectual disposition to their unattractive but logical conclusions. If as Willeford's contemporaries assumed, commercial entertainment lowered the barriers among people — producing, as Bernard Rosenberg put it, a "sodality on the lowest level" — the desire to resist the empire of mass culture and to preserve the authenticity of cultural expression became, in its most extreme form, a desire to resist community itself, and especially interracial or cross-cultural community. True art, by this reasoning, must almost necessarily be racist. Thus, at the center of *The Black Mass of Brother*

Springer Willeford placed the most dramatic and moving example of "sodality" his era produced — the civil rights movement to end legal segregation. In Willeford's narrative, that movement becomes the epitome of the postwar mass public and a prime example of the sentiment that Sam Springer feels he must resist. "As soon as you can feel sorry for someone other than yourself, you discover love," the Abbot of the CGF monastery informs Springer (145). That is precisely the celebration of pity that informed Ross Macdonald's middlebrow fiction, of course, and, as in Macdonald, it rests on the presumption that the best vehicle for common sentiment lies in the democratizing energies of mass culture. For Springer, however, those energies are less redemptive than a threat to his most basic self-definition.

Involvement in the civil rights movement is thus the natural outcome of Springer's charade as preacher — the inevitable result of the community that begins to form when he hears his congregation's prayers not as a private and abstract art, but as meaningful expressions conveying urgent desires. That exchange means, of course, that Springer must also lose the "integrity" of his "self-expression." Commenting on his success as a preacher and popular leader, Springer explains it by saying, "My voice was an independent organ I didn't fully own or control . . . and within its narrow range was a straightforward, confident sincerity" (91). That is the irony most important to Willeford — of the inauthenticity that can coexist with a too ready sincerity. For if sincerity is taken to mean direct, unrestrained communication among individuals, that intersubjectivity seems to Willeford inimical to the "integrity" demanded by authenticity. In his universe, one cannot be intimate with another and alone with oneself at the same time. To heighten the tension between these possibilities Willeford allows them temporarily to coexist in the person of Springer by rewriting the history of the Montgomery bus boycott — completed just a year before publication of Willeford's novel in 1958. Willeford sets his version of the pivotal event in Jacksonville, and most outrageously, he gives Sam Springer the role of Martin Luther King Jr. As an unwittingly dedicated minister, Springer becomes the white leader of the black popular movement to desegregate public transit. In most other respects, though, Willeford's novel gives a fairly faithful and relatively realistic account of the struggle undergone by civil rights activists, and he does nothing to downplay the violence of white resistance to integration.

It is important, in fact, for Willeford to stress the terrible struggle of the civil rights movement, the passionate commitment and courage it demanded from ordinary people, because he wants to emphasize two apparently contradictory aspects of Sam Springer's story: first that Springer can become an effective civil rights leader, even though he does not share any particular interest in the goals of the movement; and, second, that the more effective a leader he becomes, the more he will come to share a commitment to those goals, even against his own better judgment. Though Sam Springer feels only a spectator's interest in his church's pursuit of desegregation, he likewise has no sympathy for the violent defenders of Jim Crow. Like his congregation, those people, too, are motivated by a vision of community—however misguided—and Springer is as emotionally unmoved by their fears and beliefs as he is by the longings of his black followers. Neither the community of white racists, nor that of black activists, elicits any feeling from him. But the longer the bus boycott goes on, and the more deeply Springer is involved in its tactics and strategy, the more inescapably he becomes part of the community he wants only to exploit. As the boycott drags on, then, and as racial tensions in Jacksonville come to a head, Springer once again finds himself in an untenable situation, and once again he attempts to resolve it by flight. Stealing the boycott fund that his church has saved to provide for the needs of its struggling members, Springer fulfills the implications of his name and runs off to New York with Merita, the beautiful wife of his most dedicated parishioner.

Though *The Black Mass of Brother Springer* is narrated by its protagonist, Willeford leaves us in no doubt as to the depth of his hero's betrayal. "Judas is my first name," he announces without pride, and he admits ruefully that he is an "evil man" (164). Willeford shows him, too, after his departure reading of the deaths of four people in a Jacksonville race riot—in all likelihood members of his church—in order to contrast their bravery and suffering to his craven self-interest (169). And he makes it clear that Springer's flight from the boycott is a more dramatic version of his escape from his wife. In both cases, the protagonist cruelly abandons people who depend upon him emotionally and financially for the sole purpose of preserving his independence. In the final irony of the novel, Willeford shows that, like the one before it, this escape only deepens Springer's paradoxical imprisonment. Alone in New York, with the beautiful and enticing Merita, Springer discovers that, while out of danger, he is no more autonomous than he was with his wife or his congregation. He remains caught within a sexually perilous interracial relationship, and once again his only solution is flight. Springer abandons Merita, and the novel ends as he watches her leave with a black porter—a man she quickly picks up following Springer's departure and, the novelist notes sadly, far more her "kindred soul" than he was. Springer watches the happy couple walk away, laughing and hugging in "friendly" camaraderie as much as erotic fascination—an example of racial community that emphasizes by contrast the terrible solitude of the white artist—and, in the novel's concluding scene, he mourns his loss: "I was another nothing in the street. In my black uniform I had been something. The backward collar had allowed me to speak to others without permission, and it gave others the right to speak to me, to smile at me, to love me. But the church was not my way; I didn't have a way" (170).

Like the primal scene of the man ejected from the small-town movie theater, and like nearly all of Willeford's fiction, the passage is a bathetic complaint against the experience of mass society—a world, as Sam Springer sees it, where both community and individuality give way to the facelessness of the urban crowd. And, like the novel as a whole, that complaint constitutes both a critique of the macho sentimentality traditional to hard-boiled fiction and an apotheosis of the tradition. It hurts to be a lonely man, Willeford's heroes acknowledge, but their pain is only a measure of their heroic determination. The truly devastating suggestion made by *The Black Mass of Brother Springer* is not that it is difficult to maintain a macho autonomy, but that the effort is ultimately pointless. As the Abbot of the CGF monastery points out in one of the epigraphs to this chapter, Sam Springer is a terrible novelist precisely because he wants to be a radically independent man of letters. For the writer who does not know anything about people and, more importantly, does not want to learn has literally nothing to say. Indeed, as the Abbot discerns, he would prefer not to write at all, since that is the most certain way to avoid unwanted communication. Like all of the protagonists of Willeford's fiction in the 1950s, Sam Springer is left with two unsatisfactory options. He can have a public voice by inhabiting the hackneyed genres and the manipulative conventions that he sees in popular religion, or he can write badly and have no voice at all. That dilemma sums up the terrible bind created for both Willeford and Thompson by the cheap paperback market and the difficulty they saw everywhere in postwar mass culture. The popular market gave them opportunity, but it denied them authority; it both made culture democratic and robbed it of significance. Like Richard Hudson, or Harry Jordan, or Sam Springer, they could be bad artists or no artists at all.

5.

TANGIBLES

Chester Himes and the Slow Death of

New Deal Populism

American violence is public life, it's a public way of life,
it became a form, a detective story form. — Chester Himes

He was not alone; no one can ever be hurt alone. Others are
always hurt by the hurt of anyone. Had he known this, it would have
made a difference. — Chester Himes, *The Third Generation*[1]

When he set out in 1956 to write his first crime novel, Chester Himes
had few expectations for the form. Stranded in Paris and in desperate
need of cash, Himes made his first attempt at the genre only after
being prodded by Marcel Duhamel, the editor of Gallimard's *Série
noire*. "Get an idea. Start with action," Duhamel advised, offering a
handsome advance for a quick and dirty *policier*, "Give me 220
typed pages." But Himes's flair with the genre must have surprised
Duhamel as much as it did Himes himself. Less than two months
later, Himes returned with the startling *For Love of Immabelle*.
Within two years, he had produced four sequels. By the time a decade had passed, Himes had published all eight of the novels in his
"Harlem domestic" series and transformed the hard-boiled crime
novel in the process. Drawing on the genre's potential for slapstick
action and populist sentiment, Himes remade the form into an unprecedented comic literature — a vision of American society as a vio-

lent and absurd racial carnival. The result was a remarkable, and un-classifiable, literary achievement. Equal parts satire and burlesque, crime thriller and historical allegory, pulp fantasy and antiracist po-lemic, Himes's "Harlem domestic" novels are easily the most signifi-cant innovation in the postwar American crime novel and the last serious attempt to use the form as an effort to split the difference between popular literacy and literary expertise. Yet Himes down-played the originality of his achievement himself. "The detective story originally in the plain narrative form — straightforward vio-lence — is an American product," Himes told an interviewer. "I just made the faces black."[2]

Given Himes's inventiveness with the genre, that remark must be taken as one of the better examples of false modesty in the history of popular writing. For there can be little doubt of just how seriously he re-created the detective story. While Himes worked, the United States experienced the dramatic transformations of the civil rights era, and, though he wrote from Paris, Himes turned his crime novels into a running, complex meditation on America's changing political landscape. The genre's traditional preoccupation with the inade-quacy of the law — its poor fit with the demands of society, on the one hand, and those of justice, on the other — became for Himes a perfect means to dramatize the intimate relations between racism and American democracy. (He could not write a traditional detective story and would be forced to reinvent the genre, Himes claimed, because he could not "name the white man who was guilty. . . . All white men were guilty.")[3] It enabled him as well to do the most significant work of his career. Before he began the Harlem domestic series, Himes was a talented, second-rank novelist, his work consis-tently undermined by an absence of formal control and by his own, seemingly boundless self-regard. Returning time and again to the trials of an idealistic young man whose experiences were closely modeled on his own, Himes's early novels tended to spill into lugu-brious tirades of self-justification. But the built-in limits of the detec-tive novel dispensed with those flaws. Telling stories of criminals and detectives enabled Himes to escape his self-absorption, and forcing him to constrain the passions that inspired his early work within the limits of a minor genre, they made him a major talent for the first time since he had set out to become a writer.

Yet his offhand attitude toward that achievement is revealing. It makes clear that for Himes, much as for Jim Thompson, becoming a crime novelist seemed a mark of both literary surrender and political disappointment. Like Thompson, Himes had come of age in the thirties, and his thinking had been deeply shaped by the cultural politics of the Depression and especially of wartime mobilization. He too had labored on the Writers' Project of the WPA — after beginning work for the government digging sewers and dredging creeks — and the experience had been as pivotal for him as it was for Thompson. When he began working for the New Deal relief agency in 1936, Himes was still on parole after having served a seven-year prison sentence for robbery in Ohio, and although he was determined to become a writer, he had made little headway and was having a difficult time finding any sort of work. The WPA turned Himes's life around. It made it possible for him to support himself and his new wife without both partners needing to search for work — a domestic arrangement that would always seem crucial to Himes's sense of pride. It made him a disciplined and professional writer, and, as importantly, it put him in touch with the network of liberal and leftist intellectuals and philanthropic institutions that he would need in order to develop into a novelist. Years later, he looked back on that turning point as a rare moment of peace in a lifetime of anger and frustration. "We were all, black and white alike, bound together into the human family by our desperate struggle for bread."[4]

Everything that followed for Himes would seem a failure to live up to the brief happy moment. Like Thompson, Himes was drawn to Southern California after the death of the WPA, and like Thompson he found the wartime aircraft plants and shipyards around Los Angeles an enormously dismaying experience — a traducement of the promise of the New Deal. But Himes's disappointment was, if anything, more bitter and intense than Thompson's. Believing intuitively in the spirit of patriotic mobilization, Himes was shocked by the extent of racial injustice in wartime Los Angeles and shaken by the animosity he experienced from the white Southern migrants who also had been drawn to the area. It was leaving public employment for "private industry," Himes later claimed, that taught him for the first time "what racial prejudice is like," and the injury was made only more painful by the fact that it coexisted with the rhetoric of America's war against racism.[5]

Yet despite the depth of his disappointment, Himes did not cease to believe in that rhetoric for many years. His first five novels, published between 1945 and 1953, were mainly jeremiads excoriating the nation for failing to live up to its own principles — "all that stuff about liberty and justice and equality" — and they demanded a renewed commitment to the vision of interracial solidarity established during the Depression and war. It was the writer's mission, Himes argued, to challenge "the refusal of Americans as a whole to look upon the grim actualities of their own lives, the depths of their own depravities, the dangers of their dissatisfactions, and the extent of their brutalities" and to replace that "fulsome self-delusion" with a commitment to "the brotherhood of men."[6] At first, too, that prophetic stance appeared hopeful. Himes's first novel, *If He Hollers Let Him Go*, was an aesthetic, critical, and commercial success, and it seemed to augur still better chances for the writer in the future. With each following book, though, Himes appeared to lose more control over his work, to grow more strident and self-absorbed, and to speak to an ever-shrinking audience. As he strove with dwindling success to make good on his initial promise, his efforts came to seem a sign of the changing political terrain — an emblem of the decline of the politics of the New Deal and of the rise of postwar liberalism. It was only when that change appeared complete and his prophetic role seemed fully disenchanted — and after he had abandoned the United States for Paris — that Himes discovered the detective story. It became the perfect vehicle to express the volatile mix of optimism and frustration that he saw throughout the civil rights era.

THE POSTWAR PUBLIC AND THE UNUSUAL NEGRO

Himes alluded to his ambivalent attitudes in two letters he sent to his editor at New American Library in the fall of 1955. In the first, he described the previous year he had spent in the United States, where he had made nearly fruitless efforts to work out publication or re-publication of several of his books and simultaneously realized "the growing race consciousness" among both blacks and whites that followed on the decision of *Brown v. Board of Education*. It was difficult from Himes's description to disentangle his attitudes toward these events. The many rejections and then lukewarm response re-ceived by his novel *The Primitive*, the legal difficulties he experienced getting royalties for a reissue of *If He Hollers Let Him Go*, the consequent necessity of working as a porter at a Horn & Hardart automat until he could afford to rush back to Paris — all of these seemed inseparable from Himes's conviction that the United States had entered an intensely charged racial stand-off, with blacks de-manding an end to segregation and an increasingly rich and compla-cent white society digging in its heels in every way possible. For Himes, the experience was all but unbearable. "The United States was rough on me this past year," he wrote from Paris to his editor, Walter Freeman. "Rougher than anyone knows; rougher than I ever want to tell anyone." But in a characteristic gesture, he then ex-plained that the pain he had suffered was worthwhile so long as it led in some way toward racial progress. "The Negro is making great advancement," he admitted, "and must pay for it." Within weeks, though, Himes appeared to abandon even this limited hopefulness, at least so far as his own writing went. "Let's face it," Himes wrote Freeman, "people are sick and tired of the poor downtrodden Ne-gro. Their sympathy is spent; their interest left at the end of the war — even before." In such an environment there was no audience for the kind of work he had once done. "The public," he complained, "now demands that the Negro be *unusual*."[7]

Summed up in those two letters were key terms of Himes's imagina-tion and a penetrating analysis of the developing features of postwar American liberalism. Himes's sense of artistic mission had always depended on the belief that African Americans were not unusual, but rather representative figures — exemplary Americans who were un-justly denied recognition by their fellow citizens — and he had argued in essays and editorials as well as in his fiction that it was worth suffering to prove that fact. Indeed, as he implied in his reminiscence about the WPA, there was to his mind a redemptive potential in suffering itself. Violence and "hurt" (a favored term in Himes's vocabulary) were simply the core reality of American life. But if the pain they caused were communicated and made public, they might forge a common sentiment capable of overcoming exploitation and division. That was the presupposition behind Himes's claim that it "made a difference" to know that "no one can ever be hurt alone," that "others are always hurt by the hurt of anyone." A true son of the thirties, Himes suggested time and again that only by learning the pain and need of others could we overcome the legacies of racism and social division and thus aspire to a better society. ("The quality of hurt caused me to feel tenderness and pity," he later maintained, "and I wanted to record it because it was true.") But the surprising wealth of postwar America seemed to undercut that potential for shared feeling. "Everything seems to go — . . . all human values — with awesome swiftness in the struggle for the dollar." If the hope of interracial brotherhood depended on mutual suffering and a common "struggle for bread," as it seemed to Himes in the Depression, then the unexpected prosperity that began to remake the American political landscape during the late forties and the fifties appeared to doom the nation to growing racial animosity.[8]

In retrospect, it seems clear that in most ways Himes misjudged what would occur in the United States over the coming decades.[9] But his response to the civil rights movement and its transformation of American democracy shed light nonetheless on the nation's changing political temper, and it certainly illuminated his own particular way of thinking about both race and literature. As Himes himself noted, the defining event in this context was *Brown v. Board of Education*—the 1954 Supreme Court decision that declared de jure segregation of public schools a violation of the 14th Amendment and that, in doing so, not only catalyzed postwar racial attitudes but served in large measure to define them. Crystallizing legal thinking about race and civil rights that had been developing for several years, *Brown* set the terms in which arguments about the nature and effects of racism would be conceived over the coming decade. In journalist Scott Reston's objection to the decision, this transition involved a governmental foray into a psychological and subjective terrain where it was not meant to go. With *Brown*, Reston complained, "the Court insisted on equality of mind and heart rather than on equal school facilities." Although that response was particularly unsympathetic, it did point to a key feature of the decision, one to which Chief Justice Earl Warren also drew attention when he claimed that the Court's reasoning was based on "intangible considerations." In order to overturn the "separate but equal" doctrine established in 1896 by *Plessy v. Ferguson*, Warren explained, the Court had needed to presume that the question of equality could not be established solely by socioeconomic or " 'tangible' factors" — for example, "buildings, curricula, qualifications and salaries of teachers." If segregated schools were equal in every other "tangible" way, the Warren Court asserted, segregation would still be forbidden by the Fourteenth Amendment guarantee of equal protection of the law because the harmful consequences of racial discrimination appeared in their "intangible" effects — "qualities which are incapable of objective measurement."[10] In short, as Warren went on to suggest in the famous footnote eleven (in which the Court cited the research of Kenneth Clark, Gunnar Myrdal, and other social scientists), the question of whether laws that segregated on the basis of race were unconstitutional would depend henceforth primarily on the psychological effects of discrimination. Equality would be measured in relation to hearts and minds rather than to salaries and facilities.[11]

The Warren Court came to that presumption because of the particular way it approached the constitutional problem of equal protection.[12] But in a broader sense, the *Brown* decision marked a political and cultural sea change — away from efforts to see race and racism as primarily socioeconomic matters and toward the presumption that they involved mainly psychological or cultural experience. During the thirties and early forties, the dominant thinking about race in the United States had been shaped largely by the emphasis that the Depression and New Deal placed on economic issues, and well up through the war, liberal politics tended to stress a populist version of class consciousness over the preoccupation with racial and ethnic difference that had been prominent throughout American society during the twenties. The widespread notion that a healthy economy depended on a "concert of interests" fostered the perception that

the most significant political tension of the day consisted of the battle between "the common welfare" and "private, autocratic powers."[13] African Americans were thus welcomed into the New Deal,
where they formed the backbone of the new coalition of voters that
emerged during the election of 1936, but only so long as they could
be subsumed under economic categories — as members of the working class or the rural poor rather than as a distinct racial group.[14]
The same was true of the social movements shaped by the context of
the New Deal, especially industrial unionism. In the midst of its rise
to power in the late thirties and early forties, the Congress of Industrial Organizations (CIO) worked hard to stress worker unity over
the racial and ethnic division that had long crippled the labor movement, emphasizing that the only battle that counted was that between the honest working class and parasitic management. From
this perspective, racism and racial identity itself seemed the invention of capital — an invidious means of distinguishing among people
whose interests should naturally make them allies.[15] The leading
civil rights organizations of the Roosevelt years saw matters in much
the same way. Invoking the New Deal emphasis on populist class
allegiance — and later the language of wartime patriotism — black
leaders envisioned their constituency as exemplary disenfranchised
Americans who demanded "economic, political, and social equality," more or less in that order. Time and again, they denied appeals
to cultural difference in order to assert that African Americans, like
other members of the New Deal coalition, were committed to the
democratic values whose complete realization had been denied them
by prejudice and economic injustice. W. E. B. Du Bois thus claimed in
1944 that the Negro stood among "the throngs of disinherited and
underfed men" and demanded "the right to work at a wage which
will maintain a decent standard of living."[16]

    For black leaders and sympathetic liberals in the thirties and early
forties, in other words, the best strategy for racial justice was to cast
African Americans as workers and Americans first and as a distinct
minority later, if at all. By the mid-fifties, however, much of that
thinking had begun to change. The vast black migration to Northern
cities during and after the war prompted many white workers to
back away from the rhetoric of class solidarity that flourished in the

late thirties, a move echoed by Southern Democratic secession from the New Deal coalition and by growing conservative hostility to the liberal pursuit of social welfare.[17] At the same time, the developing nature of postwar liberalism and the influence of the cold war moved political opinion away from the language of economic collectivism that had been prominent during the New Deal. The role of the state in the evolving pluralist consensus of the postwar years was no longer to direct the concert of interests necessary to a "balanced economy" or to speak for the nation as a whole, but to negotiate among the country's various constituencies. From this perspective, American society appeared not the battleground of large economic blocs that it had once seemed, but an affiliation of, or struggle among, multiple interest groups — its political structure, in Robert Dahl's evocative phrase, a system of "minorities rule." The greatest danger to the health of the nation was thus not the power of the "private interests" excoriated by FDR, but the new threat of totalitarianism and the seemingly analogous danger of popular tyranny. For policy makers and opinion leaders in the postwar years, the core aspect of a liberal political order would no longer be the democratic majority, which had only recently seemed the driving force in a movement to remake both government and society, but the personal rights that prevented the triumph of conformity.[18]

In this environment, civil rights leaders and liberals in general began thinking about the problem of racism and the significance of race itself in a manner exemplified by the Warren Court's language in *Brown*. No longer would they emphasize the integral relation between race and economic disenfranchisement, which would not return to become a focus of attention until the later 1960s. Nor, with rare exceptions, would they find much use in stressing the common interests of white workers and African Americans. Freed of its subordination to questions of economic policy and patriotic commitment, the problem of racism became a prominent national concern in and of itself, and that transition had results that from the perspective of a writer like Chester Himes might well seem ambivalent or even paradoxical. On the one hand, postwar liberalism placed the problem of racism at the very center of national politics. With both the constitutional litigation that culminated in *Brown* and the emergence of a popular movement against the Southern system of Jim Crow, racial discrimination came to exemplify the core problems of American society (a place in the nation's political vocabulary previously occupied by "the labor question"). When President Dwight D. Eisenhower sent troops to Little Rock to enforce the *Brown* ruling, when Martin Luther King Jr. and his followers ground segregation in the Montgomery bus system into submission, and when the national news media began to publicize the growing violent resistance to desegregation in the South, racism began to take on the dimensions of a key national problem. Especially in the context of the cold war effort to celebrate American democracy, segregation became a national embarrassment, and, even more than during the New Deal, popular journalists and political commentators cast the South as a lamentably backward region in a nation otherwise blessed by prosperity, opportunity, and freedom. In this setting, the embattled civil rights of African Americans began to seem the epitome of American constitutional liberties in general, and black Americans became the vanguard, and the representative face, of a new political order built around a developing vision of the citizen as rights-holder.[19]

So, from one perspective predominant in the discourse of postwar liberalism, *Brown* might stand for the beginning of welcome and long-delayed attention to the national problem of racism. For a writer like Himes, though, who had been shaped by an earlier political context, the developments epitomized by the decision might seem as confusing and threatening as they were promising. If *Brown* spelled the beginning of the end for legal segregation, it did so, first, by disconnecting racial discrimination from economic oppression and, second, by stressing the value of individual rights held *against* a tyrannous popular majority. Each cut against the populist collectivism that Himes had learned during the New Deal, and, by casting civil rights as incipiently individualistic and resistant to the democratic will, they ran counter to his youthful commitment to the "brotherhood of men." In fact, rather than submerging racial identity beneath class solidarity—the promise that Himes and many black leaders saw in the liberal and leftist politics of the Roosevelt years—the growing attention to the problem of racism throughout the fifties made race itself appear enormously important. In the spotlight created by *Brown*, by Gunnar Myrdal and Kenneth Clark, and by the civil rights movement, minorities would increasingly seem less the exemplary Americans that New Deal rhetoric had made them than distinctive cultural groups, shaped by experiences and political needs that were unique rather than common. Thus, in the emerging terrain of postwar liberalism, attention to racial discrimination would appear intimately linked with a renewed commitment to personal rights and individual distinction. As Ralph Ellison explained, in the world shaped by *Brown*, "Negroes must be individuals." The Court had recognized the "human psychological complexity and citizenship" of African Americans. Indeed, by Ellison's description, they had suggested that the two were indistinguishable, and it had thus forced him to recognize that segregation could not be understood apart from "another characteristically American problem" — "the evasion of identity." In this context, the struggle against racism would be inseparable from the effort for "the only integration that counts: that of personality."[20]

This was the transition that Himes objected to when he complained that the American public had lost sympathy since the war for the "poor downtrodden Negro" and now demanded that the "Negro be *unusual*." During the thirties, when the vast majority of the black population remained Southern farm laborers, New Deal liberalism tended to cast "the Negro" as an emblem of poverty and rural privation — a representative, along with white sharecroppers and urban workers, of the most victimized portions of an entire society in need of modernization. By the mid-fifties, though, the needs of African Americans were already beginning to seem both politically central to postwar liberalism and at the same time distinctive. The needs of blacks therefore seemed to call for cultural representatives who could embody both the middle-class dignity valued throughout a newly wealthy American society and the peculiar psychological injuries created by racism. For Himes, the transition was crucial. Almost directly, *Brown* marked a caesura in his career and a transformation of his aesthetic presuppositions. Before 1954 he had written five novels, all deeply influenced by the language of social protest and the naturalist poetics that he had learned during the late thirties and early forties. After his sojourn in the United States in 1955 and the critical and commercial failure of *The Primitive*, he decided that "the old, used forms for the black American writer" would no longer avail. Taking his cue from the demands of a new public, he decided that African Americans were "more than just victims. . . . We were unique individuals."[21] The result of that discovery would turn out, strangely enough, to be Himes's reinvention of the detective story. In order to understand the significance of that transition, though, it is crucial to appreciate just how seriously he had adopted the convictions of New Deal populism and how difficult it was for him to leave those beliefs behind.

HIGHER LAWS AND LOWER PLEASURES

His first literary efforts, Himes later stressed, "were not racially oriented." Begun while he was still in the Ohio State penitentiary, they concerned the relations between individuals and institutions, criminals and the law, convicts and prison society, and they presumed in a manner typical of the *Black Mask* stories that influenced Himes at the time — as of naturalist writing from the thirties, in general — that such matters outweighed questions of racial difference. Like his contemporaries among civil rights leaders, Himes maintained a distinctly unenthusiastic attitude toward the idea of racial identity for most of his life, and like his literary hero Richard Wright, he remained unmoved by the strains of cultural nationalism that had inspired his predecessors among the Harlem Renaissance writers. He had spent his childhood like Wright in the Mississippi Delta and come north to Ohio in the 1920s, and the experience made him, much as it did his mentor, indifferent to the elite celebration of African American folk culture. But while Wright's early beliefs were inseparable from his leftist convictions, Himes rejected Marxist political theory (he was "anticapitalist but not procommunist," he later explained), and he justified his attitudes not by referring them to Wright's dream of a united proletariat, but by tracing their roots to a grim personal history.[22]

The youngest son of a terribly unhappy marriage, Himes had been raised in a volatile home that encapsulated some of the central tensions of the early-twentieth-century black community. By his telling,

Himes's parents were mismatched avatars of the educational programs of W. E. B. Du Bois and Booker T. Washington and of the segments of the African American population represented by those leaders. The dominant, and most troubling, partner in this relationship was Himes's mother. An heir to the educated middle class that had embraced bourgeois ambition as the best escape from slavery, Estelle Bomar Himes was light-skinned, well-schooled in the ways of nineteenth-century high culture, and profoundly desirous of middle-class respectability. Himes's much darker father appeared "the exact opposite" to his son—a child of the Southern peasantry who had lifted himself beyond rural poverty by becoming an instructor at the agricultural and mechanical colleges that sprang up throughout the South following Reconstruction. In Himes's recollection, their increasingly loveless marriage served almost literally to disprove the dreams of racial community that inspired an earlier generation of writers. Rather than binding folk roots and high ambition, their marriage devolved into a wildly unstable battleground, driving Himes's family from one temporary home to another and turning race itself into a weapon in an internecine warfare over class and status. Fascinated by the prestige of her white "heritage" and distrustful of darker-skinned or less-educated African Americans, Himes's intensely proud mother grew ever more bitter about the frustration of her ambitions, laying her husband's failure to rise in the world to his background and his color. His father meanwhile charged Himes's mother with hating her own people. Unlike Himes, who looked back on their sufferings from a distance of several decades, neither traced their difficulties to the racist environment in which they were forced to struggle. Their shared race and their common oppression appeared to give them little more than a motive for mutual distaste.[23]

Himes himself eventually adopted something of each of his parents' perspectives. He spent his youth repudiating his mother's obsessive pursuit of status, dropping out of college and falling into the criminal society that flourished in Cleveland's Scovil Avenue ghetto—a route that soon landed him a draconian twenty-year sentence for a bumbling attempt at armed robbery. But while he came to despise his mother's genteel ambitions, Himes absorbed much of her view of the world, adopting in particular her strict moral standards and her unyielding pride. Like his mother, he continually invoked a rigid model of personal conduct, seeing every swerve from the ideal as an example of terrible failure, and like her he described racial classification itself as an affront to his personal independence. Throughout his early fiction, he repeats time and again the canonical scene of African American autobiography and bildungsroman, the painful moment in which the protagonist discovers that he or she is a member of an excluded minority. But where in some works that experience becomes the first step in a journey toward self-discovery (as in Zora Neale Hurston's *Their Eyes Were Watching God*, for instance), Himes's heroes suffer the pain of racial identification, forget it, and then repeat the awful experience yet again — as if to prove that this is a lesson they cannot assimilate. Race almost always comes to them as a bad surprise.

That Himes set out to become a writer while in prison during the early thirties played an important role in the development of that attitude. For jail and the mode of literary protest common during the Depression each enabled him to transmute his mother's bourgeois pride into a new key. As Himes described it, prison was a world, not where special individuals might seem superior to racial distinctions, but one in which everyone was outside them. The imprisoned men in Himes's first efforts at fiction are members of a closed society, and they care far less about racial identity than about money, power, and the manly code of the convict. Thus, in his attempt to become an author, Himes cast prison in much the same role that the university, the army, or the factory would serve for other minority writers of the era. It was a total institution whose intense pressures appeared to override racial divisions. Indeed, Himes's vision of prison made it analogous to the broader environment of the Depression as the era's writers and intellectuals tended to see it. Like Steinbeck's dust bowl, or the Southern tenant farmer landscape apotheosized by James Agee, or the urban jungle portrayed in the decade's many "ghetto pastorals," Himes's prison became a laboratory in the democracy of suffering — an environment so trying that it gave rise to both leveling brutality *and* to redemptive examples of fraternity.[24] Jail taught him, Himes claimed, that given the right context, "people will do anything—white people, black people, all people." At the same time, he portrayed convicts who would endure great personal suffering in the name of brotherhood. In a scenario he would return to over and again throughout his literary career, Himes cast the tension between those two possibilities—corrosive self-interest or redemptive self-sacrifice—as the moral dilemma of his work. As if to prove that such a drama might negate racial distinctions, he made the protagonist of his first attempt at an autobiographical novel a white man from Mississippi. Like his mother, though in a determinedly anti-genteel manner that elevated the constraints of environment above bourgeois ambition, Himes seemed intent on proving that race need not be the defining force in his experience, that it could be defeated by a combination of sympathy and will.[25]

The antiracialist populism that Himes learned during the Depression would suffer an initial blow with the rejection of his first novel, when he discovered that publishers were uninterested in stories about white characters written by black authors. But Himes would never fully abandon the faith. Time and again his fiction cast race as a potent, but empty, fiction—one that could be overcome by the institutional pressures and the fraternity first exemplified for him by prison society and by the personal will represented by his own determination to become a writer. Thus, when Himes finally did undertake a novel that was "racially oriented," exploring "the lives of blacks in a white world," it remained part—this time desperately so—of an effort to deny the legitimacy of racial distinctions.[26] During the Depression, Himes's prison experience and his work on the WPA enabled him to maintain his belief in the interracial "human family." When he arrived in Los Angeles during the war, he was brutally confronted by the inconsistency between the nation's democratic rhetoric and its racist practices, and the frustration of that experience inspired his first serious literary accomplishments. They would transfer the broad approach of his prison writing to the new environment of wartime mobilization. Where he began by stressing the potential of criminal society and convict fraternity to erase inherited social divisions, the work he undertook in the early forties asserted the value of a populist style of patriotism—what historian

Gary Gerstle calls "working-class Americanism" — and, in increasingly harsh jeremiads, invoked its unrecognized potential to overcome America's racist legacy.[27]

Bob Jones, the narrator and protagonist of Himes's first published novel, *If He Hollers Let Him Go* (1945), is the frustrated embodiment of that working-class Americanism. A leaderman at a wartime shipyard in Los Angeles, he is the very image of the "worker in a CIO win-the-war poster," and he embraces without irony the language of populist virtue that ran through union rhetoric in the thirties and early forties. "Something about my working clothes made me feel rugged," he brags in the novel's opening, "bigger than the average citizen, stronger than a white-collar worker — stronger even than an executive." Imbued with that sense of virile pride, he refuses to stomach either white racists or appeals to black identity. Racists, he suggests, are the tools of an owning class, which exploits the prejudice of ignorant Southerners to keep labor feeble. Black identity, meanwhile, appears as the self-justification invented by a craven black middle class, willing to tolerate racism so long as it can take comfort in its own security and in the pomp of "black heritage." For Jones, the readiness of the black bourgeoisie to accept segregation is the moral equivalent of Vichy collaboration with the Nazis, and he demands by contrast his own immediate enfranchisement as an American worker. "That's all I ever wanted," he explains in the novel's key passage, "to be accepted as a man — without ambition, without distinction, either of race, creed, or color; just a simple Joe walking down an American street, going my simple way, without any identifying characteristics but weight, height, and gender."[28]

Like liberals and civil rights leaders of the day, in other words, Bob Jones wants to subordinate racial division to patriotism and macho populism. The central concern of Himes's novel, however, is with the various unjust forces that prevent that ambition — a variety of evils that are arrayed about the hero in a perverse version of the concert of interests. He is frustrated first of all by the racism of the Southern whites who populate the shipyard where he works, by a management uninterested in living up to the spirit of wartime nondiscrimination rules, by the Jim Crow arrangements commonly accepted throughout Los Angeles, and by his fellow black workers, who strike

him as ignorant, Uncle Tomish, and easily distracted by fleeting pleasures. The premise makes for a simple and powerful tale. Wanting
only to be accepted as a man into the industrial production he views
with Whitmanesque passion ("the hustle and bustle of moving busy
workers, trucks, plate lifts, yard cranes, electric mules, the blue
flashes of arc welders, brighter than the noonday sun . . . I loved it
like my first love"), Jones is stymied at every turn by the web of
forces that surrounds him until he erupts in self-destructive anger
and frustration (159). Yet all the obstacles he faces pale beside — and
in fact are summed up by — his obsession with one problem in particular: the untrustworthiness of black women and the illegitimate
power of white women. In a book nominally about the battle between working-class patriotism and racial segregation, everything
hinges on the protagonist's victimization by the women in his life.

The reasons for that peculiar obsession are rooted in Himes's commitment to "the brotherhood of men," a phrase made especially revealing by its alteration of the universalist "man." Despite his frustration with racial division, Himes was far from egalitarian when it
came to other kinds of discrimination, especially against women.
Indeed, he suggested that it would be in the bonds made among men
(against or in response to women) that interracial fraternity might
prosper — a belief apparent in two brief scenes of happiness in *If He
Hollers*. In the first, Jones stops for two white sailors who have been
hitchhiking. As they drive, the three men comment lasciviously on the
various women they pass, and the moment is so satisfying for Jones —
who is outraged by the racist sexual hysteria he experiences from
white Southerners on the job — that he begins to speculate about the
difference between whites who use their color as a weapon and those
who do not. In the second scene, Jones seems finally to resolve his
many prickly differences with his middle-class lover, Alice. Throughout the novel the two bicker about his ambitions and confrontational
attitude and about her ominous association with a group of lesbians,
but in this scene they make up and agree to marry. Summed up in
those two fleeting moments, the only respite Jones finds from the
novel's relentless momentum toward violence and despair, is a key
component of Himes's ideological vision — a counterpart to the rhetoric of working-class Americanism less apparent in the public writ-

ings of his contemporaries. If the only hope of escaping racism was the democracy of the common man, as civil rights leaders argued in the thirties and forties, the bonds among those men would have to be formed, Himes suggested, by the subordination of women. In the ideal world as Jones sees it, only one traditional form of social demarcation will count — "gender." To become a fully enfranchised member of American society, Jones must first join it as a man, meaning that he must feel free to demand the allegiance of his wife, to comment freely about white women in the presence of white men, and, perhaps most revealingly, "to make a polite pass at Lana Turner without having the gendarmes beat the black off [him]" (153). The most salient feature of the populist democracy that Himes envisions, in other words, is that it will be one where men will be equal by virtue of their comparison to women and where any "simple Joe" will be free to proposition any Hollywood star.[29]

In the present, of course, that democracy is denied, forestalled by the white owners who manipulate the prejudice of their workers and by a black elite that accepts its own subordinate position so long as it can enjoy personal security. The crucial feature of Himes's novel, though, is the fact that both those antidemocratic forces are represented by the illegitimate power of women. The decadence of the black elite is exemplified by the genteel pretense of Jones's fiancée, its insularity and indifference to the honest workingman embodied by her flirtation with members of the same sex. The power of white racism, meanwhile, is represented by Jones's run-in with Madge, a "cracker bitch" he encounters on the job, who baits him with the specter of white rape fantasies (27). As the novel progresses, these two forces conspire unknowingly with each other to drive Jones ever further into the trap that will destroy him — Alice demanding that Jones accept humiliation until he is on the brink of violence and Madge taunting him so relentlessly that he feels justified in very nearly raping her. In the novel's climactic chapter his nemeses finally intersect all but directly. Jones returns at Alice's insistence to humble himself on the job he had recently quit, and there, in a deeply motivated coincidence, he stumbles upon Madge, who charges him falsely with rape. The result is everything that Jones has had reason to fear all through the novel. He is set on by a lynch mob; escapes with his life, only to fall prey to the corrupt system of American justice; gets railroaded by his shipyard employer, who knows the charge against Jones to be false but who covers for his white workers; and in the novel's final lines finds himself sharing a jail cell with two Mexican prisoners who like him have been impressed into the military. The conclusion is a complete inversion of the hero's inspiring vision. Bob Jones wants to take part in the American war effort as a worker and a man. He finds himself forced into it as the second-class citizen of a racist country and as the emasculated victim of a nation seemingly ruled by women.

The Manichaean nature of that story — in which either Jones's highest ideals or his worst fears must win out — built on the moral drama that Himes first developed in his prison writing, and it remained typical of his thinking throughout his career. In an essay titled "Negro Martyrs Are Needed," published in the *Crisis* the year before *If He Hollers*, Himes made clear just how basic his tendency was to divide the world into sharply opposed conditions of good and evil, virtue and corruption. Demanding the transformation of American society, the essay called for "a Negro American revolution" to be sparked by the willing martyrdom of a self-sacrificing black leader. "Negro Americans must make the stand," Himes declared; both the status quo and the slow-moving meliorism of the war years were unacceptable. But although Himes called on the chiliastic rhetoric he had encountered in Los Angeles leftist circles, it was clear that by "revolution" he did not mean the seizure of the means of production or the abolition of private property. "There can be only one . . . aim of a revolution by Negro Americans," Himes asserted, "*the enforcement of the Constitution of the United States.*" No "better way of existence" had been discovered than that implied by the principles of liberal democracy, Himes argued. The country needed only to live up to those principles. "This is what a Negro American revolution will be: a revolution by a racial minority for the enforcement of democratic laws already in existence." For the same reason, "Negro American revolution" — at least at this stage in Himes's thinking — could not mean a nationalist struggle for self-determination. The "enforcement of the Constitution" would only be possible when "the majority of the people of the United States believed in democracy." That was what, in Himes's view, would differentiate revolution from "riot" (an allusion to the Harlem and Detroit riots of 1943) and the reason for the necessity of black martyrs. The transformation that Himes envisioned would only be successful when white citizens were led by sorrow and pity to embrace the cause sanctified by black martyrdom. "In this event a Negro American revolution will cease to be a revolution and become a movement of the people to stamp out injustices, inequalities, and violations of our laws."[30]

What Himes meant by revolution in other words was not a violent seizure of power, but a transformation of the individual and national conscience — a moral re-creation, via shared emotion, of "the manifest will of the people." It was a vision that drew on the Popular Front rhetoric of the late thirties and early forties in order to imagine something like the civil rights movement that took off in the late fifties. (The catalyst for "revolution," Himes wrote, "must be a denial of some right guaranteed to every citizen of the United States by the Constitution, such as the right of any decent, honest person to live wherever he chooses, or the right of a citizen to vote or serve on juries.") But, "Negro Martyrs" is finally most interesting less for the accuracy or inaccuracy of its historical predictions than for the light it sheds on the habits of Chester Himes's thinking. Like *If He Hollers*, and indeed like all of Himes's fiction, the document is profoundly Manichaean in argument. Revolution is necessary, Himes suggests, because American society will either live up to the "democratic laws" implicit in the Constitution or it will be hopelessly corrupt. The United States can choose to be a nation "wherein everyone is free," or it can descend inexorably toward "slavery." The pivot between those conditions, moreover, will inevitably be messianic. Democracy will either be brought about by martyrdom and by the revolution in consciousness it encourages, or it must fail.[31]

That Manichaean temper would have a decisive and lasting effect on Himes's imagination. Four decades later, he continued to speak in much the same vein, pointing to the almost hopeless effort "to reconcile the community values of Christian religion with the economic ethics of capitalism." Though here Himes spoke of Christianity rather than the Constitution, the fundamental idea, and the

Calvinist moralism behind it, remained basically the same: there is a higher law at radical odds with the world of mundane desires and interests, and we are corrupt if we do not attempt to bridge the gap. We will either live in a world where "people will do anything" or one of "decent, honest" citizens. That presumption would reappear all through Himes's fiction, where it influenced the most crucial aspects of his novels. It meant that he would consistently cast the relation between law and interest, morality and desire in starkly polar terms. And it underlay his millennial fascination with violence, which, as in "Negro Martyrs," leads to either "revolution" or to "riot" — toward the creation of a redemptive, sentimental community or to the acceptance of a chaotic, fallen society.

Perhaps most significantly, it inspired Himes to look at ordinary life and especially at black vernacular culture in a particular, acidulous way. In *If He Hollers*, the unlettered Southern migrants with whom Bob Jones works are almost as deep a disappointment to him as the black bourgeoisie. They are spirited and inventive, resilient and cunning. But the communal discourse of folk humor seems as limiting to Jones as the "black heritage" praised by the middle class. Because it gives the shipyard workers symbolic recompense for the many large and petty humiliations they must suffer, it appears in Himes's novel as a way of adapting to, rather than challenging, a racist society — a measure of the "absolute impotence" that Jones bridles at in his own experience (101). Himes's protagonist thus views his fellow workers — with the telling exception of a college-educated welder who is as stiff-necked and self-contained as Jones longs to be — as charming, but disappointing children. When he pronounces, "My people, my people," it is as much with chagrin as with ethnic pride (111).

Because he imagined that the only hope for social reform lay in profound commitment to an interracial, moral community, Himes had little option but to embrace such an attitude. Like the black middle class, the newly urbanizing Southern peasantry were bound to seem a letdown — narrow, provincial, preoccupied with the mundane demands of survival rather than the transfiguration of society. Indeed, held to the high moral standards shared by Jones and "Negro Martyrs," almost anyone would disappoint. But Himes laid particularly heavy emphasis on the dangers he saw in the urban society of the black working class and especially in the segregated community's gray market of entertainment and crime. Perhaps because of his own youthful experience among Cleveland's criminal society, Himes's early fiction cast the counterpublic of urban popular entertainment and vice as an inversion of the moral ideal he envisioned in working-class populism.

That contrast was latent in *If He Hollers* — where Bob Jones briefly and temptingly encounters the hustlers and playboys of Watts's Central Avenue — but it appears with transparent significance in a contemporaneous story. In "The Song Says 'Keep on Smiling,' " Himes tells of the dedication of Jean, a young black woman living in wartime Los Angeles who works in a shipyard and pines for her sweetheart in the merchant marine. (Not incidentally, perhaps, she has the same name as Himes's first wife.) When the story first ran in the *Crisis* in 1944, it appeared fittingly above an advertisement for war bonds. For Himes's tale is a paean to the virtues of delayed gratification and patriotic commitment, even where they seem least likely to prove rewarding. Shut out of membership in a club of white workers and unable to telegraph her boyfriend because of combat restrictions, Jean is crucially alone. She is part of an abstract, but emotionally unsatisfying, community represented by her sweetheart — and in a larger sense by the war effort in which they both partake. But she is painfully isolated from ordinary sociability, and she becomes so lonely that in desperation she visits a nightclub below her apartment. In the story's moment of crisis, she falls briefly under the sway of the club's dapper bandleader who offers pleasure and scoffs at Jean's romantic fidelity. "When I was white," he says sardonically, "I used to believe in everything. . . . But you and I are black, sugar. Now I'm just an opportunist." The statement encapsulates the moral vision of the young Himes along with his worst fears. Like Bob Jones, Jean must choose between the exacting ideal of solitary virtue and an implicit commitment to the war effort of a nation that continues to exclude her, on the one hand, and immediate, but amoral gratification in the world of the nightclub on the other. Dedication to an abstract and unrealized ethical community or the hedonistic embrace of an opportunistic society — those are the stark terms of Himes's moral compass here and throughout his career. And the anxiety at the center of Himes's story is that the injuries of racism will skew the balance — that being black will somehow become, as it does for the bandleader, an impetus and a legitimation for the latter choice. In order to avoid that implication, Jean like her analog, Bob Jones, must choose to isolate herself from the mundane black society represented by the nightclub. The final lines of Himes's story thus dramatize the antagonism between the virtue of renunciation and the pleasures of sociability. Jean sits alone in her apartment and listens to the sound of an enticing but dangerous popular community echoing up from below. "The male singer was going to town on: '*Yass-yass-yass . . .*' And the patrons were echoing: '*Oh-yass-yass-yass . . .*' The joint was rocking."[32]

The novels that Himes wrote after *If He Hollers* returned frequently to that contrast between higher laws and lower pleasures — each time to make the balance less favorable to virtue than it had initially seemed. In *Lonely Crusade* (1947), a less successful but richer and more complex novel than his first book, Himes expanded almost directly on the premise of his essay "Negro Martyrs Are Needed" to tell the story of an embattled union organizer who sacrifices his life to redeem the values of "fraternity and equality" (393). Like Bob Jones, Lee Gordon is an idealistic young man, dedicated to principles that are ignored or manipulated by the host of antagonists who surround him, and in his effort to help organize the black and white workers of a wartime aircraft plant, he dramatizes much the same problems posed by Himes's first novel. Lee Gordon is victimized by the aircraft plant's Machiavellian owner; disgusted by the union officials who hire him as a token representative of workers they cannot fully embrace; enraged by the Communist Party, which will employ any means to infiltrate the union; and disappointed by his wife's yearning for middle-class respectability. Most importantly, he is embarrassed by the uneducated and apparently undisciplined black workers he tries to organize and frustrated by the needless divisions between them and their fellow laborers. The plant's workers are all "Southern migrants," Gordon argues. "All had been born on the same baked share-croppers' farms, steeped in the same Southern traditions, the object of the same tyranny that, together, they had not only permitted but upheld. . . . Only their hatred of each other separated them, like idiots hating their own images."[33]

Despite their complex mutual enmities, all these forces are united in Himes's imagination by the simple fact that they are driven by low desires rather than high principles. Gordon's wife, his employers, his political enemies, and the workers he claims to represent are all alike in the simple fact that they seek to use him and each other instrumentally, making other people the means of satisfying their own aims and ambitions. Together they recapitulate the image of liberal society as a soulless, fragmentary, and anarchic war of all against all, and they thus conspire to teach Himes's protagonist the lesson that had always been at the center of the detective novel and that haunted both *If He Hollers* and "The Song Says 'Keep on Smiling' ": the notion that the world is organized solely by self-interest. Thus it is that at one of his lowest moments in the novel, Gordon discovers "that the one rigid rule in human behavior was to be for yourself . . . ; from then on he would believe in the almighty dollar, the cowardice of Negroes, and the hypocrisy of whites, and he would never go wrong" (238). Hence also the fact that Lee Gordon can only escape the doubts that torture him and the web of forces that surround him by embracing martyrdom. In a Christlike act of self-sacrifice, he picks up a union banner in the midst of an antilabor riot and, walking knowingly toward his death, demonstrates to himself and to all the novel's characters that high principles and fraternal spirit can triumph over divisive self-interest. In the moments before this final scene, Himes tells us of the redemption that Gordon experiences when he comes finally to a selfless dedication to the cause of labor: "he did not feel lost or black or unimportant, but a part of it, contained by it, as a ripple in the river of humanity" (393, 386).

Like all Himes's earlier fiction, in other words, *Lonely Crusade* is built on a basic contrast between principle and interest. Principle soars above the ordinary world, Himes suggests; it is universal, fraternal, impervious to racial difference or sexual manipulation. Interest, by contrast, is selfish, individualistic, and divisive. Rather than redemptive fraternity, it gives rise to corrosive appetite, needless tribalism, and erotic exploitation. In Himes's increasingly pessimistic view, only the most extraordinary acts of martyrdom could bridge the gap between these domains and bring about the victory of the good over the weak, but he seemed genuinely to believe that other people — once moved by his visions of heroic self-sacrifice — would see things as he did. Thus, it was a terrible surprise when *Lonely Crusade* did not receive the positive reaction generated by *If He Hollers*. For his contemporary audience, what stood out about Himes's second novel was its cruel rendition of the world over which Lee Gordon was to triumph. Indeed, nearly everyone could find something in the book by which to be offended: the grossly anti-Semitic light in which Himes cast the intrigues of the Communist Party, the harsh accuracy with which he dissected white liberals, the sexist portrayals of both Gordon's wife and lover, and the deep ambivalence with which Gordon regarded the uneducated migrants from the black South. Like his protagonist, Himes appeared to be "a man fighting blindly and desperately and dangerously toward a goal, and yet rejecting, denouncing, condemn each hand lifted to help him on his way — damning each slow step because he could not make it in one." Indeed, he appeared to relish the "raging fury" of the role, setting out deliberately to antagonize his readers and suggesting that only in this way could they be reminded of the high demands of the "brotherhood of men" (345).

What Himes did not appear to expect or to understand was the universal distaste with which the novel was inevitably greeted. "Everyone hated the book," Himes later recalled. "The left hated it, the right hated it, Jews hated it, blacks hated it." Rather than foster the redemptive fraternity that Lee Gordon envisioned in his final moments, the novel seemed only to illuminate how accurate its portrayal of the fragmentation of American society was becoming. And it was when he realized how widely the novel was disliked, Himes claimed in retrospect, that he "decided to leave the United States forever." For, given the intricate way in which Himes had bound together his literary and social ideas, there was no way he could prevent the terrible failure of his novel from undermining his naïve political beliefs. Like "Negro Martyrs," the conclusion to *Lonely Crusade* depended on a vision of the moral transformation of the national conscience, and the rejection of his novel thus inevitably appeared to Himes to signal the dismissal of both the ideal of populist fraternity and of the crucial role to be played in its creation by the heroic writer. Henceforth, he would cast himself and his protagonists less as martyrs and visionaries than as losers and exiles. "The whites rejected me, the blacks didn't want me," he wrote of this moment almost twenty-five years later. "I felt like a man without a country, which in fact I was."[34]

HOMAGE TO THE SQUARE

If the failure of his own novels in the late forties and early fifties spoke to Himes of a changing political and cultural climate in the United States, that impression was made still more forceful by the ascendancy of a new generation of black writers and by the development of new aesthetic canons that justified their work and marginalized his own. From his earliest publications, Himes had cast himself as the protégé and heir to Richard Wright. In the early fifties, though, he watched bemusedly as first Ralph Ellison and then James Baldwin passed him by and appeared to displace Wright in the role of exemplary black intellectual. (There always seemed room for just one such figure, Himes complained.) Baldwin he found particularly galling. For Himes had imagined himself less as someone who would repudiate Wright's example than tinker with it — adopting Wright's naturalist poetics without absorbing his theoretical convictions — and he could understand neither Baldwin's intense animosity toward Wright nor his need to see Wright as a literary father to be slain and memorialized. Indeed, by Himes's account, there were few better examples of the unfortunate atmosphere of the postwar world than Baldwin's act of literary parricide, and thus there were few events that would throw his own development as a writer into starker relief.

At the core of the frontal assault that Baldwin launched on Wright's work in the early part of the decade lay, of course, Baldwin's belief that Wright had confused "literature" with "sociology." Along with lesser imitators like Himes (who Baldwin briefly singled out for censure), Wright had been profoundly limited by his naturalist style. Obsessed with "the inequities of the social structure of America," and determined to see "the Negro" as a representative figure — "our most oppressed minority" — Wright had imagined his characters "solely in social terms," as creatures who served merely to demonstrate the action of forces far beyond their ken. Despite the fact that he had piled up "the details of slum life," then, Wright had overlooked the vital world of African American culture — the rich "dimension" of "the relationship that Negroes bear to one another." His novels depicted "no tradition, no field of manners, no possibility of ritual or intercourse, such as may, for example, sustain the Jew even after he has left his father's house," and they thereby re-created the very "dehumanization of the Negro" that Wright otherwise sought to contest. The task of the true novelist, Baldwin now argued, was to restore that humanity by turning away from the illusions of sociology for the truth of "the interior life." Only by investigating "this web of ambiguity, paradox, this hunger, danger, darkness, can we find at once ourselves and the power that will free us from ourselves."[35]

Like the Warren Court, in other words, Baldwin rejected the sociological perspective that had seemed important to reformers and writers during the thirties in favor of the nonquantifiable matters of psychology and culture. The "intangible dreams of a people," he asserted in various ways time and again, "have a tangible effect on the world."[36] But if that Jamesian conviction enabled Baldwin to dismiss Wright's example, it also dismissed some of the reasons that underlay the methods shared by Wright and Himes. Their novels had indeed focused on "social structure" at the cost of the interior life (as Himes's Lee Gordon acknowledged when he explained that he "majored in sociology" because he wanted to understand "the how and why of people" [36]). But for Wright and Himes — as for contemporaneous black political leaders — stressing the role of social environment was inseparable from the effort to dismiss the fantasies of inheritance. Their characters were the way they were because of their education and opportunities, not because of ancestry or culture. As Baldwin reported after Wright's death, for example, Wright would "snort" derisively when Baldwin brought up the subject of "roots": "Next thing you'll be telling me is all colored folks have rhythm."[37] And for Himes, as for Wright, that derisive attitude was important precisely because it seemed to allow for a freedom that Baldwin would deny, or at least sharply qualify. From Wright's perspective, "the religion and folk culture of his race" was not the source of emancipation that Baldwin imagined, but an inherently conservative power, designed to acclimate people to their world and to offer them "a compensatory nourishment" for its injuries. By contrast, as Wright reiterated many times, and as Himes suggested in the conclusion to *Lonely Crusade*, the belief that society mattered more than culture and that environment was more powerful than ancestry was powerful because it suggested that political will could triumph over racial division. Only because he had severed his roots and become a "free agent," Wright suggested, could "the American Negro" discover "the possibilities of *alliances*" with "other people possessing a kindred consciousness."[38]

By Baldwin's account, that was a shallow illusion. It was "a senti-mental error . . . to believe that the past is dead" or that it could be dismissed in favor of a utopian political future: "a truly new society [was] impossible to conceive." And thus the dream shared in dif-ferent ways by Wright and Himes — of denying the reality of race in order to unite black and white workers — was absurd. Black and white Americans could not be joined by interests or aims or institu-tions until they confronted the fact of their "*blood* relationship, per-haps the most profound reality of the American experience." Rather than fleeing the past to embrace the secondary matters of society and politics, then, every individual needed first of all to be preoccupied with the "question of identity" and to recognize its inextricable rela-tion to "inheritance." Indeed, as Baldwin repeated in various ways throughout his career, meaningful progress could begin in the United States only when every person finally realized that "his ancestors, . . . in everything they do and are, proclaim his inescapable identity."[39]

Both formally and thematically, Baldwin's fiction began from that premise. His first great novel, *Go Tell It on the Mountain* unfolds in the rich vernacular of the black revivalist church, his characters' speech and thought shaped by the language of the spirituals and the inflections of the King James Bible. That diction, though, remains inseparable from Baldwin's desire to show how profoundly his char-acters have been molded by what they have inherited and from the organizing plot of the novel — the effort made by John Grimes to come to manhood by confronting the legacy of his parents and of the church through which their past is articulated. *Go Tell It on the Mountain* attributes a particular importance to that effort, moreover, that makes for an especially revealing comparison to the later work of Chester Himes. Looking out over the streets of contemporary Harlem, John Grimes and his parents see a landscape of terrible peril—"a nervous, hollow, ringing city," lacking in moral authority or traditional guidance. And in this sense, the "sinful avenue," populated by drinkers, gamblers, and prostitutes to which the novel consistently and nervously recurs, stands for a larger danger that Baldwin recognizes in the urban North of the postwar United States. The religious tradition that gave meaning, order, and the promise of redemption to the lives of black Southerners in the past can exercise only weakened authority in contemporary Harlem, Baldwin suggests. In a racist society that holds out promises on which it refuses to deliver, offering license instead of freedom or opportunity, religion is no longer enough to hold people's lives together. It becomes instead a defensive and "fairly desperate emotional business." Thus, stranded between his father's authoritarian religion and the freedom of the street, John Grimes is not just a young boy struggling to come to manhood, but the uncertain representative of a black community imperiled both by stifling tradition and by "the decay and dislocation" of an open society.[40]

The solution to this dilemma, Baldwin suggests, comes in an intense encounter with family and inheritance. By receiving and absorbing the ancestral legacy he thought at first only to escape, John Grimes faces the future with a confidence he would otherwise lack (and he therefore seems likely to avoid the doom apparently promised his younger brother, whose stubborn rejection of their father leads toward the dangerous and violent temptations of the city). In this way, Baldwin suggests, inheritance can mediate between the church and the street, giving ballast to lives that might otherwise go astray. "The hope of salvation," as Baldwin later put it, lay in the discovery of "identity," and it depended for its achievement on "whether one would be able to decipher and describe" the "accumulated rock of ages." Like Baldwin's hypothetical Jew, in other words—who is sustained by ritual and tradition after he has left his father's house—John Grimes can find guidance in his inherited culture, even after he escapes the patriarchal authority that once seemed to embody it. The moral is emphasized by the central spatial metaphors of Baldwin's novel. Displacing the dangerous liberty implied by the horizontal movement of the city's streets with John's vertical descent to "the threshing floor" — the site of the spiritual crisis where he confronts his father's legacy — they suggest that one can climb the mountain to glimpse the promise of the future only after having gone down to encounter the mystery of the past.

Celebrating that critical encounter with tradition, Baldwin joined Ralph Ellison in the effort to develop a new black literature suitable for the emerging world of interest-group liberalism. If there was a promise in the booming consumer economy of the 1950s and in the developing public discourse of civil rights, it lay, Baldwin's writing suggested, less in the vision of interracial populist brotherhood valued by Wright and Himes, than in the prospect for black self-determination and, ultimately, in hope for the full encounter by white Americans with the history and legacies of racism. His audience should look not to the "alliances" that Wright imagined being forged across racial lines, but to the mutual self-awareness of black and white Americans — *as* people who had been fundamentally shaped by the history of racism and who were fully cognizant of its continuing force. In Himes's view, however, that project not only unjustly dismissed the example of Richard Wright; it made Baldwin seem an "opportunist" (tellingly, the same term he had used earlier to describe the amoral bandleader of "The Song Says 'Keep on Smiling'"). For Baldwin's view seemed necessarily to imply the very idea of racial identity that Himes and Wright had struggled against.[41] Indeed, so powerfully was he offended by Baldwin's work that the "Harlem domestic" novels Himes began to publish in the late fifties might be understood best as an implicit rebuttal to Baldwin's writing and to the values on which it rested.

In the first novel in his detective series, *For Love of Immabelle* (first published in France as *La Reine des Pommes* and later retitled *A Rage in Harlem*), Himes tells of the misadventures that develop when a trio of hustlers from the Deep South bring a case of fool's gold to Harlem. Their plan is to trick the city's more gullible residents into investing in a nonexistent mine — which they claim will be run as a "closed corporation," solely for "colored people" — and the novel focuses on the consequent trials of one of their victims: a naïve undertaker's assistant named Jackson who searches frantically to find and protect his fiancée Immabelle after she disappears with these men. Piling up comic incident upon incident, the narrative follows Jackson's entanglement in this effort with his ruthless brother Goldy — yet another con artist, who makes his living by impersonating a Sister of Mercy — and it adds to this complicated mix by throwing in two brutal black policemen who attempt to track the movement of these figures through the obscure passages of Harlem's demimonde. The result is nearly a direct inversion of *Go Tell It on the Mountain*. Where Baldwin's novel is earnest and lyrical, Himes stresses burlesque comedy. Where Baldwin's narrative plumbs the interior regions of character and memory, Himes's novel moves outward through the fantastic geography of the Harlem underworld. Where Baldwin is obsessed with ancestral legacy and racial identity, Himes suggests that both family feeling and black solidarity are scams, if they exist at all. The temporary alliance of *For Love of Immabelle*'s two brothers, Jackson and Goldy, depends solely on mutual necessity; each would as soon ignore or even murder as help the other. The point is reiterated by the maguffin at the center of the novel, the crate of fool's gold brought to Harlem from Mississippi (also tellingly described as a box of Immabelle's "heirlooms"). For Baldwin, the past and the ancestral terrain of the rural black South promise John Grimes a rich and essential inheritance. In Himes's world, they amount to deadly illusion.[42]

It is in this context that we can begin to see what was so appealing to Himes about the crime story and why he turned to it in 1957 in particular. Placed next to Baldwin's new way of imagining the lives of black Americans, Himes's Harlem domestic novels look like a stubborn effort to maintain his earlier convictions. Though those beliefs have lost currency and the redemptive aura they once possessed, what counts in Himes's Harlem novels is still what mattered in his earlier thinking. The importance of class and economic need far outweigh inheritance. Hence, the fact that Jackson and Goldy see each other solely as vehicles for their individual pursuits. Each brother is guided by the instrumental pursuit of self-chosen ends;

they are virtually parodic images of that "free agent," shaped less by culture or tradition than by rationally calculated self-interest, that Wright had seen as the true nature of "the American Negro." Hence, also, the description that Himes offered four years later of the two detectives, Grave Digger Jones and Coffin Ed Johnson, who would go on to become the protagonists of his series. Standing amid the Harlem crowd they seek to control, Himes's detectives look nearly indistinct from their community. Their identifying features, however, are importantly less the product of inheritance than the very tangible class markers that had mattered to Himes since the beginning of his career:

> Both of them looked just as red-eyed, greasy-faced, sweaty and evil as the other colored people gathered about, combatants and spectators alike. They were of a similar size and build to other "working stiffs" — big, broad-shouldered, loose-jointed and flat footed. Their faces bore marks and scars similar to any colored street fighter. Grave Digger's was full of lumps where felons had hit him from time to time with various weapons; while Coffin Ed's was a patchwork of scars where skin had been grafted over the burns left by acid thrown into his face.
>
> The difference was they had the pistols, and everyone in Harlem knew them as the "Mens."

Though the tone of this description has moved significantly away from the populist braggadocio of *If He Hollers*, here as before Himes's characters are most salient in their role as "working stiffs"; each resembles "a day laborer in a steel mill."[43] Where Baldwin's characters bear psychic wounds and cultural legacies, then, Himes's protagonists are marked outwardly (indeed, they seem throughout Himes's series to have almost no "interior life" whatsoever) by proletarian occupation and by the circumstances of a brutal environment. In this respect, they are representative of the whole world of Himes's Harlem. Despite, or rather because of, the fact that it is a racially segregated community, the imaginary city of Himes's novels is defined almost solely by what Baldwin might call "sociological" or economic terms. Explaining how he fell into the scam run by the novel's con artists, Jackson says, "My woman wanted a new winter coat, we want to get a place of our own, maybe buy a car. I just yielded to temptation" (9). As with all of his Harlem community, in other words, Jackson's primary experience of racism is the terrible poverty and stifled desire it creates — a fact that Himes emphasizes by building his narrative around a competitive and comically desperate struggle for money.[44] With the exception of Grave Digger and Coffin Ed, all of the major characters in *For Love of Immabelle* fight to gain possession of the elusive fool's gold at the center of the novel, and, although in varying ways, all of them share Jackson's motives: they are oppressed by economic need and driven by economic desire. No other factor counts as strongly in Himes's world — not love, faith, tradition, culture, or especially race. "All human values," as Himes had put it earlier, fall "with awesome swiftness" before "the struggle for the dollar." When he looks over his imaginary landscape, what Himes sees, then, is almost solely the urban "decay and dislocation" that Baldwin imagined could be controlled by devotion to "identity." His Harlem is "a city of black people who are convulsed in desperate living, like the voracious churning of millions of hungry cannibal fish. Blind mouths eating their own guts. Stick in a hand, draw back a nub" (133).

In this manner, Himes re-created a social fiction that he might have picked up reading *Black Mask* in the early thirties. Like the underworld envisioned by Dashiell Hammett and Carroll John Daly, Himes's Harlem is a fantastic image of society-as-open-market, a world deliberately stripped of almost every custom or value that cannot be reduced finally to appetitive self-interest. Nearly everyone is reduced to the brute struggle for survival or advantage, and everyone is thus forced to be constantly "watching everyone else, as though each one regarded his neighbor as either a potential victim or as a stool pigeon for the police" (54). Like his hard-boiled predecessors, too, Himes found this exaggerated image useful partly because it made contemporaneous ideas of racial difference or cultural hierarchy seem absurd — his brutal city is in this sense "truly democratic" — and partly because it provided a license for outlandish literary invention.[45] For Himes, in other words, Harlem is not the race capital imagined by writers during the twenties, nor the privileged vantage on the past envisioned by Baldwin, but a latter-day version of the environment he had first constructed in his prison writings:

society reduced by poverty to a surreal state of nature, where, because everyone must be desperately out for himself, anything can happen.[46]

But if this way of looking at the world — and of *not* looking at it as James Baldwin did — resembled the attitudes that Himes first adopted during the thirties and forties, in many ways his fiction registered the fact that those beliefs no longer possessed much cultural authority. The antiracialist populism at the core of Himes's earlier novels survives in the detective fiction, but it no longer possesses the redemptive tone that informed his earlier work. As before, Himes divides the world into the corrupt haves and the virtuous have-nots; his Harlem has two classes: the "elite of the underworld" and the "working strivers" (93). But, there are no uplifting images of working-class Americanism in these stories, nor paeans to swimming in "the river of humanity." The "simple Joe" of *If He Hollers* has become the scarred and lumpen "working stiff" represented by Grave Digger and Coffin Ed; the "brotherhood of men" a Hobbesian war of all against all. As the sheer extremity of his portrait of his imaginary city might suggest, moreover, Himes seemed to want to stress how rare his earlier views had become — as if he could only make his point now by overemphasizing it. His protagonists always recognize that at the root of every story lies white economic exploitation of Harlem and the tangible necessity of the city's black residents for "better housing, . . . better schools, higher wages." But they often run up against white superiors who search for, and in fact create, racial explanations for a world they would rather see as distant from their own.[47] Likewise, Grave Digger and Coffin Ed do constant battle with the various black hustlers who prey on the needs of Harlem's "working strivers" by offering them visions of heritage or racial solidarity. Beginning with the con men in *Immabelle* and continuing on through nasty denunciations of the revivalist church, black politicians and drug peddlers, the Back-to-Africa movement, Black Power, and the Black Muslims, Himes's novels reserve their worst scorn for hustlers who take advantage of Harlem's desperation by offering false hopes of redemption and racial community.[48]

Himes's protagonists find themselves, in short, on much the same slim ground that Himes imagined for himself in the fifties. They are caught between white authorities who demand—like the postwar public—that the Negro be unusual, and black opportunists, who like James Baldwin (or Baldwin as Himes imagined him), acquiesce to that demand. Their travails illustrate just how narrow Himes believed that ground was becoming and how difficult he thought it was to defend. Throughout his crime novel series, Grave Digger and Coffin Ed struggle to protect and represent the ordinary people of Harlem. Like Bob Jones or Lee Gordon in Himes's earlier novels, they are cast as enraged social prophets who see the truth of an unjust and irrational world and who strive to make it clear to a complacent audience. But where previously Himes had imagined that effort as redemptive or at least tragic, now he draws on a central feature of the hard-boiled tradition to suggest that it is merely futile. Like Hammett's Continental Op or Chandler's Philip Marlowe, Himes's detectives are useful figures for their ability to indict a law that seems rigid and inadequate, and for their capacity to delineate a kind of action in which the inertia of milieu inevitably defeats the desire for justice. Thus, embracing the detective story served Himes well if for no other reason than that it allowed him to shift his obsession with transcendent ideals to a new key—one better suited to the postwar world. Turning from Bob Jones and Lee Gordon to Grave Digger and Coffin Ed, Himes abandoned the bathos of martyrdom for the comedy of hopeless causes.

That transition is still clearer, though, in the fate of Jackson and of the many "suckers" who follow him throughout Himes's series: Sonny in *The Real Cool Killers*, Alberta in *The Big Gold Dream*, Roman in *All Shot Up*, Pinky in *The Heat's On*, and the followers of Deke O'Malley in *Cotton Comes to Harlem*. Coffin Ed and Grave Digger Jones descend from one side of the stalwart heroes who appeared in Himes's earlier protest fiction. Like Jones or Gordon or the Himes who spoke in "Negro Martyrs," they are walking superegos: men of principle, who demand justice and react in fury when they see the law sullied by greed, sloth, or racism. But another aspect of Himes's noble young men surfaces in Jackson and his descendants— as if Himes had preserved the unlikely dimensions of his heroes simply by splitting them into two kinds of characters. In Jackson's panic-stricken flights through Harlem, Himes re-creates the desperate frustrations that beset all of his early protagonists, offering a comic version of the efforts they made to maintain their bearings in a world that confounded and eluded them. Like Jones and Gordon, Jackson is a naïve and idealistic young man surrounded by obstacles and temptations. Like them, his manhood and stature hinge on his ability to bring home a woman of wandering fidelity, and, like them, he longs above all for a domestic happiness that seems to be denied him. As he did before, Himes again suggests that the very basis of decency and order is the patriarchal home, and, as before, he implies that the first injury of racism is the way that it denies that possibility to black men. In his struggle to bring home his beloved, though, Jackson redefines the story that Himes once told in earnest, replacing Himes's democratic martyrs with a comically hapless naïf.

Himes sets us up to appreciate that transition from the opening scene of *For Love of Immabelle*, in which Jackson is bilked of his money by Hank, one of the trio of Southern con men. Convinced that Hank can "raise" the denomination of $10 bills to hundreds by cooking them in the oven, Jackson turns over his rent money and waits for it to be multiplied. When Hank begins the process, however, the stove explodes, Hank and his partner disappear with Immabelle, and Jackson is left behind to be arrested by the third con man, Slim, who poses falsely as a sheriff in order to rook still more money from the befuddled sucker — a bribe that Jackson can pay only by stealing from his employer. The novel begins, in other words, with the literal explosion of the fantasies of middle-class domesticity that Jackson shares with Bob Jones, Lee Gordon, and Himes himself, and the remainder of Himes's narrative focuses on the poor man's desperate efforts to bring back his money, save his job, avoid prison, and rein in his woman.

It is that last effort that makes Himes's protagonist most pathetic. Throughout the novel, Himes stresses Jackson's panic and confusion as he chases the con men, runs from the police, and struggles to escape one slapstick calamity after the next — all of which he undergoes with a naïve innocence that singles him out from the rapacious figures of the Harlem underworld. Jackson is foolish enough to believe that his landlady should be "a Christian"; he mistakenly expects that the parasitic minister of his church will provide him with pastoral care; and, most significantly, he refuses to acknowledge what everyone else knows — that the luscious Immabelle is a golddigger who has abandoned him for better prospects. Her own sister warns Jackson that Immabelle "is a lying bitch," and in a paradigmatic dialogue Goldy tries, despite Jackson's "dogged" refusal to see his point, to explain that Immabelle is sharp enough to have "turned you in for a new model." Even the otherwise unperceptive white district attorney wonders at Jackson's gullibility (17, 88). But it is, of course, precisely that naïveté, that makes Jackson the hero of Himes's novel and the model for the many virtuous suckers who would follow him throughout Himes's detective series. For what makes Jackson admirable in Himes's eyes is a smaller-scale version of the attitude that distinguished the earlier protagonists of Himes's fiction. Like Bob Jones and Lee Gordon, Jackson is surrounded by the scheming and duplicitous and yet remains willfully innocent. A "black Don Quixote," he thus figures the ordinary residents of Harlem as people who, though mired in desperate circumstances, refuse to embrace the understandable cynicism that such a context might encourage (75).

It is a perspective that at first glance seems surprising. In many ways, Goldy appears the definitive citizen of Himes's imaginary Harlem. He is cynical, greedy, sharp-witted, and ironically aware of the rackets operating throughout his city, and, as if to indicate that his book would be written from Goldy's hip perspective on his brother, Himes initially planned to title his novel "The Five Cornered Square." But just as Himes had earlier dismissed the opportunistic bandleader of "The Song Says 'Keep on Smiling,'" here again he turns out to be a moralist who punishes hustlers and rewards the square. Goldy dies midway through the novel, and the trio of con men soon follow him to a violent end. Jackson, by contrast, survives, regains his job and room, and finally takes possession of the woman whose fidelity he has always, however mistakenly, refused to doubt.

Thus, the title that Himes eventually gave the novel, *For Love of Immabelle*, seems fitting. If his detective novels stubbornly hold on to the naturalist perspective that shaped Himes's earlier work — seeing the world only through the lens of class and social environment — the moral commitment behind that view remained much the same as it had been throughout Himes's career. Though stated more cautiously, and in a comic rather than tragic register, the message of Himes's first detective novel is much the same as the simple one that ran through his earlier fiction. Despite the fact that it no longer seemed possible to maintain such a belief without looking like a fool, Jackson's triumph taught that, given sufficient will, love can triumph over the corrosive dangers of "the struggle for the dollar."

LAW'S VIOLENCE

In short, the crime novels that Himes published during the late fifties and early sixties rewrote as farce the tragic story he had told and retold during the forties. Seeing the detective story as the natural expression of "American violence," of a society driven by brutal competition rather than fraternal spirit, Himes's Harlem domestic novels imagined a ludic inversion of the vision created in a novel like *Lonely Crusade*. In raptly fascinated depictions, they imagined Harlem as a world of sinful vitality, where "jukeboxes blared, [and] honeysuckle-blues voices dripped stickily through jungle cries of wailing saxophones, screaming trumpets, and buck dancing piano-notes," where "someone was either fighting, or had just stopped fighting, or was just starting to fight," and where "hepped-cats who lived by their wits" throve on "the hot excitement money could buy" (R 36, 60). By the terms of "Negro Martyrs," this was "riot" rather than "revolution," the lowest common denominator rather than the transfiguring force of the ideal. As Himes suggested when he quoted Milton to describe the "blind mouths" of Harlem, then, the Calvinist moral compass and the starkly Manichaean perspective of his earlier fiction persisted, but their poles now seemed reversed. He would no longer celebrate "the movement of the working people of the world," but dramatize the "cesspool of buffoonery" toward which that movement had descended.[49]

Nowhere was that transition clearer than in the most distinctive feature of Himes's crime novels — their extraordinary, carnivalesque violence. One after another, on nearly every page of the Harlem domestic novels, the images pile up: a man in a knife fight has his arm chopped off by an ax and continues furiously waving his stump, shouting at his opponent to wait until he can find his missing arm; a motorcyclist, chased by the police, is decapitated when he runs into a truck carrying sheet metal, and the headless body continues to drive the motorcycle down the street; a man stabbed in the head wanders deaf and blind through the city, where pedestrians take him for a practical joker and pass by. If the imaginary Harlem of these novels is a ravenous world of blind mouths, what makes it seem especially so is the "runaway blood" that, "surging through" the city's inhabitants, leaves it constantly on the verge of breaking into riot.[50]

Consider one scene of particularly tour-de-force invention from *Cotton Comes to Harlem.* It will be worth quoting the passage at some length in order both to grasp the conventions of Himes's rhetoric of violence and their deep roots in the Manichaean thinking that had shaped Himes's fiction from his first publications. The scene comes at the climax of the novel, when Coffin Ed and Grave Digger have finally tracked the con man Deke O'Malley to his headquarters in an abandoned church. In the opening scenes of the novel, O'Malley bilks $87,000 from the "lost and hungry black people" of Harlem by casting himself as the leader of a Back to Africa movement. As in all of Himes's Harlem domestic novels, though, that fool's gold soon goes missing, and the remainder of the novel recounts the competitive efforts of various parties to recover it. In this extended scene four of those parties come violently together. Seeking to return the lost money to O'Malley's victims (a task at which they will never succeed), Coffin Ed and Grave Digger trace the con man to the empty church. In the meantime, O'Malley's two top henchmen have turned against their boss and, hoping to force him to disclose the location of the missing loot, they imprison him in the church's basement and tie him to his former lover, Iris — who, of course, would also like the money for herself. Just as they begin to contemplate torturing their captives, however, Coffin Ed and Grave Digger enter the church above them. In the freewheeling gunfight that ensues, we see Himes's objective correlative for "the struggle for the dollar." Bring together a group of self-interested agents, the scene implies, and you get not civil society but ruthless and catastrophic violence:

A figure with burning hair loomed in the flickering red light from the burning organ with a .45 searching the gloom and Grave Digger peeped. . . . He lay on his belly beneath the benches, looking towards the sound, and made out the vague outline of trousered legs limned against the platform that had caught on fire. He took careful aim and shot a leg. He saw the leg break off like a wooden stick where the tracer bullet hit it dead center, and saw the trouser leg catch fire suddenly. Now the screaming slashed into the pool of silence like needles of flame and seared his nerves.

The burning shape of the body issuing these screams fell atop the broken leg, on the floor between two benches, and Grave Digger pumped two tracer bullets into it and watched the flames spring up. The dying man clawed at the book rack above him, breaking the fragile wood, and a prayer book fell on top of his burning body. . . .

The smoke had penetrated the hideout below, and the prisoners tied back-to-back on the two chairs had gone crazy from terror. They were spitting curses and accusations, and trying desperately to get at each other. . . .

Their legs were tied together like their arms but their feet touched the floor. They were straining with arched bodies and gripping feet to push each other into the wall. The chairs slid on the concrete floor, back and forth, rocking precariously. Arteries in their necks were swelled to bursting, muscles stretched like frayed cables, bodies twisting, breasts heaving, mouths gasping and drooling like two people in a maniacal sex act. Her make-up became streaked with sweat and her wig fell off. Deke doubled forward on his feet tied to the chair's legs, trying to bang Iris sideways against the gun rack. Her chair rose from the floor and blood-curdling screams came wetly from her scar-like mouth as his chair tilted forward from his superhuman effort and they turned slowly over in a grotesque arc. He fell forward, face downward, striking his face on the concrete floor, as she came overtop in her chair. The momentum kept them turning until her head and forehead scraped on the concrete in turn and he was lifted from the floor. They landed up against the wall, her feet touching it, his chair on top supported only by the angle of his hers on the floor. . . . Both were too spent to curse, they remained still, gasping for breath in the slowly suffocating smoke.

Upstairs in the church, light from the burning gunman on the floor lit up the figure of the gunman with his head on fire crouched behind the end of a bench ahead. . . . Now the entire platform holding the pulpit and the choir and the organ was burning brightly, lighting up the stained-glass pictures of the saints looking down from the windows. From outside came a banshee wail and the first of the cruisers came tearing into the street.[51]

As Michael Denning has noted, an "ideology of violence" informs scenes of this type in Himes's work. Central to that ideology is the assumption that the brutally wounded and broken bodies that fill them out have "become objects." Seen by others solely as instruments for realizing their own ends, the people in Himes's world are rapidly reduced, as Himes put it elsewhere, to "meat." "Given that one of the major narrative paradigms of black literature has been the movement from being an object, a thing, a slave, to being a person," Denning explains, "it is as if Himes had reversed the plot and shown the reduction of people to objects, not for the purpose of protest but for the absurd and comic incongruity."[52] But if that seems an accurate description of the gothic violence that culminates in the climax to *Cotton Comes to Harlem* — where a leg becomes "a wooden stick" and a burning man a torch — the reversal to which Denning refers can be traced more specifically to the dynamics of Himes's personal development, where its significance opens out in directions that Denning does not mention. In his earlier fiction and essays, Himes had asserted that the key to political transformation lay in "sympathy" and that this common feeling depended on an immediate awareness of the suffering of others. What is displayed in *Cotton Comes to Harlem* and throughout Himes's Harlem domestic novels is not just the instrumental reduction of people to objects, but injury without the sympathy or fraternal feeling Himes had once celebrated as the core element of political revitalization.[53] And, as the religious setting of the scene above emphasizes, the charge delivered by such violence depends on an implicit awareness of the debasement it signifies to the virtually spiritual ideals Himes and his protagonists seek to defend. The flaming pulpit, the disapproving saints, the gunman burning beneath an open prayer book all testify to Himes's disgust at the displacement of moral principle by criminal desire — an impression given still more weight by the scene tellingly located in the church's basement. Straining to injure each other while hoping simultaneously to escape personally unscathed, Iris and Deke provide Himes with a heavily eroticized emblem of perverse individual appetite. They appear prisoners of their own bodies, figures of grotesque vitality and bestial desperation, who are driven therefore to mutual self-destruction rather than common feeling.

At the core of Himes's ideology of violence, in other words, lie the elements of Menippean satire: the invocation of grotesque bodies in the defense of transcendent principles.[54] What makes that satire particularly forceful in Himes's Harlem domestic novels, however, is the fact that we know that detective stories are not supposed to work this way. Traditionally, the detective story begins with the intrusion on a stable world of an isolated example of seemingly meaningless violence and then works backward to give that violence the history and meaning that allow it to be contained. In doing so, the genre provides an allegory of the law and of liberal jurisprudence's central distinction between legitimate and illegitimate violence. If, as Austin Sarat and Thomas Kearns explain, the distinction rests on "the idea that violence can be cleansed, if not purified, by its contact with law," detective fiction traditionally makes a drama of that assumption — portraying the difficult effort to displace illegitimate violence with legitimate authority and dwelling on the ambiguities that always make the difference seem hazy or incomplete.[55] Though obliquely, this is just the drama that Himes referred to when he claimed that "American violence is public life, . . . it became a form, a detective story form." Giving public form to violence is precisely what detective stories do — or, more accurately, it is the process that they dramatize and celebrate. In the rational encounter with seemingly irrational violence, the mystery genre advances the notion that private crime can be remade into public knowledge.

The point for Himes, of course, is that in his Harlem it appears nearly impossible to imagine such a transformation — so that the detective story, and the allegory of the law behind it, seem at once indispensable and unbelievable. In the conclusion to one of the Harlem domestic novels, Coffin Ed complains about the attitude of "the public toward cops": "Folks just don't want to believe that what we're trying to do is make a decent peaceful city for people to live in." There is no sign that Himes means us to take this remark ironically. Like Bob Jones and Lee Gordon, Coffin Ed and Grave Digger want nothing more than to enable the people of Harlem to enjoy the domestic pleasures and bourgeois virtues that white Americans appear to take for granted. That possibility is denied, however, precisely because a racist system of justice makes it impossible for the residents of Harlem to think of cops as public servants; most take them, rather, as Grave Digger remarks elsewhere, for "public enemies."[56] And that reasonable assumption creates the core difficulty of Himes's crime novels. Stripped of popular legitimacy, the law can no longer serve as a counter to the ordinary injustice of society and seems instead, therefore, a mere continuation of the violence that courses through American life.

Hence the fact that Coffin Ed continues his complaint against the Harlem public by remarking that "people think we enjoy being tough, shooting people and knocking them in the head," and hence, too, Himes's barbed comment, made while comparing his protagonists to the "combatants and spectators" of Harlem street life, that the sole "difference" between his detectives and the people around them is that Coffin Ed and Grave Digger carry pistols and are commonly known as the "Mens." The indistinct popular identity of Himes's protagonists here and throughout most of the Harlem domestic novels is less a virtue than the embodiment of Himes's fundamental problem. For it signals that in their world there appears no significant difference between legitimate and illegitimate violence. Cops, even black cops, seem thugs in disguise, and, rather than cleansing or purifying violence, the law serves mainly to obscure it. Lacking a government with a monopoly on legitimate violence, Himes's Harlem thus seems, like Dashiell Hammett's Poisonville, a virtually stateless realm and always on the verge of descending into anarchy.[57]

As fierce upholders of the value of law and of the liberal principles it is supposed to represent, then, Coffin Ed and Grave Digger come to resemble *For Love of Immabelle*'s Jackson; they are heroic defenders of implausible ideals. That point is made in an especially illuminating way in a brief conversation that frames *All Shot Up* (1960), the

fifth book in Himes's group of detective novels and in some respects
the most revealing number of the series. *All Shot Up* is particularly
concerned with the relation between Harlem and its political leaders,
and it turns on the actions of the figure who controls the local Democratic party machine — a clever and autocratic man named Casper
Holmes, who is probably modeled on Harlem's famed congressman
Adam Clayton Powell Jr. In Himes's rendition, Holmes is a distinctly
ambivalent figure. As Coffin Ed explains, he is "an important man to
us colored people" — for his capacity to defend black America in the
national political system and, it is hinted, for his ability to dole out
the spoils of patronage. But he is also cravenly self-interested and
indifferent to his constituency, and Himes's narrative eventually reveals that Casper has been skimming off the very patronage he is
supposed to dole out.[58]

Even before the novel gets under way, though, Himes subtly points
to the issues raised by Casper's story. As the action of the narrative
begins, Coffin Ed and Grave Digger are eating in a soul food restaurant, where Coffin Ed briefly engages in a revealing debate. The
restaurant is owned by Mammy Louise, a recurrent character in
Himes's novels (and thus an analog to Hammett's Loop Pigatti), and
a striking representative of some of their key anxieties. An enormously fat woman, Mammy Louise is a successful entrepreneur and
a person of stern will. Her husband — the tellingly named Mister
Louise — is kept trembling in a corner by Mammy Louise's bulldog.
(In a later novel, Mister Louise is simply replaced by a "mincing
gigolo.")[59] Most significantly, Mammy Louise, as Himes pauses to
explain in some depth, is a Geechy — the descendant of "a melange of
runaway African slaves and Seminole Indians" whose insular culture
developed in isolation in the swamps of South Carolina. Mammy
Louise has grown up speaking their "mother tongue," a "mixture of
African dialects and the Seminole language," and she accordingly
pronounces English "with a strange, indefinable accent." In this conversation, she speaks with that accent to indict the actions of Himes's
protagonists:

> She was half moaning to herself. "Trouble, always trouble in dis
> wicked city. Whar Ah comes from — "

"There ain't no law," Coffin Ed cut her off as he put on his jacket. "Folks cut one another's throats and go on about their business."

"It's better than getting kilt by the law," she argued. "You can't pay for one death by another one. Salvation ain't the swapping market. . . .

"Tell it to the voters, Mammy," he said absently as he took down Grave Digger's overcoat and straightened out a sleeve. "I didn't make these laws."

"I'll tell it to everybody," she said. . . . Unnoticed by anyone but Mister Louise, the bulldog had moved over to block the curtained doorway. When Grave Digger moved toward it, the dog planted its feet and growled . . . but Mammy Louise swooped down on the dog and dragged it off before he did it injury.

"Not dem, Lawd Jim, mah God, dawg," she cried. "You can't stop dem from goin' nowhere. Them is de *mens*." (19, 20)

Concealed in this laconic dialogue is a pulp *Antigone* — a battle between matriarchal ritual and patriarchal law. Mammy Louise speaks for the wealth of custom and tradition, a fact emphasized by her rich heritage and her distinctive mother tongue; Coffin Ed defends the value of law. But the crucial feature of this meeting between maternal culture and masculine authority seems not only to be the tension between the two, but the patent inadequacy of each option and their inability to benefit from their conversation. If Mammy Louise invokes a self-contained world that seems less violent than the wicked city of Harlem, for Coffin Ed that world looks only like a lawless realm. More tellingly still, it appears indistinguishable in Himes's rendition from the emasculating kingdom of women represented by the Louises' marriage. At the same time, although Coffin Ed and Grave Digger embody the terrifying authority of "de *mens*," they cannot answer Mammy Louise's challenge. For Mammy Louise, there is no difference between the *lex talionis* of premodern tradition and the bureaucratic authority the detectives claim to represent. Each does little more than trade body for body and thus treats justice as a "swapping market." From that perspective, there seems little point to the law at all, and Himes lends Mammy Louise's point still greater weight, not only by giving Coffin Ed no strong answer to it, but by having him appeal finally to the mythical will of "the voters."

In a novel about the corruption of machine politics — and thus implicitly about the political co-optation of the people of Harlem — that parting shot seems particularly feeble, and its weakness is only emphasized by the fact that it is immediately followed by the threat of violence. Taken as whole, the conversation paints a grim picture. It casts Himes's protagonists as the defenders of a law that is indefensible precisely because it has no accountability to Harlem's black community — and that can only be maintained therefore by brute force — and at the same time, it allows them to complain reasonably that this very law is Harlem's only available means to justice and the city's sole defense against anarchy.

That dilemma is the animating problem of nearly all of Himes's Harlem domestic novels, but *All Shot Up* goes on to envision the problem in particularly revealing terms. The novel is organized by two criminal plots, which seem at first to be part of a single conspiracy but that are revealed in the novel's conclusion to be only symbolically related. Each plot depicts Harlem in terms that closely track those established by the novel's framing dialogue. In the dominant story line — as it is made finally clear by the novel's denouement — Casper Holmes plots to steal the campaign fund entrusted to him by the national offices of his party. Although he is guarded, and watched over, by the party's hired Pinkerton agents, Casper contrives to dispatch those guards by hiring a trio of gunmen — including one vicious white Southerner — to stage a mock robbery. At the same time, he double-crosses those accomplices by managing to surreptitiously pass the large bundle of cash to his homosexual lover Snake Hips as he walks in front of the Paris Bar, one of the watering holes catering to Harlem's gay subculture. Meanwhile, Casper's neglected wife, Leila, engages in a conspiracy of her own. Cross-dressing as a mysterious Harlem aristocrat, she renames herself Baron (in which role she seems to bear a resemblance to W. E. B. Du Bois: she wears "a black Homburg and a white silk scarf and has a small, bearded face like some kind of amateur magician" [6]). Along with her confederates, she then sets out to con a gullible sailor named Roman of his savings by selling him a gold Cadillac that she plans on stealing back again. In the novel's opening scenes, these two criminal plots intersect and go awry. Fleeing from the scene of their mock holdup, and enraged that they have been tricked out of the money they expected to collect, Casper's gunmen encounter Baron and Roman and immediately steal the gold Cadillac. The remainder of the novel recounts the bizarre developments that ensue as Casper and the gunmen both seek to recover the missing $50,000, as Roman hunts for his gold Cadillac, and as Coffin Ed and Grave Digger attempt to piece together the bewildering series of events that confront them as a result.

On the face of it, this complicated scenario seems little more than an excuse for generating the kind of slapstick action that Himes always favored. But the stories of Casper and Leila combine to suggest a complex symbolic logic and a substantial, if mean-spirited critique of Harlem politics. Together, Casper and Leila represent an elite political class that preys in direct and indirect ways on its own constituency, the working stiffs of Harlem who are embodied by the easily misled Roman. Each of them in that manner makes him or herself, along with their community, vulnerable to white criminal predators. The "cracker" who Casper hires to lead his mock robbery turns out to be a vicious thug who, in his determination to recover his share of the missing $50,000, goes on a violent crime spree through Harlem, and Leila's conspiracy similarly allows a white con man to profit off Roman's innocent yearning for a luxury (154). More tellingly, both Casper and Leila cast the parasitism of the black elite in terms predicted by Mammy Louise—as examples of sexual inversion and, more particularly, of a kind of erotic insularity. It is crucial, in other words, not only that both Casper as gay man and Leila as cross-dresser represent the parasite as womanly man, but that both also figure parasitism as a closed economy. Casper steals money intended for the public action of electioneering and, passing it to Snake Hips, conceals it within the obscure world of Harlem's gay demimonde—a subculture that Coffin Ed and Grave Digger repeatedly denounce for being a "clique" (169). Similarly, Leila not only preys on the vulnerable working stiff Roman, but her partner in doing so is importantly her cousin and another member of Harlem's homosexual minority—who, in carrying out their scam, cross-dresses as a woman while Leila takes on the costume of a man. In both cases, the parasitism of the black elite is represented simultaneously as a kind of gender or sexual inversion and as the secret and inward turning of a community upon itself.

So, while misogyny and homophobia run rampant all through Himes's Harlem domestic novels, where they invariably reflect Coffin Ed and Grave Digger's fury at decadence and corruption, *All Shot Up* puts the relation among these matters in an especially revealing way. What angers Himes's protagonists about Harlem's gay subculture, about its predatory women, and about its criminal parasites is that in each case they appear to represent the triumph of an effeminized privacy over the public masculinity that Coffin Ed and Grave Digger seek to represent. (It is part of the irony Casper represents that the sign for his office reads "Public Relations" even as he exemplifies hidden power [152].) As with the violence of the Harlem domestic novels, the roots of that attitude lay far back in the thinking that Himes developed during the thirties and forties. Imagining dedication to a transcendent national ideal as the necessary analog to manly autonomy, Himes's first novels likewise envisioned racial segregation as a kind of emasculation. To be minoritized in those novels was also to be feminized, and to consent to that minoritization by embracing the special rewards of black heritage or community was consequently to adopt a tacit sexual inversion. Thus, in *Lonely Crusade*, Lee Gordon objects when an academic compares "the Negro minority" to "the homosexual minority" — an analogy that he denies because he claims that it accepts the "abnormality" of "black skin" and, by extension, the special rather than representative status of African Americans.[60]

Henceforth, Himes would turn repeatedly to similar metaphors of homosexuality and effeminacy when he sought to attack the peril of invidious minoritization. The insular "clique" of Harlem's gay subculture presided over by Casper Holmes thus serves as the clearest emblem for the political emasculation that Himes attributes to Casper's leadership; like the Harlem voters patiently steered by Holmes's machine, the patrons of Harlem's gay bars enrage Coffin Ed and Grave Digger because they seem a "quiet, passive people" (32). Similar analogies run all through Himes's crime fiction — the feminization of Harlem's citizens inevitably pointing to the insularity and parasitism that Himes most feared from segregation. Thus, in *Cotton Comes to Harlem*, the swindler Deke O'Malley promises his followers a compensation for their homelessness in America. In Africa, he announces, "we'll have our own governments and our own rulers" (7). But the effect of that pronouncement is immediately to render his followers a crowd of "starry-eyed" and "helpless black people" who are most prominently represented by the female church members seduced by O'Malley. More telling still is the condition eventually suffered by O'Malley himself in the novel's climactic scene, when he is bound helplessly to the female body he once manipulated and now cannot escape. The logic at work in each of these novels is much the same as that which makes Goldy in *For Love of Immabelle* not just a con man who feeds on his own community, but by the same token a cross-dresser. To prey on the citizens of Harlem reduces them to a condition of effeminacy, Himes consistently suggests, but by the force of contagion it also strips Harlem's very parasites of masculinity and makes them the inversion of the patriarchal authority that Himes's protagonists hope to embody. As Coffin Ed explains the relation when he denounces Goldy — indicting simultaneously the con man's predatory schemes and his uncertain gender — "I hate a female impersonator worse than God hates sin" (52).

What Casper, Baron, and their analogs throughout Himes's fiction do, in other words, is to transform Himes's anxieties about the minoritization of African Americans into a drama of sexual autonomy. Like Mammy Louise, Baron, Deke, and Goldy all reject the authority of the law, and, as a consequence, all become fatally entangled in an insular community that is represented as simultaneously feminine and feminizing. The Harlem they create and represent is a world of enclosed spaces, humid interiors, and dark and twisting corridors. Like Mammy Louise's swamp, or like the church basement inhabited by Deke and Iris, in other words, it is a nightmarish female body writ large and pulsing with lethal erotic power. By contrast, the efforts that Coffin Ed and Grave Digger make to create a "decent peaceful city" are envisioned as an attempt to replace the closed spaces of a feminine community with an embattled, masculine public authority. Their investigations characteristically force them to open out Harlem, unveiling its darkened interiors and deprivatizing its concealed activities. It seems entirely fitting in this light that Himes's detectives keep their own homes in suburban Queens. For, returning from work across the Triborough Bridge after their grueling journeys through the Harlem underworld, Coffin Ed and Grave Digger not only keep faith with the determination of Bob Jones and Lee Gordon to demand their place in the fellowship of a larger, nonracial nation; like their predecessors they cast that demand as indistinguishable from the effort to recontain the private and the feminine within the limits of the domestic home.

In *All Shot Up* that effort culminates in a remarkable passage, a climactic scene that both demonstrates Himes's fascination with terrible violence and the symbolic importance he tacitly attributed to it. The scene takes place in Casper's headquarters, where the politician has been imprisoned by the gunmen he double-crossed. In a close echo of the church basement scene in *Cotton Comes to Harlem*, those gunmen, led by the especially vicious white "cracker," bind and torture Casper in order to force him to disclose the location of the missing $50,000. Once again, however, Coffin Ed and Grave Digger arrive on the scene just in time to both witness and disrupt this cruelty. Having pieced together Leila's own criminal conspiracy and her cross-dressing activities, the pair abduct Casper's wife and demand that she help them to free her husband by serving as their decoy. By the pragmatic terms of Himes's plot, Leila's role is to use her considerable sexual allure in order to gain entry to the locked, darkened, and guarded office where Casper is being held; she is then to find some way to raise the blinds, so that Grave Digger who has positioned himself on a ledge outside the office window can see Casper's torturer clearly enough to shoot him. Symbolically, however, her role is far more resonant. For what Leila does is to usher the novel's readers into a gothic installation of Himes's anxieties. Entering the closed and darkened room, she witnesses the graphic feminization of her husband toward which the novel has pointed from its beginning:

Caspar lay on his back on the dark maroon rug; his legs were spread-eagled, with his ankles lashed to the legs of the desk with halves of an extension cord. He was stripped to his underwear. . . . He was gagged with his own black silk scarf, tightly twisted and passing through his mouth to a knot behind his head. Blood trickled from his eyelids, seeped steadily from his huge, flaring nostrils, ran from the corners of his mouth and flowed down his cheeks. . . .

The white man knelt beside him with a bloodstained knife pressed tightly against his throat. He had used the knife to slit Caspar's eyelids and jab inside his nostrils and slash his tongue, and he had threatened to use it next to relieve him of his manhood. (153)

As the resemblance of this ugly moment to the analogous scene in *Cotton Comes to Harlem* suggests, this passage echoes a recurrent feature of Himes's crime novels. More tellingly still, it follows closely on a central convention of the hard-boiled tradition from which those novels descend. Like the abandoned house in *The Snarl of the Beast* or the neglected oil field in *The Big Sleep*, Caspar's office is the claustral enclosure in which the protagonists encounter a necessary tableau of degradation. Having come nearly to the end of their effort to uncover the hidden truth, Coffin Ed and Grave Digger are confronted — much like Race Williams and Philip Marlowe — with an image of "abject terror" that exemplifies the dangers that most threaten to undermine their authority (153). As in Daly and Chandler, moreover, those dangers are inseparable from the threat of feminine submission. This, of course, is what we see in Casper's supine body — whose looming emasculation points back not only to the dangers raised by Mammy Louise, but to the complaint Himes first made against the black bourgeoisie in *If He Hollers*. To turn inward on your community, Himes implies here as in that novel, is not merely to consent to a lamentable feminization but to lay yourself out before the exploitation of white predators. But beyond Casper's image alone, the scene as a whole resounds with erotic tension. Entering the room, Leila becomes "a sex pot," drenched in "aphrodisiacal perfume," her "body sway[ing] as though her pelvic girdle was equipped with roller bearings," her "breasts . . . rising and falling like bellows" (152, 154, 156). And once again that image is more significant for its symbolic resonance than for the role it plays in Himes's plot. Leila's ostensible purpose is to divide the black thugs from the white cracker holding Casper by "playing her sex along with her race"—tellingly equivalent tactics for Himes. But her more important role is to make the entire scene "swel[l] with lust," so that Casper's dark and closed office becomes a gothic image of the dangerously primal forces of fear and desire (154, 152). Just to hammer home the point, Himes adds one further element as the scene approaches its climax: "Down below in the Paris Bar someone had put a coin in the juke box, and the slow hypnotic beat of . . . *Bottom Blues* came faintly through the floor" (155).[61]

What we see in the pivotal moments of *All Shot Up*, in sum, is a near inversion of the conclusion to "The Song Says 'Keep on Smiling.'" If Jean becomes the heroine of that story for the way she chooses law over desire, ethical commitment over both erotic temptation and racial community, the scene in Casper's office dramatizes the consequences of making the opposite choice. And as the proximity of the Paris Bar, the center of the novel's gay "clique," reminds us yet again, those consequences are a combination of effeminacy and insularity. Thus, it is fitting that the scene ends when Leila finally manages to raise the blinds and Cotton Ed and Grave Digger, guns blazing, burst into the room. Displacing the threat of feminine submission with the authority of masculine violence, they simultaneously rupture, if only briefly, the private spaces of Harlem politics and open them fleetingly to public light.

MY OWN PRIVATE FEELING, MY OWN PRIVATE ACTION

As if that climactic scene were not enough to make his point, Himes closed *All Shot Up* with a denouement that made the novel's underlying issues still clearer. Discovering that Casper does not possess the missing $50,000, Coffin Ed and Grave Digger finally piece together the novel's complicated plot and realize that Casper must have passed the money to his lover, Snake Hips, in the midst of the shoot-out that begins the novel's action—just before Snake Hips himself was killed by a stray bullet. In the book's final scene, therefore, the two detectives arrive at the undertaker's office where the body is being held and discover the cash concealed in a box of stock-ings found on the corpse. For a moment, Himes teases the reader with the prospect that the detectives will keep the money for themselves, but the novel's final paragraphs offer a more fitting conclusion: "Two days later, the New York Herald Tribune Fresh Air Fund, which sends New York City boys of all races and creeds on vacations in the country during the summer, received an anonymous cash donation of $50,000" (170). The message is clear. If Casper embodies the parasitism of a black political elite — one that feminizes and isolates its community by taking its political currency out of circulation — Himes's protagonists reverse the process. They place that currency back in circulation for civic purposes that echo, though faintly, Himes's earlier antiracial populism. The money will now serve "all races and creeds," but, perhaps not coincidentally, boys alone. It is a conclusion that makes the novel's entwined difficulties — of racial separation and feminine sexuality — disappear.

As Himes continued his Harlem domestic series, that kind of resolution came to seem ever less plausible. In the best tradition of the hard-boiled crime story, Himes's detective novels had always emphasized the tenuousness of their conclusions. Neither his detectives nor the Harlem community they seek to defend and represent ever get a fair hearing from the white officials who rule Himes's city. The enormous problems of racism, crime, and poverty raised by the novels inevitably overshadow the paltry resolutions — like endorsing the Clean Air Fund — that Coffin Ed and Grave Digger manage to patch together. And, most importantly, the extreme violence wielded by Himes's detectives always points to their shaky legitimacy; the law they seek to impose, by force if necessary, always seems disappointingly more like an empty form than a principle of justice. As Himes carried his series forward into the sixties, however, each of those problems became more serious. After *All Shot Up*, Himes made the law ever less accountable to Harlem's black residents and ever more a tyrannous imposition. The sources of crime suggested by his novels became ever more complex and intractable, their roots stretching increasingly beyond Harlem into a purposefully obscured world of white power and exploitation. And, most dramatically, the violence of the novels grew increasingly extreme and increasingly immune to the kinds of order Coffin Ed and Grave Digger sought to impose. The trend came to a conclusion in the last novel in Himes's series. Inspired by the wave of riots that broke out in American cities during the mid- and later 1960s, the aptly named *Blind Man with a Pistol* (1969) redoubled the carnivalesque violence of Himes's earlier novels and turned his imaginary Harlem into a battleground between parodic images of the Black Power movement, the liberal civil rights establishment, and the revivalist church — all of them shadowed in turn by the mysterious power of "the Syndicate." The result was an extraordinary image of Harlem as "Walpurgisnacht" and a final repudiation to the law that Coffin Ed and Grave Digger once defended (28). That effort now seemed pointless.[62]

But it was in an unfinished text begun during the same period, a still more absurdly violent and brutally satiric novel, that Himes made most evident the transition that his fiction underwent during the late sixties. In *Plan B*, Himes places Coffin Ed and Grave Digger in the midst of an apocalyptic race war whose black instigators are led by a figure apparently patterned on Himes himself.[63] Beginning from the premise that "the white man's legal apparatus" is merely an obscured form of racial oppression, that nonracial allegiances are impossible, and that the only solution to injustice is violent revolution, the novel thus reverses nearly every one of the tenets that ran throughout most of Himes's career (203). Fittingly, the unfinished text trails off with the death of Himes's detective protagonists. Throwing his lot in with the black revolution, Grave Digger decides that he must murder Coffin Ed to protect the cause. At the moment he does so, however, Himes's revolutionary leader puts a bullet in the back of Grave Digger's head — as if Himes himself had stepped into his fiction to kill off the protagonists who had served him well over the previous decade.

With the death of his detective heroes, Himes's unfinished novel ends as well, perhaps because without them the underlying tension that had been central to the Harlem domestic series inevitably evaporated. From the first of his crime novels, Himes's protagonists had stood for a proposition well within the traditions of the detective novel: that however inadequate it was, however tainted by racism and injustice, a "legal apparatus" was necessary for justice as well as order. Without a commitment to the idea of a transcendent law,

Himes argued from his first writings, there could be no hope for a decent world and no prospect for a nonracial public realm — only the tribalism exemplified by figures like Mammy Louise. In different ways, each of the Harlem domestic novels had explored the tension between those unlikely principles and a world that made them seem ever less tenable. With the deaths of Coffin Ed and Grave Digger, though, Himes finally conceded to Mammy Louise's argument and suggested that Coffin Ed and Grave Digger's dedication to the law and the partnership that exemplified it were both empty.[64]

It is a denouement that *Plan B* predicts from the detectives' first appearance in the novel, where Grave Digger begins immediately to feel sympathetic to the aims of the novel's revolutionaries. Enraged by the death of a prostitute, who was herself sympathetic to the idea of a violent racial uprising, Grave Digger beats the woman's murderer to death. When Coffin Ed reproaches him, and asks, "We're a team, ain't we?" Grave Digger demurs. Tacitly embracing the very maternal culture that Himes's earlier novels had rejected, Grave Digger explains, "I did it because that woman looked something like my ma." It is an explanation, he makes clear, that not only rejects "the white man's legal apparatus" but that overthrows the long-standing commitment to a nonracial civic realm that Himes had always associated with the brotherhood of men. "This was my own private feeling," Grave Digger warns Coffin Ed, "my own private action" (20). Himes had begun his career with the conviction that "hurt" by its very nature must be made public — that so treated it could form the basis of a political community at radical odds with a society built on commerce and divided by race. Only in the late sixties did he finally abandon that faith completely. In its wake, all he could envision was the spreading absurdity of American violence.

CONCLUSION

Beyond Us, Yet Ourselves

And they said then, "But play you must
A tune beyond us, yet ourselves . . ."
— Wallace Stevens,
"The Man with the Blue Guitar," 1937[1]

The innovations that the major hard-boiled crime novelists brought
to the detective story depended on a central intuition: that the discourse of literature and that of law were analogous and that, in the
middle third of the century, each had come to an especially problematic stage in its history. What made those discourses seem alike was
a shared, fundamental paradox rooted in their common status as
simultaneously specialized and public languages. By the terms of
America's dominant traditions, both law and literature were supposed to be democratic and public — an expression of popular will or
national culture. But both were also expected to transcend mere
prejudice, custom, or interest — to defend principles or truths that
were not simply an expression of majority will. In Wallace Stevens's
formulation, the ideology of liberal democracy assumed that art and
law alike were beyond us, yet ourselves.

By the New Deal era, that paradoxical assumption had come to
seem, as Stevens implied — and as artists and intellectuals through-

out the culture recognized — a comforting but increasingly untenable myth.[2] The professionalization of legal and literary practice that had proceeded rapidly over the first third of the century made the public and democratic features of both seem less plausible. Law and literature belonged increasingly to specialists and functionaries. And while that development raised the possibility that each might be modernized and made more innovative, or efficient, or progressive, it also came to exemplify the basic problems of the liberal democracy shaped by industrial capitalism: that it was far from democratic, yet nevertheless lacked the political structures necessary to govern a complex society. American intellectuals in the decades leading up to midcentury faced a nation that was harshly divided between rich and poor, the powerful and weak, and that at the same time did not appear to have the leadership or the state capacity to render its capitalist economy more secure, let alone more just.

The various strains of reform and innovation that jockeyed for power during the New Deal were attempts to address those problems. What I have tried to show is that they were the implicit subject of hard-boiled crime fiction as well. The conflicted ambitions and uncertain professional standing of the genre's major writers made them intensely aware of the problems built into their work, and that awareness made them sensitive as well to the political tensions in their society. Like their contemporaries among legal scholars, political theorists, and politicians, the major hard-boiled writers recognized the untenable paradoxes of liberal democracy and tried to imagine solutions to those dilemmas. Like their contemporaries as well, they tended to envision resolutions that leaned to one extreme or another. For Chester Himes, the fact that both law and literature could seem to soar above ordinary prejudice promised an alternative to American racism; his detective fiction constituted an extended complaint against their failure to live up to that role. For Raymond Chandler, by contrast, the fact that legal and literary discourse tended to grow specialized and cut off from the community they were supposed to represent made each seem illegitimate; his stories consequently bemoaned the dangers of abstraction and the fragmentation of popular fellowship. Their peers raised analogous complaints. Like Chester

Himes, Dashiell Hammett praised literature for its ability to escape and clarify popular confusion — and then noted that it seemed doomed to fail in the mission. By Jim Thompson's account, the comic ugliness of the postwar world stemmed from the fact that neither literature nor the state served any longer as a civic alternative to social division and corrosive private interest.

The fact that they envisioned strong solutions to these problems made the authors of hard-boiled crime fiction both provocative and troubling writers. What now seem the most disturbing and unattractive qualities of their work are the results of that effort. The standard misogyny of the genre, its frequent racism, its penchant for violence and cruelty — these were never incidental aspects of the fiction. Rather, as I have tried to suggest, they were core features of the attempts made by the genre's writers to imagine answers to the problems of American literature and American liberalism. The fact that hard-boiled writers tended to extremes, that they were unsatisfied with the pat answers of their predecessors, is also, though, what makes their work significant. The golden age of the hard-boiled crime story coincided with a period of dramatic revision in the structures and ideologies of American government. In their stories of failed ambition and unintended consequences, the genre's major writers made their fiction a complex meditation on the rewards and dissatisfactions of literature and on the hopes and disappointments of New Deal liberalism.

NOTES

UNCIVIL SOCIETY

1   Barzun, *Of Human Freedom*, 21; Chandler, *Selected Letters of Raymond Chandler*, 159.
2   Cain, *Serenade* in *Three By Cain*, 130.
3   Cain quoted at Hoopes, *Cain: A Biography*, 382.
4   *Selected Letters of Raymond Chandler*, 181, 68; Hammett, "Tulip," *The Big Knockover*, 341; Thompson to Marc Jaffe (August 1, 1958), NAL papers, Fales Library, New York University, series 2, box 71, file 1787.
5   Cf. Poggioli, *The Theory of the Avant-Garde*, 65–66.
6   Roosevelt, *Public Papers and Addresses*, 6: 1–6.
7   See Sellers, *The Market Revolution*, 364–95. Sellers describes the expansion of commercial relations as a "bourgeois/middle-class offensive" (391); for a more celebratory account of the growth of capitalism and individualism in this era, see Howe, *Making the American Self*, 8–17, 108–35. For a provocative argument tying the genesis of the detective story to Poe's effort to reconceive the relation of the intellectual to the rapidly expanding capitalist market of Jacksonian America, see Whalen's "Edgar Allan Poe and the Horrid Laws of Political Economy."
8   Karen Haltunnen's superb recent book *Murder Most Foul* convincingly traces the emergence of the mystery story to the displacement of providential ideas of justice and social order by liberal and secular ones. Literary critics have been slower to grasp this relation. That detective fiction is closely bound up with the history of liberal democracy is a point made in passing or vaguely by a number of readers. See, e.g., Porter, *The Pursuit of Crime*, 121, 120–26; Alewyn, "The Origin of the Detective Novel," 67; Knight, *Form and Ideology in Crime Fiction*, 20–35; Miller, *The Novel and the Police*, 33–57; Moretti,

"Clues," *Signs Taken for Wonders*. Because the most thoughtful criticism of the detective story has been informed mainly by poststructuralist and Marxist theory, though, it tends to dismiss liberal principles like the rule of law and individual freedom as little more than masks for coercion and the detective story itself as an instrument of repressive ideology. Despite the fact that it is often insightful about the narratological features of detective fiction, then, the most serious criticism of the genre is indifferent or hostile to its most fundamental concerns and suggests that such matters are insignificant or illusory. D. A. Miller's argument is exemplary in this respect. Beginning from the truism that liberal societies depend on the internalization of norms, *The Novel and the Police* takes the Foucauldian position that all norms per se, even those which seem to be freely chosen, are impositions and must reflect the implicit coercion of discipline and surveillance. From that ultimately libertarian perspective (i.e., one that presumes that the only valid influences on the self are those that are thoroughly self-created), the detective story merely exemplifies the symmetry between "the detective's brilliant *super-vision*" and the omnipresent disciplinary "*supervision*" necessary to the coercive formation of the "liberal subject"—the way we all live in fear of being found out and the pleasure we may take in seeing ourselves and others brought under control. My assumption in this book will be that detective fiction actually articulates a more complex and plausible view of the problems of law: that, on the one hand, rather than coercive forces *tout court*, laws and norms are the basis of ethical claims and the grounds for any vision of social justice; and, on the other hand, that laws are nevertheless often rigidly bureaucratic and the means of abuse or exploitation. In my view, that is the core problem of the detective story—not simply the project of discipline and surveillance, but, as Thomas Roberts nicely puts it, "the conflict between the *lawful* and the *good*." *An Aesthetics of Junk Fiction*, 140.

9   Wolin, *Politics and Vision*, 324.

10   By using the term "classical liberal" I mean to refer the canonical distinction drawn between the liberal political philosophers of the eighteenth and early nineteenth centuries—who emphasized the importance of individual liberty and limitations on state power—and the liberal thinkers of the late nineteenth and twentieth centuries who have stressed not just individual liberty and political equality, but government's role in securing what T. H. Marshall called "social rights." See, e.g., Merquior, *Liberalism: Old and New*, 37–67. For an argument that the differences among these two kinds of liberalism are often overstated, see Holmes, *Passions and Constraint*, 236–66.

11   Hirschman, *The Passions and the Interests*; Manent, *An Intellectual History of Liberalism*, 65–66.

12   Joseph de Maistre, quoted in Holmes, *The Anatomy of Antiliberalism*, 25; Wilson, *Classics and Commercials*, 236–37.

13   Poe, *The Complete Tales and Poems*, 142, 167, 165, 161. Given that Poe was writing in 1840s Baltimore, it seems more than likely that the orangutan, which slaughters Madame L'Espanaye and her daughter in their bedroom, alludes to contemporary anxieties among Southern whites about slave revolts. If so, the origin of the detective story would lie revealingly in Poe's articulation of the tension basic to a society that claims to be guided by the principles of liberal democracy while in fact maintaining the virtually feudal order of a slave society. Cf. Sellers's account of slavery as "the great contradiction" that developed within "the liberal American republic" created by the expansion of capitalism. *The Market Revolution*, 396.

14   Gellner, *The Psychoanalytic Movement: The Cunning of Unreason*, 104–5; Gellner, *Reason and Culture: The Historic Role of Rationality and Rationalism*, 30–38; hence the coincidence, historically and thematically, between the detective story and both psychoanalysis and the social sciences, each of which, as Gellner explains, follow similar logics. Beginning from the skepticism inspired by liberalism — and by its epistemological corollary, empiricism — psychoanalysis and ethnography posit a chaotic world in which social cohesion is absent, reason is unreliable, and cognitive associations produce not structure, but confusion. Like the detective story, they then discover order out of this confusion. Thompson, quoted by Polito, *Savage Art*, 7.

15   Doyle, *Sherlock Holmes Detective Stories*, Book II, 38.

16   Ibid., Book I, 181.

17   Poe takes care to emphasize that Dupin is an aristocrat déclassé who has made his peace with post-Revolutionary democratic society. He is "of an excellent family, but, by a variety of untoward events, had been reduced to such poverty that the energy of his character succumbed beneath it" (143.) As with Watson and Holmes, his friendship with the narrator becomes an emblem of free association that both raises and then dismisses the threat of social disarray. "Our seclusion was perfect," the narrator reports. "Had the routine of our life . . . been known to the world, we should have been regarded as madmen — although, perhaps, as madmen of a harmless nature" (144). Though the two seem to "exist within ourselves alone," they become figures of civil society through their social usefulness. In both these respects, they form a myth of the liberal intellectual, who is presumed to be both individually free and ultimately beneficial to society. Indeed, as a repre-

sentation of the aristocratic thinker who reluctantly admires and contributes to the democratic order, Dupin might well be compared to his contemporary Tocqueville.

18   Porter, *The Pursuit of Crime*, 125, 25.
19   Ibid., 126.
20   Gellner, *Conditions of Liberty: Civil Society and Its Rivals*, 94.
21   See, e.g., Kloppenberg, *Uncertain Victory: Social Democracy and Progressivism in European and American Thought, 1870–1920*.
22   Roosevelt, *Public Papers and Addresses*, 6: 3; 1: 753, 755.
23   Hartz, *The Liberal Tradition in America*. Hartz's account of the Lockean nature of American liberalism has been challenged many times over, of course — especially by the school of civic republicanism led by J. G. A. Pocock and Gordon Wood. It has also received some qualified reassertions in recent years. See, e.g., Diggins, *The Lost Soul of American Politics*, and Kramnick, "Republican Revisionism Revisited." In any case, critics of liberalism in the interwar decades certainly assumed a perspective very much like Hartz's.
24   Robinson, *Law and the Lawyers*, 322.
25   Cain, *Our Government*, vii, viii; Hammett, "The Boundaries of Science and Philosophy," unpublished manuscript, Hammett collection, Harry Ransom Humanities Research Center, University of Texas.
26   Alewyn, "The Origin of the Detective Novel," 67.
27   Chandler, *The Big Sleep*, 103.
28   Cain, quoted by Hoopes, *Cain: A Biography*, 546.
29   Ibid., 385, 37.
30   Cain, *Serenade*, in *Three By Cain*, 50, 57.
31   Cain, preface to *The Butterfly*, in *Three By Cain*, 353.
32   Cain, quoted by Hoopes, *Cain*, 405, 316, 161, 241, 301; see also, Fine, *James M. Cain and the American Authors' Authority*, 31–45.
33   Ibid., 262, 234, 546.
34   Cain, *Three By Cain*, 77, 78, 79.
35   See, e.g., Greenfeld, *Nationalism: Five Roads to Modernity*, 293–302, 344–52, 460–72; Kedourie, *Nationalism*, 35–43; for a sympathetic version of this argument in relation to a particularly American context that might have influenced Cain, see, Blake, *Beloved Community*, 1–9.
36   Cain, quoted by Hoopes, *Cain*, 549.
37   Ibid., 180.
38   Apart from this moralism, Cain's analysis anticipates the classic sociological accounts of the making of the modern art world. See, e.g., Bourdieu, *The Field of Cultural Production*; Bürger, *Theory of the Avant-Garde*; Graña, *Bohemia Versus Bourgeois*; Huyssen, *After the Great Divide: Modernism, Mass Culture, Postmodernism*; the conflict between institutional authority and popular legitimacy central to

these analyses was crucial to Cain's work from his first writing. His early essay "The Labor Leader" portrayed the corruption that undermines union men when they become bureaucratic officials rather than working-class tribunes, emphasizing the irony of their alienation from the constituency out of which they emerged.

39 Roosevelt, *Public Papers and Addresses*, 1: 754, 749, 743, 751; see also, Kesler, "The Public Philosophy of the New Freedom and the New Deal."

40 Roosevelt, *Public Papers and Addresses*, 1: 743.

41 Ibid., 6: 3; Brinkley, *The End of Reform: New Deal Liberalism in Recession and War*, 3.

42 Roosevelt, *Public Papers and Addresses*, 1: 752; FDR, quoted by Brinkley, *The End of Reform*, 10. On the diverse policies of the Roosevelt administration from 1933 to 1938 and their common preoccupation with reforming the structure of industrial capitalism, see especially, Hawley, *The New Deal and the Problem of Monopoly*, and Brinkley, *The End of Reform*, 3–37; my description here follows Brinkley's argument closely.

43 Adelstein, " 'The Nation as an Economic Unit': Keynes, Roosevelt, and the Managerial Ideal"; Brinkley, *The End of Reform*, 265–71; Jeffries, "The 'New' New Deal: FDR and American Liberalism"; Katznelson, "Was the Great Society a Lost Opportunity"; McCraw, "The New Deal and the Mixed Economy."

44 Landis, *The Administrative Process*, 5.

45 Ibid., 23; Roosevelt, *The Public Papers and Addresses*, 1: 646, 642; Merriam, *Political Power: Its Composition and Incidence*, 326.

46 Grierson, *Grierson on Documentary*, 123, 124, 150, 127, 149, 166, 126; Lilienthal quoted in Leuchtenburg, *Franklin D. Roosevelt and the New Deal, 1932–1940*, 86.

47 Dewey, *The Public and Its Problems*, in *The Later Works*, 2: 277; emphasis added.

48 Finegold and Skocpol, *State and Party in America's New Deal*, 20, quoting Otis L. Graham Jr.

49 Lowi, *The End of Liberalism: Ideology, Policy, and the Crisis of Public Authority*, 86.

1. CONSTRUCTING RACE WILLIAMS

The Klan and the Making of Hard-Boiled Crime Fiction

1 Frost, *The Challenge of the Klan*, 110; Hammett, *Red Harvest*, 209.

2 Letters to the editor, *Black Mask* (henceforth cited as *BM*), September 1924, 128, *BM*, January 15, 1924, 127; "Behind this Cover," *BM*,

October 1929, vi; Nebel, "Graft," 25; Daly, "Tainted Power," 5; Shaw, introduction to "The Cleansing of Poisonville," 9; Shaw, "Greed, Crime, and Politics," 9.

3   See, e.g., Porter, *The Pursuit of Crime*, 161–85; Ruehlmann, *Saint with a Gun*; and, esp., Slotkin, *Gunfighter Nation*, 228.

4   Hammett, "Women, Politics, and Murder."

5   See, e.g., Kazin, *The Populist Persuasion*, chaps. 1 and 2 and pp. 101–6.

6   *BM*, June 1, 1923, 32; *BM*, August 15, 1923, 117; during 1923, the magazine's editors were George W. Sutton Jr. and his associate, H. C. North, along with "circulation director" P. C. Cody; in the following year, Sutton would be replaced by Cody, who pushed the magazine toward tales of macho adventure; in 1926, Joseph T. Shaw, the most renowned of the magazine's editors and the champion of hard-boiled crime fiction especially—and Hammett in particular—would take Cody's place.

7   *BM*, August 15, 1923, 128; *BM*, June 1, 1923, 32; *BM*, December 1, 1923, 128.

8   Frost, *The Challenge of the Klan*, 1; Evans, "The Klan's Fight for Americanism," 92; the authoritative accounts of the Klan, especially its incarnation in the twenties, are Chalmers, *Hooded Americanism: The History of the Ku Klux Klan*; Wade, *The Fiery Cross: The Ku Klux Klan in America*; Jackson, *The Klan in the City, 1915–1930*; see also, Blee, *Women of the Klan: Racism and Gender in the 1920s*; Lay, ed., *The Invisible Empire in the West: Towards a New Historical Appraisal of the Ku Klux Klan of the 1920s*; MacLean, *Behind the Mask of Chivalry: The Making of the Second Ku Klux Klan*; Moore, *Citizen Klansmen: The Ku Klux Klan in Indiana, 1921–1928*.

9   Evans, "The Klans's Fight for Americanism," 100; *BM*, July 1, 1923, 47–48, 51; *BM*, April 1927, 128; see Goulart, *The Dime Detectives*, 24–36; Nolan, introduction, *The Black Mask Boys*, 20–24.

10 Hammett's "The Crusader" appeared in the August 1923 edition of *The Smart Set*, where it mocked Klan fantasy and regalia; *The Maltese Falcon* began life as a manuscript titled "The Secret Emperor," which in turn grew out of the story "The Vicious Circle," published in *Black Mask* one issue after its special Klan number. The story of a man named Gutman who is driven to amass influence because, "being a Jew, he may not be President," "The Secret Emperor" steals the Klan's language of Invisible Empire and its paranoia about aliens and concentrated power for what would eventually become a novel that cut against Klan presuppositions. See Johnson, *Dashiell Hammett: A Life*, 56–57; Layman, *Shadow Man: The Life of Dashiell Hammett*, 31, 81.

11 Coben, *Rebellion Against Victorianism*, 136–41; see also Higham,

Strangers in the Land: Patterns of American Nativism, 1860–1925, 264–99; Karl, *The Uneasy State: The United States from 1915 to 1945,* 62–65.

12   H. K. S., *BM,* November 15, 1923, 127; Troy, Ohio, *BM,* November 1, 1923, 127; "What the Klan Really Is," *BM,* September 1, 1923, 123; Christopher N. Cocoltchos, 'The Invisible Empire and the Search for the Orderly Community: The Ku Klux Klan in Anaheim, California," *The Invisible Empire in the West,* ed. Lay, 97–120, emphasis added; "Another Real Live Klansman," *BM,* December 1, 1923, 128; "Pan-American," *BM,* December 1, 1923, 127; on Klan membership, see esp., MacLean, *Behind the Mask of Chivalry,* 52–74; Moore, *Citizen Klansman,* 44–75.

13   J.S., "Department of Investigation," *BM,* February 1925, 127. On the Klan's protocommunitarianism, see Blee, *Women of the Klan,* 157–73; Moore, *Citizen Klansman,* 76–106; on Klan costume and ritual, see Fry, *The Modern Ku Klux Klan,* 82–93; MacLean, *Behind the Mask of Chivalry,* 19–21; see also Carnes, *Secret Ritual and Manhood in Victorian America,* 17–36; on Klan vigilantism, see MacLean, 149–73.

14   Ohmann, *Selling Culture: Magazines, Markets, and Class at the Turn of the Century;* Dumenil, *The Modern Temper: American Culture and Society in the 1920s,* 89; Cohn, *Creating America: George Horace Lorimer and the "Saturday Evening Post";* Peterson, *Magazines in the Twentieth Century;* Marchand, *Advertising the American Dream: Making Way for Modernity, 1920–1940;* Schneirov, *The Dream of a New Social Order: Popular Magazines in America, 1893–1914;* Wilson, "The Rhetoric of Consumption: Mass-Market Magazines and the Demise of the Gentle Reader, 1880–1920." The phrase "consumption mobility" is Lawrence Levine's description of the message of the interwar era's developing consumer culture, *The Unpredictable Past: Explorations in American Cultural History,* 223.

15   Hersey, *Pulpwood Editor: The Fabulous World of the Thriller Magazines Revealed By a Veteran Editor and Publisher,* 35. For a more extensive discussion of the economics of pulp publishing and their effects, see McCann, " 'A Roughneck Reaching for Higher Things': The Vagaries of Pulp Populism"; also, Smith, *Reading Pulp Fiction: Hard-Boiled Writing Culture and Working-Class Life;* Mullen, "From Standard Magazines to Pulps and Big Slicks: A Note on the History of U.S. General and Fiction Magazines"; Peterson, *Magazines in the Twentieth-Century,* 293–317; Tebbell, *A History of Book Publishing in the United States,* 1: 240–251, 2: 481–511; Gruber, *The Pulp Jungle.* The pulps did carry some minor advertising, but this was mainly for low-end products (hernia belts and depilatories) and for correspon-

dence school courses targeted to working-class men. According to Hersey, these advertisements played a negligible role in the magazines' budgets.

16   Pratt, "The Million-Word-a-Year Man," *American Mercury*, February 1939, 161; Hersey, *Pulpwood Editor*, 2–3, 8, 9. A rare survey conducted by the pulp distributor Popular Publications found that "their typical reader was a young, married man in a manual job who had limited resources and lived in an industrial town"; quoted in Bold, *Selling the Wild West: Popular Western Fiction, 1860–1960*, 7–8, 34. Inconclusive evidence of the magazines' working-class readership can also be seen in Waples, *Research Memorandum on Social Aspects of Reading in the Depression*, 143, 150–54, 210. There also were pulp magazines targeted to women readers — especially the true confession magazines — but the market tended to be sharply divided by gender, with *Black Mask* usually addressing an implicitly (and heavily) masculine audience.

17   Shaw, "Help Yourself," 7; Chandler, *Selected Letters*, 7, 11, 45, 461; see also, Gruber, *The Pulp Jungle*; Hersey, *Pulpwood Editor*; n.a., "A Penny a Word," *American Mercury*, March 1936, 285–92; Gardner, "Getting Away with Murder" and "Speed Dash." Erin Smith's *Reading Pulp Fiction* offers a different perspective on these issues, stressing the way the pulps negotiated, rather than repudiated, consumer culture for a working-class audience.

18   There were very large pulp publishing firms like Street and Smith, which published dozens of magazines, but these were more fiction factories than large editorial operations. They tended to diversify their products horizontally, spinning off many small magazines, rather than building up large magazines like those common in the world of the slicks.

19   Gruber, *The Pulp Jungle*, 89; Shaw, editorial, *BM*, September 1928, iv; Shaw, introduction, *The Hard-Boiled Omnibus*, ix; Hersey, *Pulpwood Editor*, 94; *BM*, November 1, 1923, 70; *BM*, March 1927, iv; *BM*, July 1, 1924, 4; *BM*, July 1, 1923, 49; *BM*, February 1927, 97; *BM*, February 1, 1924, 127.

20   Hersey, *Pulpwood Editor*, 26, 11, 136, 87; *BM*, December 1933, 7.

21   Hersey, *Pulpwood Editor*, 105. In reality, the pulps tended to have even smaller audiences than this advertisement suggested. At its peak in the early thirties, *Black Mask*, among the most successful magazines in the industry, sold only 103,000 copies per issue; by 1935, circulation had dropped to 63,000. Nolan, "History of a Pulp: The Life and Times of *Black Mask*," in *The Black Mask Boys*, 29; Publisher's Statement of Circulation, *Black Mask*, June 1935, 105.

22   Peterson, "Call Out the Klan," 7, 31.

23 *BM*, December 1, 1923, 128; *BM*, August 15, 1923, 121, 122; "What the Klan Really Is," 122; *BM*, November 15, 1923, 128.

24 "A Nurse and Kentuckian," *BM*, November 1, 1923, 128; "An American," *BM*, November 15, 1923, 127; "Dallas," 128; "Gary, Indiana," *BM*, August 15, 1923, 119; "Pan-American," *BM*, December 1, 1923, 127; "Another Real Live Klansman," *BM*, December 1, 1923, 128.

25 Klan pamphlet quoted at MacLean, *Behind the Mask of Chivalry*, 132; Evans, "The Klan's Fight for Americanism," 92, 96, 100, 107; "What the Klan Really Is," 123; Christopher Sandstone, "The Knights of the Ku Klux Klan," *BM*, June 1, 1923, 67.

26 Stoddard, *Re-Forging America*, 309; Evans, "The Klan's Fight for Americanism," 96; *BM*, December 1, 1923, 126–27.

27 Johnson, *Dashiell Hammett: A Life*, xviii; Daly, "Three Thousand to the Good," 33; J.S., "Department of Investigation," *BM*, February 1925, 125–28; *BM*, September 1928, iv; Shaw, "Greed, Crime, and Politics," 9; *BM*, November 1927, 9; Shaw, "Stop Thief!" 85; Shaw, "Dillinger et al.," 5; Shaw, "Crime and the Law," 7; Shaw, "Do You Ever Find Fault With the Police?" 7; *BM*, January 1935, 7; *BM*, June 1935, 7; Shaw, "What's In a Name?" 97; *BM*, November 1924, 128.

28 Daly, "Knights of the Open Palm," 46; Stoddard, *Re-Forging America*, 302; Daly's story was not his first in *Black Mask*, nor his first to feature a protagonist with the characteristics exemplified by Race Williams, but it was the one where Daly created the protagonist he would use for dozens of stories over the subsequent decade and who is generally recognized as the first successful private-detective narrator. Race Williams's debut in *Black Mask*'s special Klan issue also marked a turning point in Daly's fortunes in the magazine. The editor at the time, George Sutton, did not much care for Daly's stories, but he found it impossible to argue with the way they boosted sales figures after Race Williams began appearing in the magazine. Goulart, *The Dime Detectives*, 29.

29 Daly, "Knights of the Open Palm," 46, 36, 44, 38.

30 Ibid., 39, 37, 43.

31 Ibid., 35, 33; *BM*, August 15, 1923, 118.

32 Daly, "Knights of the Open Palm," 37.

33 Ibid., 46, 34.

34 Evans, "The Klan's Fight for Americanism," 96, 95, 103.

35 *BM*, August 15, 1923, 118, 120, 121; "Another Real Live Klansman," 128. In effect, Daly arranges to have things both ways. He allows Mick Clancy to denounce the Klan by saying it "ain't no order for an Irishman," but he gives Race Williams no particularly ethnicized sentiments.

36 In this respect, Daly's vision of race resembles that of his contemporary D. H. Lawrence, who, as Walter Benn Michaels points out, uses "the

technologies of racial identity" to imagine a primitivism that "cross[es] racial lines." In Lawrence, the result is an antinativist and "universalist" racialism. *Our America: Nativism, Modernism, and Pluralism*, 103–9.

37   Daly, "Three Thousand to the Good," 31–42; "I'll Tell the World," 28; emphases added.

38   *BM*, June 1927, iii; *BM*, October 1928, vi; *BM*, November 1926, 85; *BM*, October 15, 1923, 34; Peterson, "One Dried Head," 55–69.

39   See Daly, "South Sea Steel," 21; Hammett, "The Gutting of Couffignall," and "This King Business," *The Big Knockover*, 6, 115–70; Hammett, "Creeping Siamese," 39–47.

40   Ignatieff, "Jungle Shadows," 37; Rex Parson, "Where There Ain't No Ten Commandments," *Argosy-Allstory Weekly*, September 10, 1921, 741, 743; Feak, "The Reaper of Regret"; Harper, "A Melanesian Holiday," *BM*, December 1, 1923, 32; Fisher, "Fungus Isle"; compare the descriptions of an earlier type of imperial adventure in Kaplan, "Romancing the Empire: The Embodiment of American Masculinity in the Popular Historical Novel of the 1890s," and Slotkin, *Gunfighter Nation*, 106–22; 194–221.

41   Ayotte, "White Tents," 71, 74, 77, 82; Evans, "The Klan's Fight for Americanism," 93, 98; the intellectual source of Evans's description of the Great War can be seen in Stoddard's *The Rising Tide of Color Against White World Supremacy*, 183.

42   *BM*, November 1, 1923, 70; on the "family" as "the indispensable model for the new [nativist and racialized] conception of American identity" prevalent in the social discourse of the twenties, see Michaels, 40–52 and passim.

43   Hammett, "Zigzags of Treachery," 89.

44   Chandler, *Farewell, My Lovely* 3; Hammett, *The Maltese Falcon*, 94; Michael O'Shaughnessy, an Irish-born immigrant, was San Francisco city engineer from 1912 through 1934 and a central figure in municipal government—especially in his role as manager of the Hetch Hetchy reservoir and pipeline project, a massive engineering feat that took two decades to complete and gave O'Shaughnessy great personal power over the city's politics and landscape. Among other things, he was responsible for creating the Stockton Street tunnel near which Brigid kills Miles Archer. In an earlier story, "Women, Politics, and Murder," Hammett implicitly associated him with graft and autocratic power.

45   Ignatieff, "Jungle Shadows," 37. That distinction is especially significant since it was during the early twenties that American courts began to broaden antimiscegenation laws that already outlawed marriages between whites and African Americans and "Mongolians" to prohibit marriages between whites and Filipinos and other members of "the

Malay race" as well. The pulp fiction of foreign adventure, with its central preoccupation with miscegenation and Oriental corruption, echoed those developments. The hard-boiled crime fiction of writers like Hammett, by contrast, made them seem foolish. Osumi, "Asians and California's Anti-Miscegenation Laws," 1–37.

46 *BM*, December 1, 1923, 128; *BM*, August 15, 1923, 125.

47 Hammett, "Creeping Siamese," *BM*, March 1926, 47. A similar point about the convenient use of vulnerable ethnic outsiders as scapegoats for domestic criminality is made in "Night Shots," where Hammett mocks a pair of old-stock Americans who suspect all Italians and Mexicans of various evils, believing that "nearly all crimes of violence were committed by foreigners." *BM*, February 1, 1924, 37.

48 Hammett, "Dead Yellow Women" [1925], *The Big Knockover*, 196–97, 190, 241, 242, 238. That Hammett's story was intended to both invoke and ridicule the melodramatic conventions of the period's exotic fiction can be seen by comparing it to *Black Mask*'s description of a contemporaneous tale. George C. Peterson's "Who Shot?," the magazine announced, would investigate "the mysterious purlieus of San Francisco"—i.e., Chinatown—and would feature "a beautiful princess who wears a royal title." In Hammett's fiction, "mysterious purlieus" turn out not to be mysterious, and royal titles are charades. *BM*, October 15, 1923, 34.

49 See, e.g., Weber, "From Limen to Border."

50 See also Sol Caspar of Cain's 1942 novel *Love's Lovely Counterfeit*, who has "a six-pointed star on his ring and a mazuza on the door casing; these, however, were caprices, or possibly affectations for business reasons. Actually, he had no Hebraic connections, for his real name was Salvatore Gasparro, and no doubt it was his origin that prompted him to name his hotel for Columbus, a popular hero with Italo-Americans." *Three By Cain*, 202.

51 Cain, *The Postman Always Rings Twice*, 85, 3, 12, 7.

52 See, for example, this renowned bit of dialogue:

> We didn't do anything. We just lay on the bed. She kept rumpling my hair, and looking up at the ceiling, like she was thinking.
> "You like blueberry pie?"
> "I don't know. Yeah. I guess so."
> "I'll make you some."

The point of the scene is not merely to indicate the characters' triviality, but to suggest that their only possible moment of happiness is in a condition of near wordless enchantment. Sex is primal and immediate; language merely leads to confusion and antagonism. The scene is thus set up to contrast with all the frantic and failed efforts at communication and coordination that the lovers will make through the remainder of the novel. Cain, *Postman*, 11.

53 See the discussion of Cain's novel in Klein, *Foreigners*, 113–14.

54 Cain, *Postman*, 91.

55 Ibid., 93.

56 Evidence toward that conclusion can be seen in those infrequent hard-boiled crime stories from the period that *do* put a heavy emphasis on racial conflict. Not coincidentally, in those stories, the protagonist typically finds it easier to reach reliable conclusions and, more importantly, to establish fraternal bonds with other men. See, e.g., Hammett, "The House in Turk Street," *The Continental Op*, 93–119.

57 "What the Klan Really Is," 124; Evans, "The Klan's Fight for Americanism," 103; Frost, *The Challenge of the Klan*, 110; Dixon, *The Leopard's Spots*, 281.

58 Klan newspaper, quoted in Moore, *Citizen Klansman*, 123.

59 Shaw, introduction to Hammett's "$106,000 Blood Money," 9; Hammett, *Red Harvest*, 154; Dick O'Neill, "Too Many Murders," *Saturday Review of Literature*, February 11, 1939, 9.

60 Carl Freedman and Christopher Kendrick point out that "by the standards of its genre, this mystery novel is both too successful and not successful enough." In a description that helps underline the novel's relation to Klan politics of the twenties, they also note that it provides "an antifascist allegory of fascism." "Forms of Labor in Dashiell Hammett's *Red Harvest*," 219, 218.

61 *Red Harvest*, 3, 10, 18, 45, 203; Evans, "The Klan's Fight for Americanism," 86, 87; Shaw, editor's introduction, *BM*, November 1927, 9.

62 *Red Harvest*, 203, 67, 157; Roberts, *An Aesthetics of Junk Fiction*, 142–45; see also Klein, *Easterns, Westerns, and Private Eyes: American Matters, 1870–1900*, 178–94.

63 *Red Harvest*, 13, 123; on Thaler's consistency with anti-Semitic—and effeminate—images of gangsters from the twenties, see Ruth, *Inventing the Public Enemy: The Gangster in American Culture, 1918–1934*, 13; "Another Real Live Klansman," *BM*, December 1, 1923, 128.

64 *Red Harvest*, 4, 51, 7, 6, 144, 49, 84, 31.

65 Stoddard, *Re-Forging America*, 235, 241, 237, 249; *Red Harvest*, 12, 115.

66 *Red Harvest*, 143, 162–64; "This King Business," *The Big Knockover*, 143.

67 Whitfield, *Green Ice*, 30; Daly, *The Hidden Hand*, 19.

68 Himes, *The Quality of Hurt*, 3. Himes claimed that he learned this attitude in prison. It's fitting that while he was imprisoned during the late twenties and early thirties, he had a subscription to *Black Mask*.

69 Cohen, "Transcendental Nonsense and the Functional Approach,"
    837.

2. "MYSTIC RIGMAROLE"
Dashiell Hammett and the Realist Critique of Liberalism

1 George Soule, "Hard-Boiled Radicalism," 262, 263, 265; Hammett,
   "Tulip," *The Big Knockover*, 347.
2 Hammett, *The Maltese Falcon*, 12–13.
3 Hammett, "From the Memoirs of a Private Detective," *Smart Set*,
   March, 1923, quoted in Johnson, *Dashiell Hammett: A Life*, 48; *The
   Maltese Falcon*, 7, 15.
4 On this therapeutic mission of the detective story, see esp. Halltunen,
   Murder Most Foul, 131–34; an interesting account of the key role
   of the classic detective's eccentricity can be found in Žižek, *Looking
   Awry*, 62.
5 *The Maltese Falcon*, 215.
6 See Orvell, *The Real Thing: Imitation and Authenticity in American
   Culture, 1880–1940*, 141–56.
7 Hellman, *An Unfinished Woman*, 39. On the transformation of publishing in the period, see Tebbel, *A History of Book Publishing in the
   United States*, 2: 185–480 and 3: 76–200; Boyer, *Purity in Print: The
   Vice Society Movement and Book Censorship in America*, 70–149; on
   the contemporary emergence of an American literary intelligentsia and
   the development of institutional and economic structures to support intellectual dissent, see esp. Coben, *Rebellion Against Victorianism*, 36–
   58, and Sklar, *The United States as a Developing Country: Studies in
   U.S. History in the Progressive Era and the 1920s*, 170–96. It was
   especially the development of that institutional structure that differen-
   tiated the literary professionalism of the interwar years from that of the
   Gilded Age and Progressive Era described by Borus, *Writing Realism:
   Howells, James, and Norris in the Mass Market*; Kaplan, *The Social
   Construction of American Realism*; and Wilson, *The Labor of Words:
   Literary Professionalism in the Progressive Era*. For late-nineteenth-
   and early-twentieth-century fiction writers, being professional tended
   to mean vending literary products to the middle-class readership catered to by the new mass-circulation magazines. Professionalism was
   thus mainly defined against the genteel hostility to the market associated with the nineteenth century's elite "general" magazines. For writers in the twenties, increasing segmentation of the literary world and
   new systems of patronage meant that tensions could exist between at
   least three styles of professionalism: the celebrity authorship that con-

tinued to be associated with the mass-circulation "big slicks" and with the new prominence of book clubs and bestseller lists; the anonymous craftsmanship fostered by the pulps; and the ideal of the specialist's expertise encouraged, in particular, by the return, via foundations and universities, of noncommercial patronage. The best account of the ideological transformations that accompanied this patronage version of literary professionalization can be found in Menand, *Discovering Modernism: T. S. Eliot and His Context*, 97–132; Hoffman, *The Twenties: American Writing in the Postwar Decade* also remains invaluable on these developments; and see Douglas, *Terrible Honesty: Mongrel Manhattan in the Twenties*. Because of the trajectories of their careers, all of the major hard-boiled writers were forced to contend with the disparities among these diverse ideas of literary professionalism. For an account of one writer's extensive efforts to come to grips with this problem, see Fine, *James M. Cain and the American Author's Authority*.

8   Johnson, *Dashiell Hammett: A Life*, xviii; Hammett to Blanche Knopf (3/20/28, Knopf files at the Harry Ransom Humanities Research Center at the University of Texas, Austin (henceforth cited as HRHRC), Box 691, folder 9; Hammett to Margaret Kober (2/24/51, 3/19/51); Hammett to Lillian Hellman (1/7/57), Hammett corres., HRHRC; Hammett, "Tulip," *The Big Knockover*, 328; a representative combination of such attitudes, and of Hammett's fondness for cultural rebels of the 1920s like Mencken and James Branch Cabell, can be seen, for example, in "Seven Pages," an unpublished story written in either the early or middle twenties, Hammett works, HRHRC. Another sign of the young Hammett's intellectual attitudes can be seen in the fact that during the twenties he kept a subscription to the Haldeman-Julius Little Blue Books, controversial pamphlets published by Emanuel Haldeman-Julius that discussed such progressive subjects as atheism, birth control, psychoanalysis, and socialism. Hammett later made a tongue-in-cheek reference to these pamphlets in *The Thin Man*, 44.

9   Hammett, undated letter to Phil Cody (from late 1925 or early 1926), Hammett corres., HRHRC; Hammett in *Writer's Digest*, June 1924, quoted in Layman, *Shadow Man: The Life of Dashiell Hammett*, 70.

10   Thus, the bits of slang that Hammett claims to find expressive are remarks like "two-time loser" that show the injured lives of their speakers. Hammett, "From the Memoirs of a Private Detective," *Smart Set*, March 1923, 88–90; Hammett, "Jargon of the Underworld" (1931), unpublished notes, Hammett papers, misc., HRHRC; Hammett, *Red Harvest*, 3; Chandler, *Selected Letters*, 85, 155.

11   Hammett, "The Advertisement IS Literature," *Western Advertising*, October 1926, quoted in Johnson, *Dashiell Hammett: A Life*, 54.

12   Hammett's review of Albert T. Poffenberger's *Psychology in Advertising* in *Western Advertising*, December 1925, quoted in Johnson, *Dashiell Hammett: A Life*, 55; Hammett to Lillian Hellman (1/5/44), Hammett to Margaret Kober (7/31/44), Hammett corres., HRHRC; *The Thin Man*, 45.

13   Denning, *The Cultural Front: The Laboring of American Culture in the Twentieth Century*, 7; Peeler, *Hope Among Us Yet: Social Criticism and Social Solace in Depression America*, 264–85.

14   Hammett, "Tempo in Fiction," address to the Third American Writers Congress, *Fighting Words*, ed. Stewart, 56; Hammett to Lillian Hellman (1/2/44), Hammett corres., HRHRC; Hammett had already integrated this sentiment into his screenplay for Hellman's play *Watch on the Rhine*, in which the protagonist, Kurt Muller, explains: "All men are good soldiers when they know for what they fight." *Watch on the Rhine*, typed screenplay (5/20/42), Hammett, works, HRHRC.

15   Lillian Hellman, undated letter to Alfred A. Knopf Publishers, Knopf files, HRHRC, Box 435, folder 2; Hammett to Blanche Knopf (3/20/28), Knopf files, HRHRC, Box 691, folder 9.

16   Hammett to Harry Block (6/16/29), Knopf files, HRHRC, Box 691, folder 9.

17   Hammett to Harry Block (7/14/29), Knopf files, HRHRC, Box 691, folder 9; Hammett to Alfred Knopf (4/27/31), Knopf files, HRHRC, Box 714, folder 1; Hammett, undated letter to Hellman (from the fifties), Hammett corres., HRHRC; Hammett, "Tulip," *The Big Knockover*, 347.

18   Hammett, "Magic," unpublished story, Hammett papers, HRHRC; the story is undated, but according to the address on the MS, must have been written before July 1926.

19   Hammett, *The Maltese Falcon*, 215.

20   Hammett, "The Advertisement IS Literature," quoted in Johnson, 55; "Magic" explicitly points to the threatening implications of evaluating "Art" in the same pragmatic terms used for advertising or commerce. The story's protagonist "snort[s] at the idea that the authenticity of his work was to be measured by its consequences." The temptation toward such a standard, he suggests, marks the difference between "trickery" and "True Magic." In his chapter, "Dashiell Hammett, Copywriter," William Marling contends that Hammett's brief career in advertising was the most significant influence on his literary predilections. Marling suggests that Hammett's objective style, his instrumentalist epistemology, and his sensitivity to the features of an urbanizing, consumerist society, were all rooted in his experience as a copywriter. Marling, *The American Roman Noir*, 93–147.

21 Sandel, *Democracy's Discontent: America in Search of a Public Philosophy*, 118.

22 Llewellyn, "A Realistic Jurisprudence — The Next Step," 461.

23 Soule, "Hard-Boiled Radicalism," 263; on the central role of a Lamarckian account of national evolution to pre-World War I Progressivism, see Eisenach, *The Lost Promise of Progressivism*; Lustig, *Corporate Liberalism: The Origins of Modern American Political Theory, 1890–1920*; Reed, *W. E. B. Du Bois and American Political Thought: Fabianism and the Color Line*, 15–26, 107–25.

24 Soule, "Hard-Boiled Radicalism," 264, 265; Robert Westbrook calls Soule's essay the "closest thing to a manifesto of [the] technocratic progressivism" that "controlled the command posts of liberal opinion in the thirties." *John Dewey and American Democracy*, 455.

25 William F. Ogburn, "The Folkways of a Scientific Sociology" (1930), quoted by Ross, *The Origins of American Social Science*, 431; see also, Ross, 390–470; Purcell, *The Crisis of Democratic Theory: Scientific Naturalism and the Problem of Value*; Ricci, *The Tragedy of Political Science: Politics, Scholarship, and Democracy*.

26 Llewellyn, "A Realistic Jurisprudence," 464; Llewellyn, *The Bramble Bush*, 3; Robinson, *Law and the Lawyers*, 321. On legal realism generally, see, Horwitz, *The Transformation of American Law, 1870–1960: The Crisis of Legal Orthodoxy*, 213–46; Kalman, *Legal Realism at Yale, 1927–1960*; Summers, *Instrumentalism and American Legal Theory*; Wiecek, *The Lost World of Classical Legal Thought: Law and Ideology in America, 1886–1937*, 197–200. In his critique of Thurman Arnold's particular version of realist critique, which more than any other brought realist premises to matters of public policy, Sidney Hook noted how it served the needs of an administrative state: "the social interest which gives a philosophy such as Arnold's driving force is the vocational need of the intellectual worker and professional who make a career in public service or the business of government — a group which regards itself as independent of other classes, in fact as a special class whose function is to mediate between others." Hook, *Reason, Social Myths, and Democracy*, 50.

27 Adelstein, " 'The Nation as an Economic Unit' "; Gerstle, "The Protean Character of American Liberalism"; Kidd, "Collectivist Intellectuals and the Idea of National Economic Planning, 1929–33"; Pells, *Radical Visions and American Dreams: Culture and Social Thought in the Depression Years*, 10–21, 43–95.

28 Arnold, *Symbols of Government*, 288, 270; Cohen, "Transcendental Nonsense and the Functional Approach"; Chase, *A New Deal*, 232.

29 Chase, *A New Deal*, 219; Arnold, *The Folklore of Capitalism*, 45, 391, 161–62, 393, 385. Though their reactions to him differ sharply,

both Richard Hofstadter and Christopher Lasch contend that this atti-
tude made Arnold, in Lasch's phrase, "the quintessential New Dealer."
Hofstadter, *The Age of Reform: From Bryan to FDR*, 319–24; Lasch,
The True and Only Heaven: Progress and Its Critics, 430.

30 See Karl, *The Uneasy State*, 58, 65–66; Potter, *War on Crime: Bandits,
G-Men, and the Politics of Mass Culture*, 31–74; Ruth, *Inventing
the Public Enemy: The Gangster in American Culture, 1918–1934*,
11–62.

31 Particularly illuminating on this point is the 1928 story, "This King
Business," a satirical revision of the turn-of-the-century adventure
novels, like Richard Harding Davis's *Soldier of Fortune* or, more famously, Mark Twain's *Connecticut Yankee in King Arthur's Court*,
that depicted the heroic efforts of Americans to bring modernity to
backward European monarchies. Hammett's story revises that genre
by seeing it through the lens of the contemporary American fascination
with Mussolini's strong-arm politics. The story sends the Continental
Op to the fictional Balkan republic of Muravia where he works to save
a wealthy American who has been duped into believing that a popular
revolution will make him king. Hammett's story disabuses this young
man of both his aristocratic fantasies and of his false belief in the
legitimacy of the popular will. The Op reveals that what seems to be
popular consent results from a combination of brute force and "spectacular, theatrical" manipulation of the "mob." He leaves Muravia
having helped install a giant police commandant in power — a "strong
man" who is admirable because he stands for the value of "admin-
is[tration]" and because, refusing to tolerate "inefficiency," he "insists
on an organization that will keep crime down to a minimum." If only
in the exotic world of the Balkans, the story thus depicts the historical
displacement of the illusions of both monarchy and democracy by the
efficiencies of dictatorship. Hammett, "This King Business," *The Big
Knockover*, 143, 169, 164, 161, 141. Compare the fascination among
American managerialists with Italian fascism described by Diggins,
Mussolini and Fascism: The View from America.

32 The phrase "cynical acid" comes from Oliver Wendell Holmes's influential 1897 essay "The Path of the Law" and was taken up by the later
generation of realists as a motto for their work. See, e.g., Cohen,
"Transcendental Nonsense," 830; Llewellyn, "A Realistic Jurisprudence," 456.

33 Hammett, "The Boundaries of Science and Philosophy," unpublished
Ms, Hammett collection, HRHRC.

34 Dumenil, *The Modern Temper*, 147; Purcell, *The Crisis of Democratic
Theory*, 47–73.

35 Frank, *Law and the Modern Mind*, 130, 102, 104, 126.

36   Hammett, *Red Harvest*, 117, 118, 178.

37   Frank, *Law and the Modern Mind*, 10, 19, 18.

38   Hammett, untitled fragment (Nelson Redline?) in Hammett collection, HRHRC; *The Dain Curse* (New York: Vintage, 1989), 181. Subsequent references are given parenthetically in the text. As Karl Llewellyn put the same point: "categories and concepts, once formulated and once they have entered into thought processes, tend to take on an appearance of solidity, reality, and inherent value which has no foundation in experience." "A Realistic Jurisprudence," 453.

39   Marcus, *Representations: Essays on Literature and Society*, 311–31. Marcus's essay, and its emphasis on Hammett's rendition of "the work of the detective" as "a fiction-making activity," is still the best critical account of Hammett's innovations (323). My aim is to supplement Marcus's argument by situating those innovations in Hammett's intellectual and political context and by showing how that context might further illuminate the underlying concerns of his stories.

40   Halttunen, *Murder Most Foul*, 132.

41   The Op even echoes the Veblenesque assumptions that were a key part of neoprogressive dogma, drawing a sharp distinction between profit and technical expertise: "I like being a detective, like the work," he explains in a famous passage, "And liking work makes you want to do it as well as you can. . . . You can't weigh that against any sum of money." *The Big Knockover*, 33.

42   Hammett made this dialogue doubly coy by modeling Fitzstephen on himself. Like the young Hammett, he is "long, lean, sorrel-haired" and "a man who pretended to be lazier than he was" (16). Thus, *The Dain Curse* turns out to be a classic example of modernist self-consciousness—and an apparent warning about the author's own literary ambitions. In his pulp creation, the Continental Op, Hammett invents a character who rebukes and eventually imprisons his own fictional counterpart.

43   Lon Fuller emphasized this problem in his fierce attacks on legal realism during the later thirties and forties. See, e.g., Fuller, "American Legal Realism" and *The Law in Quest of Itself*; see also Sidney Hook's similar critique of Thurman Arnold, along with Arnold's reply and a rejoinder by Hook, in Hook, *Reason, Social Myths, and Democracy*, 41–61.

44   Arnold, *Symbols of Government*, 268; *The Folklore of Capitalism*, 393; Cohen, "Transcendental Nonsense," 841.

45   Hammett later had Nick Charles make the point explicit while speaking of a woman who echoes the qualities of Brigid (and of women in general in Hammett's world): "When you catch her in a lie, she admits it and gives another lie to take its place and, when you catch her in that one, admits it and gives you still another, and so on. . . . She keeps

trying and you've got to be careful or you'll find yourself believing her, not because she seems to be telling the truth, but simply because you're tired of disbelieving her." *The Thin Man*, 141.

46 Hammett, "Tulip," *The Big Knockover*, 304, 318, 340, 329, 346, 347. Hammett emphasizes his protagonist's belittled fatherly role by also surrounding him with a friend's family of young children. They are tellingly divided by gender. Pop enjoys a kind of paternal relation with a preadolescent boy, Tony, whose ability to understand hunting and engineering problems eases Pop's isolation: "Talking through Tony had seemed to make things easier for me" (337). But their camaraderie is constantly interrupted, first by Tulip and then by Tony's sisters. In a postscript to the unfinished Ms, Hammett further emphasized the unlikely combination of Tulip's macho bluster and his symbolic effeminacy — and revealingly tied that status to the lack of paternal guidance he receives from Pop: "Two or three months later I heard Tulip was in a Minneapolis hospital where he had had a leg amputated. I went out to see him and showed him this [Ms]." When Tulip replies that Pop "seem[s] to have missed the point," he underlines *Hammett's* point — that Tulip suffers bodily dismemberment because he cannot benefit from the abstract symbolic work done by Pop. He is pure body and thus subject to physical decay, while the disembodied intelligence of Pop disappears into the empty abstraction of the Möbius strip.

47 Ibid., 347.

48 Soule, *A Planned Society*, 283.

49 Layman, *Shadow Man*, 121.

50 Ibid., 118.

51 Schudson, *The Good Citizen: A History of American Civic Life*, 185, 182.

52 Arnold, *Symbols of Government*, 271, 105–27; cf. Soule, *A Planned Society*, 28–70 ff.

53 Ohmann, *Selling Culture*, 15; Hammett, "From the Memoirs of a Private Detective," quoted in Johnson, *Dashiell Hammett: A Life*, 46.

54 Daly, *The Snarl of the Beast*, 14, 40, 31, 227.

55 In this respect, both novels draw on the conventional association between marriage and liberal contractualism pointed out by Werner Sollors in *Beyond Ethnicity: Consent and Descent in American Culture*.

56 Park, *On Social Control and Collective Behavior*, 63, 65; Park, *Human Communities*, 34.

57 Park, *On Social Control*, 203.

58 Dewey, *The Public and its Problems* (1927), *The Later Works*, 2: 324–25; Mumford, *The Culture of Cities*, 492, 481–82.

59 This is not to say that the political views of Dewey and Mumford (who each valued democratic community) were at all the same as those of

writers like Arnold and Soule (who valued expert leadership) — only that all shared with Park and with the hard-boiled crime story an underlying sense that American society was poised between custom and rationality and the conviction that political reform should lead the nation from the former toward the latter. Their methods of envisioning that transformation differed sharply.

60   *The Maltese Falcon* offers one striking revision of the convention when Sam Spade forces Brigid to submit to a strip search near the novel's climax. Here, Spade is tellingly both torturer and witness, and the scene, like the novel's conclusion, dramatizes both the difficulty of submitting Brigid to control and the high ethical price Spade will pay for his victory. Another elaboration of the form can be seen in *The Big Sleep*, when Marlowe watches the naked Carmen Sternwood from outside the pornographer Geiger's house. Of course, this convention was not new in Daly's use but had a long pedigree in Gothic fiction and sensational journalism. For a superb account of an earlier stage in its history, see Halttunen, *Murder Most Foul*, 60–90, 172–207.

61   Daly, *The Snarl of the Beast*, 216.

62   Marcus, *Representations*, 323.

63   This is not necessarily the implication of the many masochistic scenes that run through the hard-boiled genre, though it is probably the case that each time those scenes crop up they thematize the tension between egalitarian, consensual relations (which in the hard-boiled story inevitably seem asexual, even when they are romantic) and relations of dominance (which are almost invariably eroticized — even when, as is usually the case, they refer to the hierarchical relations among clannish or aristocratic groups of men). Compare, for example, the scene in *Farewell, My Lovely* where Marlowe is beaten at the same time the gigolo Lindsay Marriot is murdered. Chandler's aim in this scene seems to be to contrast Marlowe's fraternal bonds with Moose Malloy, to Marriot's place in the Grayle's aristocratic chain of parasitism and abuse. That difference is marked by the fact that Marlowe survives the violence that kills Marriot, much as Race Williams overcomes the paralysis that kills Danny Davison. In other words, Chandler draws much the same distinction that Daly makes and that Hammett minimizes.

3. THE PULP WRITER AS VANISHING AMERICAN
Raymond Chandler's Decentralist Imagination

1   Lilienthal, *TVA Democracy on the March*, 145–46, original emphasis; Pratt, "The Million-Word-a-Year Man," *American Mercury*, February 1939, 161.

2   Chandler, *The Lady in the Lake*. Subsequent citations are given paren-
    thetically in the text.

3   Starr, *Endangered Dreams: The Great Depression in California*,
    276; J. B. Priestly, "Arizona Desert: Reflections of a Winter Visitor,"
    Harper's, March 1937, 365.

4   Chandler was probably alluding to the dam at Big Bear Lake, which
    had been built by private enterprise during the 1910s.

5   Theodore White, "Building the Big Dam," *Harper's*, June 1935, 120;
    Starr, *Endangered Dreams*, 290–308.

6   On the "decentrist elements in the New Deal political imagination"
    generally, and the diverse aims that informed it during the later thirties
    and early forties especially, see Rodgers, *Atlantic Crossings: Social
    Politics in a Progressive Age*, 446–84; Brinkley, *The End of Reform*,
    106–36; Kloppenberg, *The Virtues of Liberalism*, 100–124; on the
    particular role that industrialists, bankers, and politicians in the West-
    ern states played in supporting the revitalization of antimonopolist
    rhetoric in the late thirties and the associated rise of Keynesian policy
    during the Roosevelt administration, see Brinkley, *End of Reform*, 77–
    84, 94–98; Nash, *World War II and the West: Reshaping the Econ-
    omy*, 2–17; Schlesinger, *The Age of Roosevelt: The Politics of Up-
    heaval*, 411.

7   Davis, *City of Quartz: Excavating the Future in Los Angeles*, 384–97.

8   Hawley, *The New Deal and the Problem of Monopoly*, 328.

9   Further evidence of this conviction can be seen in Chandler's screenplay
    for *The Blue Dahlia*, which turns on the conflict between wartime
    camaraderie and domestic consumerism. An interesting comparison
    can also be drawn to James M. Cain's wartime novel, *Love's Lovely
    Counterfeit* (1942), which like *The Lady in the Lake* uses corruption in
    Santa Monica to consider the role of New Deal reformism in Califor-
    nia. Offering an implicit allegory of Culbert Olsen's 1938 gubernato-
    rial victory, *Love's Lovely Counterfeit* dismisses New Deal politicians
    as weak sentimentalists and suggests that only wartime commitment
    has the power to call forth civic sacrifice and personal regeneration.

10 G. Gordon Whitnall, quoted in Fogelson, *The Fragmented Metropolis:
    Los Angeles, 1850–1930*.

11 Himey, *Raymond Chandler: A Life*, 53; see also MacShane, *The Life
    of Raymond Chandler*. "If people could deal with one another hon-
    estly, they would not need" middlemen and go-betweens, Chandler
    argued in the fifties. But the crude agents of profit maximization and
    the bureaucratic forces of "elaborate organization" always tended to
    creep back into the picture, interfering with "once personal, kindly,
    and intimate" connections, turning popular culture into mass industry,
    and making art "a question of dealing more or less at arm's length with

someone you never entirely trusted." Chandler, "Ten Percent of Your Life," *Atlantic*, February 1952, 48, 50, 51.

12　Chandler, *Selected Letters*, 86.

13　Ibid., 152, 337, 87, 200, 172, 52, 43.

14　Ibid., 52; Chandler, *The Notebooks of Raymond Chandler*, 21, 56.

15　Kazin, *The Populist Persuasion*, chap. 6; Klein, *Foreigners*, 35–38, 130–45, and passim; Marquis, *Hopes and Ashes: The Birth of Modern Times, 1929–1939*; Matthews, "Art and the People: The New Deal Quest for Cultural Democracy."

16　Chandler, "The Simple Art of Murder: An Essay," *The Simple Art of Murder*, 15.

17　Knight, *Form and Ideology in Crime Fiction*, 138, 136, 151; Porter, *The Pursuit of Crime: Art and Ideology in Detective Fiction*, 66. Knight in particular is scathing about these qualities. For him, Chandler's fiction is not just unfortunately aestheticized; it is "conservative and elitist." Assuming these are inextricable qualities, Knight misses the alternate possibilities that may best describe both Chandler and his predecessor—i.e., that Chandler was a conservative populist, while Hammett was a radical elitist. Knight, 136.

18　For a more detailed discussion of Chandler's critical assumptions and their roots in his pulp career, see McCann, " 'Small, Private Notions: Chandler and the Literary Market."

19　Chandler, Introduction, *Trouble Is My Business*, viii; Chandler, *Selected Letters*, 115; Chandler to Neil Morgan, August 8, 1956, Chandler Collection, UCLA Special Collections; for accounts of the way that classic detective fiction exemplifies what Peter Brooks calls "the double logic" of narrative—its synthesis of story and plot, or *histoire* and *discourse*—see, e.g., Porter, *The Pursuit of Crime: Art and Ideology in Detective Fiction*, 29–30; Brooks, *Reading for the Plot: Design and Intention in Narrative*, 23–29.

20　Macdonald, *Self-Portrait: Ceaselessly into the Past*, 4, 120, 16, 8–9; emphasis in original.

21　Anderson, *Puzzled America*, x; Lilienthal, *TVA—Democracy on the March*, 76, 121, 198.

22　Dewey, *The Later Works*, 11:296, 217–18; 14:91.

23　Ibid., 9:110, 399, 400. These views also significantly influenced the thinking of the directors of the Federal Arts Project of the WPA, whose idea of a democratic culture in many ways echoed Chandler's. Westbrook, *John Dewey and American Democracy*, 400; Matthews, "Art and the People," 322–23.

24　Chandler, "The Simple Art of Murder," 10, 12, 14, 15.

25　Dewey, *Later Works*, 9:27.

26 Chandler, "Try the Girl," *Trouble Is My Business*, 153, 181. Subsequent citations are given parenthetically in the text.

27 Perhaps in keeping with his tendency to attribute cultural corruption to the evils of middlemen and agents, and with the muted anti-Semitism that ran through his fiction, Chandler gave a subtle racial cast to his rendition of Marineau. The radio manager appears "Levantine," and in moments of shock he does not turn "white as a sheet" because, as Carmady notes, he does not "have the right kind of skin" (152, 154).

28 Chandler himself could be extremely moralistic about similar scenes in the work of Mickey Spillane. See, *Selected Letters*, 310–11, 476.

29 Knight, *Form and Ideology in Crime Fiction*, 155; Marling, *Raymond Chandler*, 98.

30 As if to directly contradict the claim that Marlowe does not see African Americans "as people struggling with their own problems, let alone in simple social terms as a class faced with repressive forces of various sorts, economic and ideological," Chandler shows Marlowe doing exactly that in the meeting between Malloy and the bouncer he badly injures. Marlowe notes the desire of the bouncer to protect his club from white slumming (even suggesting that the bouncer takes umbrage when he mistakes Malloy's search for Velma as a pursuit of interracial sexual adventure). He then notes the reasons the bouncer fails to take Malloy's obvious strength into account: "He had his job, his reputation for toughness, his public esteem to consider. He considered them for a second and made a mistake." Nearly all of Marlowe's sympathy is, of course, with Malloy's failure to appreciate the rules of a changed society, but that does not prevent him from engaging in a lesser variety of the empathy that Chandler's critics want to deny. "I felt a little sorry for him," Marlowe notes just before the fight begins. Later, he describes the result with characteristically Marlovian pity: "He was crawling along the baseboard like a fly with one wing. He was moving behind the tables wearily, a man suddenly old, suddenly disillusioned." *Farewell, My Lovely*, 6, 8.

31 On this feature of Chandler's fiction, see Stowe, "From Semiotics to Hermeneutics: Modes of Detection in Doyle and Chandler," 378–82.

32 See, e.g., Stott, *Documentary Expression and Thirties America*, 67–118; Levine, "The Historian and the Icon: Photography and the History of the American People in the 1930s and 1940s," *The Unpredictable Past*, 252–90; Natanson, *The Black Image in the New Deal: The Politics of FSA Photography*. For a different interpretation of the meaning of New Deal paternalism, focusing on the way it was created by the urban working class as much as by state activists, see Cohen, *Making a New Deal*, 267–89.

33   Barone, *Our Country: The Shaping of America from Roosevelt to Reagan*, xi–xii; Brinkley, *The End of Reform*, 164–70; McElvaine, *The Great Depression: America, 1929–1941*, 221–23, 337–43.

34   Roosevelt, *Public Papers and Addresses*, 1: 750, 751–52. FDR's remarks are from the famed Commonwealth Club speech given in 1932 in which he aimed to articulate the work of "Progressive Government," but they articulate an economic theory that would gain still more credibility in the late 1930s and that would be dethroned from the position of reigning wisdom only with the enormous growth that occurred during the wartime and postwar years. See Brinkley, *The End of Reform*, 131–35; Kennedy, *Freedom from Fear: The American People in Depression and War, 1929–45*, 372–77; Jeffries, "The 'New' New Deal," 401–6; Rosenof, *Economics in the Long Run: New Deal Theorists and Their Legacies, 1933–1993*, 44–65. Jim Thompson's phrase is from his 1946 populist story of the Nebraska frontier, *Heed the Thunder*, 23. Robert Polito points out that Thompson took the phrase from a pamphlet to which Thompson contributed when he worked on the Oklahoma Writers' Project during the thirties; Polito, *Savage Art: A Biography of Jim Thompson*, 245–48.

35   Chandler, *Selected Letters*, 87.

36   Chandler, *The Big Sleep*, 39. Subsequent citations are given parenthetically in the text.

37   Roosevelt, *Public Papers and Addresses*, 1: 752.

38   Chandler's most astute critic, Fredric Jameson, points to this difference by labeling the first four novels "the synoptic Chandler." The last three novels (*The Little Sister*, *The Long Goodbye*, and *Playback*) belong to a different order. Jameson, "The Synoptic Chandler."

39   Chandler, *Selected Letters*, 172.

40   Chandler himself liked to make such a distinction, speaking for example of English as used in England as "a class language" and American English as "a mass language." *The Notebooks of Raymond Chandler*, 20. On the political and intellectual environment broadly, see Pells, *The Liberal Mind in a Conservative Age: American Intellectuals in the 1940s and 1950s*, 130–82; Patterson, *Grand Expectations: The United States, 1945–1974*, 61–81, 311–74.

41   Cain, "Preface to *The Butterfly*," *Three By Cain*, 353.

42   Hofstadter, The *American Political Tradition and the Men Who Made It*, xxxvii.

43   Blum, *V Was for Victory: Politics and American Culture During World War II*, 96; Davis, *Two-Bit Culture: The Paperbacking of America*, chaps. 3 and 4; Peterson, *Magazines in the Twentieth Century*, 223–24, 285–317; Pratt, "The Million-Word-a-Year Man," 161, 167–70.

44   Brinkley, "World War II and American Liberalism," 320.

45 Katznelson, "Was the Great Society a Lost Opportunity?" 191; Gobel, "Becoming American: Ethnic Workers and the Rise of the CIO"; Davis, *Prisoners of the American Dream: Politics and Economy in the History of the U.S. Working Class*, 52–101; Fraser, "The 'Labor Question,' " 55–84; Lichtenstein, "From Corporatism to Collective Bargaining: Organized Labor and the Eclipse of Social Democracy in the Postwar Era," 122–52.

46 *The Little Sister*, 184. Subsequent citations are given parenthetically in the text.

47 Arendt, *Between Past and Future*, 200.

48 Macdonald, "A Theory of Mass Culture," 61.

49 In a striking passage in *The Long Goodbye*, therefore, the police seek to justify their abuse of power by claiming that they represent "the little guy . . . the lad that stops off with his pay envelope in his pocket and loses the weekend grocery money" against "the big racket." For Marlowe, that aim, which would surely have seemed noble in *The Big Sleep* or *Farewell, My Lovely*, represents both the foolishness of the police and the overextension of their authority: "cops are all the same. They all blame the wrong things. If a guy loses his paycheck at a gambling table, stop gambling. If he gets drunk, stop liquor. If he kills somebody in a car crash, stop making automobiles" (350–51).

50 Luce, quoted by Dallek, "The Postwar World," 32; Rosenberg, "Mass Culture in America," 4, 12; Greenberg, "Avant-Garde and Kitsch," *Art and Culture: Critical Essays*, 6.

51 *Partisan Review*, May–June 1952, 284; see also, Lears, "A Matter of Taste: Corporate Cultural Hegemony in a Mass-Consumption Society," 38–57; Fearing, *The Big Clock*, 8. Fearing makes a particularly good comparison to Chandler, since far more than Chandler he wrote as a champion of a leftist class populism during the thirties, but, like Chandler, turned after the war toward a critique of mass culture. Like *The Long Goodbye*, *The Big Clock* is deeply concerned about the possibility for "authentic" culture in a mass-consumption society—a concern that figures, among other ways, in a painting that strikingly anticipates the "portrait of Madison" in Chandler's novel: "The canvas showed two hands, one giving and the other receiving a coin. That was all. It conveyed the whole feeling, meaning, and drama of money." As in *The Long Goodbye*, the painting is important for the way it represents money, but also translates money into the higher values of art. Thus, the protagonist agrees that the painting "is either worth ten dollars or a million times that much" (46, 50, 52).

52 On anxieties about legal and illegal Mexican immigration at this time and the U.S. government's program Operation Wetback in the early 1950s, which sought to pacify angry Southwestern Anglos by sys-

tematically deporting migrants, see Paterson, *Great Expectations*, 379–80.

53 Even the location of Terry's foxhole in Norway is significant in this light. As Eileen Wade suggests, by the terms of her own thinking, it should indicate the epitome of the Nordic ideal and a kind of purity that would be exemplified by the beautiful death of the chaste young man. The corruption of the postwar world begins with the fact that, instead, Norway becomes merely the site of injury and corruption: "He should have died young in the snow of Norway, my lover that I gave to death. He came back a friend of gamblers, the husband of a rich whore, a spoiled and ruined man" (329).

54 Arthur Vandenberg, quoted by Diggins, *The Proud Decades*, 76.

55 Greenberg, *Art and Culture*, 16.

56 Schiller, *On the Aesthetic Education of Man*, 41.

57 Chandler, *The Little Sister*, 227.

4. LETDOWN ARTISTS

Paperback Noir and the Procedural Republic

1 Harris, "A Liberal Economic Program," *Saving American Capitalism*, 370; Willeford, *The Black Mass of Brother Springer*, 142.

2 Chandler was especially annoyed by Macdonald, claiming that his effort to combine "highly . . . sophisticated" themes and methods with "the public for the mystery story" made him a "literary eunuch." He seemed not to realize that in this respect Macdonald might resemble him more than Chandler liked. Chandler, *Selected Letters*, 311, 164, 476.

3 Thompson to Marc Jaffe (November 9, 1958), New American Library Papers, Series 2, Box 781, file 1787, Fales Library, New York University; Thompson, *Savage Night*, 14, 106; Goodis, *Cassidy's Girl*, 148; *Nightfall*, 79; for discussion of an analogous transition in the contemporaneous film western, see Slotkin, *Gunfighter Nation*, 379–82.

4 The phrase "CIO working-class" is Denning's, *The Cultural Front*, 39, 21–37.

5 Willeford, *The Black Mass of Brother Springer*, 11.

6 David Dempsey, Kurt Enoch, Bernard De Voto, and Dwight Macdonald, quoted by Davis, *Two-Bit Culture: The Paperbacking of America*, 178, 179, 185.

7 "The developmental state" is Ira Katznelson and Bruce Pietrykowski's term for a government that "organizes markets by direction, decided either by executive officials or by a process of negotiation among the state, capital, and labor." In their usage, that view of the state subsumes

the various collectivist, corporatist, and regulatory visions that competed for control of the Roosevelt administration during the first and second New Deals. It was displaced during and after the war, they argue, by the Keynesian "fiscalist state," which "shapes markets through the instrumentalities of fiscal and monetary policy." Katznelson and Pietrykowski, "Rebuilding the America State: Evidence from the 1940s," 306.

8   Mickey Spillane, quoted by David Halberstam, *The Fifties*, 148.

9   Spillane, *I, the Jury*, 236, 245–46.

10 Ibid., 17–18, 145, 244, 236, 82.

11 Ibid., 4; Spillane, quoted by Halberstam, *The Fifties*, 61; on Spillane's anticommunist nationalism, see Whitfield, *The Culture of the Cold War*, 34–37; on Spillane's recasting of populist masculinity for the world of postwar consumerism, see Jesse Berrett's unpublished dissertation, "The Secret Lives of Consumer Culture: Masculinity and Consumption in Postwar America."

12 Michael Arlen, quoted by Halberstam, *The Fifties*, 234; Macdonald, *The Three Roads*, 11, 73; "The Bearded Lady," *The Name is Archer*, 67.

13 Macdonald, *The Galton Case*, 224, 28, 199, 202.

14 Ibid., 238.

15 Ibid., 29, 32, 8; *The Three Roads*, 71.

16 Brinkley, *The End of Reform*, 10; Macdonald, *Meet Me at the Morgue*, 119, 117; *The Chill*, 158–59.

17 Macdonald, *The Three Roads*, 72.

18 Spillane, *I, the Jury*, 6; Macdonald, *Meet Me at the Morgue*, 61, 63; *The Chill*, 158–59.

19 It is sometimes noted that Spillane's faith as a Jehovah's Witness corresponds with the moralism and violence of his fiction. An equally important echo occurs in the egalitarian ethos implicit in that faith, which holds that all believers are ministers and thus equally important to the work of the church.

20 Although Spillane agreed to publish his novels in cloth with E. P. Dutton, that arrangement was largely for the sake of propriety. His closest editorial relationship was with the people at New American Library who shepherded his career and who recognized that a nearly "magic" sympathy existed between his fiction and the paperback market. Acknowledging that magic, Spillane cultivated his paperback editors and took pleasure in rebuking or ignoring his clothbound publishers. New American Library Papers, Fales Library, New York University, General Correspondence, Box 68, file 1700; see also Davis, *Two-Bit Culture*, 180–85.

21 Newton, quoted by Bold, *Selling the Wild West*, 21.

22 Dahl, *A Preface to Democratic Theory*, 143; Riesman et al., *The Lonely Crowd: A Study of the Changing American Character*, 223.

23 Greenberg, *Art and Culture*, 157.

24 MacShane, *The Life of Raymond Chandler*, 74; Polito, *Savage Art*, 338. In paperback reprints during the forties and fifties, hundreds of thousands of copies of Chandler's and Hammett's titles were sold. The point, though, is that Thompson and other writers of paperback originals matched these sales and vastly outnumbered the major writers' initial hardback audiences, even though they had none of Chandler or Hammett's established reputations. Of course, none of these writers approached the unprecedented sales achieved by their contemporary, Mickey Spillane, whose books sold in the millions.

25 Thompson to Marc Jaffe (May 9, 1959), New American Library papers, Series 3, Box 82, File 2689, Fales Library, New York University.

26 Polito, *Savage Art*, 341, 364–65.

27 Marc Jaffe to Victor Gollancz (January 3, 1958), New American Library papers, Series 2, Box 71, file 1789, Fales Library, New York University.

28 Thompson, *The Killer Inside Me*, 188.

29 Thompson, *Heed the Thunder*, 297.

30 Thompson, *Now and On Earth*, 259, 162, 161, 123.

31 In his classic thriller from this same period, *The Big Clock*, Kenneth Fearing made a similar implication. Like Thompson a left-wing populist who turned to the crime novel during the forties when the American political climate began to change, Fearing created in the parody of Time/Life at the center of his novel, an acid portrait of a social order that combined the hypnosis of the mass media with omnipresent surveillance and a meritocratic system of social welfare. "The substance of" this vision, Fearing's nasty satire suggests, "was the capitalization of gifted people in their younger years for an amount sufficient to rear them under controlled conditions, educate them, and then provide for a substantial investment in some profitable enterprise through which the original indebtedness would be repaid. . . . The social implications of such a project, carried to its logical conclusions, meant the end of not only poverty, ignorance, disease, and maladjustment, but also inevitably of crime." Its corollary in Fearing's novel is inhuman competition and paranoia. Fearing, *The Big Clock*, 28–29.

32 The novel also refers to the decline of the political vocabulary of the thirties in an apostrophe to Marx. Musing on the profound unhappiness of his family, Dillon asks: "Why, Karl? And what will you do about it?" Thompson had first encountered leftist thought while working in the Oklahoma oil fields and had been educated in Marxism while he worked on the Writers' Project during the thirties, where

"Marx had given him," Thompson later told a friend, "the words to understand his life." By the late 1940s, however, Thompson was already suggesting that Marxism did not provide the analytic tools needed to understand the institutional structure of the postwar world. As his remarks about the "intolerable self" and as the title of one never-written novel — "Compulsion to Confess" — suggest, Thompson's crime novels suggested a more nearly Foucauldian reaction to the disciplinary powers of bureaucratic agencies. Thompson, *Now and On Earth*, 237–38, 221, 233, 150, 141; Polito, *Savage Art*, 229; Thompson to Marc Jaffe (May 9, 1959), New American Library Papers, Series 3, Box 82, File 2689.

33 Polito, *Savage Art*, 229, 128, 260, 261.

34 Thompson, *Now and On Earth*, 275.

35 Thompson, "Sympathy," 109–11.

36 Thompson, quoted in Polito, *Savage Art*, 261. Compare the description of the goal of the American Guide series later offered by the Writers' Project coordinating editor, Jerre Mangione: "the hope of portraying the nation in such an honest and effective way that it would help create a more noble standard of social behavior." Mangione, *The Dream and the Deal: The Federal Writers' Project, 1935–1943*, 193–94; Alfred Kazin likewise noted at the time that the WPA guides reflected "a need to give the whole spirit of social inventory in New Deal America a basic foundation in the reclaimed American inheritance." The key point here is the assumption that a "collective self-consciousness" was required to ground "social inventory." What Thompson's postwar fiction depicts is the procedures of inventory shorn of the redemptive spirit of collective will. Kazin, *On Native Grounds*, 502, 496.

37 Sandel, *Democracy's Discontent*, 203.

38 By "transitivity," Haskell refers to the fact that we cannot regard any cause-and-effect relationship as discrete. "Anything we call a 'cause' (including even the voluntary choices and actions of apparently free human agents) can upon logical reflection be regarded as the *effect* of prior causes, thereby compromising its causal status." Haskell, "Persons as Uncaused Causes: John Stuart Mill, the Spirit of Capitalism, and the 'Invention' of Formalism," 444.

39 Ibid., 495, 453, 475.

40 Copjec, "The Phenomenal Nonphenomenal: Private Space in Film Noir," 167–79. Historian Carlo Ginzburg makes an exactly contrary claim in his admiring description of the detective story — that it exemplifies a kind of "low intuition" whose freedom from "deadly abstraction" places appropriate emphasis on the "animality" of human beings. Ginzburg, *Clues, Myths, and Historical Method*, 125. Of course, both descriptions are accurate. What makes the detective story

interesting is the way that it mediates between these two positions and raises—in order to dispatch—the dangers of both excessive abstraction and imprisoning bodiliness. It is not surprising that a historian, on the one hand, and a psychoanalytic theorist (who has described herself as being "against historicism"), on the other, should emphasize different aspects of this pattern.

41   Lippmann (1931), quoted in Ruth, *Inventing the Public Enemy*, 18; Ruth points out that Lippmann's remark was part of a widespread discourse that used the ostensible crime wave of the 1920s to argue over the extent of personal free will in an industrial economy, *Inventing the Public Enemy*, 11–36.

42   Brinkley, "The New Deal and the Idea of the State," 92–94.

43   Brinkley, *The End of Reform*, 227–71; Jeffries, "The 'New' New Deal: FDR and American Liberalism, 1937–1945," 397–418; Karl, *The Uneasy State*, 155–81; Katznelson and Pietrykowski, "Rebuilding the America State: Evidence from the 1940s," 301–39.

44   Adelstein, " 'The Nation as an Economic Unit,' " 160–87.

45   On this point, see esp. Jeffries, "The 'New' New Deal," 410. Alan Wolfe points out that the American adaptation of Keynes placed far less emphasis on social welfare and far more value on the ameliorative qualities of economic growth alone than Keynes himself envisioned. Wolfe, *America's Impasse: The Rise and Fall of the Politics of Growth*, 3–13.

46   Rodgers, *Atlantic Crossings: Social Politics in a Progressive Age*, 445.

47   See Szalay's groundbreaking account of the relation between the aesthetic and political forms of the welfare state, *New Deal Modernism*; throughout the present book, but especially on this subject, my analyses have benefited from Szalay's arguments and from conversations with him about the literature and politics of the New Deal era.

48   Arendt, *The Human Condition*, 43.

49   Thompson, *The Killer Inside Me*, 182, 131, 143.

50   Haskell, "Persons as Uncaused Causes," 453.

51   Thompson, *Nothing More Than Murder*, 142, 174; Freud, *Beyond the Pleasure Principle*, 16.

52   As his nemesis explains to Dusty, his father had "taught you how to write. . . . Probably set down examples for you [to copy]." In this context, Dusty's forgery—as his dropping out of school, his ultimate hostility to his father in general, and his illicit lust for his mother all emphasize—represents a refusal of the Oedipal narrative of character formation. Thompson, *A Swell-Looking Babe*, 85.

53   Willeford, *The Black Mass of Brother Springer*, 22, 23.

54   Ibid., 23.

55 Willeford, *Wild Wives*, 102. Subsequent citations are given parenthetically in the text.

56 Willeford, *The Woman Chaser*, 152, 103.

57 Thompson, *A Hell of a Woman*, 183; *Savage Night*, 148. The point is
only emphasized by the fact that those visions of castration typically
appear in Thompson's first-person narratives as hallucinatory visions
whose reality is never certain. The reader cannot be sure whether Dolly
Dillon or Little Bigger has been physically mutilated or whether they
have simply descended into madness. For Thompson, though, the distinction is ultimately insignificant. Castration and delusion, like criminality, each indicate the impotence and privatization that invert the
collective public voice that has disappeared from Thompson's fiction.

58 Willeford, *Pick-Up*, 63, 26, 11, 166. Subsequent citations are given
parenthetically in the text. Willeford's revelation of Harry's racial
identity may have been inspired by a similar plot in Hammett's story
"Night Shade," published in *Mystery League Magazine* in 1933; see
Layman, *Shadow Man: The Life of Dashiell Hammett*, 137.

59 Harry's fulminations about an excess population of professional and
amateur painters reflect an explosion of popular interest in painting
during the fifties, whose dynamics closely approximated the contro-
versies over the paperback revolution. Amateur painting was a faddish
hobby in the period, popularized by Sunday painters like Eisenhower,
Churchill, and Frank Sinatra and institutionally supported by a wide
range of corporations and professional associations. Karal Ann Marling suggests that the epitome of this trend — which, as with the paperbacks, was denounced by contemporary intellectuals as a debasement
of artistic standards — was the fad for "painting-by-numbers." See
Marling, *As Seen on TV: The Visual Culture of Everyday Life in the
1950s*, 50–85.

60 See Doss, "The Art of Cultural Politics: From Regionalism to Abstract
Expressionism," *Re-Casting America*, 195–220; Guilbaut, *How New
York Stole the Idea of Modern Art: Abstract Expressionism, Freedom,
and the Cold War*.

61 Willeford created another version of this story in *The Burnt Orange
Heresy*–the story of James (or Jaime) Figueras, an art critic who, in a
complex plot, is able to enter the "limited visionary world" of art only
after he has killed off the artist about whom he writes and has fab-
ricated a counterfeit art to criticize. Again, cultural ambition is con-
strued as antithetical to a kind of racialization. To be part of the visionary world for Figueras is to cease being — in a way that he describes
as desirable — ethnically marked: "The man who achieves success in
America must pay for it. It's the American way, and no one knows this

fact of life any better than I, a de-islanded Puerto Rican." Willeford, *The Burnt Orange Heresy*, 3, 144.

5. TANGIBLES
Chester Himes and the Slow Death of New Deal Populism

1   *Conversations with Chester Himes*, ed. Fabre and Skinner, 48; Himes, *The Third Generation*, 238.

2   Himes, *My Life of Absurdity*, 102; *Conversations with Chester Himes*, 48; Himes's debt to the work of Hammett and Chandler is discussed at length in Robert E. Skinner's definitive survey, *Two Guns from Harlem: The Detective Fiction of Chester Himes*; see also Milliken, *Chester Himes: A Critical Appraisal*; Nelson, "Domestic Harlem: The Detective Fiction of Chester Himes." By far the most insightful account of Himes's detective fiction is Michael Denning's structuralist reading, "Topographies of Violence: Chester Himes's Harlem Domestic Novels." Denning sees Himes's use of the hard-boiled form as the vehicle for a Fanonist critique of colonial oppression. This is a plausible view of some of the later work in the series, but, as I will attempt to show in this chapter, it misconstrues much of Himes's writing by reading it through remarks that Himes made late in life—after he had abandoned ideas that first inspired his detective fiction.

3   Himes, *My Life of Absurdity*, 102.

4   Himes, *The Quality of Hurt*, 72.

5   Ibid., 72–75; on Himes's experience in wartime industry in Los Angeles, see also Lipsitz, *Rainbow at Midnight: Labor and Culture in the 1940s*, 20–44.

6   Himes, *If He Hollers Let Him Go*, 151; Himes, undated letter to Victor Weybright, New American Library Papers, New York University, Fales Library, General Corres. Series 2, Box 46, File 931; Himes, "Dilemma of the Negro Novelist in the U.S.," 1948 lecture, quoted by Lipsitz, *Rainbow at Midnight*, 39.

7   Himes, *My Life of Absurdity*, 25; Himes, undated letter (September 1955) to Walter Freeman, NAL papers, General Corres. Series 2, Box 46, File 931; letter (October 1, 1955) to Freeman, NAL papers, File 933.

8   *Conversations with Chester Himes*, 106; Himes, *My Life of Absurdity*, 9; on the key role of common sentiment in the cultural politics of the thirties and the assumption that it could be stimulated by writers, artists, and documentarians to compensate for the limits of traditional liberalism, see Stott, *Documentary Expression in Thirties America*.

9   Though his sense that *Brown* would lead to the intensification of racial

conflict was accurate; see Klarman, "How *Brown* Changed Race Relations: The Backlash Thesis."

10   Reston, quoted by Branch, *Parting the Waters: America in the King Years, 1954–63*, 113; *Brown et al. v. Board of Education of Topeka et al.*, in *The Eyes on the Prize Civil Rights Reader: Documents, Speeches, and Firsthand Accounts from the Black Freedom Struggle, 1954–1990*, 71, 70; in its emphasis on the importance of civil liberties, *Brown* descended from Justice Harlan Fiske Stone's famed *Carolene Products* footnote (1937) — which sought to distinguish judicial protection of civil liberties from judicial restraint in regard to economic regulation — and from *West Virginia v. Barnette* (1943), which found a "preferred position" for civil liberties in the Bill of Rights, a decision that made constitutional law of Stone's distinction and created a division in the "New Deal majority" on the Court. As legal historian Morton Horwitz argues, the distinction would be central to the legal discourse of the fifties and a key aspect of the transition away from the progressivism prominent among legal thinkers during the thirties and early forties. Horwitz, *The Transformation of American Law*, 250–68.

11   Hence the position of a writer like Zora Neale Hurston, who disliked the *Brown* decision and argued that increased spending for social workers and truant officers would be more beneficial than a court order forcing "somebody to associate with me who does not wish me to be near them." For Hurston, as for white critics of *Brown*, the law could not reasonably hope to address the intangible realm of personal feelings; it could and should, however, address the tangible matters of government spending. Hurston, "Court Order Can't Make Races Mix," 956.

12   Kateb, "*Brown* and the Harm of Legal Segregation," 91–109.

13   Leuchtenberg, *Franklin D. Roosevelt and the New Deal, 1932–1940*, 84; Roosevelt, *Public Papers and Addresses*, 6: 1–6. See, for example, the representative remark made by Harold Ickes — the member of the Roosevelt administration most concerned with the needs of African Americans — at the dedication in 1934 of the first housing project for blacks: "discrimination against a section, a race, a religion or an occupation is harmful to the people as a whole," Ickes claimed, "and disturbing to any attempts to work out a balanced economy." Quoted in Kirby, *Black Americans in the Roosevelt Era*, 23.

14   Gerstle, "The Protean Character of American Liberalism," 1044–45; Sitkoff, "The New Deal and Race Relations," 93–112.

15   Cohen, *Making a New Deal*, 323–68; Kazin, *The Populist Persuasion*, 135–63.

16   Du Bois, "My Evolving Program for Negro Freedom," *What the Negro*

Wants, ed. Rayford W. Logan, 65, 69. Du Bois was himself not in full agreement with the position he summarized in these remarks — advocating instead a nationalist effort for black economic self-sufficiency — but statements more characteristic of the thinking of black leadership during the Depression and war can be found throughout Logan's volume. See also *Black Protest Thought in the Twentieth Century*, ed. Meier et al., 122–269; Kirby, *Black Americans in the Roosevelt Era*; Cooney, *Balancing Acts: American Thought and Culture in the 1930s*, 117–28.

17   Boyle, *The UAW and the Heyday of American Liberalism, 1945–1968*, 107–31; Katznelson, Geiger, and Kryder, "Limiting Liberalism: The Southern Veto in Congress, 1933–1950"; Sugrue, "Crabgrass-Roots Politics: Race, Rights, and the Reaction against Liberalism in the Urban North, 1940–1964."

18   Brinkley, *The End of Reform*, 3–14; Pells, *The Liberal Mind in a Conservative Age: American Intellectuals in the 1940s and 1950s*, 83–96; Schudson, *The Good Citizen*, 231–64.

19   Gewirtz, "The Triumph and Transformation of Anti-Discrimination Law," *Race, Law, and Culture*, 110–34; Brinkley, *Liberalism and Its Discontents*, 99–102; Patterson, *Grand Expectations*, 375–406, 562–92, 637–77. On the notion that the "labor question" served as "the animating problem of national politics" from the Progressive Era through the New Deal — whose institutional and political realignments dispatched it — see Fraser, "The 'Labor Question,' " and Foner, *The Story of American Freedom*, 118.

20   Ellison to Morteza Sprague (May 19, 1954), " 'American Culture Is of a Whole': From the Letters of Ralph Ellison," ed. John F. Callahan, *New Republic*, March 1, 1999, 38–39. Ellison's remarks make plausible Carol J. Greenhouse's claim that following *Brown* race would become "the paradigm" of an expanding attention to the significance of personal "identity." Greenhouse, "A Federal Life: *Brown* and the Nationalization of the Life Story," 185; see also Michael Schudson's remark that "in the postwar world, the struggle of blacks for inclusion in the body politic would prove the fountainhead for a new understanding of citizenship." *The Good Citizen*, 231.

21   Himes, *My Life of Absurdity*, 36.

22   Ibid., 13.

23   Himes, *The Quality of Hurt*, 5. Himes discusses his background briefly in his memoirs, but his most revealing treatment of his family and his childhood is in the autobiographical novel *The Third Generation*.

24   On the genre of the "ghetto pastoral," see Denning, *The Cultural Front*, 230–58.

25   Himes, *The Quality of Hurt*, 65. Himes's prison novel was eventually

published in a heavily revised version as *Cast the First Stone* in 1953. The original version is now available as *Yesterday Will Make You Cry.*

26   Himes, *The Quality of Hurt*, 65.

27   Gerstle, *Working-Class Americanism: The Politics of Labor in a Textile City, 1914–1960.*

28   Himes, *If He Hollers Let Him Go*, 164, 8–9, 151, 152, 153.

29   On comparable rhetoric in contemporaneous union politics, see Faue, *Community of Suffering and Struggle: Women, Men, and the Labor Movement in Minneapolis, 1915–1945*, 69–99.

30   Himes, "Negro Martyrs Are Needed," *Crisis* 51 (May 1944): 159, 174; emphasis in original.

31   Ibid., 174, 159.

32   Himes, *The Collected Stories of Chester Himes*, 89, 90.

33   Himes, *Lonely Crusade*, 393, 391, 392.

34   Himes, *The Quality of Hurt*, 100–101, 103. Himes wrote one last significant novel in the naturalist protest vein before abandoning the genre, but this time he did so less to defend the principles of his earlier novels than to complain about their evisceration. *The Primitive* (1955) (republished in Himes's unedited version as *The End of a Primitive*) tells of the abusive relationship between Jesse, another in the series of Himes's angry young men, and Kriss, a white liberal who works tellingly for a philanthropic institute based on the Ford Foundation. Set in 1951, the novel takes place in the context of the displacement of the New Deal by Truman's Fair Deal, the developing Korean War, and the looming election of Eisenhower, and it looks back with nostalgia on the pivotal election of 1944 — the "greatest time in the history of the Republic for interracial lovemaking." In the novel's present, that erotic alliance among the races has been displaced by white liberalism's predatory racial exoticism. The sterile and dissatisfied Kriss explains that when she sleeps with black men, she treats them not as equal partners, but as a virtual extension of her foundation work: "I wan[t] to know what they [a]re like inside." Her story thus serves as Himes's allegory of American liberalism. Disconnected from the virility of the labor movement, postwar liberals turn to African Americans less for alliance than for curiosity and a source of vitality. In Himes's rendition, that leads to violent antagonism between the races and ultimately drives the black man to murder the white woman. *The End of a Primitive*, 64, 146.

35   Baldwin, *Notes of a Native Son*, 19, 32, 33, 34, 15.

36   Baldwin, *Nobody Knows My Name*, 23.

37   Baldwin, *Notes*, 35; *Nobody*, 158.

38   Wright, "How 'Bigger' Was Born," *Native Son and How "Bigger" Was Born*, 513, 512, 520, 515; emphasis in original.

39   Baldwin, *Notes*, 29, 21, 42; emphasis in original. *Nobody*, 18, 87.

40   Baldwin, *Go Tell It on the Mountain*, 163, 50; *Notes*, 65, 64.

41   *Conversations with Chester Himes*, 8.

42   Himes, *A Rage in Harlem*, 62, 40. Michael Denning points out the crucial structural role that some version of "fool's gold" plays in nearly all of Himes's "Harlem domestic" novels: "everyone is searching for the same thing, they all think that someone else has it, and they are all convinced of its great value. It circulates from one unwitting character to another, but invariably it proves to be worthless, or, if there is something valuable, it turns out to have been removed from circulation very early" (14). What might be added to this description is that in every instance—just as in *The Maltese Falcon*, from which Himes may have taken this motif—the fool's gold is also an allusion to the misprisions of cultural legacy: e.g., the map of treasure buried on an African farm in *The Heat's On*, the "mojos and potions and charms" or Confederate money in *The Big Gold Dream*, the bale of cotton from the Deep South in *Cotton Comes to Harlem*.

43   Himes, *The Heat's On*, 25; *Cotton Comes to Harlem*, 13.

44   In a later novel, Grave Digger Jones explains Himes's view of the principal effects of racism, one that echoes the earlier thinking Himes shared with Wright. Segregation is evil—not, as Baldwin has it, because it injures the self-image of blacks—but because it "force[s] colored people to live in vice-and-crime-ridden slums." *The Real Cool Killers*, 65. Note also the explanation of Harlem's violence that Grave Digger Jones offers to one of his white superiors: "We got the highest crime rate on earth among the colored people in Harlem. And there ain't but three things to do about it: Make the criminals pay for it— you don't want to do that; *pay the people enough to live decently*— you ain't going to do that; so all that's left is let 'em eat one another up." *Cotton Comes to Harlem*, 14; emphasis added.

45   Himes, *The Big Gold Dream*, 26.

46   Thus, even as he emphasizes the unique suffering and, therefore, the unique hysteria of his imaginary Harlem, Himes takes care to emphasize that the response made to that suffering by Harlemites is *not* unique. When Grave Digger Jones asserts that "folks in Harlem do things for reasons nobody else in the world would think of," for example, Himes subtly corrects him. Jones's example is the double murder of "two hard working colored jokers" who "got to fighting in a bar . . . and cut each other to death about whether Paris was in France or France was in Paris." His superior, Sergeant Brody, responds, "That ain't nothing. . . . Two Irishmen over in Hell's Kitchen got to arguing and shot each other to death over whether the Irish were descended

from the gods or the gods descended from the Irish." Himes's point is much the same as the one that rang through *If He Hollers* and *Lonely Crusade*: that poverty and the hard realities of working-class life should departicularize people, bringing out commonalities that the appeal to cultural difference otherwise obscures. Indeed, like Brody's Irishmen, Himes's characters tend to look most absurd, and vulnerable, when they imagine ethnic lineages that might compensate for their suffering. Himes, *The Crazy Kill*, 56.

47 Himes, *Plan B*, 60.

48 Himes attacks predatory revivalist preachers in *The Big Gold Dream*; he lampoons the Back-to-Africa movement in *Cotton Comes to Harlem*; he satirizes Harlem political operatives, and perhaps Adam Clayton Powell Jr. in particular, in *All Shot Up*; he attacks heroin dealers in *The Heat's On*, and, by having them use stories of African repatriation as a cover for their smuggling network, tellingly associates the traffic in drugs with the traffic in heritage; he alludes parodically to the Black Muslims in *The Real Cool Killers* and later offers a more ambivalent portrait of them and of Malcolm X in *Blind Man with a Pistol*. While writing this last novel, Himes was increasingly smitten by the Black Nationalist rhetoric he absorbed from American readers who were beginning to champion him, and accordingly he offered a far more sympathetic account of defiant or separatist racial leaders than he had in his previous works. Even here, though, Himes prefaced his book by championing ordinary people against "loudmouthed leaders" who were "urging our vulnerable soul brothers on to getting themselves killed" (5).

49 Himes, *Lonely Crusade*, 397; *My Life of Absurdity*, 126.

50 Himes, *The Real Cool Killers*, 50.

51 Himes, *Cotton Comes to Harlem*, 7, 143–45.

52 Himes, *The Heat's On*, 92; Denning, "Topographies of Violence," 10, 14.

53 Himes had fittingly predicted this attitude earlier in his career. When Charles Taylor, the autobiographical protagonist of *The Third Generation*, drives into a crowd in a traffic accident, he falls momentarily into a sense of alienation, feeling "no connection . . . with the resulting pain and awful hurt and terrible consequences." For a brief time, then, Charles's attitude and the violence he recalls point ahead toward the world of the Harlem domestic novels—the "tragedy" of the accident disappearing into a "grotesquerie," the "victims . . . recalled as adagio dancers executing comic pantomime." But Himes leaves us in little doubt about his own distaste for this attitude: "There was something monstrous, inhuman, in his mental rejection of the horror." And he

makes it clear that Charles has reached a moral turning point when he discovers that "no one can ever be hurt alone." *The Third Generation*, 198, 199, 238.

54   See Bakhtin, *Rabelais and His World*, 62–63.

55   Sarat and Kearns, "Making Peace with Violence: Robert Cover on Law and Legal Theory," 212–13; see also, Cover, "Violence and the Word," 1601–29.

56   Himes, *The Heat's On*, 174, *The Big Gold Dream*, 43.

57   Here, too, a revealing comparison can be drawn between Himes and Baldwin. For Baldwin, the Harlem riot of 1943 signaled the frightening power of popular myth. Sparked by a mistaken story about the police murder of a black soldier, the riot began for Baldwin from a "concerted surrender to [the] distortion" of "legend." In effect, the riot testified — though in a terrifying fashion — to the common identity and collective myths of Harlem's people, and it thus had for Baldwin a collective protagonist: "Harlem had needed something to smash." *Notes of a Native Son*, 110, 111. For Himes, by contrast, riot rarely signals popular identity, dramatizing instead the ubiquitous, rapacious individualism that breaks out when law offers no counter to society.

58   Himes, *All Shot Up*, 146.

59   Himes, *Cotton Comes to Harlem*, 102.

60   Himes, *Lonely Crusade*, 36.

61   Compare the analogous scene in *The Heat's On*. There Coffin Ed confronts the enticing prostitute Ginny in an effort to find the location of a shipment of heroin and subjects her to a brutal strip search. The "tight, close, abnormal contact of their bodies" is "aphrodisiacal in a sadistic manner, and both [a]re shaken with an unnatural lust." But when Ginny offers to share both the heroin and her body with Coffin Ed, he is "caught for a moment in a hurt as terrible as any he had ever known" and responds with outrage: "You think because I'm a cop I've got a price. But you're making a mistake. You've got only one thing I want. The truth" — a truth he literally extracts from her by the threat of torture. As in the scene from *All Shot Up* — or as in *The Maltese Falcon*, from which both novels drew — the criminal market is exemplified by feminine sexuality. As in those novels, too, the detective proves his legitimacy by refusing that seduction and by answering it with righteous violence, so that the victory of law over crime becomes inseparable from the victory of violent authority over feminine seduction. Significantly, Coffin Ed hears "a saxophone solo by Lester Young" playing throughout the scene, so that jazz once again registers the appeal and the danger of lawless popular community: "It was like listening to someone laughing their way to death. . . . Colored people's laughter." Himes, *The Heat's On*, 144–46.

62   Michael Denning points to this transition as well, but explains it as a kind of consciousness-raising. A "major shift occurs in Himes's work" when he "employs Fanon's hermeneutic to re-understand his early work and reorient his writing." For Denning, then, the later novels make good on a potential latent in the earlier ones. It seems more plausible to me to see them as involving a serious alteration in both ideological premise and point of view. Denning, "Topographies of Violence," 16.

63   See Skinner and Fabre's introduction to *Plan B*, xxviii.

64   Even here, though, Himes remained ambivalent. The revolution falls into chaos because the ordinary people do not become a disciplined fighting force as their leader expects, thus undermining the very separatism the novel seems to want to endorse: "Why should black men act any different from white men in a similar situation? Did black men value their lives any more than white men? Did black men value freedom any less? What was the difference between a black man and a white man whose antecedents had lived under the same society and with the same values and beliefs for three and a half centuries?" Himes, *Plan B*, 200.

CONCLUSION

Beyond Us, Yet Ourselves

1   Wallace Stevens, *The Palm at the End of the Mind*, 133.

2   Stevens suggests that the anonymous audience he depicts is the philistine mass worried over by his realist contemporaries. Just before demanding "a tune beyond us, yet ourselves," they complain to the-man-with-the-blue-guitar that, "You do not play things as they are."

BIBLIOGRAPHY

Adelstein, Richard P. " 'The Nation as an Economic Unit': Keynes, Roosevelt, and the Managerial Ideal." *Journal of American History* 78 (June 1991): 160–87.

Alewyn, Richard. "The Origin of the Detective Novel." In *The Poetics of Murder: Detective Fiction and Literary Theory*. Ed. Glenn W. Most and William W. Stowe. New York: Harcourt Brace Jovanovich, 1983.

Anderson, Sherwood. *Puzzled America*. New York: Charles Scribner's Sons, 1935.

Arendt, Hannah. *Between Past and Future: Eight Exercises in Political Thought*. 1961. Reprint, New York: Penguin, 1968.

——. *The Human Condition*. Chicago: University of Chicago Press, 1958.

Arnold, Thurman. *The Folklore of Capitalism*. New Haven, Conn.: Yale University Press, 1937.

——. *Symbols of Government*. New Haven, Conn.: Yale University Press, 1935.

Ayotte, John. "White Tents." *Black Mask*, November 1, 1923, 70–82.

Bakhtin, Mikhail. *Rabelais and His World*. Trans. Helene Iswolsky. Bloomington: Indiana University Press, 1984.

Baldwin, James. *Go Tell It on the Mountain*. 1953. Reprint, New York: Dell, 1985.

——. *Nobody Knows My Name*. New York: Dell, 1961.

——. *Notes of a Native Son*. 1955. Reprint, Boston: Beacon, 1984.

Barone, Michael. *Our Country: The Shaping of America from Roosevelt to Reagan*. New York: Free Press, 1990.

Barzun, Jacques. *Of Human Freedom*. Boston: Little, Brown, 1939.

Blake, Casey Nelson. *Beloved Community: The Cultural Criticism of Randolph Bourne, Van Wyck Brooks, Waldo Frank, and Lewis Mumford*. Chapel Hill: University of North Carolina Press, 1990.

Blee, Kathleen M. *Women of the Klan: Racism and Gender in the 1920s*. Berkeley: University of California Press, 1991.

Blum, John Morton. *V Was for Victory: Politics and American Culture During World War II*. New York: Harcourt Brace Jovanovich, 1976.

Bold, Christine. *Selling the Wild West: Popular Western Fiction, 1860–1960*. Bloomington: University of Indiana Press, 1987.

Borus, Daniel. *Writing Realism: Howells, James, and Norris in the Mass Market*. Chapel Hill: University of North Carolina Press, 1989.

Bourdieu, Pierre. *The Field of Cultural Production*. New York: Columbia University Press, 1993.

Boyer, Paul. *Purity in Print: The Vice Society Movement and Book Censorship in America*. New York: Scribner's, 1968.

Boyle, Kevin. *The UAW and the Heyday of American Liberalism, 1945–1968*. Ithaca, N.Y.: Cornell University Press, 1995.

Bürger, Peter. *Theory of the Avant-Garde*. Trans. Michael Shaw. Minneapolis: University of Minnesota Press, 1984.

Branch, Taylor. *Parting the Waters: America in the King Years, 1954–63*. New York: Simon & Schuster, 1988.

Brinkley, Alan. *The End of Reform: New Deal Liberalism in Recession and War*. New York: Vintage, 1996.

———. "The New Deal and the Idea of the State." In *The Rise and Fall of the New Deal Order*. Ed. Steve Fraser and Gary Gerstle, 85–121. Princeton, N.J.: Princeton University Press, 1989.

———. *Liberalism and Its Discontents*. Cambridge, Mass.: Harvard University Press, 1998.

———. "World War II and American Liberalism." In *The War in American Culture*. Ed. Lewis A. Erenberg and Susan E. Hirsch, 313–30. Chicago: University of Chicago Press, 1996.

Brooks, Peter. *Reading for the Plot: Design and Intention in Narrative*. New York: Vintage, 1984.

Cain, James M. *Double Indemnity*. 1936. Reprint, New York: Vintage, 1989.

———. "The Labor Leader." *American Mercury* 1 (1924): 196–200.

———. *Our Government*. New York: Knopf, 1930.

———. *The Postman Always Rings Twice*. 1934. Reprint, New York: Vintage, 1989.

———. *Three By Cain*. New York: Vintage, 1989.

Carnes, Mark C. *Secret Ritual and Manhood in Victorian America*. New Haven, Conn.: Yale University Press, 1989.

Carson, Clayborne, ed. *The Eyes on the Prize Civil Rights Reader: Documents, Speeches, and Firsthand Accounts from the Black Freedom Struggle, 1954–1990*. New York: Penguin, 1991.

Chalmers, David. *Hooded Americanism: The History of the Ku Klux Klan*. Durham, N.C.: Duke University Press, 1987.

Chandler, Raymond. *The Big Sleep*. 1939. Reprint, New York: Vintage, 1988.

——. *Farewell, My Lovely.* 1940. Reprint, New York: Vintage, 1988.

——. *The High Window.* 1942. Reprint, New York: Vintage, 1988.

——. *The Lady in the Lake.* 1943. Reprint, New York: Vintage, 1988.

——. *The Little Sister.* 1949. Reprint, New York: Vintage, 1988.

——. *The Long Goodbye.* 1952. Reprint, New York: Vintage, 1988.

——. *The Notebooks of Raymond Chandler and "English Summer: A Gothic Romance."* Ed. Frank MacShane. New York: Ecco Press, 1976.

——. *Selected Letters of Raymond Chandler.* Ed. Frank MacShane. New York: Columbia University Press, 1981.

——. *The Simple Art of Murder.* New York: Vintage, 1988.

——. *Trouble is My Business.* 1950. Reprint, New York: Vintage, 1988.

Chase, Stuart. *A New Deal.* New York: Macmillan, 1932.

Coben, Stanley. *Rebellion Against Victorianism: The Impetus for Cultural Change in 1920s America.* New York: Oxford University Press, 1991.

Cohen, Felix. "Transcendental Nonsense and the Functional Approach." *Columbia Law Review* 35 (1935): 809–49.

Cohen, Lizabeth. *Making a New Deal: Industrial Workers in Chicago, 1919–1939.* New York: Cambridge University Press, 1990.

Cohn, Jan. *Creating America: George Horace Lorimer and the* Saturday Evening Post. Pittsburgh: University of Pittsburgh Press, 1989.

Cooney, Terry A. *Balancing Acts: American Thought and Culture in the 1930s.* New York: Twayne, 1995.

Copjec, Joan. "The Phenomenal Nonphenomenal: Private Space in Film Noir." *Shades of Noir: A Reader.* Ed. Copjec, 167–97. New York: Verso, 1993.

Cover, Robert. "Violence and the Word." *Yale Law Journal* 95 (1986): 1601–29.

Dahl, Robert S. *A Preface to Democratic Theory.* Chicago: University of Chicago Press, 1956.

Dallek, Robert. "The Postwar World." *Estrangement: America and the World.* Ed. Sanford J. Unger, 27–50. New York: Oxford University Press, 1985.

Daly, Carroll John. *The Hidden Hand.* 1928. Reprint, New York: Harper Perennial, 1992.

——. "I'll Tell the World." *Black Mask,* August 1925, 3–41.

——. "Knights of the Open Palm." *Black Mask,* June 1, 1923, 33–47.

——. *The Snarl of the Beast.* 1927. Reprint, New York: Harper Perrenial, 1992.

——. "South Sea Steel." *Black Mask,* May 1926, 3–41.

——. "Tainted Power." *Black Mask,* June 1930, 5–40.

——. "Three Thousand to the Good." *Black Mask,* July 15, 1923, 31–42.

Davis, Kenneth. *Two-Bit Culture: The Paperbacking of America.* Boston: Houghton Mifflin, 1984.

Davis, Mike. *City of Quartz: Excavating the Future in Los Angeles.* New York: Verso, 1990.

———. *Prisoners of the American Dream: Politics and Economy in the History of the U.S. Working Class.* London: Verso, 1986.

Denning, Michael. *The Cultural Front: The Laboring of American Culture in the Twentieth Century.* New York: Verso, 1996.

———. "Topographies of Violence: Chester Himes's Harlem Domestic Novels." *Critical Texts: A Review of Theory & Criticism* 5 (1988):10–18.

Dewey, John. *The Later Works.* 17 vols. Ed. Jo Ann Boydston. Carbondale: Southern Illinois University Press, 1981–90.

Diggins, John Patrick. *The Lost Soul of American Politics: Virtue, Self-Interest, and the Foundations of Liberalism.* New York: Basic Books, 1984.

———. *Mussolini and Fascism: The View from America.* Princeton, N.J.: Princeton University Press, 1972.

———. *The Proud Decades: America in War and in Peace, 1941–1960.* New York: Norton, 1989.

Dixon, Thomas. *The Leopard's Spots.* New York: Doubleday, 1902.

Erika Doss, "The Art of Cultural Politics: From Regionalism to Abstract Expressionism." *Re-Casting America: Culture and Politics in the Age of the Cold War.* Ed. Lary May, 195–220. Chicago: University of Chicago Press, 1989.

Douglas, Ann. *Terrible Honesty: Mongrel Manhattan in the Twenties.* New York: Knopf, 1995.

Doyle, Arthur Conan. *Sherlock Holmes Detective Stories.* New York: Murray Book, 1930.

Dumenil, Lynn. *The Modern Temper: American Culture and Society in the 1920s.* New York: Hill and Wang, 1995.

Eisenach, Eldon J. *The Lost Promise of Progressivism.* Lawrence: University of Kansas Press, 1994.

Evans, Hiram Wesley. "The Klan's Fight for Americanism." In *The Culture of the Twenties,* ed. Loren Baritz, 85–107. Indianapolis: Bobbs-Merrill, 1970.

Fabre, Michel, and Robert E. Skinner, eds. *Conversations with Chester Himes.* Jackson: University Press of Mississippi, 1995.

Faue, Elizabeth. *Community of Suffering and Struggle: Women, Men, and the Labor Movement in Minneapolis, 1915–1945.* Chapel Hill: University of North Carolina Press, 1991.

Feak, Donald. "The Reaper of Regret." *Black Mask,* July 1, 1923, 39–47.

Fearing, Kenneth. *The Big Clock.* 1946. Reprint, New York: Harper & Row, 1980.

Fine, Richard. *James M. Cain and the American Authors' Authority.* Austin: University of Texas Press, 1992.

Finegold, Kenneth, and Theda Skocpol. *State and Party in America's New Deal*. Madison: University of Wisconsin Press, 1995.

Fisher, Philip M. "Fungus Isle." *Argosy*, October 27, 1923, 340–65.

Fogelson, Robert. *The Fragmented Metropolis: Los Angeles, 1850–1930*. Berkeley: University of California Press, 1967.

Foner, Eric. *The Story of American Freedom*. New York: Norton, 1998.

Frank, Jerome. *Law and the Modern Mind*. 1930. Reprint, New York: Tudor, 1936.

Fraser, Steve. "The 'Labor Question.' " In *The Rise and Fall of the New Deal Order*. Ed. Steve Fraser and Gary Gerstle, 55–84. Princeton, N.J.: Princeton University Press, 1989.

Freedman, Carl and Christopher Kendrick. "Forms of Labor in Dashiell Hammett's *Red Harvest*." *PMLA* 106 (March 1991): 209–21.

Freud, Sigmund. *Beyond the Pleasure Principle*. Trans. and ed. James Strachey. New York: Norton, 1975.

Frost, Stanley. *The Challenge of the Klan*. Indianapolis: Bobbs-Merrill, 1923.

Fry, Henry P. *The Modern Ku Klux Klan*. 1922. Reprint, New York: Negro Universities Press, 1969.

Fuller, L. L. "American Legal Realism." *University of Pennsylvania Law Review* 82 (1934): 429–62.

———. *The Law in Quest of Itself*. Chicago: Foundation Press, 1940.

Gardner, Erle Stanley. "Getting Away with Murder." *Atlantic Monthly*, January 1965, 72–75.

———. "Speed Dash." *Atlantic Monthly*, June 1965, 55–57.

Gellner, Ernest. *Conditions of Liberty: Civil Society and Its Rivals*. New York: Penguin, 1994.

———. *The Psychoanalytic Movement: The Cunning of Unreason*. 2nd ed. Evanston, Ill.: Northwestern University Press, 1996.

———. *Reason and Culture: The Historic Role of Rationality and Rationalism*. Oxford: Blackwell, 1992.

Gerstle, Gary. "The Protean Character of American Liberalism." *American Historical Review* 99 (1994): 1043–73.

———. *Working-Class Americanism: The Politics of Labor in a Textile City, 1914–1960*. New York: Cambridge University Press, 1989.

Gewirtz, Paul. "The Triumph and Transformation of Anti-Discrimination Law." In *Race, Law, and Culture: Reflections on* Brown v. Board of Education, ed. Austin Sarat, 110–34. New York: Oxford University Press, 1997.

Ginzburg, Carlo. *Clues, Myths, and Historical Method*. Baltimore: Johns Hopkins University Press, 1992.

Gobel, Thomas. "Becoming American: Ethnic Workers and the Rise of the CIO." *Labor History* 29 (1988): 173–98.

Goodis, David. *Cassidy's Girl*. 1951. Reprint, New York: Vintage, 1992.

——. *Nightfall*. 1947. Reprint, New York: Vintage, 1991.

Goulart, Ron. *The Dime Detectives: A Comprehensive History of the Detective Fiction Pulps*. New York: Mysterious Press, 1988.

Graña, César. *Bohemia Versus Bourgeois: French Society and the French Man of Letters in the Nineteenth Century*. New York: Basic Books, 1964.

Greenberg, Clement. *Art and Culture: Critical Essays*. Boston: Beacon Press, 1989.

Greenfeld, Liah. *Nationalism: Five Roads to Modernity*. Cambridge, Mass.: Harvard University Press, 1992.

Grierson, John. *Grierson on Documentary*. Ed. Forsyth Hardy. London: Collins, 1946.

Gruber, Frank. *The Pulp Jungle*. Los Angeles: Sherbourne Press, 1967.

Guilbaut, Serge. *How New York Stole the Idea of Modern Art: Abstract Expressionism, Freedom, and the Cold War*. Trans. Arthur Goldhammer. Chicago: University of Chicago Press, 1983.

Halberstam, David. *The Fifties*. New York: Fawcett Columbine, 1994.

Haltunnen, Karen. *Murder Most Foul: The Killer and the American Gothic Imagination*. Cambridge, Mass.: Harvard University Press, 1998.

Hammett, Dashiell. *The Big Knockover*. Ed. Lillian Hellman. 1972. Reprint, New York: Vintage, 1989.

——. "Bodies Piled Up." 1923. Reprint, in *The Black Mask Boys: Masters in the Hard-Boiled School of Detective Fiction*, ed. William Nolan, 80–91. New York: Mysterious Press, 1985.

——. *The Continental Op*. Ed. Steven Marcus. New York: Vintage, 1989.

——. "Creeping Siamese." *Black Mask*, March 1926, 39–47.

——. *The Dain Curse*. 1930. Reprint, New York: Vintage, 1989.

——. "From the Memoirs of a Private Detective." *Smart Set*, March 1923, 88–90.

——. *The Glass Key*. 1932. Reprint, New York: Vintage, 1989.

——. *The Maltese Falcon*. 1929. Reprint, New York: Vintage, 1989.

——. *Red Harvest*. 1929. Reprint, New York: Vintage, 1989.

——. *The Thin Man*. 1934. Reprint, New York: Vintage, 1989.

——. "Women, Politics, and Murder." *Black Mask*, September 1924, 67–83.

——. *Woman in the Dark*. 1933. Reprint, New York: Vintage, 1989.

——. "Zigzags of Treachery." *Black Mask*, March 1, 1924, 80–102.

Harper, Thomas DeV. "A Melanesian Holiday." *Black Mask*, December 1, 1923, 32.

Harris, Seymour E., ed. *Saving American Capitalism: A Liberal Economic Program*. New York: Knopf, 1948.

Hartz, Louis. *The Liberal Tradition in America: An Interpretation of American Political Thought Since the Revolution*. New York: Harcourt Brace, 1955.

Haskell, Thomas L. "Persons as Uncaused Causes: John Stuart Mill, the Spirit of Capitalism, and the 'Invention' of Formalism." In *The Culture of the Market: Historical Essays*, ed. Haskell and Richard F. Teichgraeber, 441–502. New York: Cambridge University Press, 1993.

Hawley, Ellis. *The New Deal and the Problem of Monopoly*. Princeton, N.J.: Princeton University Press, 1966.

Hellman, Lillian. *An Unfinished Woman*. Boston: Little, Brown, 1969.

Hersey, Harold Brainerd. *Pulpwood Editor: The Fabulous World of the Thriller Magazines Revealed by a Veteran Editor and Publisher*. New York: Frederick A. Stokes, 1937.

Higham, John. *Strangers in the Land: Patterns of American Nativism, 1860–1925*. New Brunswick, N.J.: Rutgers University Press, 1955.

Himes, Chester. *All Shot Up*. 1960. Reprint, New York: Thunder's Mouth Press, 1996.

———. *The Big Gold Dream*. 1960. Reprint, New York: Thunder's Mouth Press, 1996.

———. *Blind Man with a Pistol*. 1969. Reprint, New York: Vintage, 1989.

———. *The Collected Stories of Chester Himes*. New York: Thunder's Mouth Press, 1990.

———. *Cotton Comes to Harlem*. 1965. Reprint, New York: Vintage, 1988.

———. *The Crazy Kill*. 1959. Reprint, New York: Vintage, 1989.

———. *The End of a Primitive*. New York: Norton, 1997.

———. *The Heat's On*. 1966. Reprint, New York: Vintage, 1988.

———. *If He Hollers Let Him Go*. 1945. Reprint, New York: Thunder's Mouth Press, 1986.

———. *Lonely Crusade*. 1947. Reprint, New York: Thunder's Mouth Press, 1997.

———. *My Life of Absurdity: The Autobiography of Chester Himes, the Later Years*. 1976. Reprint, New York: Paragon House, 1990.

———. *Plan B*. Ed. Michael Fabre and Robert E. Skinner. Jackson: University Press of Mississippi, 1994.

———. *The Quality of Hurt: The Autobiography of Chester Himes*. 1971. Reprint, New York: Thunder's Mouth Press, 1989.

———. *A Rage in Harlem*. Originally *For Love of Immabelle*, 1957. Reprint, New York: Vintage, 1989.

———. *The Real Cool Killers*. 1959. Reprint, New York: Vintage, 1988.

———. *The Third Generation*. 1954. Reprint, New York: Thunder's Mouth Press, 1982.

———. *Yesterday Will Make You Cry*. New York: Norton, 1998.

Himey, Tom. *Raymond Chandler: A Life*. New York: Atlantic Monthly Press, 1997.

Hirschman, Albert O. *The Passions and the Interests: Political Arguments for Capitalism Before Its Triumph*. Princeton, N.J.: Princeton University Press, 1977.

Hoffman, Frederick J. *The Twenties: American Writing in the Postwar Decade*. New York: Viking, 1955.

Hofstadter, Richard. *The Age of Reform: From Bryan to FDR*. New York: Vintage, 1955.

———. *The American Political Tradition and the Men Who Made It*. 1948. Reprint, New York: Vintage, 1989.

Hook, Sidney. *Reason, Social Myths, and Democracy*. New York: John Day, 1940.

Hoopes, Roy. *Cain: A Biography*. New York: Holt, Rinehart and Winston, 1982.

Holmes, Stephen. *The Anatomy of Antiliberalism*. Cambridge, Mass.: Harvard University Press, 1993.

———. *Passions and Constraint: On the Theory of Liberal Democracy*. Chicago: University of Chicago Press, 1995.

Horwitz, Morton J. *The Transformation of American Law, 1870–1960: The Crisis of Legal Orthodoxy*. New York: Oxford University Press, 1992.

Howe, Daniel Walker. *Making the American Self: Jonathan Edwards to Abraham Lincoln*. Cambridge, Mass.: Harvard University Press, 1997.

Hurston, Zora Neale. "Court Order Can't Make Races Mix." 1955. Reprint, in *Folklore, Memoirs, and Other Writings*. New York: Library of America, 956–58.

Huyssen, Andreas. *After the Great Divide: Modernism, Mass Culture, Postmodernism*. Bloomington: Indiana University Press, 1986.

Ignatieff, Ivan. "Jungle Shadows." *Black Mask*, July 1, 1924, 32–46.

Jackson, Kenneth T. *The Klan in the City, 1915–1930*. New York: Oxford University Press, 1967.

Jameson, Fredric. "The Synoptic Chandler." In *Shades of Noir: A Reader*, ed. Joan Copjec, 33–56. New York: Verso, 1993.

Jeffries, John W. "The 'New' New Deal: FDR and American Liberalism." *Political Science Quarterly* 105 (1990): 397–418.

Johnson, Diane. *Dashiell Hammett: A Life*. New York: Fawcett Columbine, 1983.

Kaplan, Amy. "Romancing the Empire: The Embodiment of American Masculinity in the Popular Historical Novel of the 1890s." *American Literary History* 2 (1990): 659–90.

———. *The Social Construction of American Realism*. Chicago: University of Chicago Press, 1988.

Kalman, Laura. *Legal Realism at Yale, 1927–1960*. Chapel Hill: University of North Carolina Press, 1986.

Karl, Barry D. *The Uneasy State: The United States from 1915 to 1945*. Chicago: University of Chicago Press, 1983.

Kateb, George. "*Brown* and the Harm of Legal Segregation." In *Race, Law, and Culture: Reflections on* Brown v. Board of Education, ed. Austin Sarat, 91–109. New York: Oxford University Press, 1997.

Katznelson, Ira. "Was the Great Society a Lost Opportunity." In *The Rise and Fall of the New Deal Order*. Ed. Steve Fraser and Gary Gerstle, 185–211. Princeton, N.J.: Princeton University Press, 1989.

—— and Bruce Pietrykowski. "Rebuilding the America State: Evidence from the 1940s." *Studies in American Political Development* 5 (1991): 301–39.

——, Kim Geiger, and Daniel Kryder, "Limiting Liberalism: The Southern Veto in Congress, 1933–1950." *Political Science Quarterly* 108 (1993): 283–306.

Kazin, Alfred. *On Native Grounds: An Interpretation of Modern American Prose Literature*. 1942. Reprint, New York: Harcourt Brace, 1982.

Kazin, Michael. *The Populist Persuasion*. New York: Basic Books, 1995.

Kedourie, Elie. *Nationalism*. 4th ed. Cambridge: Blackwell, 1993.

Kennedy, David M. *Freedom from Fear: The American People in Depression and War, 1929–45*. New York: Oxford University Press, 1999.

Kesler, Charles R. "The Public Philosophy of the New Freedom and the New Deal." In *The New Deal and Its Legacy: Critique and Reappraisal*, ed. Robert Eden, 155–66. New York: Greenwood Press, 1989.

Kirby, John B. *Black Americans in the Roosevelt Era: Liberalism and Race*. Knoxville: University of Tennessee Press, 1980.

Kidd, Stuart. "Collectivist Intellectuals and the Idea of National Economic Planning, 1929–33." In *Nothing Left to Fear: New Perspectives on America in the Thirties*, ed. Stephen W. Baskerville and Ralph Willett, 15–35. Manchester: Manchester University Press, 1985.

Klarman, Michael. "How *Brown* Changed Race Relations: The Backlash Thesis." *Journal of American History* 81 (June 1994): 81–118.

Klein, Marcus. *Easterns, Westerns, and Private Eyes: American Matters, 1870–1900*. Madison: University of Wisconsin Press, 1994.

——. *Foreigners: The Making of American Literature, 1900–1940*. Chicago: University of Chicago Press, 1981.

Kloppenberg, James T. *Uncertain Victory: Social Democracy and Progressivism in European and American Thought, 1870–1920*. New York: Oxford University Press, 1986.

——. *The Virtues of Liberalism*. New York: Oxford University Press, 1998.

Kramnick, Isaac. "Republican Revisionism Revisited." *American Historical Review* (1982): 629–64.

Knight, Stephen. *Form and Ideology in Crime Fiction*. Bloomington: Indiana University Press, 1980.

Landis, James M. *The Administrative Process*. New Haven, Conn.: Yale University Press, 1938.

Lasch, Christopher. *The True and Only Heaven: Progress and Its Critics.* New York: Norton, 1991.

Lay, Shawn, ed. *The Invisible Empire in the West: Towards a New Historical Appraisal of the Ku Klux Klan of the 1920s.* Urbana: University of Illinois Press, 1992.

Layman, Richard. *Shadow Man: The Life of Dashiell Hammett.* New York: Harcourt Brace Jovanovich, 1981.

Lears, Jackson. "A Matter of Taste: Corporate Cultural Hegemony in a Mass-Consumption Society." In *Recasting America: Culture and Politics in the Age of the Cold War,* ed. Lary May, 38–57. Chicago: University of Chicago Press, 1989.

Leuchtenburg, William E. *Franklin D. Roosevelt and the New Deal, 1932–1940.* New York: Harper & Row, 1963.

Levine, Lawrence. *The Unpredictable Past: Explorations in American Cultural History.* New York: Oxford University Press, 1993.

Lichtenstein, Nelson. "From Corporatism to Collective Bargaining: Organized Labor and the Eclipse of Social Democracy in the Postwar Era." In *The Rise and Fall of the New Deal Order,* ed. Steve Fraser and Gary Gerstle, 122–52. Princeton, N.J.: Princeton University Press, 1989.

Lilienthal, David. *TVA: Democracy on the March.* New York: Harper & Brothers, 1944.

Lipsitz, George. *Rainbow at Midnight: Labor and Culture in the 1940s.* Urbana: University of Illinois Press, 1994.

Llewellyn, Karl. *The Bramble Bush.* New York: Columbia University Press, 1930.

———. "A Realistic Jurisprudence — The Next Step." *Columbia Law Review* 30 (April 1930): 431–65.

Logan, Rayford W., ed. *What the Negro Wants.* Chapel Hill: University of North Carolina Press, 1944.

Lowi, Theodore J. *The End of Liberalism: Ideology, Policy, and the Crisis of Public Authority.* New York: Norton, 1969.

Lustig, R. Jeffrey. *Corporate Liberalism: The Origins of Modern American Political Theory, 1890–1920.* Berkeley: University of California Press, 1982.

Macdonald, Dwight. "A Theory of Mass Culture." In *Mass Culture: The Popular Arts in America,* ed. Bernard Rosenberg and David Manning White, 59–73. Glencoe, Ill.: Free Press, 1957.

Macdonald, Ross. *The Chill.* 1963. Reprint, New York: Vintage, 1991.

———. *The Galton Case.* 1959. Reprint, New York: Vintage, 1991.

———. *Meet Me at the Morgue.* 1953. Reprint, New York: Warner, 1991.

———. *The Name Is Archer.* 1955. Reprint, New York: Bantam, 1987.

———. *The Three Roads.* 1948. Reprint, New York: Warner, 1991.

———. *Self-Portrait: Ceaselessly into the Past*, ed. Ralph B. Sipper. Santa Barbara, Calif.: Capra Press, 1981.

MacLean, Nancy. *Behind the Mask of Chivalry: The Making of the Second Ku Klux Klan*. New York: Oxford University Press, 1994.

MacShane, Frank. *The Life of Raymond Chandler*. New York: E. P. Dutton, 1976.

Manent, Pierre. *An Intellectual History of Liberalism*, trans. Rebecca Balinski. Princeton, N.J.: Princeton University Press, 1995.

Mangione, Jerre. *The Dream and the Deal: The Federal Writers' Project, 1935–1943*. Boston: Little, Brown, 1972.

Marchand, Roland. *Advertising the American Dream: Making Way for Modernity, 1920–1940*. Berkeley: University of California Press, 1985.

Marcus, Steven. *Representations: Essays on Literature and Society*. New York: Columbia University Press, 1990.

Marling, Karal Ann. *As Seen on TV: The Visual Culture of Everyday Life in the 1950s*. Cambridge, Mass.: Harvard University Press, 1994.

Marling, William. *The American Roman Noir: Hammett, Cain, and Chandler*. Athens: University of Georgia Press, 1995.

———. *Raymond Chandler*. Boston: Twayne, 1986.

Marquis, Alice G. *Hopes and Ashes: The Birth of Modern Times, 1929–1939*. New York: Free Press, 1986.

Matthews, Jane DeHart. "Art and the People: The New Deal Quest for Cultural Democracy." *Journal of American History* 62 (1975): 316–39.

McCann, Sean. " 'A Roughneck Reaching for Higher Things': The Vagaries of Pulp Populism," *Radical History Review* 61 (1995): 4–34.

———. " 'Small, Private Notions: Chandler and the Literary Market." In *Critical Essays on Raymond Chandler*, ed. Robert Merrill. Boston: G. K. Hall, forthcoming.

McCraw, Thomas K. "The New Deal and the Mixed Economy." In *Fifty Years Later: The New Deal Evaluated*, ed. Harvard Sitkoff, 37–68. New York: Knopf, 1985.

McElvaine, Robert S. *The Great Depression: America, 1929–1941*. New York: Times Books, 1984.

Meier, August, et al., eds. *Black Protest Thought in the Twentieth Century*. 2nd ed. Indianapolis: Bobbs-Merrill, 1971.

Menand, Louis. *Discovering Modernism: T. S. Eliot and His Context*. New York: Oxford University Press, 1987.

Merquior, J. G. *Liberalism: Old and New*. Boston: Twayne, 1991.

Merriam, Charles Edward. *Political Power: Its Composition and Incidence*. New York: McGraw-Hill, 1934.

Michaels, Walter Benn. *Our America: Nativism, Modernism, and Pluralism*. Durham, N.C.: Duke University Press, 1995.

Miller, D. A. *The Novel and the Police*. Berkeley: University of California Press, 1988.

Milliken, Stephen F. *Chester Himes: A Critical Appraisal*. Columbia: University of Missouri Press, 1976.

Moore, Leonard J. *Citizen Klansmen: The Ku Klux Klan in Indiana, 1921–1928*. Chapel Hill: University of North Carolina Press, 1981.

Moretti, Franco. *Signs Taken for Wonders: Essays in the Sociology of Literary Forms*. London: Verso, 1983.

Mullen, R. D. "From Standard Magazines to Pulps and Big Slicks: A Note on the History of U.S. General and Fiction Magazines." *Science Fiction Studies* 22 (March 1995): 144–56.

Mumford, Lewis. *The Culture of Cities*. New York: Harcourt Brace, 1938.

Nash, Gerald D. *World War II and the West: Reshaping the Economy*. Lincoln: University of Nebraska Press, 1990.

Natanson, Nicholas. *The Black Image in the New Deal: The Politics of FSA Photography*. Knoxville: University of Tennessee Press, 1992.

Nebel, Frederick. "Graft." *Black Mask*, May 1929, 19–41.

Nelson, Raymond. "Domestic Harlem: The Detective Fiction of Chester Himes." *Virginia Quarterly Review* 48 (1972): 260–76.

Nolan, William, ed. *The Black Mask Boys: Masters in the Hard-Boiled School of Detective Fiction*. New York: Mysterious Press, 1985.

Ohmann, Richard. *Selling Culture: Magazines, Markets, and Class at the Turn of the Century*. New York: Verso, 1996.

Orvell, Miles. *The Real Thing: Imitation and Authenticity in American Culture, 1880–1940*. Chapel Hill: University of North Carolina Press, 1989.

Osumi, Megumi Dick. "Asians and California's Anti-Miscegenation Laws." In *Asian and Pacific American Experiences: Women's Perspectives*, ed. Nobuya Tsuchida, 1–37. Minneapolis: University of Minnesota Press, 1982.

Park, Robert E. *Human Communities: The City and Human Ecology*. Glencoe, Ill.: Free Press, 1952.

——. *On Social Control and Collective Behavior: Selected Papers*, ed. Ralph H. Turner. Chicago: University of Chicago Press, 1967.

Patterson, James T. *Grand Expectations: The United States, 1945–1974*. New York: Oxford University Press, 1996.

Peeler, David. *Hope Among Us Yet: Social Criticism and Social Solace in Depression America*. Athens: University of Georgia Press, 1987.

Pells, Richard. *The Liberal Mind in a Conservative Age: American Intellectuals in the 1940s and 1950s*. 2nd ed. Middletown, Conn.: Wesleyan University Press, 1989.

——. *Radical Visions and American Dreams: Culture and Social Thought in the Depression Years*. 2nd ed. Middletown, Conn.: Wesleyan University Press, 1984.

Peterson, Herman. "Call Out the Klan." *Black Mask*, June 1, 1923, 5–31.

———. "One Dried Head." *Black Mask*, November 1, 1923, 55–69.

Peterson, Theodore. *Magazines in the Twentieth Century*. 2nd ed. Urbana: University of Illinois Press, 1964.

Poe, Edgar Allan. *The Complete Tales and Poems*. New York: Vintage, 1975.

Poggioli, Renato. *The Theory of the Avant-Garde*, trans. Gerald Fitzgerald. New York: Harper & Row, 1971.

Polito, Robert S. *Savage Art: A Biography of Jim Thompson*. New York: Knopf, 1995.

Porter, Dennis. *The Pursuit of Crime: Art and Ideology in Detective Fiction*. New Haven, Conn.: Yale University Press, 1981.

Potter, Claire. *War on Crime: Bandits, G-Men, and the Politics of Mass Culture*. New Brunswick, N.J.: Rutgers University Press, 1998.

Purcell, Edward. *The Crisis of Democratic Theory: Scientific Naturalism and the Problem of Value*. Lexington: University Press of Kentucky, 1973.

Reed, Adolph L., Jr. *W. E. B. Du Bois and American Political Thought: Fabianism and the Color Line*. New York: Oxford University Press, 1997.

Ricci, David M. *The Tragedy of Political Science: Politics, Scholarship, and Democracy*. New Haven, Conn.: Yale University Press, 1984.

Riesman, David, with Nathan Glazer and Reuel Denney. *The Lonely Crowd: A Study of the Changing American Character*. New Haven, Conn.: Yale University Press, 1950.

Roberts, Thomas J. *An Aesthetics of Junk Fiction*. Athens: University of Georgia Press, 1990.

Robinson, Edward S. *Law and the Lawyers*. New York: Macmillan, 1935.

Rodgers, Daniel T. *Atlantic Crossings: Social Politics in a Progressive Age*. Cambridge, Mass.: Harvard University Press, 1998.

Roosevelt, Franklin D. *The Public Papers and Addresses of Franklin D. Roosevelt*. 13 vols. Ed. Samuel I. Rosenman. New York: Random House, 1938–50.

Rosenberg, Bernard. "Mass Culture in America." In *Mass Culture: The Popular Arts in America*, ed. Rosenberg and David Manning White, 3–12. Glencoe, Ill.: Free Press, 1957.

Rosenof, Theodore. *Economics in the Long Run: New Deal Theorists and Their Legacies, 1933–1993*. Chapel Hill: University of North Carolina Press, 1997.

Ross, Dorothy. *The Origins of American Social Science*. New York: Cambridge University Press, 1991.

Ruehlmann, William. *Saint with a Gun: The Unlawful American Private-Eye*. New York: New York University Press, 1974.

Ruth, David E. *Inventing the Public Enemy: The Gangster in American Culture, 1918–1934*. Chicago: University of Chicago Press, 1996.

Sandel, Michael. *Democracy's Discontent: America in Search of a Public Philosophy*. Cambridge, Mass.: Harvard University Press, 1996.

Sarat, Austin, and Thomas R. Kearns. "Making Peace with Violence: Robert Cover on Law and Legal Theory." In *Law's Violence*, ed. Sarat and Kearns, 211–50. Ann Arbor: University of Michigan Press, 1992.

Schudson, Michael. *The Good Citizen: A History of American Civic Life.* New York: Free Press, 1998.

Schiller, Friedrich. *On the Aesthetic Education of Man*, trans. Reginald Snell. Bristol, Eng.: Thoemmes Press, 1994.

Schlesinger, Arthur. *The Age of Roosevelt: The Politics of Upheaval.* Boston: Houghton Mifflin, 1957.

Schneirov, Matthew. *The Dream of a New Social Order: Popular Magazines in America, 1893–1914.* New York: Columbia University Press, 1994.

Sellers, Charles. *The Market Revolution: Jacksonian America, 1815–1846.* New York: Oxford University Press, 1991.

Shaw, Joseph T. "Crime and the Law." *Black Mask*, August 1934, 7.

———. "Dillinger et al." *Black Mask*, July 1934, 5.

———. "Do You Ever Find Fault with the Police?" *Black Mask*, October 1934, 7.

———. "Greed, Crime, and Politics." *Black Mask*, March 1931, 9.

———. "Help Yourself." *Black Mask*, June 1931, 7.

———. Introduction to "$106,000 Blood Money," by Dashiell Hammett. *Black Mask*, May 1927, 9.

———. Introduction to "The Cleansing of Poisonville," by Dashiell Hammett. *Black Mask*, November 1927, 9.

———. "Stop Thief!" *Black Mask*, November 1926, 85.

———. "What's In a Name?" *Black Mask*, February 1927, 97.

———., ed. *The Hard-Boiled Omnibus: Early Stories from* Black Mask. New York: Simon & Schuster, 1946.

Sitkoff, Harvard. "The New Deal and Race Relations." In *Fifty Years Later: The New Deal Evaluated*, ed. Sitkoff, 93–112. New York: Knopf, 1985.

Skinner, Robert E. *Two Guns from Harlem: The Detective Fiction of Chester Himes.* Bowling Green, Ohio: Bowling Green State University Popular Press, 1989.

Sklar, Martin J. *The United States as a Developing Country: Studies in U.S. History in the Progressive Era and the 1920s.* New York: Cambridge University Press, 1992.

Slotkin, Richard. *Gunfighter Nation: The Myth of the Frontier in Twentieth Century America.* New York: Harper Collins, 1992.

Smith, Erin. *Reading Pulp Fiction: Hard-Boiled Writing Culture and Working-Class Life.* Philadelphia: Temple University Press, 2000.

Sollors, Werner. *Beyond Ethnicity: Consent and Descent in American Culture.* New York: Oxford University Press, 1986.

Soule, George. *A Planned Society.* New York: Macmillan, 1932.

———. "Hard-Boiled Radicalism." *New Republic*, January 21, 1931, 261–65.

Spillane, Mickey. *I, the Jury*. 1947. Reprint, New York: New American Library, 1986.

Starr, Kevin. *Endangered Dreams: The Great Depression in California*. New York: Oxford University Press, 1996.

Stevens, Wallace. *The Palm at the End of the Mind: Selected Poems and a Play*, ed. Holly Stevens. New York: Vintage, 1972.

Stewart, Donald, ed. *Fighting Words*. New York: Harcourt Brace, 1940.

Stoddard, Lothrop. *Re-Forging America*. New York: Scribner's, 1927.

——. *The Rising Tide of Color Against White World Supremacy*. New York: Scribner's, 1920.

Stott, William. *Documentary Expression and Thirties America*. Chicago: University of Chicago Press, 1973.

Stowe, William. "From Semiotics to Hermeneutics: Modes of Detection in Doyle and Chandler." In *The Poetics of Murder: Detective Fiction and Literary Theory*, ed. Glenn W. Most and William W. Stowe. New York: Harcourt Brace Jovanovich, 1983.

Sugrue, Thomas J. "Crabgrass-Roots Politics: Race, Rights, and the Reaction Against Liberalism in the Urban North, 1940–1964." *Journal of American History* 82 (September 1995): 551–78.

Summers, Robert S. *Instrumentalism and American Legal Theory*. Ithaca, N.Y.: Cornell University Press, 1982.

Szalay, Michael. *New Deal Modernism*. Durham, N.C.: Duke University Press, 2001.

Tebbell, John. *A History of Book Publishing in the United States*. 5 vols. New York: R. R. Bowker, 1972–1981.

Thompson, Jim. *Heed the Thunder*. 1946. Reprint, New York: Vintage, 1994.

——. *A Hell of a Woman*. 1954. Reprint, New York: Vintage, 1990.

——. *The Killer Inside Me*. 1952. Reprint, New York: Quill, 1984.

——. *Nothing More Than Murder*. 1949. Reprint, New York: Vintage, 1991.

——. *Now and On Earth*. 1942. Reprint, New York: Vintage, 1994.

——. *Savage Night*. 1953. Reprint, New York: Vintage, 1991.

——. *A Swell-Looking Babe*. 1954. Reprint, New York: Vintage, 1992.

——. "Sympathy," ed. Robert Polito. *Bomb*, Fall 1998, 109–11.

Wade, Wyn Craig. *The Fiery Cross: The Ku Klux Klan in America*. New York: Simon & Schuster, 1987.

Waples, Douglas. *Research Memorandum on Social Aspects of Reading in the Depression*. New York: Arno, 1972.

Weber, Donald. "From Limen to Border," *American Quarterly* 47 (September 1995): 525–36.

Westbrook, Robert. *John Dewey and American Democracy*. Ithaca, N.Y.: Cornell University Press, 1991.

Whalen, Terence. "Edgar Allan Poe and the Horrid Laws of Political Economy." *American Quarterly* 44 (1992): 381–417.

Whitfield, Raoul. *Green Ice*. 1930. Reprint, New York: Quill, 1986.

Whitfield, Stephen. *The Culture of the Cold War*. 2nd ed. Baltimore: Johns
Hopkins University Press, 1996.

Wiecek, William M. *The Lost World of Classical Legal Thought: Law and
Ideology in America, 1886–1937*. New York: Oxford University Press,
1998.

Willeford, Charles. *The Black Mass of Brother Springer*. Originally *Honey
Gal*, 1958. Reprint, Berkeley, Calif.: Black Lizard Press, 1989.

———. *The Burnt Orange Heresy*. 1971. Reprint, New York: Vintage, 1990.

———. *High Priest of California*. San Francisco: RE/Search, 1995.

———. *Pick-Up*. 1955. Reprint, New York: Vintage, 1990.

———. *Wild Wives*. 1956. Reprint, New York: RE/Search, 1987.

———. *The Woman Chaser*. 1960. Reprint, New York: Carroll and Graf,
1990.

Wilson, Christopher P. *The Labor of Words: Literary Professionalism in the
Progressive Era*. Athens: University of Georgia Press, 1985.

———. "The Rhetoric of Consumption: Mass-Market Magazines and the Demise of the Gentle Reader, 1880–1920." In *The Culture of Consumption*,
ed. Richard Wightman Fox and T. J. Jackson Lears. New York: Pantheon,
1983.

Wilson, Edmund. *Classics and Commercials*. New York: Vintage, 1962.

Wolfe, Alan. *America's Impasse: The Rise and Fall of the Politics of Growth*.
New York: Pantheon, 1981.

Wolin, Sheldon. *Politics and Vision*. Boston: Little, Brown, 1960.

Wright, Richard. *Native Son and How "Bigger" Was Born*. New York:
Harper Perennial, 1993.

Žižek, Slavoj. *Looking Awry: An Introduction to Jacques Lacan Through
Popular Culture*. Cambridge, Mass.: MIT Press, 1992.

INDEX

Sean McCann is
Associate Professor of English
at Wesleyan University.

Library of Congress Cataloging-in-Publication Data

McCann, Sean.
Gumshoe America : hard-boiled crime fiction
and the rise and fall of New Deal liberalism /
Sean McCann.
p. cm. — (New Americanists)
Includes bibliographical references and index.
ISBN 0-8223-2580-2 (cloth) —
ISBN 0-8223-2594-2 (pbk.)
1. Detective and mystery stories, American —
History and criticism. 2. Politics and literature —
United States — History — 20th century.
3. American fiction — 20th century — History
and criticism. 4. Liberalism — United States —
History — 20th century. 5. Political fiction,
American — History and criticism. 6. New Deal,
1933–1939. 7. Crime in literature. I. Title.
II. Series.
PS374.D4 M38 2000
813'.087209358 — dc21   00-010992

DATE DUE

HIGHSMITH #4511